the

NOVEL CURE

the

NOVEL CURE

FROM *ABANDONMENT*

TO *ZESTLESSNESS*:

7 5 1 BOOKS TO CURE

WHAT AILS YOU

ELLA BERTHOUD *and*

SUSAN ELDERKIN

THE PENGUIN PRESS

New York

2013

THE PENGUIN PRESS
Published by the Penguin Group
Penguin Group (USA) LLC
375 Hudson Street
New York, New York 10014

USA · Canada · UK · Ireland · Australia
New Zealand · India · South Africa · China
penguin.com
A Penguin Random House Company

First published by The Penguin Press, a member of Penguin Group (USA) LLC, 2013

LIBRARY OF CONGRESS CATALOGING-IN-PUBLICATION DATA
Berthoud, Ella.
The novel cure : from abandonment to zestlessness: 751 books to cure what ails you / Ella Berthoud
and Susan Elderkin.
pages cm
Includes index.
ISBN 978-1-59420-516-3
1. Fiction—History and criticism—Theory, etc.   2. Reading, Psychology of.   3.
Bibliotherapy.   4. Best books.   I. Elderkin, Susan.   II. Title.
PN3352.P7B47 2013
809.3'9353—dc23   2013017177

Printed in the United States of America
1   3   5   7   9   10   8   6   4   2

Designed by Gretchen Achilles

To Carl and Ash

and in memory of Marguerite Berthoud and David Elderkin,

who taught us to love books—
and build the bookshelves

One sheds one's sicknesses in books—repeats and presents again one's emotions, to be master of them.

—D. H. LAWRENCE
(The Letters of D. H. Lawrence)

CONTENTS

INTRODUCTION

bib·lio·ther·a·py *noun*
\bi-blē-ə-'ther-ə-pē, -'the-rə-py
: the prescribing of fiction for life's
ailments
—Berthoud and Elderkin, 2013

This is a medical handbook—with a difference.

First of all, it does not discriminate between emotional pain and physical pain—you're as likely to find a cure within these pages for a broken heart as a broken leg. It also includes common predicaments you might find yourself in, such as moving house, looking for Mr. or Mrs. Right, or having a midlife crisis. Life's bigger challenges, such as losing a loved one or becoming a single parent, are in here too. Whether you've got the hiccups or a hangover, a fear of commitment or a sense of humor failure, we consider it an ailment that deserves a remedy.

But there's another difference too. Our medicines are not something you'll find at the drugstore, but at the bookshop, in the library, or downloaded onto your electronic reading device. We are bibliotherapists, and the tools of our trade are books. Our apothecary contains Balzacian balms and Tolstoyan tourniquets, the salves of Saramago and the purges of Perec and Proust. To create it, we have trawled two thousand years of literature for the most brilliant minds and restorative reads, from Apuleius, second-century author of *The Golden Ass*, to the contemporary tonics of Ali Smith and Jonathan Franzen.

Bibliotherapy has been popular in the form of the nonfiction self-help book for several decades now. But lovers of literature have been using novels as salves—either consciously or subconsciously—for centuries. Next time you're feeling in need of a pick-me-up or require assistance with an emotional tangle, reach for a novel. Our belief in the effectiveness of fiction as the purest and best form of bibliotherapy is based on our own experience with patients and bolstered by an avalanche of anecdotal evidence. Sometimes it's the story that charms; other times it's the rhythm of the prose that works on the psyche, stilling or stimulating. Sometimes it's an idea or an attitude suggested by a character in a similar quandary or jam. Either way, novels have the power to transport you to another existence and see the world from a different point of view. When you're engrossed in a novel, unable to tear yourself from the page, you are seeing what a character sees, touching what a character touches, learning what a character learns. You may *think* you're sitting on the sofa in your living room, but the important parts of you—your thoughts, your senses, your spirit—are somewhere else entirely. "To read a writer is for me not merely to get an idea of what he says, but to go off with him and travel in his company," said André Gide. No one comes back from such a journey quite the same.

Whatever your ailment, our prescriptions are simple: a novel (or two), to be read at regular intervals. Some treatments will lead to a complete cure. Others will simply offer solace, showing you that you are not alone. All will offer the temporary relief of your symptoms due to the power of literature to distract and transport. Sometimes the remedy is best taken as an audiobook, or read aloud with a friend. As with all medicines, the full course of treatment should always be taken for best results. Along with the cures, we offer advice on particular reading issues, such as being too busy to read or what to read when you can't sleep, along with the ten best books to read in each decade of life; and the best literary accompaniments for important rituals or rites of passage, such as being on vacation—or on your deathbed.*

We wish you every delight in our fictional plasters and poultices. You will be healthier, happier, and wiser for them.

---

* As P. J. O'Rourke said, "Always read something that will make you look good if you die in the middle of it."

A

Plainsong
KENT HARUF

ABANDONMENT

If inflicted early, the effects of physical or emotional abandonment—whether you were left by too busy parents to bring yourself up, told to take your tears and tantrums elsewhere, or off-loaded onto another set of parents completely (see: Adoption)—can be hard to shrug. If you're not careful, you might spend the rest of your life expecting to be let down. As a first step to recovery, it is often helpful to realize that those who abandon you were most likely abandoned themselves. And rather than wishing they'd buck up and give you the support or attention you yearn for, put your energy into finding someone else to lean on who's better equipped for the job.

Abandonment is rife in *Plainsong*, Kent Haruf's account of small-town life in Holt, Colorado. Local schoolteacher Guthrie has been abandoned by his depressed wife, Ella, who feigns sleep when he tries to talk to her and looks at the door with "outsized eyes" when he leaves. Their two young sons, Ike and Bobby, are left bewildered by her unexplained absence from their lives. Old Mrs. Stearns has been abandoned by her relatives, either through death or neglect. And Victoria, seventeen years old and four months' pregnant, is abandoned first by her boyfriend and then by her mother, who, in a backhanded punishment to the man who'd abandoned them both many years before, tells her, "You got yourself into this, you can just get out of it," and kicks her out of the house.

Gradually, and seemingly organically—although in fact it is mostly orchestrated by Maggie Jones, a young woman with a gift for communication—other people step into the breach. Most astonishing are the McPheron brothers, a pair of "crotchety and ignorant" cattle-farming bachelors who agree to take the pregnant Victoria in: "They looked at her, regarding her as if she might be dangerous. Then they peered into the palms of their thick callused hands spread out before them on the kitchen table and lastly they looked out the window toward the leafless and stunted elm trees." The next thing we know they are running around shopping for cribs, and the rush of love for the pair felt by Victoria, as well as the reader, transforms them overnight. As we watch the community quicken to its role as extended family—frail Mrs. Stearns teaching Ike and Bobby to make cookies, the McPherons watching over Victoria with all the tender, clumsy tenacity they normally reserve for their cows—we see how support can come from very surprising places.

If you have been abandoned, don't be afraid to reach out to the wider community around you—however little you know its inhabitants as individuals. They'll thank you for it one day.

ACCUSED, BEING

True History of the Kelly Gang
PETER CAREY

If you're accused of something and you know you're guilty, accept your punishment with good grace. If you're accused and you didn't do it, fight to clear your name. And if you're accused and you know you did it but you don't think what you did was wrong, what *then*?

Australia's Robin Hood, Ned Kelly—as portrayed by Peter Carey in *True History of the Kelly Gang*—commits his first crime at ten years old when he kills a neighbor's heifer so his family can eat. The next thing he knows, he's been apprenticed (by his own mother) to the bushranger, Harry Power. When Harry robs the Buckland Coach, Ned is the "nameless person" who blocked the road with a tree and held the horses so "Harry could go about his trade." And thus Ned's fate is sealed: He's an outlaw forever. He makes something glorious of it.

In his telling of the story—which he has written down in his own words for his baby daughter to read one day, knowing he won't be around to tell her himself—Ned seduces us completely with his rough-hewn, punctuation-free prose that bounds and dives over the page. But what really warms us to this Robin Hood of a boy/man is his strong sense of right and wrong: Ned is guided at all times by a fierce loyalty and a set of principles that happen not to coincide with those of the law. When his ma needs gold, he brings her gold; when both his ma and his sister are deserted by their faithless men, he'll "break the 6th Commandment" for their sakes. And even though Harry and his own uncles use him "poorly," he never betrays them. How can we not love this murdering bushranger with his big heart? It is the world that's corrupt, not him, and we cheer and whoop from the sidelines as pistols flash and his Enfield answers. And so the novel makes outlaws of its readers.

Ned Kelly is a valuable reminder that just because someone has fallen foul of society's laws, he's not necessarily bad. It's up to each one of us to decide for ourselves what is right and wrong in life. Draw up your personal constitution, then live by it. If you step out of line, be the first to give yourself a reprimand. Then see: Guilt.

ADDICTION TO ALCOHOL

See: Alcoholism

ADDICTION TO COFFEE

See: Coffee, can't find a decent cup of

ADDICTION TO DRUGS

See: Drugs, doing too many

ADDICTION TO GAMBLING

See: Gambling

ADDICTION TO SEX

See: Sex, too much

ADDICTION TO SHOPPING

See: Shopaholism

ADDICTION TO THE INTERNET

See: Internet addiction

ADDICTION TO TOBACCO

See: Smoking, giving up

The Catcher in the Rye
J. D. SALINGER
· · ·
Who Will Run the Frog Hospital?
LORRIE MOORE
· · ·
In Youth Is Pleasure
DENTON WELCH

ADOLESCENCE

Hormones rage. Hair sprouts where previously all was smooth. Adam's apples bulge and voices crack. Acne erupts. Bosoms bloom. And hearts—and loins—catch fire with the slightest provocation.

First, stop thinking you're the only one it's happened to. Whatever you're going through, Holden Caulfield got there first. If you think everything is "lousy," if you can't be bothered to talk about it, if your parents would have "two hemorrhages apiece" if they knew what you were doing right now, if you've ever been expelled from school, if you think all adults are phonies, if you drink/smoke/try to pick up people much older than you, if your so-called friends are always walking out on you, if your teachers tell you you're letting yourself down, if the only person who understands you is your ten-year-old sister, if you protect yourself from the world with your swagger, your bad language, your seeming indifference to whatever happens to you next—if any of these is true for you, *The Catcher in the Rye* will carry you through.

Adolescence can't be cured, but there are ways to make the most of it. Lorrie Moore's *Who Will Run the Frog Hospital?* is full of the usual horrors. The narrator, Berie, is a late developer who hides her embarrassment by mocking her "fried eggs" and "tin cans run over by a car," and she and her best friend, Sils, roll about laughing when they remember how Sils once tried to shave off her pimples with a razor. In fact, laughing is something they do a lot of together—and they do it "violently, convulsively," with no sound coming out. They also sing songs together—anything from Christmas carols to TV theme tunes and Dionne Warwick. And we applaud that they do. Because if you don't sing loudly and badly with your friends when you're fourteen and fifteen, letting the music prepare your heart for "something drenching and big" to come, when do you get to do it?

A teenage boy who makes no friends at all yet lives with incredible intensity is Orvil Pym in Denton Welch's *In Youth Is Pleasure*. This beautifully observed novel, published in 1945, takes place over the course of one languid summer against the backdrop of an English country hotel, where Orvil, caught in a state of pubescent confusion, holidays with his father and brothers. Aloof and apart, he observes the flaws in those around him with a pitiless lens. He explores the countryside, guiltily tasting the communion wine in a deserted church, then falling off his bike and crying in despair for "all the tortures and atrocities in the world." He borrows a boat and rows down a river, glimpsing two boys whose bodies "glinted like silk" in the evening light. New worlds beckon, just beyond his reach, as he hovers on the edge of revelation. And for a while, he considers pretending to be mad, to avoid the horrors awaiting him back at school. Gradually he realizes that he cannot leap the next ten years—that he just has to survive this bewildering stage and behave in "the ordinary way," smiling and protecting his brothers' pecking order by hiding his wilder impulses.

Adolescence doesn't have to be hell. Remember that your peers are struggling to cross the chasm too. If you can, share the struggles together. Friends or no friends, be sure to do the silly, crazy things that only adolescents do. Then, when you're older, at least you'll be able to look back at these heady, high, hormonal times and laugh.

See also: Bed, inability to get out of · Internet addiction · Irritability · Rails, going off the · Risks, taking too many · Teens, being in your

ADOPTION

Children's literature is strewn with adoptees. Mary Lennox in *The Secret Garden* is a spoiled adoptee who learns to love in her new cold climate; Mowgli in *The Jungle Book* is brought up by wolves; Tarzan in the novels of Edgar Rice Burroughs is reared by apes. A romance seems to surround these lost and found—and indeed who, as a child, hasn't had a run-in with their parents and

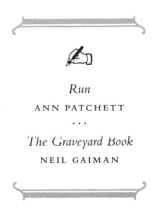

Run
ANN PATCHETT
· · ·
The Graveyard Book
NEIL GAIMAN

fantasized that they too were a foundling? Adoptees find their way into adult literature too: there's James in Grant Gillespie's *The Cuckoo Boy*, a novel with some disturbing views on adoption but a riveting read nonetheless; Heathcliff in *Wuthering Heights*, who upsets the delicate balance of his adoptive family; "Wart" in T. H. White's *The Once and Future King*, who is one of the rare success stories in this list—an adoptee who turns out to be Arthur, King of Camelot.

In reality, adoption is less romantic and can be hard for all concerned—for the natural parents who decide to give their child away; for the child who finds out in a nonideal way (see: Abandonment); for children who blame their adoptive parents for their confusion and who may seek out their natural parents, only to be disappointed; and for the adoptive parents who have to decide when to tell their children that they are "special" and not blood related. The whole matter is fraught with pitfalls, but also with love, and it can bring an end to childless grief (see: Children, not having). Anyone involved would do well to explore its complexity via those who have been there before.

One of the loveliest novels featuring adoptees is Ann Patchett's *Run*. Bernard Doyle, the white ex-mayor of Boston, has three sons: Sullivan, Teddy, and Tip. One is a white redhead, and two are black, athletic, and extremely tall. Bernard's fiery-haired wife, Bernadette, Sullivan's mother, is dead. Teddy and Tip's real mother is "the spy who came in from the cold"—she has watched her sons grow up from a distance, aware of their successes and failures, their friendships and rivalries, and presiding over them like a guardian angel.

When eleven-year-old Kenya—the runner of the title—unexpectedly comes to live in the Doyle household, the complex family dynamics begin to move in new directions. Teddy and Tip seem to be successful, as a scientist and a would-be priest, but Doyle wishes they had followed him into politics. Sullivan has been in Africa for some time trying to help in the battle against AIDS, running away from a terrible incident in his past. With the new issues raised by Kenya's presence, the stories of the brothers' different origins gradually emerge, and it is Kenya's simple but overwhelming need to run—beautifully portrayed by Patchett: "She was a superhuman force that sat outside the fundamental law of nature. Gravity did not apply to her"—that brings them all together. The overall message of the novel is clear, and delivered without sentimentality: blood matters, but love matters more.

Confirmation that even the most unconventional parents can make a good job of adopting a child is found within the pages of *The Graveyard Book* by Neil Gaiman. When a toddler goes exploring one night, he manages to evade death at the hands of "the man Jack," who murders the rest of his family. Ending up in a nearby graveyard, he's adopted by a pair of ghosts. The dead Mr. and Mrs. Owens never had children of their own in life and relish this unexpected chance to become parents. They name him "Nobody" but refer to him as Bod. During his eccentric childhood, Bod picks up unusual skills such as "Fading, Haunting, and Dream Walking," which turn out to be very useful later on.

Bod's ghostly parents do an excellent job. "You're alive, Bod. That means you have infinite potential. You can do anything, make anything, dream anything. If you can change the world, the world will change." Their wisdom from the grave gives Bod the impetus to live his life to the fullest, despite the tragedy of his early years. And he certainly does.

Adoption is never a simple thing. Honesty on all sides is essential to allow those involved to come to terms with who they are and what relationship they have to whom. Whatever part you play, these novels will show you you're not alone. Read them and then pass them around your family—however that family is defined.

See also: Abandonment • Outsider, being an

ADULTERY

The temptation to have an affair generally starts when those who are one half of a pair feel dissatisfied with who they are—or who they feel themselves perceived to be—within their current relationship. If only they could be with someone new, they think, they would be a sparklier, wittier, sexier version of themselves. Perhaps they justify their betrayal by telling themselves that they married too young, when they were not fully grown into themselves, and now their real self wants its moment on the stage. And maybe they *will* be that sexier, shinier person—for a while. But affairs that break up long-term relationships usually go the same way in the end, as

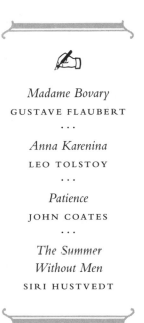

Madame Bovary
GUSTAVE FLAUBERT
. . .

Anna Karenina
LEO TOLSTOY
. . .

Patience
JOHN COATES
. . .

*The Summer
Without Men*
SIRI HUSTVEDT

the old self and habits catch up, albeit within a slightly different dynamic. Often insecurities creep in too. Because if the relationship began as a clandestine affair for at least one of you, it's easy to become paranoid that infidelity will strike again.

For Emma Bovary, the temptation to stray comes almost immediately after tying the knot with doctor Charles, stuck as she is in her adolescent preconceptions of what a marriage should be. While expecting love to be "a great bird with rose-colored wings" hanging in the sky, instead she finds her marriage to her adoring husband stifling and oppressive. Such absurdly sentimental notions of marriage, we are slightly embarrassed to admit, were picked up from literature—Sir Walter Scott is named and shamed—for at the age of fifteen Emma swallowed down a great number of romantic novels, riddled with tormented young ladies "fainting in lonely pavilions" and gentlemen "weeping like fountains."* When she meets the lustful, false Rodolphe, full of clichéd flattery and the desire to serenade her with daisies, she is putty in his hands. If you suspect you are harboring similarly unrealistic ideas of romantic love and marriage, you need to dose yourself up with some contemporary realists: the works of Jonathan Franzen and Zadie Smith are a good place to start.

Anna Karenina is not actively looking for a way out of her marriage to the conservative Karenin, but she certainly finds the full expression of her vivacious self with Vronsky. When, on the way back to St. Petersburg after having met the young officer on her visit to Moscow, she sees him on the platform, she is unable to stop the animation bubbling forth. And when she next sets eyes on her husband, she can't bear the customary "ironical" smile with which he greets her (or, now she comes to think of it, his "gristly" ears). More strongly than ever, she feels that she is pretending, that the emotion between them is false—and she feels dissatisfied with herself as a result. Now that she has seen herself around Vronsky, how can she go back to being the Anna she is with cold Karenin?

What Anna also finds, of course, is that loving Vronsky involves guilt. In fact (and this time we take pleasure in pointing it out), it is while she is reading a novel about a guilty baron that she first becomes aware that the emotion has hatched within herself. Guilt and self-hatred ultimately bring the stricken heroine crashing down, for she can never shake the principles and

---

* Novels are not the only culprit, however: she knows by heart all the love songs "of the last century," glories in the heady rites and rituals of the Catholic Church, and likes the countryside only when it involves ruins—the responsibility for which we lay squarely at the foot of eighteenth-century Romantic art.

values that formed her—particularly with regard to the love she owes her son. Whatever the rights and wrongs of the situation, be aware that guilt is hard to live with. See: Guilt, for how to survive a stricken conscience and still come out standing.

A more devious way of dealing with guilt is to ride in the slipstream of a partner who has been unfaithful first. In 1950s London, the eponymous heroine of *Patience* is a contentedly married woman whose stuffy husband, Edward, expects little more from her than keeping house, cooking regular meals, and performing her duties in the bedroom, which she does while planning what vegetables to buy for tomorrow's lunch. The revelation that Edward is having an affair with the not so Catholic Molly leaves her feeling oddly relieved. Her sense of imminent liberation rapidly finds a focus in the form of Philip, a handsome, intriguing bachelor who awakens her to what sex can be. Patience brings about the end of her marriage and embarks on a new life with Philip, somehow in an almost painless way. Even her three young children remain unscathed. Her suggestion that Philip keep his bachelor flat—where he works and where they sometimes have an assignation—seems to be particularly full of foresight. Perhaps a second home is the secret to an enduring second love.

Sadly, Edward doesn't come off so lightly: he is deeply thrown, his whole tidy world turned upside down, and is landed, somewhat unfairly, we feel, with the blame for it all. There is a chance that adultery may free you from a loveless marriage and catapult you into a fine romance. But there's a chance it won't. You may simply take your problems with you, be capsized by religious or personal guilt, and leave at least one wreckage behind, apart from yourself. The fact is, unless you married late or were very lucky—or are one of the fortunate few whose parents raised you to be fully in your skin by age twenty—you probably will hit a time when you feel there is more to you than your marriage, at present, allows (see also: Midlife crisis).

Having an affair does not always destroy a long-term partnership, and if you're the aggrieved spouse who suspects or knows that your partner is having an affair, it's worth taking courage from Siri Hustvedt's *The Summer Without Men*, an intriguing take on the cliché of older man leaves wife of thirty years to try a younger version on for size. When her husband, Boris, announces he wants a "pause" in their relationship, Mia feels all the things you'd expect, and which you may feel too: humiliated, betrayed, and enraged. She ends up spending time in a psychiatric unit. (For help in dealing with this phase and to avoid temporary madness yourself, see: Anger; Rage; and Broken heart.) But then she takes herself off to the backwater town in Minnesota where she grew up, and where her mother still lives in an old folks' home. Surrounded by various women who for one reason or another are living without men, Mia heals a vital part of herself. Sometimes, a relationship can be better for a dramatic "pause" in which grievances are aired—by both parties. And if you don't want to return to a partner who has abandoned you, temporarily or otherwise, a summer without men (or women) may well give you the strength to forge ahead alone (see: Divorce).

The breaking of trust causes deep wounds, and for many couples recovery is just too hard. If your partner has been unfaithful, you have to be honest with each other and decide between you if your trust can be rebuilt. If you're the one having an affair (or tempted by it), have a go at unleashing your unexpressed self within your marriage instead (to get some ideas, see: Stuck in a rut). You'll save everyone a lot of pain and trouble if you achieve it, and it may make both of you feel better about yourselves.

See also: **Dissatisfaction** · **Guilt** · **Jump ship, desire to** · **Midlife crisis** · **Regret** · **Trust, loss of**

AGE GAP BETWEEN LOVERS

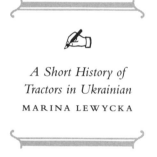

A Short History of Tractors in Ukrainian
MARINA LEWYCKA

A May-to-December romance tends to worry those observing the relationship more than those actually having it. But the disapproval and suspicion of others can be undermining, and if you are on the verge of falling into the arms of someone significantly older or younger than yourself, it's worth asking whether your relationship will be strong enough to withstand the ingrained cultural prejudice against large age gaps that persists in the West.

The first thing to establish is what you're both in the relationship for—and whether either of you is in any sort of denial about your own or your partner's motivation. When Nadia's eighty-six-year-old father in *A Short History of Tractors in Ukrainian* announces his engagement to Valentina—a thirty-six-year-old Ukrainian divorcée with "superior breasts" and an ambition to escape her drab life in the East—she gets straight to the point: "I can see why you want to marry her. But have you asked yourself why she wants to marry *you?*" Papa knows, of course, that she's just after a visa and a posh car in which to drive her fourteen-year-old son to school, but he sees no harm in rescuing her and Stanislav in return for a little youthful affection. She will cook and clean for him, and care for him in his old age. That she'll also clean out his meager life savings and bring them all to their knees with boil-in-the-bag cuisine is something he refuses to acknowledge, however, and it takes a good deal of teamwork between Nadia and her estranged "Big Sis" Vera to persuade him to open his rheumy eyes to the damage this "fluffy pink grenade" of a woman is doing to their family.

Yet you'd have to be a bit mean-spirited to begrudge the elderly tractor expert the new lease on life that Valentina, for all her faults, gives him. As long as both parties understand and accept each other's motivations, a relationship between two people at opposite ends of the innocence-experience spectrum can be a wonderfully symbiotic thing. There needs to be openness on both sides, though, and no game playing. If you've got that, you have our blessing. Fall away—whatever the age of those arms.

AGING, HORROR OF

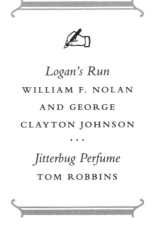

Logan's Run
WILLIAM F. NOLAN
AND GEORGE
CLAYTON JOHNSON

. . .

Jitterbug Perfume
TOM ROBBINS

In an age where almost every person in the public eye has ironed away their wrinkles, Botoxed their frowns, and banished gray hair forever, we can understand the impulse to flee the first signs of aging the way a rabbit would run from a fox. Growing old gracefully is a lovely idea . . . for your grandparents. But when it starts happening to you, it's hard to see where gracefulness enters into the picture.

Several novels—generally in the realm of science fiction and fantasy—indulge the notion of banishing old age forever. In *Logan's Run*, for instance, billed as a "terrifying novel of the twenty-third century," the authors William F. Nolan and George Clayton Johnson have invented a seemingly carefree (though postapocalyptic) world in which smooth-skinned young people indulge in no-strings-attached sensual romps in between bouts of cosmetic surgery. Work, such as it is, amounts to little more than hobbies, and there are no frowning oldies to scold the slackers to behave themselves and grow up. All this may sound like delicious, escapist wish fulfillment, until it dawns upon you that, even in the fanciful world of sci-fi, avoiding old age means dying young. (You knew there had to be a catch, right?) Yep. Youth's stuff will not endure, and the frivolous denizens of Nolan and Johnson's futurama are put to sleep—*permanently*—on their twenty-second birthdays. A fleet of enforcers called "Sandmen" hunt and trap the "runners" who perversely decide, as the deadline looms, that they wouldn't mind a few crow's-feet after all. Logan, the title character, is one of the most dedicated of these Sandman vigilantes—until his own twenty-second birthday looms. Which prompts, of course, his "run." But where can you run to in a world without old folks' homes? Whenever you get depressed about being physically past your peak, medicate with a dose of *Logan's Run* and be grateful for your comparative longevity.

King Alobar, the hero of *Jitterbug Perfume*, Tom Robbins's exploration of a similar scenario (set not in the future but a fictional eighth century of the past), has very good reason to dread the approach of senescence. It is customary for his tribe to commit regicide with a poisoned egg at the king's first sign of middle age. Here we distill the essence of *Jitterbug Perfume* in order to give you Alobar's recipe for eternal youth. For a fuller exposition, read the novel in its entirety.

INGREDIENTS
1 eighth-century king on the brink of middle age
1 immortal, goaty god giving off a strong stench
1 vial of perfume that has the power to seduce whole cities when released
1 measure of Jamaican jasmine, procured by the beekeeper Bingo Pajama
1 most vital part of beetroot

METHOD
Fold ingredients earnestly inside a French perfumery until combined, adding at the last moment your beetroot's vital part. Breathe in a never-ending loop while you fold. Now ensure that the Bandaloop doctors preside over your potion while you take a hot bath. Then achieve orgasm with your sexual partner, drawing all the energy from this act up into your brain stem. Repeat daily for a thousand years.

If you have not by then achieved your aim, take Alobar's best advice of all: lighten up.

See also: **Baldness** • **Birthday blues** • **Old age, horror of**

AGING PARENTS

The Corrections
JONATHAN FRANZEN
. . .
Family Matters
ROHINTON MISTRY

We wish this ailment on all of you. To have aged parents is something to celebrate, the alternative being to have faced their deaths before their time (see: Death of a loved one). However, one can't deny that people sometimes get annoying when they get old. They become crankier, more opinionated, less tolerant, more set in their ways. And on top of it all, they become physically incapacitated and need looking after, forcing a quite disconcerting reversal of the parent-child relationship. To that end, we address aging parents as a condition requiring a salve as well as a celebration. We recommend two excellent novels with this theme at their heart, revealing the practical and psychological effects of aging parents on the caring—or uncaring—children.

All three children veer heavily toward the latter in Jonathan Franzen's painfully funny *The Corrections*—though maybe Alfred and Enid Lambert had it coming. We first meet the Lambert parents in the final, most troubled stage of their lives. Alfred has Alzheimer's and dementia, and Enid joins the children in worrying about how to look after him (he has taken, among other things, to peeing in bottles in his den, because it's too far to get to the toilet). The driving force behind the narrative is Enid's desperation that all her children and grandchildren should come home for Christmas, as if this alone will reassure her that life is still worth living. Her eldest son, Gary, pretends that one of his children is ill in order to avoid the trip home. Daughter Denise has her own fish to fry with her new restaurant, and Chip, the youngest, has fled about as far away as you can get—Lithuania—on the back of a highly dubious Internet business.

As we move toward the inevitable Christmas showdown, we revisit significant moments in this seemingly conventional family's past: Alfred refusing—out of meanness—to sell a patent that could have made his fortune, Alfred dominating Enid in an increasingly worrisome fashion, and Enid taking out her misery on her children by feeding them the food of revenge (rutabaga and liver). Perhaps it's the memory of this meal that persuades these three grown children to put Alfred into a retirement home—which, never one to miss an opportunity for a joke, Franzen names Deepmire. It works well for everybody except Alfred. The terrorizing experience of reading this novel will remind you that avoiding such poor parent-child relations in the first place is highly recommended.

Mistry's Bombay novel begins with a celebration: the seventy-ninth birthday of the patriarch of the Vakeel family, Nariman. Nariman is a Parsi, whose religion prevented him from marrying the woman he loved for thirty years, and in fact lived with for many of these, until he gave in to his family's dogma and married a woman of his own faith. Now widowed and suffering from Parkinson's disease, he finds himself increasingly dependent on his two stepchildren, Jal and Coomy, who have always resented him because of his imperfect love for their mother. When one day on his daily excursion he breaks his leg, he's forced to put himself in their hands entirely. Soon he is lying in bed wishing that one of them would wash him, change his clothes, and play him some music, but he is too worried about disturbing them to ask for help. When they hear him crying at night, they realize he is depressed. Finding the management of his personal hygiene intolerable—loathing the details of bedpans and bedsores they know come from their own neglect—they send him to live with his blood daughter, Roxana, in the tiny flat she shares with her husband and two sons.

Here Grandpa Nariman has to sleep on the settee with Jehangir, the nine-year-old, while Murad, the older boy, sleeps in an improvised tent on the balcony—which, luckily, he finds a wonderful adventure. Roxana and her husband do an infinitely better job, compassionately embracing Grandpa and his fastidiousness over his dentures. Years later, Jehangir remembers with fondness and affection the time that his grandfather lived with them.

Family Matters is a wonderful example of how to look after one's aging parents with compassion—and how not to. And even though Nariman's stepchildren do a poor job, at least they take him in. In our Western world of dependence on nursing homes and hospitals, we would do well to take note of this example of a family caring for its elderly at home. Aged parents: don't be so objectionable that your children and spouse want to hole you up somewhere you can't embarrass them. Children of these parents: listen to their pleas for dignity and privacy, and do your utmost to help them retain these last vital assets. Both parties: try to forgive one another's different moralities and expectations. And, if possible, make it home for Christmas (for some survival tips, see: Christmas).

AGORAPHOBIA

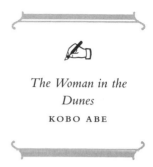

The Woman in the Dunes

KOBO ABE

Agoraphobics experience great discomfort when they find themselves in new places. Surrounded by the unfamiliar, the fear that they could lose control can trigger a panic attack (see: Panic attack). And so they prefer to stay at home—resulting in isolation, depression, and loneliness. Kobo Abe's novel is the perfect antidote.

Jumpei Niki, an amateur entomologist, takes a trip to a coastal desert at the end of the railway line, on the hunt for a new species of insect. While he searches for invertebrates, he stumbles upon a village hidden among eternally shifting dunes. Here he finds a unique community of people who live in houses nestled at the bottom of holes fifty feet deep in the buff terrain. To prevent their homes from being submerged, the residents must dig bucketfuls of golden dirt every day, which they send up on ropes to the villagers above.

Their work takes place in the moonlight, as the sun makes their shafts unbearably hot. Jumpei is lured into one of the burrows for the night, where he helps a young widow in the endless battle against the fluid sand. In a twist of fate, Jumpei wakes the next morning to find the ladder that should have been his exit has been removed. His escape attempts are alternately heroic, sadistic, and desperate. Slowly he accepts his fate as one who must work all day, sending buckets of sand up on ropes to helpers above—in between eating, sleeping, and having sex with the widow. By the end of the novel you have shared Jumpei's humiliation—for the villagers above find his inadvertent life change highly amusing—and his gradual acceptance of his bizarre new existence. And it's not all bad, for he does make a discovery under the sand.

Let Jumpei teach you to submit to the unexpected. And once you've experienced being hemmed in by imaginary walls of sand, you may be glad to take some tentative steps beyond your own, less imprisoning walls.

See also: **Anxiety** · **Loneliness**

Alcoholics knock around in the pages of novels like ice cubes in gin. Why? Because alcohol loosens tongues. And because it's always the old soaks who collar us to tell a tale. When they're on the page, we can enjoy their ramblings without having to smell their beery breath. But let's agree to keep them on the page. Nobody wants a real one in their home, and if you find yourself heading that way, we suggest you terrify yourself with a couple of graphic portrayals of bottle-induced ruin. Our cure is to be imbibed in three parts: two heady cocktails that will show you a glimpse of your potential fate to sober yourself up quick smart, followed by an enticing shot that will prompt you to put on your trainers and run yourself into a new, clean life.

Jack Torrance, the writer in Stephen King's spine-chilling *The Shining*, has been on the wagon for some years. Though his wife has stayed with him, he lost her trust when he broke his son Danny's arm in a drink-fueled rage. By working through the winter as caretaker of the Overlook Hotel in the Colorado Rockies, he hopes he can reconnect with his wife and now five-year-old son, and get his career back on track by writing a new play.

The two big obstacles to Jack's happiness have been an excessive reliance on alcohol and an explosive temper—not a good combination to take to a vast, spooky hotel where you are likely to be cut off from the outside world for several weeks once the snow hits. Jack starts his work in the firm conviction that he will stay sober. But one of the Overlook's ghostly attributes—apart from architecture that redesigns itself regularly—is an ability to produce cocktails from out of nowhere.

At first these are merely imaginary, but soon Jack is confronted with a genuine gin served to him by the (deceased) bartender, Lloyd (see: Haunted, being). Looking into the gin is "like drowning" for Jack: the first drink he's held to his lips in years. In the company of increasingly malign spirits, the specter of Jack's lurking alcoholism is delighted to break out and let rip. Observing Jack's disintegration will put the fear of the demon drink into you in more ways than one and will have you heading for the orange juice rather than the hooch.

Drunks tend to be either intoxicating or infuriating. Malcolm Lowry's

Under the Volcano, set on the Day of the Dead in the Mexican town of Quauh-nahuac, shows us both aspects of the psyche in dipsomaniac hero Geoffrey Firmin. The British consul of this volcano-shadowed town, he spends the day juggling his drinking needs with the complicated reappearance of his estranged wife, Yvonne. This ought to be the most important day of his life, he suspects, but all he can do is drink, telling himself he's downing a beer "for its vitamins" (he doesn't really bother with food), and dread the arrival of guests that fail to bring fresh supplies of liquor with them.

The events cover just one day and take place largely inside the consul's head, but the scope of this enormously powerful novel attains to the epic. As the Day of the Dead celebrations build to their feverish climax, the consul plunges tragically and irredeemably toward self-destruction, his thoughts laced always with whiskey and mescal. His musings are at times blackly funny, and references to Faust are frequent. Firmin is heading gleefully to hell, and his last words—"Christ, what a dingy way to die," foretold at the opening of the novel by Firmin's filmmaker friend Laruelle—echo with a ghastly reminder of what a horrible route this is to take in life.

Enough warnings! Those seeking to break such damaging habits need a glowing, inspirational model too—an alternative way to live. To this end, we urge you to read *Once a Runner* by John L. Parker, Jr. An underground classic when the author self-published it in 1978, it was taken up as a sort of novel-manual for competitive runners (bibliotherapy at work in the world). It tells the story of Quenton Cassidy, a member of Southeastern University's track team, training under Olympic gold medal winner Bruce Denton to run the mile. Denton pushes him and his running cronies to limits they never even knew existed. Quenton revels in the countless laps that Denton forces him to run, pushing himself so much that he urinates blood and openly weeps, his "mahogany hard legs" pounding the track all the while. At his peak, he is "vital, so quick, so nearly immortal" that he knows that life will never be "quite so poignant" as it is now.

Let *Once a Runner* inspire you to change your relationship with your body completely. Push it to the limit in a positive way. Put it to work and see what it can do. While Firmin in Lowry's novel wishes away the minutes between drinks, Cassidy in John Parker's breathes space into every second, getting the most out of each. The pure joy—and pain—of running, the sweat and ruthless determination of the race are as far a cry as you can get from the nihilism of the alcoholic. Buy yourself a pair of sneakers and serve this novel up to yourself instead of after-dinner drinks. May it be a symbol of your commitment to ditching the booze.

ALOPECIA

AMBITION, TOO LITTLE

The Crimson Petal and the White
MICHEL FABER

If you find yourself watching everybody else's race but your own, or even that you're still standing on the starting line, you need a novel to galvanize you into setting some finishing posts, then pelting toward them. There's no better novel for the job than *The Crimson Petal and the White*.

Our young heroine starts life in a place most would say was so far from the possibility of even competing that she might as well give up before she starts. Sugar was forced into prostitution by her mother at the tender age of thirteen and grows up believing she has no choice but to submit to the gentlemen who come to her bed "to keep her warm." But she yearns to rise above this base existence. Her way of going about it is to become the best in the brothel—and then the best in Britain. Soon not only has she acquired phenomenal accomplishments in the bedroom, but she knows how to make a man feel eloquent, witty, and full of vitality, simply by the way she listens and flirts. But underneath her charming exterior, she still finds her work grotesque and pours her disgust into a novel she writes in secret at her desk.

Her big break comes when she meets William Rackham of Rackham Perfumeries, who discovers her through the pages of the gentleman's magazine *More Sprees in London*. Rackham is so smitten with Sugar that he arranges to keep her for his exclusive use. Eventually she becomes invaluable to him, not just for her charms and beauty, but for her brains, being more astute and more in touch with her customer's needs than he is himself. It's not long before Sugar is the guiding force behind his advertising campaigns and overall business strategy.

Faber portrays in minute detail a Victorian world of social inequality and rigid convention. "Watch your step. Keep your wits about you; you will need them," he exhorts at the start of the novel. Follow Sugar (though not into prostitution), and rise wisely, determining your own fate rather than those of others. As Oscar Wilde put it: "Our ambition should be to rule ourselves, the true kingdom for each one of us."

See also: Apathy • Bed, inability to get out of • Lethargy

AMBITION, TOO MUCH

Great Expectations
CHARLES DICKENS

Some of us have too little of it, others too much. According to the Taoist philosopher Lao-Tzu, ambition—in its best ratio—has one heel nailed in well, "though she stretch her fingers to touch the heavens." When neither heel is nailed down firmly, and we overreach our innate talents and social limitations, we are in danger of losing our purchase completely.

This is what happens to Pip in *Great Expectations*. Orphaned Pip lives with his older sister, the harsh and unsympathetic Mrs. Joe, whose face looks as if it has been "scrubbed with a nutmeg grater" and who believes in bringing him up "by Hand" (though she is tempered by her gentle husband, Joe, who shows kindness to Pip throughout his turbulent life). When Pip meets Estella, the beautiful but ice-hearted ward of eccentric Miss Havisham, who is still wearing the wedding dress in which she was jilted at the altar forty years ago, Pip is encouraged by his sister to nurture a hope that this strange old lady has plans to groom him for Estella. The hope turns to a conviction, giving him the green light to behave "like a gentleman"—not necessarily of the best sort—and look down on his origins, including his friend Biddy, who sees the way that Pip is going and doesn't like it.

Pip and his sister are proved horribly wrong. Though Pip does land a surprise inheritance, and outwardly this makes him a "gentleman," worldly success is shown to be naught to success in love. Fortunes can be lost as easily as they are won. Pip would have saved a lot of time and heartache if he had never been "raised up." Let Pip's mistake stand as a warning. By all means look to the skies. But keep at least one foot on the terra firma of your origins.

See also: **Greed** · **Selling your soul** · **Social climbing** · **Workaholism**

READING AILMENT   *Amnesia, reading associated*

CURE   *Keep a reading journal*

Sufferers of reading-associated amnesia have little or no recollection of the novels they have read. They come home from the bookshop, excited by the crisp new novel in their hands, only to be struck five or twenty pages in by a sense of déjà vu. They join a conversation about a classic novel they believe they've read, only to be posed a question they can't answer—usually what happened at the end.

What you need, blancmange-brained reader, is a reading journal. A small notebook to carry with you at all times, ideally one that's beautiful and pleasing to the touch. Dedicate one page to each book you read, and on the day you turn the last page write down the book's title and author, the date, and the place you read it. You might like to sum up the story in one headline-grabbing line: MAN MURDERS PAWNBROKER, FEELS GUILTY FOR NEXT FIVE HUNDRED PAGES, for example. Or you might opine at length on the motivations of a character you found particularly intriguing. You may also want to make a note of how the book left you feeling—uplifted or downhearted? Like taking a walk on the windy moors, or emigrating to New Zealand? If words don't come easily, use images to summarize your feelings, or give it marks out of ten, or write a list of the words that you found in the book and liked.

This journal will be a record of your reading journey. Over

(continued)

---

the years you can flip back and recollect the highs and the lows. And if an author or title eludes you midconversation, make an excuse to go to the bathroom and look it up.

AMPUTATION

See: Limb, loss of

ANALLY RETENTIVE, BEING

The Life and Opinions of Tristram Shandy

LAURENCE STERNE

If you're anally retentive, you'll know all about the importance of order, logic, and neatness. A maker of lists, your life consists of accomplishing tasks that you can then tick off. Anything that comes between you and your task—an unexpected telephone call, a sunlit field calling you to take a stroll, an uninvited guest dropping by for tea—is grossly unwelcome. Your single-track mind cannot wander from its course. Now is your moment to swap psyches with Tristram Shandy. After 480 pages of living inside the head of this lovable philosopher and accompanying him on his remarkably prolix ramblings, you will be cured of your anal retentiveness forever.

Published in successive volumes from 1760 to 1767, *Tristram Shandy* is perhaps the first interactive novel, inviting the reader to take Sterne's proffered hand and join in the author's game. Like Italo Calvino two hundred years later, the authorial voice intrudes often and merrily, asking readers to consider the ways in which he has advanced their understanding of a character.

Shandy's determination to write his memoirs is unstinting, but it takes him until volume three to arrive at his birth. Because this memoir, and indeed his life, consists entirely of diversions from the point. While he was still a mere homunculus inside his mother's womb, the road to his existence was disturbed, at the very moment of procreation, by his mother asking his father if he had remembered to wind the clock. This interruption to the act of conception results, he believes, in his prenatal self falling prey to "melancholy dreams and fancies" even before he came to fully exist. And when his name, which his father considered of enormous importance to his nature and fortunes, is accidentally mangled by the time it reaches the curate, and he is inadvertently christened Tristram—apparently the least auspicious of names—rather than Trismegistus as intended, he believes himself to be even less blessed by the fates.

All of which, perhaps, explains why Shandy's/Sterne's prose is so unruly—a page left blank for readers to draw their own version of Widow Wadman, the paramour of Uncle Toby; asterisks where the reader is invited to imagine what a character is thinking; and an entirely black page that supposedly "mourns" the loss of Parson Yorick. There are even squiggly loops indicating the shape of the narrative digressions themselves.

One cannot help but come under the spell. "Digressions, incontestably, are the sunshine. They are the life, the soul, of reading!" says Tristram at the start of the novel. We wholeheartedly agree. Interrupt the reading of this book by opening *Tristram Shandy*. Go on, just for a chapter. Although after a few pages, perhaps, it'll be time for a cup of tea. And then a spontaneous excursion might take your fancy. You might forget you were reading this book in the first place. (That's okay; you can come back to it in the middle of some other task some other day.) A digression a day keeps the doctor away—and so will *Tristram Shandy*.

See also: **Control freak, being a · Give up halfway through, refusal to ·
Humorlessness · Organized, being too · Reverence of books, excessive ·
Single-mindedness**

ANGER

*The Old Man and
the Sea*
ERNEST HEMINGWAY

Because even after eighty-four consecutive days of going out in his boat without catching a single fish, the old man is cheerful and undefeated. And even when the other fishermen laugh at him, he is not angry. And even though he now has to fish alone—because the boy who has been with him since he was five, and whom he loves, and who loves him, has been forced by his family to try his luck with another boat—he holds no grudge in his heart. And because on the eighty-fifth day he goes out again, full of hope.

And even though, when he does hook a big fish—the biggest fish that he or anyone else has ever caught—it pulls on his line so fiercely that the skin on his hand is torn, he still lets the fish pull him farther out. And though he wishes to God that the boy were with him, he is grateful that at least he has the porpoises that play and joke around his boat. And even when it's been a day and a night and another day stretches ahead, and it's only him and the fish and there's no one to help, still he keeps his head. And even when he has been pushed further than he has ever been pushed in his life, and he begins to feel the edge of despair, he talks himself around, because he must think of what he has, and not what he does not have, and of what he can do with what there is. And though his hand becomes so stiff it is useless, and though he is hungry and thirsty and blinded by the sun, he still thinks of the lions he once saw on the beach in Africa, like some sort of heavenly vision. Because he knows that there is nothing greater, or more beautiful, or more noble than this fish that tugs him ever on. And even when it is dead, and the sharks come to feast—first one, then half a dozen—and the man loses his harpoon and then his knife in his attempts to fend them off; and even when he has ripped out the keel of his boat to use as a club; and even though he fails to save the flesh of the fish, and the ordeal leaves him so tired and weak he is nearly lost himself; and even though when he finally makes it to shore all that is left of the fish is a skeleton, he accepts what has happened, and is not broken, nor angry, but goes, rather gratefully, to bed.

Because by immersing yourself in the simple, calming prose of this story, you too will rise above your emotions. You will join the old man in his boat, witness firsthand his love for the boy, for the sea, for the fish, and allow it to fill you with peace and a noble acceptance of what is, leaving no space for what was or what you would like to be. Sometimes we all go out too far, but it doesn't mean we can't come back. And just as the old man is made happy by his vision of lions on a beach, you too can have your vision—perhaps of the old man and the way he talks himself around. And after you have read it, you will keep this novel on your shelf, somewhere you will see it whenever you feel angry. And you'll remember the old man, the sea, the fish, and you'll be calm.

See also: Rage · Road rage · Turmoil · Vengeance, seeking · Violence, fear of

Siddhartha
HERMANN HESSE

As anyone who has stood at the top of a cliff will tell you, alongside the fear of falling to your death is an equally strong and entirely conflicting emotion: the urge to jump. The knowledge that nothing is stopping you from making that leap, the leap into possibility—the realization that you have absolute freedom of will, infinite power to create and to destroy—fills you with horror and dread. It is this horror, according to Soren Kierkegaard, that lies at the root of existential angst.

If you are unlucky enough to have been struck with this debilitating affliction, you will be in urgent need of spiritual refreshment. You need to pare back the possibilities, to renounce the world, and join, at least for a while, the ascetics. You need *Siddhartha*.

Siddhartha, the young son of a fictional Brahmin in ancient India, brings joy and bliss to everyone—except himself. Leading a seemingly idyllic existence surrounded by a family who loves him, he appears destined for great things. But despite his material and spiritual wealth, young Siddhartha feels that something is missing.

And so, as young men in ancient India were wont to do, he goes on a spiritual quest. First he joins the Samana, a band of self-flagellating ascetics who deny the flesh and seek enlightenment through renunciation. Fully flagellated but still discontented, he encounters Gotama, the Buddha, who teaches him the eightfold path that illuminates the way to the end of suffering. Not content with this knowledge alone, and wanting to reach his goal through his own understanding, he meets Vasudeva, a ferryman with an astonishing inner light, who seems content with his simple life. But this, too, fails to satisfy. Even after living a sensual and happy life for many years with the beautiful Kamala, still something is missing for Siddhartha. For a while he contemplates death by drowning. But then he remembers the astoundingly happy ferryman, Vasudeva, and learns that he must study the river.

Here he finds revelations to last a lifetime—including the true cycle of life and death, and what it is to be part of a timeless unity. And from that day on he radiates transcendent understanding, self-knowledge, and enlightenment. From all over the world, people come to him to seek wisdom and peace. People like you.

See also: Anxiety • Despair • Dread, nameless • Pointlessness

ANGST, TEENAGE

See: Adolescence • Teens, being in your

ANOREXIA NERVOSA

See: Eating disorder

ANTISOCIAL, BEING

Being not the most sociable person in the world doesn't have to mean you're a sad excuse for a human being. Greta Garbo—no slouch, she—famously got an Oscar nomination for declaring "I want to be alone" (three times) in the movie *Grand Hotel.*

The Accidental Tourist
ANNE TYLER
. . .
We Have Always Lived in the Castle
SHIRLEY JACKSON

Since novelists spend days, weeks, months, and even years inside their own invented worlds, it's not surprising that many of them focus on characters who aren't exactly clubbable. One of the best novels about loners is Anne Tyler's *The Accidental Tourist,* whose introverted lead character, Macon Leary, wants mostly to be left in peace. "It's nice to be so unconnected," he tells his sister, Rose, when his wife leaves him, fed up with his "little routines and rituals, depressing habits, day after day." Macon likes his life when it's free of attachments. "I wish things could stay that way a while," he tells Rose. Macon writes travel guides for businesspeople who don't like traveling and who, as he does, like to "pretend they had never left home." Macon carries this mind-set to such an extreme that he envies his older brother, Charles, when Charles gets stuck in the pantry of the family home, where Macon's grown-up siblings still live. "Macon imagined how safe the pantry must feel, with Rose's jams lined up in alphabetical order and the black dial telephone, so ancient that the number on its face was still the old Tuxedo exchange. What he wouldn't give to be there!"

If you identify with Macon, you may be surprised to find yourself warming to Anne Tyler's story of his transformation to a friendlier sort of person. When Macon meets a bighearted, effusive divorcée named Muriel, her kooky coaxing gradually persuades him to connect more enthusiastically with the world outside his head. Through Muriel, he discovers that he can enjoy the world beyond his own doorstep. Macon's cure can be yours.

If, however, you find yourself stroppily chafing at the idea of interacting more energetically with your fellow man, you might want to prescribe yourself sterner medicine: Shirley Jackson's dark novella *We Have Always Lived in the Castle*. In this cautionary tale, Mary Katherine Blackwood and her sister Constance live, by choice, in a secluded house outside a village. Their family's sinister unfriendliness has made them pariahs among the locals. For Mary Katherine, the thought of speaking to any non–family member—even a librarian—fills her with dread, and a visit to the local grocery store is for her a ghastly ordeal. When she picks up bread and sugar, she senses that the "women in the store were watching," and longs to kick them. "It's wrong to hate them," Constance tells her. "It only weakens you." But Mary Katherine hates them all the same, and even wonders "why it had been worthwhile creating them in the first place." Reading the spooky results of their self-imposed solitary confinement might well shake you out of yours.

See also: Cynicism • Dinner parties, fear of • Killjoy, being a • Misanthropy • Read instead of live, tendency to

ANXIETY

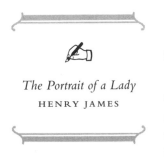

The Portrait of a Lady
HENRY JAMES

To live with anxiety is to live with a leech that saps you of your energy, confidence, and chutzpah. A constant feeling of unease or fearfulness—as opposed to the sense of frustration that characterizes stress (see: Stress)—anxiety is both a response to external circumstances and an approach to life. While the external circumstances cannot be controlled, the internal response can. Laughter, or a big intake of oxygen (the former leading to the latter), usually relieves systems at least temporarily, as well as offering an encouragement to relax. The cause of the anxiety, however, determines whether laughter or breathing and relaxing is the appropriate cure. Luckily, our cure offers all three.

Of the fourteen causes of anxiety that we have identified,[*] the first chapter of *The Portrait of a Lady* by Henry James can be expected to ameliorate ten. Opening as it does with a description of the civilized and serene institution of afternoon tea in an English country garden—complete with "mellow" late afternoon light, long shadows, tea cups held "for a long time close to [the] chin," rugs, cushions, and books strewn on the lawn in the shade of the trees—its indirect invitation to slow down and have a cup yourself (helpful for causes 2, 3, 4, 7, 10, 11, 12, and certain elements of 13) is reenforced by James's unhurried, elegant prose, a balm for anxiety arising from all of the preceding causes, and also serves to begin the complete eradication of anxiety arising from cause number 8.

To say that James's prose spreads itself thickly, like butter, is not intended to suggest turgidness, but rather creaminess—and let us make that *salted* butter. For the pleasures of both prose and afternoon tea are made complete by James's dialogue, which contains both frankness and sharpness of wit (a curative for causes 1 through 4, and also excellent for cause 7). For the banter between the three men—the elderly chair-bound American banker Mr. Touchett, his "ugly, sickly" but charming son Ralph, and the "noticeably handsome" Lord Warburton with his quintessentially English face—is always aiming to trigger a chuckle, and the characters are not afraid of teasing (note Lord Warburton's markedly un-English reference to Mr. Touchett's wealth). Freed of the chains of propriety and form that had been shackling dialogue on similar lawns three quarters of a century earlier, it is the sort of conversation that puts you at your ease (again, addressing causes 1 through 4 and 7, while also ameliorating causes 6 and 9 through 12).

Once the little party is joined by Ralph's American cousin Isabel Archer, recently "taken on" by Mrs. Touchett, the conversation loses some of its ease, but gains in spirit—for Isabel, at this stage in her life, has a lightness, a boldness, and a confidence both in herself and in others that cannot fail to rub off on the reader. Those suffering anxiety from cause 9 will find her presence in the story especially curative.

[*] (1) Trauma, including abuse, or death of a loved one; (2) relationship problems, either at home or at work; (3) work/school; (4) finances; (5) natural disaster; (6) lack of oxygen at high altitude; (7) taking life too seriously; (8) gnawing feeling that you should have read more of the classics; (9) negative self-talk; (10) poor health/hypochondria; (11) taking too many drugs; (12) being late/too busy; (13) inadequate food, water, heat, or comfort; (14) threat of attack by wild animal/person.

Indeed, we recommend this novel for all sufferers of anxiety except those made anxious by causes 5 and 14 (for the latter, in particular, a novel of any sort is unhelpful, except perhaps to use as a weapon), though readers suffering anxiety from causes 1 and 2 should be warned that the ending may backfire and prompt their symptoms to get worse. In which case, they should immediately turn back to the beginning for another dose of afternoon tea.

See also: **Angst, existential** • **Panic attack** • **Turmoil**

APATHY

*The Postman Always
Rings Twice*
JAMES M. CAIN

Although it can manifest as physical sluggishness—like its heavy-limbed cousin, lethargy—apathy is essentially a mental condition, characterized by an attitude of indifference toward outcomes, both for oneself and for the world at large. Its cure, however, is best tackled by addressing the physical sluggishness first, thus further distinguishing it from its other near relations, pessimism and existential angst, which require an overhaul of the mind. This is because apathy is also characterized by a suppression of positive emotions, and to reengage them and rekindle the desire for things to turn out well, one has to stir up the sediment at the bottom of the too sedentary soul.

It's not that it all ends well for Frank Chambers, the itinerant chancer and jailbreaker in James M. Cain's 1934 masterpiece *The Postman Always Rings Twice*. Indeed, if you were to adopt his philosophy of life, you'd end up (as he does) with a price on your head and several angry women in hot pursuit. But the novel is written with such rattling exuberance that it's impossible to read without becoming physically buzzed. By the end, you'll be up and about with a bounce in your step, throwing caution to the wind in your determination to have a hand in fate, setting you on a more spontaneous and proactive—if slightly reckless—new tack.

From the moment Frank Chambers is thrown off the hay truck, the story is up and running. Within three pages he has swindled the honest owner of the Twin Oaks Tavern into fixing him a colossal breakfast (orange juice, cornflakes, fried eggs, bacon, enchilada, flapjacks, and coffee, if you're interested), got himself hired as a mechanic, and set covetous won't-take-no-for-an-answer eyes on Cora, the tavern owner's sullenly sexy wife. One thing leads to another—and then another—and Cain does a splendid job of keeping up with Frank, capturing his immoral inability to say no in short, snappy sentences laced with slang. The combination of story and style hits you like a triple espresso, and at only a little over a hundred pages it's also a very quick fix. Rip through it in an afternoon, then jack your apathy onto your back and chuck it out on the street as you go. You'll be inspired by Frank's irrepressible interest in each new moment—even when things aren't going so well—and determined not to blow, as he does, the opportunities that arise.

See also: Ambition, too little • Bed, inability to get out of • Lethargy • Pessimism • Pointlessness • Zestlessness

APPETITE, LOSS OF

The Leopard
GIUSEPPE TOMASI
DI LAMPEDUSA

Losing one's appetite is a terrible thing. For one's appetite for food is part and parcel of one's appetite for life. A result of various kinds of physical and emotional sickness (the latter including lovesickness, depression, heartbreak, and bereavement), total loss of appetite can lead in only one direction. To bring it back, and solicit a reengagement with life, whet and tempt with one of literature's most sensual novels.

The Leopard, Don Fabrizio Corbèra, Prince of Salina, feels as if he has been dying for years. But even now, in his old age, he is Appetite writ large. He still has the energy, at seventy-three, to go to brothels, and is still delighted to see his favorite dessert—a rum jelly in the shape of a fortress, complete with bastions and battlements—on the dining table (it's rapidly demolished beneath the assault of his large, equally lusty family). There are ravishing descriptions of desire of many different kinds: the daily pursuit of a hare in the "archaic and aromatic fields," and the intense and overwhelming attraction of young Tancredi and Angelica as they chase each other around the palace, forever finding new rooms in which to yearn and dream, for "these were the days when desire was always present, because always overcome."

One cannot help but revel in the old patriarch's appreciation for the sensual world. This is a novel that will help you rediscover your appetite—for food, for love, for the countryside, for Sicily with all its history and rampant beauty. And, most important, for life itself.

ARROGANCE

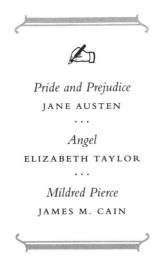

Pride and Prejudice
JANE AUSTEN
. . .

Angel
ELIZABETH TAYLOR
. . .

Mildred Pierce
JAMES M. CAIN

Arrogance is one of the greatest crimes in literature. We know this because when Mr. Darcy snubs Elizabeth Bennet at Bingley's ball—refusing to dance with her, dismissing her beauty as just "tolerable," and generally turning sour on the inhabitants of Longbourn—he is immediately written off by everyone, even Mrs. Bennet, as the "proudest, most disagreeable man in the world." And this is despite being much more handsome than the amiable Mr. Bingley, despite his having a large estate in Derbyshire, and despite his being by far the most eligible man for a twenty-five-mile radius—which, as we know, means a great deal to Mrs. Bennet, with five daughters to marry off.

Luckily, the playful Elizabeth Bennet, Jane Austen's heroine in *Pride and Prejudice*, knows how to bring him down to size. She uses a combination of teasing ("I am perfectly convinced . . . that Mr. Darcy has no defect," said to his face) and blunt, hyperbolic rejection ("I had not known you a month before I felt that you were the last man in the world whom I could ever be prevailed on to marry"), which not only corrects his flaws but displays the "liveliness of [her] mind" to such a degree that he falls in love with her all over again—and properly this time. If you are inflicted with similar arrogance, learn from this novel how to spot intelligent teasing and courageous honesty—and welcome it. You should be so lucky to be turned into the perfect man/woman by someone like Elizabeth.

Sometimes, however, the arrogance is so deeply instilled that nothing and no one can shift it. The eponymous heroine of *Angel*, by Elizabeth Taylor—not the Hollywood actress but the mid-twentieth-century British writer—is just fifteen years old when we meet her, and to say she thinks she's the bee's knees is an understatement. An incorrigible liar, this strange child is vain, bossy, and utterly devoid of humor. She feels nothing but contempt for her classmates, is unmoved when one of them is taken to the hospital with diphtheria, and fantasizes about a future in which, dressed in emeralds and a chinchilla wrap, she'll be able to employ her own, tiresome mother as her maid. Naturally, her mother is pretty appalled by the daughter she's raised—just as Mildred is horrified by her similarly monstrous daughter Veda in James M. Cain's *Mildred Pierce*. Veda drains the family coffers to support her extravagant lifestyle and steals her mother's new man. It's not hard to see why Mildred tries to kill the monster she's created.

Fascinatingly, Angel's über-confidence carries her a long way—all the way to those emeralds, in fact. Veda, too, gets exactly what she wants. Neither discovers humility. Rejection—in Angel's case, from publishers and critics; in Veda's, by her own mother—has no sobering effect on either of them.

Do not be an Angel or a Veda. When you inspire rejection, question what you might have done to deserve it. Instead, be a Darcy. Though he's initially angered and mortified by Elizabeth's refusal of his proposal—and her accusations against his character—he knows the difference between right and wrong and craves the good opinion of someone he admires. Be glad when others pull your leg—chances are, they'll be improving you.

See also: **Confidence, too much** • **Vanity**

ATTENTION, SEEKING
See: **Neediness**

B

BAD BLOOD

See: Anger • Bitterness • Hatred

BAD MANNERS

See: Manners, bad

BAD TASTE

See: Taste, bad

BAD TEMPERED, BEING

See: Grumpiness • Irritability • Killjoy, being a • Querulousness

BALDNESS

If you have a shiny pink pate on which nothing grows—and you catch glimpses of its outward spread reflected in windows as you pass—you may feel dismay at the passing of your locks, and perhaps with them, a sense of virility. You envy the thick manes you see around you and wish that some of their excess could be transferred to you. But think of the evolution of man from ape to

Blow Fly
PATRICIA CORNWELL
(continued)

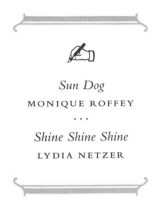

Sun Dog
MONIQUE ROFFEY
. . .
Shine Shine Shine
LYDIA NETZER

nearly hairless human. You are the superior being, your high-domed forehead more evolved. It is the mop-headed brutes who should feel shifty in your presence and who would surely shave it all off if they had enough brains to think it through.

If these sentiments don't reassure you, Patricia Cornwell's seventeenth novel, *Blow Fly*, will. Jean-Baptiste Chandonne was born with a fine down of black hair—not just on his head but covering every inch of his body. As a child, he was treated as a worrying curiosity, hidden from the public by his embarrassed parents. As an adult he has assumed the role of monster, a "wolfman" repellent to the eye—not merely because of his pelt, but because the condition brings with it a deformed body and a terrifyingly bestial face.

Hair hangs around this novel, clogging sinks, coming out in tufts in people's hands, and left incriminatingly on dead bodies. Forensic science brings a magnifying lens to these hairs with medical examiner Kay Scarpetta on the case (and in fact she has met this hirsute beast before). As Scarpetta and Chandonne sharpen their claws on each other's armory, you will be increasingly repelled by the sheer ickiness of all the hair and will run your hand over your smooth scalp with untold relief.

And if you need further convincing that bald is best, read Monique Roffey's *Sun Dog*. Her protagonist, August, is a man who can change his bodily attributes with the seasons. In the autumn he has blood orange hair that leaps from his head "as if from a burning attic." In winter he turns blue and emits snowflakes. In spring, buds emerge from his armpits, nipples, and ears. And in summer his hair comes off in swathes. It is then, at his baldest and most vulnerable, that August meets his true love. Luckily, she has no interest in whether he's tufty or smooth; she loves him for himself.

It was the alopecia of Sunny Mann, the bald heroine of Lydia Netzer's novel *Shine Shine Shine*, that endeared her to her first love, and later husband, Maxon Mann, a math-minded astronaut with a touch of Asperger's. He and Sunny fell in love as teenagers, when they would sit in their local planetarium looking up at the stars. Maxon longed to draw the constellations on Sunny's smooth skull and was fond of imagining her head lighting up like a celestial globe. Sunny is comfortable in her own scalp, and she secretly looks "askance" at women with long hair, feeling they are somehow "overcompensating." All the same, she can't help dreaming of a miracle cure, and after she and Maxon marry, she starts wearing a blond wig so as to fit in with the other wives in her neighborhood. When that wig accidentally flies off, Sunny feels wildly liberated: "She woke up out of her sleep, she dropped out from her orbit, scattered across the sky on every different vector, every crazy angle." She becomes, in short, her genuine, glorious, undisguised self, which her friends turn out to like just as much as her bewigged incarnation. "Own it," Sunny says to herself. "Own the bald." If baldness is your bugbear, be like Sunny: Fear it no longer. Accept your shining pate.

See also: Aging, horror of

BEANS, TEMPTATION TO SPILL THE

Tess of the d'Urbervilles
THOMAS HARDY

For reasons medical science has never explained (although, naturally, we have our own hypothesis; see below), it's physically uncomfortable to keep a secret bottled up, and a great relief to let it out. And confessing—or spilling the beans—can bring not only immense relief, but also sometimes a sadistic pleasure. The look on someone's face during the moment of spillage can be both entertaining and gratifying (see: Schadenfreude). But these positive emotions are usually short-lived, particularly if the spilling of the beans has caused pain or anguish in the spillee, or the beans were not yours to spill. Before such spillages are indulged in, therefore, the short-term gain (for you) of spilling must be weighed against the long-term consequences (for you and others). Because beans, once spilled, cannot be unspilled, and it may be better for everyone if you live with the discomfort of keeping them pent up inside instead.

If Tess Durbeyfield had lived with her beans—as her mother Joan advised her to—her marriage could have been saved and a happy ending secured. Tess's confession to her husband, Angel Clare, on their wedding night about her tarnished past with Alec d'Urberville is made after Angel owns up to a previous liaison of his own. She, understandably enough, sees this as the perfect moment for them both to clear their consciences. But Angel, to his great discredit, fails to forgive Tess as she has forgiven him. He rejects his sullied Tess and heads off to Brazil in a serious sulk.

All might have been well if Tess had kept her beans inside her and waited until such time as Angel was man enough to see the situation for what it was—she as the victim, Alec as the assailant. By this time she would also have realized (as she eventually does) that the beans were not hers to feel guilty about in the first place—that they were in fact Alec d'Urberville's beans and should have been his all along. Tess is an innocent victim of nineteenth-century patriarchy, of course, but the emotional truth still holds: she should have kept those beans inside.

A word of warning, though. If your secret is a guilty one through and through, and having weighed the pros and cons you've decided to keep the secret inside, be prepared that the discomfort may get worse over time—whether it indicts you or someone else. Bottled-up beans, like actual beans, give off a sort of gas that expands, producing flatulence and indigestion until they eventually erupt without warning, usually at the very worst possible moment. This is a situation worth avoiding at all costs and indicates that your secret has more guilt attached than you may have realized. If you suspect that your beans might turn gaseous, find an intermediary on whom to off-load them, who can then spill them in a more considered and controlled fashion—or help you to. See: Guilt, for an example of an intermediary at work in this way.

See also: **Goody-goody, being a** • **Regret**

Bed
DAVID WHITEHOUSE

BED, INABILITY TO GET OUT OF

Perhaps you have a headache or a hangover (see: Headache; Hangover). Perhaps you hate your job and have declared a Duvet Day. Perhaps your central heating is on the blink and you can't get warm. Perhaps everything seems pointless (see: Pointlessness) or you're depressed (see: Depression, general). Whatever the reason, if you know that sometimes staying in bed seems a much better idea than emerging into your day, keep this volume under your pillow (so you don't have far to stretch). Read it once, and then during subsequent attacks of the condition you will need only a brief dip to send you leaping out from under your duvet and thence into anything other than the small suburban bedroom and freak show of a life depicted within its pages.

Malcolm Ede has stayed in bed for so long that his skin is as "white as an institution." He is deprived of sunlight and drained of life. Weighing in at more than half a ton, he is pinned to the bed by an "umbrella of fat." After deciding, for complex reasons, on his twenty-sixth birthday to simply never get out of bed again, he's been there ever since. Cared for and fed by his hopelessly devoted mother, his dreamy dad, and his broken brother, he is the planet around which they orbit. A great big hot-air balloon of a planet.

Malcolm escapes his carapace of flesh in the end. But unless you want to be living in your parents' bedroom at age forty-three, unless you want blisters and sores on parts of your body that you can't even see, unless you fancy being unable to even meet your hands together to pray for escape, read this. Then get up, out of bed, right now.*

See also: Ambition, too little • Lethargy • Read instead of live, tendency to

BEREAVEMENT

See: Broken heart • Death of a loved one • Widowed, being • Yearning, general

BIOLOGICAL CLOCK TICKING

See: Children, not having • Children, under pressure to have • Shelf, fear of being left on the

BIRTHDAY BLUES

So you're about to be one year older and you don't like it at all. You may fear the loss of your looks (see: Vanity; Baldness). You may fear the loss of your health and marbles (see: Senile, going). Well, you're not the only one (see: Aging, horror of; Old age, horror of). In fact, at this very mo-

Midnight's Children
SALMAN RUSHDIE

---

* And that means *now*.

ment, one million seventy-six thousand two hundred and eighty* other people on this planet are also experiencing the birthday blues. Just like Saleem Sinai, the hero of *Midnight's Children*, who shares his birthday (midnight on August 15, 1947) with the birth of a newly independent India and one thousand others, so you too took your first breath on the same day in the same year as an awful lot of other people around the world.

You don't have to believe in astrology (or magical realism) to see that you have a special connection to these people—just as Saleem's life is yoked to the history of his country, and to the other "children of midnight" with whom he shares a strange telepathy and magical gifts. Think of it this way: it's already an uncanny coincidence to be alive on this planet with anyone else at all, given how long the universe has been in existence and how long it is likely to remain so into the future. To think that there are other people born the *very same day, the very same year*—well, they're practically your siblings! Doesn't it make you want to rush out into the world and wish them all a happy birthday?

On the eve of your big day, tuck in to *Midnight's Children* along with all the other birthday boys and girls your age. Raise your glass to your extended family. Experience, simultaneously, the vibrancy and color of this delightful novel, chuckle in tandem at its goofy humor and attention to the craziness of life. As you laugh, you will feel young again, together. Keep reading all night, as you used to do years ago. It's a long novel. From over the top of the page, watch those blues turn pink with the dawn.

See also: **Dissatisfaction**

Oroonoko
APHRA BEHN

BITTERNESS

If you feel you have been dealt an unfair hand and deserve better, that everybody else but you has it easy, if you are outraged when things do not go your way, you may have succumbed to the scourge of bitterness. It may well be true that you were dealt a bad hand. But life is what we make it and nobody said it would be fair. Besides,

* Give or take a few.

people tend to shun bitter characters—in life as well as literature—as they exude anger and ill will. Unless you want to make your life even harder, we urge you to take a lesson from the magnificent Prince Oroonoko, hero of a tale of betrayal, true love, and stoicism published in 1688.

Prince Oroonoko, tall, proud, and strikingly regal, loves Imoinda. She loves him too—and marries him—but she is so beautiful that the King of Coramantien (present-day Ghana) falls in love with her as well and forces her to join his harem. She and Prince Oroonoko manage to escape together, but are caught and sold into slavery. Miraculously, they find each other, in Surinam, and even conceive a child, but their plea to return to their homeland is ignored. Abandoned and betrayed, they tackle head-on the political forces that keep them enslaved, and things go from bad to worse—and then to even worse still.

No one has greater reason to be bitter than Oroonoko. Not only is his wife taken from him, but he is caught up in the terrible injustice of slavery. Right at the end, when all is lost, Oroonoko faces a final, horrific ordeal: the dismemberment of his limbs, one by one. But having recently discovered the consolation of the tobacco pipe, he bears the torture by calmly smoking, sanguine and pensive. We don't recommend that you take up smoking. But we do recommend that you emulate Oroonoko's ability to rise above life's unfairness and live his life without a grudge.

See also: Anger • Cynicism • Hatred • Jealousy • Regret • Scars, emotional • Schadenfreude

BLOCKED, BEING

See: Constipation • Writer's block

BLUSHING

Blushing is something we dread. Occurring when adrenalin generated by a rush of embarrassment makes the blood vessels just under the surface of the skin expand, it turns the visage a bright, unnatural crimson that nobody can fail to notice. We all suffer the horror of blushing as

Lady: My Life as a Bitch
MELVIN BURGESS

teenagers, and it can happen occasionally as adults (see: Shyness). But a few continue to suffer from it chronically through adulthood, to the point where it becomes a vicious circle—fearing the blush so much that the fear creates it.* The truth is that blushing is something we respond to warmly; recent research has shown that those who blush are seen in a positive light by their peers. But if you feel that your blushing is a hindrance to your enjoyment of social situations, we prescribe one of Melvin Burgess's unashamedly dirty teenage novels, *Lady: My Life as a Bitch*.

Sandra Francy is a girl of seventeen who is seriously hot for boys. She's been hanging around with a lot of them recently, loving every minute. But two pages in, she loses her feminine charms in a rather shocking way. It happens by accident. An "alchie" in the street whom she annoys by knocking over his beer calls her a "bitch." Suddenly she's down on all fours, baring her teeth at him, and when she runs away, she's delighted by her unaccustomed speed. She has lived up to his accusation—not that she realizes it for a while. Wondering why her family keeps shouting at the mad dog that seems to be just behind her, she finally sees a mongrel in her bedroom mirror—and realizes it's her.

Burgess handles the weirdness of the situation with consummate skill. Sandra tries to speak to her parents, and they can half hear her trying to form words. She does her best to walk on her hind legs to show them she's really human, and while they begin to believe her, they are still creeped out by the freak before them. Soon she finds herself out on the street.

And so Sandra discovers the joys of canine fun. "Life at the edge tastes so sweet! It's steal or starve, life or death . . . Glorious days!" She fluctuates between doggy hilarity, hunting cats in clever half-human ways, and trying to find a way back to humanity. When she sees the picture of her human self on a MISSING poster, she remembers her past and longs for home. But might she in fact be better off as a dog?

Certainly a constant blusher might. Immerse yourself in the uninhibitedness of this novel. Get hairy. Lose that self-consciousness that is unique to humanity. Run with the pack, clatter through deserted streets, take no heed of human laws. Dash until your pads bleed, then lick them dry. Discover your doggy nature and your roseate cheeks will no longer concern you.

---

* The technical name for this is "erythrophobia."

READING AILMENT *Book buyer, being a compulsive*

CURE *Invest in an e-reader and/or create a "current reading" shelf*

We know your type. You love the look and feel of books so much that you yearn to possess them. Just walking into a bookshop turns you on. Your greatest pleasure in life is bringing the new books home and slipping them onto your immaculate shelves. You stand back to admire them, wonder what it will be like to have read them—then you go off and do something else instead.

Invest in an e-reader. By reducing a book to its words—no elegant cover, no fashionable or esoteric author name for others to notice—you will soon discover whether you really want to read the book or whether you just want to own it. If it passes the test, wait until you're actually ready to read it before you press "download" (keeping it on a wish list in the meantime). If, and only if, you love it when you read it on your e-reader, then you may allow yourself a beautiful hard copy to keep on your shelves, to read and reread, to love and touch and drool over, to show off to your friends, and just *have*.

If an e-reader is not for you, designate one shelf in your house a "current reading" shelf. This should be near your bed, or wherever you like to read most, and contain the half dozen books next up on your to-read list. Keep the turnover on this shelf brisk. Because rule number one is that you can only buy a new book when one of the other books on your current reading shelf has been read and returned to its place on your general shelves. Rule number two is that you must read the books on this shelf in the order in which they arrive there, more or less. And rule number three is that if any of the books are leapfrogged more than once or stay on the shelf for more than four months, they go to a friend or a charity shop.

No cheating! You'll be cured of your habit within the year.

Desperate Characters
PAULA FOX

If you suffer from boredom, whether you live in London, Shanghai, Yaroslavl', or a tiny mountain hamlet, it might just be your own boring fault. "When a man is tired of London, he is tired of life," Samuel Johnson said—or at least James Boswell said he said it, in his *Life of Johnson*, more than two hundred years ago. Johnson knew it wasn't fair to blame boredom on geography: each of us is responsible for whipping up our own interest in the world.

In *Desperate Characters*, a dark gem of a novel by the American writer Paula Fox, a bite from a feral cat in Brooklyn shakes a bourgeois New York couple out of their congealed routine. The setting is New York in the last years of the 1960s. "We are all of us dying of boredom," a pompous playwright tells Sophie and Otto Bentwood at a neighborhood party, and the Bentwoods do not disagree. "Boredom," the playwright goes on, "is the why of the war, the why of the assassinations, the why of why." Is she right? In the wake of the deaths of the Kennedys and Martin Luther King, Jr., the calm, coherent backdrop of the Eisenhower era had been replaced by a noisome collage of cultural change in which Vietnam, hippies, the Pill, and the civil rights movement jostled in the collective unconscious. Amid such confusion, can the sense of pointlessness the Bentwoods and their friends feel truly be put down to boredom?

Set in their ways and childless in their early forties, Otto and Sophie have bought a town house in a gentrifying part of Brooklyn, as have many of their friends. But at this early stage of transition, the neighborhood has rejected the transplants—or, at least, is not accepting the new organs easily. Seamy remnants of the neighborhood's previous population linger on the sidewalks, throwing rocks, drunkenly colliding with trash cans, leering and lurching to show the newcomers they're not welcome. You might think that fear for their own safety would keep the Bentwoods at a pitch of alertness that would stave off ennui. Apparently not.

As the novel begins, Otto has fallen out with his longtime law partner, Charlie Russel, whom he considers hypocritically sentimental and has come to hate. Otto dislikes people who display "unseemly emotions," he dislikes the lurking bums on his Brooklyn block, and he doesn't like gentrifiers such as himself any better. As he tells his wife as they leave a neighborhood gathering, "I'm tired of parties. I get so bored." More interesting to them both is whether the stray cat that bit Sophie is rabid. Sophie delays going to the hospital, and their anxiety about her possible rabies gradually brings them to a greater appreciation of their previous comfort. As they flee the city for a restorative visit to their country place, Sophie is on the verge of needling Otto when she catches herself and thinks, "Why interrupt the pleasant boredom of the drive?"

Desperate Characters is a useful reminder that boredom can be a good thing; it may mean that nothing is terribly wrong with your life, which ought to give you a boost and encourage you to stoke your enthusiasm. "The sky was all clear now, a bland, washed blue, and the occasional house that could be glimpsed from the road looked freshly painted and prosperous and eternal," Sophie thinks, her mood lifting. If you find yourself experiencing the malaise of feeling fitfully bored, it's probably an occasion to celebrate. Follow the example set by Chloe in Harriet Beecher Stowe's *Uncle Tom's Cabin*, and "tink ob yer marcies."

See also: Apathy • Dissatisfaction • Lethargy • Mundanity, oppressed by • Stagnation, mental

BORING, BEING

See: Anally retentive, being • Humorlessness • Organized, being too • Risks, not taking enough • Sci-fi, stuck on • Teetotaler, being a

BOSSINESS

See: Bully, being a • Control freak, being a • Dictator, being a

BRAINY, BEING EXCEPTIONALLY

Franny and Zooey
J. D. SALINGER

"I don't know what good it is to know so much and be smart as whips and all if it doesn't make you happy." So says Mrs. Glass in J. D. Salinger's novella *Franny and Zooey*—and she should know. Mother of seven precocious prodigies who have all featured as panelists on the popular radio show *It's a Wise Child*, she has since lost her eldest (Seymour) to suicide, and is now watching her youngest (Franny) have a suspected nervous breakdown on the living room couch.

Being brainier than everyone else should, in theory, be a positive thing. But there's nothing mediocre people hate more than having their mediocrity exposed. Unfortunately, this sentences the exceptionally brainy child to a lifetime of alienation. The Glass children find themselves branded either "a bunch of insufferably 'superior' little bastards that should have been drowned or gassed at birth" or the kinder but distrustful "bona fide underage wits and savants." And if the exceptionally brainy are not pushed away by others, they often end up pushing others away. Clever people are easily bored and disappointed by their peers. Franny's apparent breakdown is triggered by a weekend date with her college beau Lane, during which she finds herself criticizing him relentlessly. "I simply could *not* keep a single opinion to myself," she laments to her brother Zooey. "It was just horrible. Almost from the very second he met me at the station, I started picking and picking and picking at all his opinions and values and—just *everything*." It makes her hate herself.

In life, it's usually the Lanes of this world who get the sympathy—those "normal" people on the receiving end of "abnormal" behavior. But literature likes to side with the freaks, and the exceptionally brainy will find great relief in Franny's description of her torment. Luckily, readers adore characters like the Glass siblings for the very traits for which their peers dislike them, and the exceptionally brainy should take some comfort from this.

If, like Franny and Zooey, your cleverness has cut you off from the world, it's vital not to hate the world for it (see: Bitterness). Franny and Zooey eventually find a way out of their disaffection via an epiphany that allows them to see God in everyone. You may prefer to leave God out of it; the invocation really is just to love others. This charming novella will fill you with a sense of solidarity and replenish your tank of love whenever it threatens to run dry.

See also: **Different, being**

BREAKING UP

High Fidelity
NICK HORNBY

As the songs say, breaking up is hard to do. And whether you're the dumper or the dumped, you should never go through it alone. Ideally, you need your hand held by a friend who has also been battered and bruised by relationship bust-ups and knows how it feels (for more of which, see: Broken heart). We offer you the hand of Rob, the music-mad hero of Nick Hornby's paean to pop, *High Fidelity*. In our list of all-time best breakup novels (see below), this holds the number one spot. For though the vinyl may have dated, the experience, the emotions, the lessons, and the truths have not.

In order to make sense of his latest breakup—with live-in girlfriend Laura—Rob revisits his all-time top five most memorable splits, from the "first chuck" inflicted by twelve-year-old Alison Ashworth (who, for reasons that remain as unfathomable as they were then, decided to snog Kevin Bannister after school instead of him) to the humiliation of Charlie Nicholson upgrading to someone called Marco. Every page jangles with bells of recognition: who hasn't experienced the initial wave of tentative optimism—part liberation, part nervous excitement—that washes over you in the immediate aftermath of a breakup, only to have it wiped out by a crushing sense of loss the minute it hits you that she or he is not coming back? And who hasn't wondered which comes first—the music or the misery—as heartache plays out to the accompaniment of "Love Hurts" or "Walk on By"?

One of the hard truths Rob learns is that breakups do not get easier the more we go through. "It would be nice to think that as I've got older times have changed, relationships have become more sophisticated, females less cruel, skins thicker, reactions sharper, instincts more developed . . . ," bemoans thirty-five-year-old Rob. And yet, with some help from Hornby, one can try to do it a bit better than the time before. The main lesson for Rob is one of commitment (see: Commitment, fear of), but as you watch him pick through the shards of his broken loves, you'll soon know which lessons are meant expressly for you. Are you the sort, like the twentysomething Rob, to react to your bust-ups by flunking college and going to work in a record shop (or today's equivalent)? Do you beat yourself up, like the older Rob, for being a rejection magnet, when, in fact, you've left your own fair share of broken hearts in your wake? The wisdom of this novel may be from a decidedly masculine point of view, but there are patterns here that will map onto almost any breakup and that you can use to help recognize the part you played. Girls will do well to remind themselves that boys cry into their pillows too. And the spurned may get a kick from the fortysomething woman who tries to flog her husband's priceless record collection for fifty pounds because he's run off to Spain with a twenty-three-year-old friend of her daughter's. (Before you get any similar ideas, note Rob's impressively disciplined response and see: Vengeance, seeking.)

Read *High Fidelity* and allow your heart to absorb the lessons from Rob's—and your own—past mistakes. Are you going for the wrong sort of guys/girls? Are you failing to be the solid rock that your partner needs? Or are you living your love life to the wrong sound track? Get it right, and this breakup will be your last.

See also: **Appetite, loss of** • **Bed, inability to get out of** • **Cry, in need of a good** • **Lovesickness** • **Sadness** • **Shelf, fear of being left on the** • **Tired and emotional, being**

THE TEN BEST BREAKUP NOVELS

Call Me by Your Name	ANDRÉ ACIMAN
Wuthering Heights	EMILY BRONTË
The End of the Story	LYDIA DAVIS
This Is How You Lose Her	JUNOT DÍAZ
Heartburn	NORA EPHRON
The Love of My Youth	MARY GORDON
The End of the Affair	GRAHAM GREENE
High Fidelity	NICK HORNBY
Important Artifacts and Personal Property from the Collection of Lenore Doolan and Harold Morris, Including Books, Street Fashion, and Jewelry	LEANNE SHAPTON
Anna Karenina	LEO TOLSTOY

BROKE, BEING

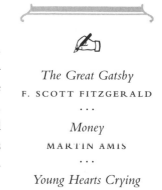

The Great Gatsby
F. SCOTT FITZGERALD

. . .

Money
MARTIN AMIS

. . .

Young Hearts Crying
RICHARD YATES

So you're out of cash. That's half the problem. Maybe you're out of work (see: Unemployment; Depression, economic) or maybe you're spending more than you earn (see: Extravagance). Either way, you're convinced that if only you had a bit more money in the bank, all your problems would be solved. That's the other half of the problem. We'll deal with that half first.

James Gatz—aka Jay Gatsby—had the same stupid idea: that money would bring him what he most longed for, in this case, Daisy Buchanan. In ill-begotten ways, he amassed a fortune, bought the flashiest house on West Egg, then hurled his hundreds on stupendously extravagant parties to lure the lovely Daisy back into his arms, like a moth to an enchanted flame.

Gatsby is one of literature's most powerful dreamers (hence the "great"), and his passion and longing for Daisy is as gorgeous to behold as the little green light at the end of her dock. But the fact is, having more money than we need to cover the essentials in life (food, clothes, shelter, and, of course, books) causes more problems than it solves. Not only does it fail to bring Gatsby lasting happiness with Daisy, but the making of it causes him to abandon and defile his true self. What does he think he's doing calling everyone "old sport" in a fake English accent, owning more shirts than he can possibly wear, and holding parties that he doesn't enjoy? And what does he expect Daisy to do when she discovers how he earned it all? When the flame sputters, and Gatsby goes out, he has no one to blame but himself.

As for being broke, our cure comes in three parts. First, read *Money* by Martin Amis to remind yourself of the horrible ways in which money can taint and corrupt. Then read *Young Hearts Crying* by Richard Yates to see how an inherited fortune can obscure the path to a life of purpose and a sense of self-worth. Finally, return to *The Great Gatsby* and do what James Gatz should have done: inhabit and accept your impoverished self and find someone who loves you as you are. Then quit wasting money on lottery tickets, downsize, and learn to budget. If your job still doesn't bring in enough for the basics, get another one. If it does, stop whining and get on with living happily ever after within your modest means.

See also: **Tax return, fear of doing**

BROKEN CHINA

Utz
BRUCE CHATWIN

The percussive smash of china hitting the floor is a dramatic shock of a sound that is always impressive. Unfortunately, the satisfaction it brings doesn't last long, and is quickly superseded by dismay. Broken china is strangely symbolic of the human heart—one minute so robust and whole, and the next so irreparably damaged. Luckily, unlike a broken heart, broken china can often be glued back together.

But if your broken Davenport sugar bowl, handed down through the generations, is beyond repair, read *Utz*. Kaspar Utz is a Czechoslovakian connoisseur of Meissen porcelain with compulsive collecting habits who becomes a prisoner to his own pieces. Jewish, he risks his life by staying in Russia under Stalin, because he cannot take his priceless artifacts with him. Such is the danger and tyranny of beautiful possessions.

But when Utz dies, having left his collection to the Rudolfine Museum in Prague, his china is nowhere to be found. Various theories are offered as to where his fine china has vanished to, and we will not spoil the ending by giving away the one that proves correct. Suffice it to say, Professor Utz was finally liberated of his obsession. If, through Utz, you can learn to accept the essentially transitory nature of both lives and material possessions, you will be liberated of your upset too.

BROKEN DREAMS

Requiem for a Dream
HUBERT SELBY, JR.

To witness the destruction of a loved one's dreams—or to resign yourself to the loss of your own—is a terrible thing to go through. And it's much more common than you'd think. Having a dream is easy, but finding the right way to make it come true is much harder—and success or failure can make or break you. If you've given up on your dreams, ask yourself if you ever really gave them a chance. As this hard-hitting novel shows, it's possible to choose the wrong way to achieve them.

Everyone has a dream in this novel. Harry and Marion dream of having their own little business, a café with art for sale on the walls, including Marion's own. Harry's best friend, Tyrone, simply wants to escape the ghetto. And Sara, Harry's mother, has hopes for the mystic realms of live television, in the beam of which she spends most of her waking life.

The dreams are innocent enough. It's the way they go about realizing them that's the problem. Because the key to escaping their bottom-rung lives in New York, so Harry and Marion believe, is a particularly potent type of heroin they plan to sell at a massive profit. They test the heroin for quality, and before they know it, they're hooked. Tyrone too. Meanwhile, Sara sits on her couch simultaneously eating chocolate and popping slimming pills, convinced she will make it onto the weight loss show she's glued to. She never gets there.

Instead of achieving their dreams, each character descends into a living hell. Read this devastating, shocking novel. It's too late for Harry, Marion, Tyrone, and Sara—but it's not too late for you. Think of a practical, realistic way to achieve your dreams—one that doesn't involve the sale of narcotics (see: Drugs, doing too many). Keep your eyes on the dream, but also on each rung of the ladder.

See also: Disenchantment • Hope, loss of

BROKEN FRIENDSHIP
See: Friend, falling out with your best

As It Is in Heaven
NIALL WILLIAMS
...
Jane Eyre
CHARLOTTE BRONTË

Rare is the person who goes through life with his or her heart intact. Once the arrow has flown from Cupid's bow and struck its target, quivering with a mischievous thrill, there begins a chemical reaction that dispatches its victim on a journey filled with some of life's most sublime pleasures but also its most tormented pitfalls. (See: Love, doomed; Love, unrequited; Lovesickness; Falling out of love with love; and, frankly, most of the other ailments in this book.) Nine times out of ten,* romance is dashed on the rocks and it all ends in tears.

Why so cynical? Because literature bursts with heartbreak like so many aortic aneurisms. You can barely pick up a novel that does not secrete the grief of a failed romance or the loss of a loved one through death, betrayal, or some such unforeseen disaster. Heartbreak doesn't just afflict those on the outward journey; it can strike even when you thought you were safely stowed (see also: Adultery; Divorce; and Death of a loved one). When afflicted you have no choice, at least not initially, but to sit down with a big box of tissues, another of chocolates, and a novel that will open up the tear ducts and allow you to cry yourself a river. Heartrending music could accompany your read; some would say this is crucial, especially if you have a tendency to keep your emotions under tight control (see: Emotions, inability to express).

It works for the father and son in Niall Williams's seriously hanky-drenching *As It Is in Heaven*, both still brokenhearted and stunned by the deaths in a car crash of Philip's wife, Anne, and their ten-year-old daughter some years before. Both cut from the same cloth, retired tailor Philip and his shy, history teacher son, Stephen, have retreated into their separate, solitary worlds, shutting their hearts to each other and everyone else. Indeed Philip can think of little else but giving his money away to the poor and joining his wife as quickly as possible, aided and abetted by the cancer with which he's been diagnosed.

But once a month, when they meet to play chess, they are enveloped by the music of Puccini. And as we meet the other inhabitants of Ennis, the

---

* Studies have shown that accurate numbers aren't any more useful than the ones you make up.

small town in Ireland where they live, we watch how Stephen finds himself compelled to go to a concert despite driving his car into a ditch on the way. Everything changes overnight. For at the concert he hears Italian violinist Gabriella Castoldi, causing "pools" of "clear black sadness" to fill inside him, and he begins to let out his grief at last. When a thirst for the music becomes a thirst for the musician herself, Stephen's father plays a pivotal role—romantic love is the most powerful motivation in his life too. Now his greatest desire is to help Stephen find happiness with Gabriella. And as the symphony builds to its uplifting conclusion, we see how Stephen's healing brings healing to his father too. Let yourself be swept along for the ride. As this novel shows, the passage of time—and love—does heal.

Broken hearts can be redeemed—and for those refusing to give up on their lost love, we prescribe *Jane Eyre*. When Jane and Rochester's marriage ceremony is interrupted by the announcement that the owner of Thornfield Hall has a wife already, Jane is too shocked to cry: "I seemed to have laid me down in the dried-up bed of a great river," she says, though the "full heavy swing" of the torrent does come later. Bereft, she forgives Rochester in an instant when he shows that he still loves her as much as ever. But the better part of her knows that there is neither "room nor claim" for her, and despite the "cracking" of her heartstrings, she tells him she must go. At which point it's Mr. Rochester's turn to be heartbroken: "Jane! . . . Jane, do you mean to go one way in the world, and to let me go another?" Has there ever been a more heartrending spelling out of the pain of parting?*

All is not lost, however. Jane gets her dark hero in the end—but on her own terms and with her self-respect intact. Mr. Rochester, true, is a charred ruin of his former self by this time, but it doesn't seem to matter. Jane has a fortune of her own now, which enables them to meet as equals, and she never gets tired of reading out loud to him. Follow Jane's example: On no account must you attempt to mend your broken heart by compromising your integrity. Better to suffer with dignity than to self-placate in shame. And you never know who might notice and love you all the more for your strength of character and ability to endure.

It's vital to grieve when love is lost. Drop out for a while to do it. (See: Cry, in need of a good, for our ten best weepies.) Don't compromise unwisely in an attempt to make yourself feel better. Cupid will strike again, either with new love or the same love, in new circumstances. And if you

* If there is, send it to us on a postcard, damp with tears.

decide that you're better off on your own, there are plenty of solitary pleasures to be had in this book.

See also: **Appetite, loss of** · **Despair** · **Hope, loss of** · **Sadness** · **Turmoil** · **Yearning, general**

BROKEN LEG

Cleave
NIKKI GEMMELL

Being able to move—to walk, to run, by extension to run away—is overrated. There's much more sense in staying put. But if you've broken your leg and are wondering how you will stay sane lying in one place or hobbling around on crutches for the next few weeks, turn to *Cleave* by Australian novelist Nikki Gemmell. The title of Gemmell's debut—written in crisp, inventive prose ever aware of its sounds and contours—is an antagonym, a word that, by a freakish accident of linguistic evolution, also means its own opposite. Muse as you read on the relationship of *cleave* ("to split") to *cleave* ("to stick fast to"). It will help you visualize the cleft nature of your bone and therefore speed up its new cleaving.

Snip—"thin and bitten from too much life on the run"—had her first taste of being on the move when her father took her from her mother twenty-five years earlier. He cut her hair (hence, Snip) to make her look like a boy so no one would find her. Now thirty, Snip has made sure that the men in her life have always had the feeling she'll be out the door any minute, so that while they're with her they're hooked. Then, when she decides it's over, out the door she goes. "No number. No forwarding address. A new town, another rupture."

That is, until she meets Dave, a city boy who answers her ad for a companion to drive her and her Holden Ute from Sydney to Alice. Snip is quick to dismiss him as not her type. His face is "too open," too untroubled. He "blares" good health. He shows all the signs of having been loved very much in his life, like a rock that's been sitting in the sun. She runs away again, of course, but headlong into an experience that forces her to reevaluate her habit.

Don't be a Snip. Be a Dave. Lie in that hospital bed with the expanse of the Australian desert unfolding in your mind (you'll particularly appreciate, no doubt, the image of "the great stretch of blue arching above . . . [with] the shin-bone beauty of a lone ghost gum against a reddened hill") and be like a rock emanating heat to those who come to your bedside. Not only will you get lots of attention, but you'll end up with new friends to go see once you're up and about again. The reader invests a lot in Dave and ardently hopes for Snip to find a way to cleave to him—a desire that will manifest itself in the reknitting of your bones.

See also: Hospital, being in the • Pain, being in

BROKEN PROMISE

See: Trust, loss of

BROKEN SPIRIT

The Grapes of Wrath
JOHN STEINBECK
. . .
The House of Mirth
EDITH WHARTON

There's a reason they called the global economic crisis of the 1930s the Great Depression, beyond depressed stock prices and failed banks. The Great Depression was also a time of misery, sadness, and despair as the afflicted populace saw its prosperity and prospects come crashing down. These days, in the new millennium's Great Recession, that bleak mood is felt by many who agonize that the present, and future, are chancy. If you're feeling frightened, pessimistic, and whipped by fate, mend your broken spirit by reading John Steinbeck's novel *The Grapes of Wrath*. It's about the desolate Joads, a family of tenant farmers from Depression-era Oklahoma who travel to California looking for crop-picking work.

After serving four years in prison for manslaughter, Tom Joad emerges to discover that the Dust Bowl has ruined his family's fortunes. Bad as things are, he struggles to get work to help his family. A young migrant worker he meets on the road tells Tom that men like them have to put up with whatever employers dish out because work is so scarce, and it's best not to get a reputation as a complainer. Tom retorts, "So we take what we can get, huh, or we starve; an' if we yelp we starve." That is not how Tom rolls;

he may be an ex-con living in a tent city and warming himself by a trash fire, but he has his pride. "I ain't gonna take it," he says. "Goddamn it, I an' my folks ain't no sheep. I'll kick the hell outa somebody." Tom won't let a stranger demoralize him and he won't give up. When work comes his way, he tells his sister Ruthie, "I got a chance at a job, an' I'm a-goin' for it." Even as calamity after calamity continues to befall the luckless Joads, Tom's resolve is unshaken. He determines to bring the workers together to defend their rights. However rough a road you may be on, you can take heart in recognizing that the Joad family's was surely worse, and find inspiration in Tom Joad's convictions and courage.

But what if your broken spirit is not a product of evil times but of your own outsize ambition, which has led you to aim for greater glory than you were likely to attain, resulting in dashed dreams and frustrated hopes? Rather than stew, mope, and give up on yourself, recalibrate your desires and reconceive your achievable potential by reading Edith Wharton's wickedly perceptive social novel *The House of Mirth*. Wharton's beautiful, haughty, and calculating antiheroine, Lily Bart, wrecks her own happiness by setting the bar too high. Lily was born to wealth, but after her father's bankruptcy and death, she loses both her money and her status. Nearing thirty, she determines to regain both through marriage. She stubbornly refuses to accept reality, turning down eligible men because they're not rich enough or sophisticated enough, until there's hardly anyone left for her to reject. Even as her romantic career circles the drain, she continues showing callousness to the few men who still come knocking. One of those, a former suitor named George Dorset, who has a philandering wife, asks Lily to save his reputation and mend hers by marrying him. She refuses him. "I'm sorry; there's nothing in the world that I can do," she says. That is because she, unlike you, is not capable of being flexible and adjusting her views to match her possibilities. Don't be like Lily. Shore up your spirits by inventing for yourself a realizable future. Then fight your way there, like Tom Joad.

See also: Hope, loss of • Identity crisis

BULIMIA
See: Eating disorder

BULLIED, BEING

ullying comes in many forms. Among boys, it tends to be aggressive and physical. Among girls, spiteful and verbal. And although we tend to think of it as a childhood phenomenon, it happens just as much among adults—in the workplace and at home. Both our cures are about bullying among young people, but they capture an ingredient common to all: the shame or bewilderment of the victims, which, at least initially, prevents them

Cat's Eye
MARGARET ATWOOD
. . .
Tom Brown's School Days
THOMAS HUGHES

from seeing the situation for what it is. If you suspect you are being bullied, these novels will give you some perspective. Perhaps you'll recognize the techniques the bullies use to assert their authority. And depending on whether you're the sort to crumble or fight back, you may recognize one or the other response. If you do, speak out.

When middle-aged Elaine returns to Toronto for a retrospective of her paintings in Margaret Atwood's chilling *Cat's Eye*, she wonders whether she'll bump into her old friend Cordelia, and, if so, what she will say. Cordelia was the most powerful and alluring of a trio of girls at school (the others being Carol and Grace) to whom she became joined at the hip—the one Elaine most wanted to please. Whenever Cordelia had a "friend day," putting her arm through Elaine's and singing and laughing together, Elaine would feel gratitude—and anxiety. Sooner or later she knew Cordelia would turn from friend to foe and, as the ringleader of the group, encourage Carol and Grace to do the same. In Toronto, when Elaine finds a marble like a cat's eye, given to her years earlier by her brother Stephen, it brings to the surface a traumatic memory she's long blanked out.

Anyone who has been bullied will recognize Elaine's emotional numbness and won't be surprised by her failure to remove herself from the damaging trio. Victims of bullying often don't realize they're being bullied at first, and in a perverse act of complicity, the bullied may even be drawn to the bully, craving acceptance while dreading rejection and scorn. Like Elaine, the bullied can become so browbeaten that they lack the strength and belief in themselves to overcome their abusers (if this applies to you, see: Self-esteem, low). Only when things finally go too far does Elaine wake up and discover the power to walk away, if she wants to: "It's like stepping off a cliff, believing the air will hold you up. And it does." If Elaine's story resonates with you, learn to walk away before the numbness occurs.

No such crumbling goes on between Tom and his bully Flashman in Thomas Hughes's *Tom Brown's School Days*. No sooner has Tom arrived at Rugby School than the appalling Flashman does his best to make Tom's life a misery. Flashman threatens and physically attacks Tom, and it all comes to a head when the older boy instigates a "burning" of Tom in front of an open fire. It is at this point that Tom decides to do something about the injustices he and his fellows have experienced at the hands of all the school bullies. It helps that Tom has become strong and feisty and, crucially, that he has earned the respect of older boys, one of whom comes to his aid in bringing Flashman down.

Tom's triumph over his oppressors will leave you elated and inspired. It is Hughes's acknowledgment of the lasting damage inflicted on Tom, though, you may find most cathartic: it takes Tom months to undo Flashman's blackening of his name among his peers, even after the bullying has stopped. And who knows how long the emotional scars will remain (see: Scars, emotional)? For Elaine in *Cat's Eye* they last into middle age, but by revisiting the scene of her childhood trauma, she achieves redemption. Take heart from these two literary victims. They may struggle with the effects of bullying for a long time, but they come out stronger in the end.

See also: Anxiety · Left out, feeling · Nightmares · Superhero, wishing you were a

BULLY, BEING A

A Death in the Family
JAMES AGEE

You may not think of yourself as a bully. But if you ever purposefully inflict pain on someone more vulnerable than you—even in an unthinking way, and perhaps verbally rather than physically—you may well be guilty of this shameful practice. If you know deep down that you do, we ask you to read *A Death in the Family*, winner of the Pulitzer Prize in 1958 and one of the most moving accounts of bullying that we know.

Rufus lives on a "mixed sort of block" in Knoxville, Tennessee. It's a place where supper's at six and over by half past, at which point the children go out to play while the mothers clean the kitchen and the fathers hose down the lawns. Rufus, not yet old enough for school himself, likes to watch the older children going back and forth to school. First he watches them from the front window, then from the front yard, and then from the sidewalk outside his house. Finally he dares to stand on the street corner, where he can see them coming from three directions. He admires their different pencils and lunch boxes, and the way the boys swing their books in the brown canvas straps—until, that is, they start swinging them at his head. The bullying quickly builds to daily mockery and humiliation. Desperate to believe that they can be trusted—that their pretense of friendship is for real—Rufus walks into the traps they set for him again and again, much to the bullies' mounting hilarity. He is younger than all of them, and their violation of his guileless trust is exquisitely painful to witness.

Agee was a poet first and foremost and his agile prose delves into emotional crevices previously unexplored. When Rufus suffers a tragedy he is too young to fully comprehend—and the bullies make no amends—the reader's heartbreak is complete.

If you're guilty of exploiting another's weakness—whether on the playground, in the home, or at work—and have never paused to think about the effects of your behavior on your victim, we defy you to read this novel and remain a bully thereafter. If you know you were a bully in your youth, see: Guilt, and then move on. Sadly, you may know only too well what it's like to be bullied—many bullies were bullied themselves first. If you belong in this camp, switching sides is not the answer. See our cure for Bullied, being, above.

See also: Dictator, being a

BURNING THE DINNER

The Belly of Paris
ÉMILE ZOLA

Domestically speaking, there are few things more catastrophic than burning the dinner. Whether you have slaved for hours over a *daube de boeuf* or rustled up some *crêpes suzette*, a scorched, acrid offering fit only to be flung out onto the garden path for scavenging animals will leave you not just hungry, but ill-humored. On such occasions, grab *The Belly of Paris*, the third novel to be published in Zola's multigenerational Rougon-Macquart saga.

It tells the story of Florent Quenu, who returns to his native Paris to live with his family in an apartment on the edge of the newly rebuilt Les Halles food market. As you wander with him here, you will find meat, vegetables, fruit, and cheese, all laid out before you with mouthwatering voluptuousness. Take your pick from stuffed Strasbourg tongues "red and looking as if they had been varnished," pâtés, casseroles, pickling jars of sauces and stocks, preserved truffles, salmon "gleaming like well-buffed silver," and peaches with "clear, soft skin like northern girls." Soon you'll be dribbling with desire and rushing to your nearest farmers' market for more.

Even if you hadn't burned it, your dinner would not have been as tasty as the delicacies offered up to us by Zola. Tell this to your guests; convince them by reading from this novel aloud. And next time you go shopping, stock up on glorious fruits and fish and cheeses—you can serve them up without needing to turn the oven on.

BURNING WITH DESIRE

See: Lust

BUSY, BEING TOO

This Is Your Life
MEG WOLITZER
. . .
The Poisonwood Bible
BARBARA
KINGSOLVER

You've got a company to run (see: Dictator, being a), a music lesson and a gymnastics meet to drive to (see: Children, having), dinner to cook for twenty, and your mother is in the hospital (see: Hospital, being in the). You're underslept, overscheduled, and feel like you're about to fall to pieces. Well . . . join the club! Being excessively busy is the universal contemporary human plight—boosted to turbo speed lately by the Internet, cell phones, and twenty-four/seven wiredness. Unsurprisingly, this epidemic of busyness is a popular subject among wise and mordant writers who not only recognize the prevalent Joan of Arc–like compulsion toward self-perfection, but the attendant risks of self-immolation. Not to mention the burning fallout.

In Meg Wolitzer's novel *This Is Your Life*, Dottie Engels is an overweight single mother and stand-up comic whose career is exploding, in a good way. Dottie's daughters, rather than exulting in their mother's new fame and applauding her impressive array of gigs, sulk and pout as her star rises. They would rather have a mother who is miserable, weeping, and thwarted, but *at home* with them, instead of one who is ecstatically fulfilled on a spotlit stage taking bow after bow. We're all for mothers who work, but there's a limit to the successfulness of success, it seems. If your life is busy because you've taken on multiple roles, it's worth asking whether the success of one might be preventing the success of another.

In Barbara Kingsolver's *The Poisonwood Bible*, it's a father, an overzealous missionary named Nathan Price, whose fanatical zeal to convert Congolese forest dwellers to Christianity brings him, his wife, and four daughters to Africa. Price's quixotic spiritual goals force his family to endure endless privations—including hunger, drudgery, discomfort, and disease on hostile territory. While he works tirelessly, and wrongheadedly, to "improve" the lives of the natives—planting crops that won't germinate in the region, trying to persuade the natives to be baptized in a river riddled with crocodiles—he neglects his own flesh and blood. There's an old expression in Spanish to describe such a man: *luz en la calle, oscuridad en la casa*—one who sheds light on strangers on the street, but keeps his own family in the dark. Busyness in and of itself, Kingsolver's novel suggests, is not a virtue.

If stand-up comedy and bushwhacking don't feature in your crowded schedule, you and your family can count your blessings. But as you look askance at the frenetic activity of these characters, ask yourself this question: "Is this really so different from my life?" If the answer is no, examine as honestly as you can how much of your to-do list is *really* crucial, and find ways to pare your *horaire*.

See also: **Busy to read, being too** · **Children requiring attention, too many** · **Exhaustion** · **Live instead of read, tendency to** · **Stress**

READING AILMENT   *Busy to read, being too*

CURE   *Listen to audiobooks*

Your life is one big to-do list, and living is about ticking things off. You don't have time to phone your best friend, let alone to sit down with a book. But one thing we know you can do is multitask. So we suggest you learn to inhale a book on the hoof. Stock up on a supply of audiobooks (see: Noise, too much, for our list of Ten Best Audiobooks to get you started). Order a set of comfortable headphones. And next time you're busy doing something with your body that is not taxing to your mind—ironing, gardening, washing the dishes, pounding the treadmill, walking to work—listen to a novel while you're at it. You'll find that you use a different part of your brain to take in the story than you need for whatever task is at hand—and, suddenly, the menial, workaday aspect of your life will be transformed. You'll soon be on the lookout for more chores to tackle. Any task will do, just as long as it earns you another half hour—and then another—with your audiobook.

C

CANCER, CARING FOR SOMEONE WITH

When someone you love is diagnosed with cancer and you suddenly find yourself in the role of carer, it can be a tremendously difficult time. Not only will you need to give your loved one emotional support, absorbing his or her distress as well as managing your own, but you may need to acquire the practical skills of a nurse, as well as a cook, cleaner, accountant, social secretary—indeed all the domestic duties your loved one cannot manage at this time. You will find you are called upon to help make choices about treatment, to engage with doctors, and to act as the go-between with concerned relatives and friends. You may have to deflect or encourage visits depending on how well your loved one feels. And you may find it difficult to tell others when you need a break. Who is going to support you, while you're doing all this work, giving all this care, and shouldering all these worries?

It helps enormously during times of stress to read about other people who are going through similar things: watching how other people cope or fail to cope will make you feel less alone and give you strength. To this end, here

The Spare Room
HELEN GARNER

. . .

The Sickness
ALBERTO BARRERA
TYSZKA

. . .

A Monster Calls
PATRICK NESS

are three excellent novels that explore the impact of cancer on the lives of those nearest to the patient.

The Spare Room by Helen Garner deals with both the agonizing and the (albeit darkly) humorous sides of caring for someone with cancer. When the narrator, Hel, hears that her old friend Nicola is coming to Melbourne to undergo alternative treatment for her end-stage bone and liver cancer, she prepares her spare room. It is very quickly apparent to Hel that Nicola is dying—and in denial about it. Hel is furious with the "quack" clinic that's taking Nicola's money so freely and giving her false hope. She begins to feel she must tell her friend what the clinic's therapists, with their bogus vitamin C treatments, are not. As her increasing duties as carer start to take over her life, her rage escalates and she battles against self-hatred—reaching the point where she is desperate for Nicola to get on with her dying somewhere else. Garner shows immense understanding and compassion for her characters, but it is the bitter humor alongside the horror of the situation that makes this such a gripping read. This is a novel for those inclined to beat themselves up when they struggle to care for their patient nonstop. However much you want to help, you still need to be healthy in your own life. It's also a reminder that, however serious things are, it helps to laugh.

Bodies have few secrets these days, and in the light of our ever increasing ability to detect and predict the course of an illness, the question of honesty, and how much information is too much, is pressing. Surgeon Dr. Andrés in Alberto Barrera Tyszka's *The Sickness* is in the unusual position of diagnosing his own father's cancer. The X-rays show that, without a shadow of a doubt, his father, Javier, has a stage IV spinocellular carcinoma, and there is nothing that can be done. Having spent years informing his patients of their terminal illnesses—quite brutally, he now realizes—he simply cannot find the right moment to tell his father. Thus begins his questioning of the whole notion of knowledge. Is it, in fact, better for the patient not to know? His relationship with his beloved father has always been strong; now, for the first time, it becomes strained.

He decides to take his father on a weeklong holiday to the Isla Margarita, where his father took him when his mother died. There he will calmly tell his father the news. But when it comes out, it comes at a moment of high emotion. Javier is horrified that Andrés has been keeping it from him and by the burden his illness will place on others. The old man is anguished and distressed, and as his health rapidly deteriorates, he wishes it could all be over swiftly. The shattering of the father-son relationship is painful to watch, and serves as a reminder of how much an illness can strain a bond, however loving. The message to take away, perhaps, is to try to maintain a sense of "business as usual" in your relationship with your loved one—particularly if that relationship is good. The cancer brings with it enough change as it is.

The question of how to help and protect children when someone in the family is diagnosed with cancer is a fraught one. When and what should they be told? And how will the child be affected outside the home? In Patrick Ness's *A Monster Calls*, Conor O'Malley's mother is diagnosed with cancer soon after his father has left the family to live in America with a new partner. When his mother's hair falls out following chemotherapy, Conor starts being bullied at school—about her bald head, and about his increasingly odd behavior. When his peers realize his mother is dying, they avoid him completely.

One night Conor is visited by a monster in the form of an ancient walking, talking yew tree. The looming tree insists that Conor must call upon his own inner reserves of strength in order to face the months ahead. The yew tree tells him stories, parables that teach him how to deal with the bullies at school, and also with his grandmother, who is helping, badly, to look after him. The monster acts as a catalyst, bringing Conor to confront his woes and, ultimately, helping him find a way to accept his mother's death. Incredibly moving, this novel is not for the fainthearted. It has the power to force you to face mortality—and will hold your hand as it does so.

Looking after someone with cancer is difficult, both practically and emotionally. For a start, isolate the emotion you battle with most, and see, for instance: Grumpiness; Guilt; Empathy, lack of; Anxiety; Sadness; Stress; and Worry. These novels will help you to stand back from your particular experience and see that others have been there too. And they'll remind you that being gentle on yourself is just as important as caring for your loved one.

See also: **Busy, being too** • **Cope, inability to** • **Tired and emotional, being** • **Waiting room, being in a**

CANCER, HAVING

When you're sitting through chemo, when you're feeling weak, when your brain refuses to work, when you haven't the strength for company . . . what you need is a short and perfectly formed piece of prose.

See also: Hospital, being in the • Pain, being in • Waiting room, being in a

THE TEN BEST NOVELLAS

To the Wedding .... JOHN BERGER
Breakfast at Tiffany's .... TRUMAN CAPOTE
Do Androids Dream of Electric Sheep? .... PHILIP K. DICK
A Simple Heart .... GUSTAVE FLAUBERT
Tinkers .... PAUL HARDING
Daisy Miller .... HENRY JAMES
Train Dreams .... DENIS JOHNSON
An Imaginary Life .... DAVID MALOUF
Flush .... VIRGINIA WOOLF

The Sisters Brothers
PATRICK DEWITT

CAREER, BEING IN THE WRONG

It's no small thing to change career when you suspect you're in the wrong one. For a start, you're probably too exhausted from doing your current job to have much time to figure out what you could be doing instead. And the thought of all those years of training and experience going down the drain makes you feel faint. As does kissing that nice silver Audi good-bye. As does the thought of the expression on your partner's face when you let drop that you've had enough of your lucrative career and fancy opening a hat shop instead.

It would spoil one of the many delightful sentences in this unputdownable novel to divulge the exact line of work the brothers Charlie and Eli Sisters are engaged in. But suffice it to say it is not an easy one to get out of alive. Set during the crazed days of the California gold rush, younger brother Eli starts to admit to himself that he is ill suited to his profession after passing through a doorway around which a hairless old crone with blackened teeth has hung a string of beads—the sure sign of a hex. The beads may or may not have anything to do with it, but from that point on, Eli finds himself increasingly ashamed of who he is and what he does, and develops a tendency to make decisions that surprise his unsentimental elder brother (see:

{64}   CAREER, BEING IN THE WRONG

Sibling rivalry). When Providence offers him a fine, strong black horse, he rejects it in order to remain loyal to his trusty Tub, a dangerously slow ride and blind in one eye. Soon he is giving his money away to strangers, newly aware of its power to corrupt.

When he comes into contact with Hermann Kermit Warm, a man who has allowed his own interests and ingenuity—plus a desire for honest friendship—to lead him to work he is passionate about, he is filled with admiration and envy. As he watches Hermann reap the benefits, both monetary and spiritual, of his labors, Eli has his Damascene moment. Initiating a shift in the balance of power between himself and his domineering older brother, he persuades Charlie that they should join Warm in his work. Then Eli experiences a moment of pure ecstasy, partly because the physical nature of the work is so pleasant (standing in a river in dappled sun, with a warm wind "pushing down from the valley"), and partly because he is being himself—a self he likes.

Stand with Eli in that river and take inspiration from Hermann Warm. If you, too, could find a way of earning money that brought you spiritual as well as financial rewards—and allowed you to spend your days full of joy— what would it be?

See also: Dissatisfaction • Monday morning feeling • Seize the day, failure to • Stuck in a rut

CARELESSNESS

The Little Prince
ANTOINE DE SAINT-
EXUPÉRY

If you lived on a planet as small as the Little Prince's planet, Asteroid B-612—so small that if you took a herd of elephants there you'd have to pile them on top of one another; so small that you'd have to take great care, after you'd finished washing and dressing each morning, to dig out any baobab shoots that had appeared overnight lest they take over your planet; so small that one day you watched the sunset forty-four times, just by moving your chair— you'd be living a simple life that would instill in you the habit of carefulness. You would water the one flower that grew on your planet every day, and never forget. You would take the trouble, before you went away on a trip, to rake out your volcanoes, even the extinct one. Because you would know that it's the time and care you spend on things that make them important. And if you didn't take this care, you'd wake up one day to find that everything around you was sad, feeling as unimportant as you made it feel.

Whatever the size of your planet when you begin reading *The Little Prince*, we guarantee it will have shrunk and become much more like Asteroid B-612 by the end. And afterward you will live your life with more care.

See also: **Risks, taking too many** • **Selfishness**

CARNIVOROUSNESS

Under the Skin
MICHEL FABER

When you pass by those fields in the springtime, do you see frolicking lambs or do you see so many Sunday roasts? Or an uncomfortable collision of the two? Whatever your take on the consumption of animal protein—whatever your religious, political, or ethical stance—this novel will shatter any veneer you might have conveniently placed between yourself and the slab of meat on your plate.

To reveal exactly why Michel Faber's genre-defying novel is a cure for eating meat would be to spoil the delicious pleasure of savoring it. But we can hint. The unforgiving beauty of the Scottish landscape, with its "glimpses of rain two or three mountains away," is the only uplifting feature in the deeply disturbing events that unfold. Isserley is an attractive but strange woman who spends her days driving around the countryside. Her job is mysterious, but seems to involve picking up hitchhikers, and her car has been specially adapted for her duties. Disconcertingly, Isserley herself is uncomfortable in her car seat and travels with the heat turned incredibly high. And the people she lives with seem afraid of her.

Essential reading for anyone debating the ethics of the food they eat, for those considering shacking up with a vegetarian and wishing to avoid culinary conflict, or for those who suffer spasms of guilt whenever they bite into what was once a cute, fluffy, innocent creature, *Under the Skin* will continue to live with you long after you finish the final page—and long after you have learned to love tofu.

CARSICKNESS

If you suffer from carsickness, hop out and take the train instead. Train journeys offer unparalleled opportunities for immersing yourself in a book. When else does one have a guilt-free few hours to do nothing but read in the anonymous company of other readers and with an ever changing view out the window? Trains are beloved of writers too, it seems, whisking characters off as they do to unknown futures. And there's always the chance of an unexpected liaison en route . . .

See also: Nausea

THE TEN BEST NOVELS TO READ ON A TRAIN

Possession	A. S. BYATT
Murder on the Orient Express	AGATHA CHRISTIE
Stamboul Train	GRAHAM GREENE
Love on a Branch Line	JOHN HADFIELD
The Great Fire	SHIRLEY HAZZARD
Strangers on a Train	PATRICIA HIGHSMITH
Mr. Norris Changes Trains	CHRISTOPHER ISHERWOOD
The Railway Children	EDITH NESBIT
The Train	GEORGES SIMENON
The Wheel Spins	ETHEL LINA WHITE

CHANGE, RESISTANCE TO

Are you one of those people who will put up with almost anything rather than shake up your routine? Do you rationalize reasons to stay in a horrible job? Do you soldier on in a marriage that features endless bickering and joylessness? Do you ignore the irritations of living in a collapsing flat but make no plans to move out? You are not alone. Tolerating less than ideal circumstances has been humanity's default

Empire Falls
RICHARD RUSSO

setting since long before Hamlet pondered the virtue of bearing those ills he had rather than fly to others he knew not of. But as scary as it is to contemplate change, avoiding it bears its own dangers. Chew on this thought as you read Richard Russo's beautiful and forgiving novel *Empire Falls*, about a man in a washed-up industrial town in Maine who, rather than attempt to improve his lot, lets life get away from him.

As a boy, Miles Roby was ambitious and resolved to escape his depressing blue-collar village. But when he's away at college and his mother gets sick, he dutifully drops out and returns home to run the family business, the Empire Grill. Mrs. Whiting, a rich, manipulative old local woman, owns part of the grill; early on, impressed by Miles's conscientiousness, she promises to bequeath him her share. But under Miles's stewardship, the diner, which was "never terribly profitable," goes into a "long, gentle decline almost imperceptible without the benefit of time-lapse photography." When the diner starts losing money, Miles, now in middle age, faces losing everything. Mrs. Whiting threatens to alter her will, and Miles's energetic wife has tired of his paralysis and found a way to evolve. Life is changing around Miles, whether he wants it to or not. By staying in place, he risks being left behind.

If, like Miles, "surviving not thriving" is pretty much your MO, let *Empire Falls* suffuse you with a rueful understanding of the perils of inertia. Don't let life happen to you. To survive *and* thrive, take a proactive role in what happens next.

See also: **Control freak, being a** • **Single-mindedness**

CHEATING
See: **Adultery**

The Birth of Love
JOANNA KAVENNA

CHILDBIRTH

If you're facing the great unknown of childbirth for the first time, you're probably keen to prepare yourself mentally. You may have the urge to ask anyone who looks like a mother what it entails and how it feels, and for any tips on how to get through it with minimum pain and maximum joy. But anyone who has given birth knows that it is almost impossible to convey the experience, as it is, by its nature, unique every time. For a less didactic approach than the latest pregnancy manual, women on the verge of delivering are encouraged to turn to fiction to find out what it's all about. Besides, it's a great time to rest on the sofa with a good novel (see: Pregnancy).

The Birth of Love by Joanna Kavenna tackles head-on the varied nature of childbirth through four interweaving stories. In the present, Brigid is going through her second labor. As we accompany her through ever agonizing contractions all the way to an eventual C-section, we watch her dream of a home birth shatter. In the past is real-life scientist Ignaz Semmelweis, struggling to hold on to his sanity in a Viennese asylum after coming to the horrifying realization that the high rate of "childbed fever" fatalities could have been prevented if only the doctors had washed their hands before examining their patients. Michael Stone, a novelist telling Semmelweis's story, goes through his own version of birthing pangs as he watches his first novel, *The Moon*, go out into the world to stand or fall on its own merits. And in a laboratory of the future, Darwin C, where people are kept and bred in cells, their wombs closed off and their eggs harvested at the age of eighteen, a female escapee successfully manages to bear a child in the natural way.

Giving birth—or watching a partner give birth—is perhaps the closest any of us will get to witnessing a miracle. Read this novel to prepare yourself for the intensity of the experience, but also so you can appreciate doing it amid the high hygiene standards of today. Kavenna's graphic and vivid storytelling does not spare the squeamish, but it will remind you that, the minute your baby has arrived, you'll be so swept away on a tidal wave of love that you'll forget all the pains of pregnancy at once. Giving birth is a physical, messy, joyous, and agonizing affair, and *The Birth of Love* will help you live the experience to the fullest.

See also: Hospital, being in the • Motherhood • Pain, being in

CHILDREN, HAVING

See: Broke, being • Busy, being too • Busy to read, being too • Childbirth • Children requiring attention, too many • Cope, inability to • Family, coping with • Fatherhood • Motherhood • Mother-in-law, being a • Noise, too much • Single parent, being a • Trapped by children

Waterland
GRAHAM SWIFT
· · ·
She
H. RIDER HAGGARD

Pondering the positives of not having children is easy for those who are already encumbered. Acres of limitless time to read novels. Sleeping in on Sunday mornings. No modeling clay or mashed banana in your hair. The simple luxury of having an uninterrupted thought, let alone a bath.

But when you have that negative space in your life, the luxury of doing what you want with your time may not have the same appeal. And for those who want to have children but are unable to—for whatever reason—the absence of a child can bring acute feelings of grief and longing. Certainly it does for Mary, the wife of history teacher Tom Crick in Graham Swift's masterful *Waterland*. Mary's botched abortion in the hands of a reputed witch when she was just sixteen led to her subsequent infertility. For years she and Tom seem to get along fine without children, but at the age of fifty-three Mary shocks everyone by kidnapping a baby left in its pram by the turnstiles at the supermarket.

Swift's gorgeous, whimsical novel meanders eellike through several generations of Cricks and Atkinsons on the watery Fens of eastern England. As it unfurls, the tale makes a magnificent case for people being so molded by the landscape from which they come that their destinies are written in its mud. Because this is a place of "unrelieved and monotonous" flatness where, like the silted rivers, spirits are so "sluggish" with phlegm that suicide, drinking, madness, and acts of violence are inescapable. Mary, it seems, cannot escape her roots. Of course one can't change the past. But one can change one's vision of the present and the future. The message here is that, unlike Mary, we can choose to let go of what we imagined our lives to be. If things haven't turned out the way you thought they would, don't dwell on your preconceptions. Start afresh. Be someone else. (See: Change, resistance to.)

To that end, we offer you a thrillingly positive outlook on childlessness in the form of H. Rider Haggard's *She*, the fantastical nineteenth-century tale of a white queen ruling over a lost kingdom in an undiscovered realm of Africa. She, or Ayesha to her friends, uses her child-free years to become a goddess among men. Not only does she not lose her looks, but she manages to stay alive for two thousand years. With that much time to put into her career, it's true, she does become something of a megalomaniac, earning herself the nickname *She-who-must-be-obeyed*. But Ayesha makes the most of her thirst for knowledge and eventually holds the enigmas of the universe at her fingertips.

She and its companion piece, *Ayesha: The Return of She*, are royal adventures and rollicking reads—all the better enjoyed for not having constant interruptions from any progeny. Let these spirited novels show you how to glory in your child-free life and use your time and energy to develop other qualities—wisdom, worldly success, and never-ending desirability, for a start. What else will you add to the list?

See also: Children, under pressure to have • Empty-nest syndrome • Fatherhood, avoiding • Yearning, general

---

READING AILMENT   *Children requiring attention, too many*

CURE   *Designate a reading hour*

If you are like the old lady who lived in a shoe, with an excess of children at your feet requiring love, food, and cleansing, the only real option is to do as the Victorians did and declare a quiet hour after lunch when everybody reads a book. If the mites are too young to read by themselves, settle them down to an audiobook. During reading (or listening) hour, no one is allowed to make a noise, except to giggle or weep in response to the written (or spoken) word. Once it's over, they can demand your attention once more, and you can enjoy telling one another about what you have read (or heard). You might be surprised by how much they come to enjoy it. If your children struggle to last an hour, try reading aloud together. Sharing a book you love with your children, particularly if it's around a fire, is probably the most idyllic way to spend restful time together that we know of.

CHILDREN, TRAPPED BY

See: **Trapped by children**

We Need to Talk About Kevin
LIONEL SHRIVER

CHILDREN, UNDER PRESSURE TO HAVE

If you are sick of justifying your childlessness, if you are happy with your life as it is and don't want to spoil things, if you think the world is populated enough already, if you know that you'd make a useless parent, if you like your nights uninterrupted and your cream sofa without fingerprints, then the next time someone asks you when they're going to hear the patter of tiny feet in your house, send them this novel for Christmas. They won't ask you about it again.

See also: **Children, not having** • **Thirtysomething, being**

A Christmas Carol
CHARLES DICKENS

CHRISTMAS

Christmas can be a time when all your afflictions seem to come at once. If you have a big family, you'll be stuck under one roof with a big bunch of relatives (see: Family, coping with), which may include a number of overexcited children (see: Motherhood; Fatherhood; Trapped by children). You will probably spend as much in one month as you normally spend in three (see: Broke, being; Tax return, fear of doing). You'll certainly eat too much (see: Gluttony; Obesity) and get wind and maybe even diarrhea (see: Diarrhea) or the opposite (see: Constipation) and end up paying the penalty for an excess of drink (see: Hangover; or, if you're a veteran of many punishing Christmases, see: Alcoholism). If you're married or have a partner, one of you will no doubt have a few run-ins with the in-laws (see: Mother-in-law, having a), which may result in a run-in with one another (see: Married, being). If you have a boyfriend/girlfriend, you will probably be forced to answer personal questions about this relationship (see: Coming out; Children, under pressure to have). And if you are single, you will be asked why, which may make you wish you weren't (see: Shelf, fear of being left on the) and leave you feeling unbearably lonely (see: Loneliness). If you don't have a large family, or are spending Christmas with just the dog, you may indeed feel lonely (again, see: Loneliness) or miss your family (Family, coping without). All in all, Christmas is an experience very likely to lead to loss of faith (see: Faith, loss of) and a desire to lock yourself in a dark closet all alone (see: Misanthropy).

In these pages you will find cures for all of the above. As preventative medicine, read them slowly, over the course of the year, to steel yourself for the big day. And when it comes, announce to your family, partner, Granny, or potted plant that instead of a film on Christmas Day you will be reading aloud to them, around the fire, mulled wine and roasted chestnuts at hand, the multigenerationally appealing *A Christmas Carol* by Charles Dickens.

It is a brilliant ghost story, and however familiar it may be, it doesn't cease to satisfy children and adults alike. Revel in those ghostly apparitions. Gasp at Scrooge's greed and cry tears of pity for Tiny Tim. Jubilate with all at the end. And make Dickens an annual tradition. A lovely sense of warmth will pervade your heart as you read—and the hearts of all those to whom you read.

CITY FATIGUE

The City and the City
CHINA MIÉVILLE

Life in the city can grind you down. The commuting, the hoards, the rush, the anonymity. The drab dreariness of unending concrete, the flashing billboards, the litter, the crime. If your city is making you sick, we implore you: do not step foot outside your door again without first medicating yourself with *The City and the City* by China Miéville. Quite simply the best novel we know of that deals with living in a city, Miéville's deeply unsettling yet wholly familiar tale will put a 3-D lens on what you had only before seen in 2-D.

Because when you walk down the streets of the fictional city Besźel, you must "unsee" those people who are walking next to you on the street but are in a different city—a second city, called Ul Qoma, which occupies the same geographical space. To inhabit these overlapping cities successfully, you must study the architectural quirks, the clothing, and even the gait and mannerisms of those living in your city, and how they differ from those living in the parallel city. If you cross from one city to another, you are "in breach"; if you commit breach, you disappear.

Inspector Tyador Borlú has been called to investigate the murder of a female student named Mahalia, which takes place in Besźel. A thoughtful and intelligent man, Borlú soon realizes that the murder breaches all the rules of living in either city. An academic named Bowden is summoned; he once claimed there was a third, unseen city—Orciny—between Besźel and Ul Qoma. Mahalia seems to have stumbled upon this third city and was conducting her own investigations into it when she was sucked into a dangerous underworld.

The brilliance of this gripping novel—part detective story, part conceptual thriller—rests on the chilling familiarity of a subconscious state of "unnoticing." How many times have we, too, ignored people in our own city because we think interacting with them may be unsafe? Miéville messes with your brain so immeasurably that you will never be able to look at your own urban sprawl in the same way again. The metropolis you thought you knew will take on a completely new sense of space, reality, and possibility. And you might find yourself seeing a lot of people you somehow missed before.

CLAUSTROPHOBIA

Little House on the Prairie
LAURA INGALLS
WILDER

If you've a tendency to suffer from claustrophobia, never enter an enclosed space without *Little House on the Prairie*, second of the nine novels in the much loved series of settler life by frontierswoman Laura Ingalls Wilder. In an instant, you'll be taking up the reins on the high seat of the covered wagon and riding over the enormous, open Kansas prairies, grasses "blowing in waves of light and shadow" and a great blue sky overhead. There you'll find Pa—crystallized forever in our minds with the helmet of thick black curls on actor Michael Landon's head—splitting logs with swings of his ax, while Ma sits in the shade of the cabin stitching a patchwork quilt and Laura and her sisters hunt for bird's nests in the long grass, their sunbonnets bouncing against their backs. Before long, you'll be so plumb tuckered out you'll be needing a scrub in the tin washbasin, with freshwater brought from the creek. Then you'll sit down to an open-air supper of cornmeal mush and prairie hen gravy while the notes of Pa's fiddle wind up into the huge starry sky.

And you'll have forgotten you are crammed into an immobile* elevator with fifteen other people, your nose pressed into someone else's armpit and no EXIT sign or ventilation duct in sight.

See also: Anxiety • Panic attack

COFFEE, CAN'T FIND A DECENT CUP OF

The Coffee Story
PETER SALMON

Many of us are familiar with the rage that descends upon us when in dire need of a decent cup of coffee. The very suggestion that such crimes against nature as "instant" coffee or "camp" coffee could be a reasonable substitute are enough to send the coffee addict into a paroxysm of gut-clenching withdrawal (see: Cold turkey, going). Can literature help at such times? We suggest holing up with some gentle encouragement to steer clear of the rocket fuel—or at least cut down—because if it's a choice between bad coffee or none, you might as well abstain. The following novel offers you a lot of reasons for not drinking java, but it can't help but sing a paean to the bean at the same time. So you will be consoled by this cure as well as encouraged to hold back.

In *The Coffee Story*, Theodore T. Everett lies propped up on his deathbed, sipping a coffee "so weak you could read a book through it." He is determined to tell us the tempestuous story of his life—a life that contained "a wife here and a wife there," dreams of Africa, Africa itself, an awful memory of bullets hitting flesh, a broken coffee table, a dead child. Among it all, the one constant is coffee, the drink that made it possible to keep going. Teddy is the last in a line of white coffee moguls who built their wealth on the back of the aromatic bean.

Everett's intimate knowledge of what coffee does to us physiologically is fascinating and horrifying. How coffee neutralizes the neural inhibitor, adenosine, throughout the body, so that the consumer experiences a rise in nervous activity. So far, so good, thinks the coffee lover. But also how the body reacts by creating additional adenosine, in the expectation that this will be neutralized by more coffee. If more coffee does not come, then the coffee lover begins to experience light-headedness, nausea, and flushing. All of which gives a jolt to the gut not unlike the first hit of coffee of the day. On top of which, we learn of the rotten roots of the coffee trade.

Everett's story is a grim one, reveling in addiction while scorning it too. It will work on you like a sobering draft of cold water. At the very least, you'll be reminded to make sure your coffee is from a nonexploitative source. And it may well plant the bean of the idea that alternative beverages would be better for your spiritual and physical health.

Now let that percolate through your system.

See also: **Concentrate, inability to** • **Constipation** • **Cope, inability to** • **Headache** • **Irritability** • **Lethargy**

COLD, COMMON

There is no cure for the common cold. But it is an excellent excuse to wrap up with a blanket, a cup of hot tea, and a comforting, restorative read.

See also: **Man flu**

THE TEN BEST NOVELS FOR
WHEN YOU'VE GOT A COLD

A Study in Scarlet .... ARTHUR CONAN DOYLE
Jamaica Inn .... DAPHNE DU MAURIER
The Princess Bride .... WILLIAM GOLDMAN
Journey to the River Sea .... EVA IBBOTSON

COLD TURKEY, GOING

To combat the physical and emotional agony of weaning yourself off an addiction, you need books that hook, compel, and force you to search your weather-beaten soul. Full immersion is recommended, as is the option of aural administration. These books are unafraid to heave you through withdrawal.

See also: Anxiety • Appetite, loss of • Concentrate, inability to • Headache • Insomnia • Nausea • Paranoia • Sweating

THE TEN BEST NOVELS FOR GOING COLD TURKEY

Journey to the End of the Night .... LOUIS-FERDINAND CÉLINE
Stuck Rubber Baby .... HOWARD CRUSE
The Gathering .... ANNE ENRIGHT
Ask the Dust .... JOHN FANTE
Neverwhere .... NEIL GAIMAN
Oblomov .... IVAN GONCHAROV
Blood Meridian .... CORMAC MCCARTHY
Charming Billy .... ALICE MCDERMOTT
Nausea .... JEAN-PAUL SARTRE
Last Exit to Brooklyn .... HUBERT SELBY, JR.

*Oranges Are Not
the Only Fruit*
JEANETTE
WINTERSON
· · ·
Like People in History
FELICE PICANO

If you're lesbian, gay, bisexual, or transgender, coming out—first to yourself and then to other people—can take years, and sometimes a lifetime. Indeed, it may never happen at all. But however hard it is, it can't be harder than for Jeanette in Jeanette Winterson's heavily drawn-from-life novel *Oranges Are Not the Only Fruit*. Jeanette's fundamentalist Christian mother adopted her for the express purpose of raising her as a "servant of God." When Jeanette's preference for girls is discovered, she is forced to undergo an exorcism by the church to which she and her mother belong.

Jeanette does not want to shock her mother, or push her away. And when she tries to tell her mother what it is she feels for Melanie, her difficulty in getting the words out will ring bells for many readers: her mother, "very quiet, nodding her head from time to time," clearly just does not want to know. She has erected an impenetrable wall between herself and her daughter, and as soon as Jeanette stops speaking, her mother says, "Go to bed now." Then she picks up her Bible, as if it were a literal manifestation of this wall. In a way it is, for when she eventually turns her daughter out of the house, leaving her with no home, no money, and no friends (if this is familiar, see: Abandonment), it is the church that she evokes as her justification. Jeanette's mother's response is so clearly absurd, so clearly lacking in empathy, that it will strengthen your resolve to assert who you are to the world. If other people can't handle it, that's their problem, not yours.

Thankfully, there are more inspiring coming out tales to latch on to in literature. One of our favorites is the delightful, rich gay epic *Like People in History* by Felice Picano, a tale that spans the fifties to the eighties. The coming out experiences of its two male protagonists are almost entirely celebratory, occurring in the context of the newly emerging gay rights scene in sixties America and being part and parcel of the hedonistic, drug-drenched party culture.

Cousins Roger and Alastair first meet at the age of nine, when Alastair is precociously cool and camp—already at ease with his burgeoning sexuality—while the baseball-playing Roger has yet to recognize his own. Alastair comes out to his family when caught rather marvelously in flagrante with the Italian gardener. For both men, stepping into their homosexuality is associated with joy, compassion, and tenderness—wishful thinking for some, maybe, but certainly an inspiration. If you take as an example the confident Alastair, who does not care what others think of him, leading the way by being blasé and untroubled by his homosexuality, you can even see how you might plant the idea of a nonchalant acceptance into the minds of those you are telling.

Though Roger lives for a while in Alastair's shadow, he eventually falls for an "Adonis," a macho navy veteran with a damaged leg who writes poetry (does it get any better?) *and* who loves him back (yes, it does!). Even with its inevitable complications, their deep love lasts a lifetime and must be one of the best examples of enduring love in literature, gay or straight. Every would-be out and proud gay man or woman fearful of announcing himself or herself to the world—and of finding true, lasting love—should commit this vital, exultant novel to heart.

See also: **Homophobia**

COMMITMENT, FEAR OF

Blindness
JOSÉ SARAMAGO

When you begin a sentence by the Portuguese writer José Saramago, you are making a commitment to follow it wherever it goes, because this ingenious writer does not follow the normal rules of grammar, but uses commas in unexpected ways, ways that will have your inner grammarian's jaw dropping open as your arm reaches for a red pen, surely that was a clause and this is another, shouldn't there be a period in between or at the very least a semicolon, and your inner grammarian is right, of course, but Saramago is right as well, he knows exactly what he's doing, and by the end of the first two paragraphs he will have you hopelessly ensnared by these sentences which flow from one to the other with an unstoppability that mimics the silent and terrifying epidemic of blindness which gives this novel its title and the cause of which nobody can explain.

In an unnamed city at an unspecified moment in history, the inhabitants begin to go blind, quite suddenly, one by one. And as the narrative moves between one unnamed character and the next, from the young prostitute with the dark glasses to the car thief to the ophthalmologist and his wife, we submit to the surreal and powerful accumulation of sentences, and any resistance to Saramago's unconventional style that we might have felt at the start is soon forgotten.

The rewards of commitment—whether to a sentence, a novel, a relationship, or indeed to anything you believe has value and in which you decide to put your faith—are great, as this story demonstrates. In the mental asylum where the blind are quarantined in an attempt to stem the epidemic, and where armed guards stand at the gates ready to shoot anyone who tries to escape, conditions quickly descend into squalor and disorder as the helpless inmates fight over the limited rations of food. In the midst of all this, a wife looks after her husband, tenderly, carefully, devotedly. In a moment of great foresight shining out from all the horror, the eye doctor's wife, her vision mysteriously intact, has managed to sneak into the asylum with him, pretending to be blind herself so that she can stay by her husband's side. When he goes to the bathroom, she washes him. When he needs to move, she guides him. She realizes that if anyone discovers she is sighted, they might use her for their own ends, so she takes great care to continue to act as if blind—not just to protect herself but also so she can continue to look after her husband.

The wife's selfless actions are those of a woman for whom loyalty, love, and commitment come first, unconditionally. From the moment her husband is struck blind, she is fighting first for him. Then she helps the others who share their ward, and they form a familial bond, one that is maintained and strengthened by acts of kindness and support. If they survive, we know it is because of their commitment to one another. Their commitment is also what enables them to keep their humanity while everyone around them is losing theirs.

Whatever it is you're struggling to commit to, let this novel guide you. And maybe even get some practice with it: When you begin the first sentence, commit to all the others. When you put the book down, commit to the rest of Saramago's oeuvre. And from there commit to . . . reading Proust? You never know—reading Saramago might just help you transform from commitment-phobe to one willing—nay, *eager*—to jump into anything with two feet.

See also: **Coward, being a** • **Give up halfway through, tendency to** • **Starting, fear of**

COMMITMENT, FEAR OF

COMMON SENSE, LACK OF

Cold Comfort Farm
STELLA GIBBONS

Common sense is the ability to make sound decisions about the everyday matters of life. Such as cleaning the floor with a mop rather than a toothbrush. Or going through the empty field rather than the one with the bull. If you lack common sense, you may find that you lead a rather inconvenient, though not to say frightening, life. To cure this lamentable lack, read Stella Gibbons's much loved spoof *Cold Comfort Farm*, which will introduce you to an unforgettable character from whom you have a lot to learn.

Nineteen-year-old Flora Poste is full of good, practical common sense, which she is determined to inflict upon her less sensible relatives. Finding herself an orphan, she feels a need to sort out stray members of her family and thus writes to all her living relatives to ask if she can go to live with them. The most intriguing reply comes from family members at Cold Comfort Farm in the village of Howling, Sussex, who claim that "there have always been Starkadders at Cold Comfort" and that because these Starkadders did some nameless wrong to her father, they would be pleased to give her a home and redress it. Flora had averred that she would not go if she had any cousins at the farm named Seth or Reuben, because "highly sexed young men living on farms are always called Seth or Reuben, and it would be such a nuisance." But in the end she doesn't have a chance to find out their names in advance. Off Flora goes, carrying, as she always does, a copy of *The Higher Common Sense* by Abbé Fausse-Maigre under her arm, sending a telegram to her friend on arrival: "Worst fears realized darling Seth and Reuben too send gumboots."

What she finds is that Aunt Ada Doom has been lurking in the attic at Cold Comfort ever since, as a small child, she "saw something nasty in the woodshed." Running the farm with an iron rod from this safe haven, she frankly has a rather good life up there, being brought three meals a day and not having to do any work. Flora conquers her fear of Ada, and cleverly uses a copy of *Vogue* as a means of luring her out into the world. With her breezy, optimistic, commonsense solutions, she goes on to sort out pretty much everyone, herself included, and we forgive her for being shallow, bossy, and opinionated.

Flora really does leave her relatives a lot better off than she found them, and you, too, will be far less likely to get yourself foolishly impregnated, left to run a farm, or live out the rest of your days in an attic (see: Agoraphobia) after reading this hilarious tome. Give it to all your unsensible friends and relations, and if anyone gives it to you, you'll know exactly what they think of you.

See also: **Risks, taking too many**

READING AILMENT *Concentrate, inability to*

CURE *Go off grid*

When so many ways of bamboozling our brains are available to us, from the constant visual stimuli of the Internet to the audio assault of podcasts, the tactile temptations of tablets, and the compulsion of social networks—all offering tasty nuggets that can be gulped rather than savored—it is out of step with the zeitgeist to focus on a book. What's worse, many of us seem to have lost the skill of concentrating on one thing for long stretches at a time. We are so accustomed to leaping from one brightly colored flower to another, moving on as soon as we feel the smallest twinge of boredom or mental exertion, that sitting down with a book—which may take some time before it offers up its precious nectar—is uncomfortable and hard.

Don't let your brain fragment. Declare an afternoon a week to go off grid. Two hours minimum, no upper limit. Switch off phones and disconnect from all possible sources of distraction. Then go somewhere else entirely, with a good book. It doesn't matter where you go, although a reading nook is recommended (see: Household chores, distracted by). The key is to have guaranteed hours of interruption-free thought. Slowly, your brain will piece itself back together, and continuity and calm will return.

CONFIDENCE, TOO LITTLE

See: Bullied, being • Confrontation, fear of • Coward, being a • Neediness • Pessimism • Risks, not taking enough • Seduction skills, lack of • Seize the day, failure to • Self-esteem, low • Shyness

CONFIDENCE, TOO MUCH

The Golden Ass
APULEIUS

So you reckon you're something. A mover-shaker. You can deal with anything life throws at you. You know how to do it all, don't need any help, thanks very much. You are the King of Karaoke, the Queen of Comedy, and, frankly, you can do it on your head with aplomb.

We applaud you. Confidence can be self-fulfilling and infectious, after all. But being overconfident can easily stray into the realms of arrogance (see: Arrogance). It is not quite the same thing, though, because the overconfident tend to do what they do with a grin rather than a smirk. They are delighted with themselves, rather than pleased they are better than everyone else. Which makes them much more likable. But what do your friends, O overconfident one, say about you behind your back? Do they think you are a bit cocky? If so, rein yourself in with the help of Lucius Apuleius's *The Golden Ass.*

Written in the second century AD, this adaptation of an earlier Greek fable is the only Latin novel to survive in its entirety. According to Pliny the Younger, historian and philosopher of this period, storytellers would preface their street corner entertainments with a shout of "Give me a copper and I'll tell you a golden story." This, then, is a golden story, designed to be engrossing, full of extravagant language, and containing a moral at the end.

Its hero, also named Lucius, is waylaid while on business to Thessaly by a desire for a magical experience. He has always been curious about the arts of personal transformation, and when he meets an attractive slave girl named Fotis, he begins a sexually athletic affair with her, not just because he likes her, but because he has heard that she may have access to ointments and spells that could transform him into an owl. Desperate to try his hand at metamorphosing himself, Lucius persuades Fotis to obtain some of her mistress's powerful ointment. He rubs this onto his skin, saying the magic words—and seconds later he can only communicate his fury to Fotis by rolling his huge, watery donkey eyes. It turns out that she muddled her ointments. But she reassures him that all he needs to do is find some roses to eat, and they will bring him back to human form.

As it transpires, Lucius spends twelve months in the ass's skin, roaming in search of the restorative flower from one rose season to the next. And though he delights in the unaccustomed enormity of his masculine organ and enjoys his hirsute state (he was going bald as a man),* he is constantly thwarted in any opportunities he might have for fun. His inner voice is wry and self-deprecating, always humorous but vividly descriptive of his strange and troubling state. His adventures as an ass, under almost constant threat of death from bandits and cruel masters as well as the fruits of his own foolhardy escapades, bring him closer and closer to true humility.

Luckily, his transformation doesn't last forever. And as a symbol of having renounced his vain affectations, he decides that he will now wear his human baldness with pride. By the end of this frequently hilarious and constantly entertaining novel, you will feel as though you too have worn the ears of the ass for long enough to have attained the humility that Lucius gains himself. The moral of the tale for both the Romans and for you is that, in time, the overconfident will indeed be brought low.

See also: Optimism • Risks, taking too many

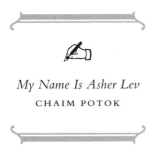

CONFRONTATION, FEAR OF

My Name Is Asher Lev
CHAIM POTOK

We who fear confrontation are the natural peacemakers—or, to put it less kindly, the pushovers, the oh-let's-just-do-it-your-way types. We give in at the slightest sign of disagreement. Yes, we do! Well, if you say so, we don't. But our greatest fear is an argument. And we will do anything to avoid one. We will eat our words, smile through our rage, mutter self-deprecatingly, and let the other party take all. Then we are left seething internally, the unresolved conflict festering until

* If this strikes a chord with you, see: Baldness.

it either erupts more violently another day (see: Rage) or simmers for several decades, causing intangible but real pain.

Overcoming your fear of confrontation is essential if you have any hope of dealing with conflicts when they arise. We suggest you study the eponymous hero of Chaim Potok's *My Name Is Asher Lev*. Asher finds himself in conflict with his parents from a very young age because of his prodigious talent for painting. Hasidic Jews, his parents don't think art is a worthwhile thing to do. But Asher is unable to control his own talent. He draws constantly, sometimes without even realizing he is doing it. One day at school a face appears in fountain pen on an inside page of his Chumash. Fellow pupils are outraged at this desecration of the holy book, and Lev's parents are mortified and take it as a personal insult. But Asher has gotten so used to repressing his artistic ability that he has no memory of drawing the picture.

The conflict within the family is painful to behold, as Asher's parents strive to understand their complicated son. His mother, Rivkeh, traumatized by the loss of her brother, is terrified that she will one day lose Asher too; he does not assuage her fears when he stays out late at the museum drawing, unbeknownst to her. His father, Aryeh, is permanently disappointed with Asher's choices, and things are often explosive when the two do spend time together. The leader of the Ladover Hasidic community has a guiding influence over all of them. A wise and powerful man, he speaks to Asher in ways that make him listen, gently reminding the young man where his loyalties should lie. "They tell me the world will hear of you one day as an artist," he says. "I pray to the Master of the Universe that the world will one day also hear of you as a Jew. Do you understand my words?" The rebbe does not disapprove of Asher's artistic pursuits, but he at least wants the young man to be as committed a Jew as he is an artist. Asher deals with all these conflicts by ignoring them as much as possible, but, alas, he is left tormented by them for years.

Whether your conflict is born of differing beliefs, ambitions, approaches to life, or simply domestic issues, face it before it escalates into estrangement or worse.

See also: **Violence, fear of**

CONSTIPATION

Shantaram
GREGORY DAVID
ROBERTS

Some novels make you want to keep it all in; others make you want to let it all come out. This sprawling, voluminous novel set in the poverty-stricken slums of Bombay, written by Australian ex–bank robber Gregory David Roberts, will have you unblocked in no time at all. Read it for its narrator's great warmth, its embrace of all that is spirited and lawless inside. Read it for the ease with which the words tumble out, raising up this city of twenty million with its choking heat and dirty mirages, its acre upon acre of shantytown in which people go about their lives: eating, smoking, arguing, copulating, haggling, singing, shaving, birthing, playing, cooking, dying—and relieving themselves—all in full view of one another. Read it for its lovely list of soft fruits that may loosen your small intestines like a lexical laxative: pawpaw, papaya, custard apples, *mosambi* (sweet lime), grapes, watermelon, banana, *santra* (orange), mango. And above all read it for Prabaker's description of the male slum dwellers' morning "motions," which occur en masse off the side of a jetty, young men and boys squatting with their buttocks to the ocean in convivial harmony, able to spectate at will on one another's progress, or lack of it. "Oh, yes!" says Prabaker, the narrator's friend, urging him to come to the jetty, as he knows other people are waiting for them. "They are a fascinating for you. You are like a movie hero for them. They are dying to see how you will make your motions."

With this image of bare buttock cheeks doing their business in public engraved on your memory, you will be forever grateful for your own private toilet, and eager to make use it. And if, when you get there, the long-awaited "motions" fail to motate, this doorstopper of a novel will keep you marvelously entertained while you wait.

See also: Irritability

The Way of All Flesh
SAMUEL BUTLER
...
*The Man Who Loved
Children*
CHRISTINA STEAD

You know the way you like things. So you like to keep things that way. And you like to tell everyone around you the way you like things, so that they can keep things that way too. Why should you listen to anybody else when you already have things under control?

We'll tell you why. Because you're a control freak and nobody likes you. Because being a control freak is hard, endless work that rarely yields good results. And because your children, should they grow up to be famous writers, will expose your domineering ways and tell everyone what an awful person and parent you were. No writer has more thoroughly itemized and weighed his parents' soul-crushing character flaws than the surprisingly levelheaded Samuel Butler (who fled to New Zealand in the 1850s to get out from under the parental thumb). His semi-autobiographical novel *The Way of All Flesh* offers so many lessons in recovering from damage wrought by control freak parents that it ought to be prescribed to psychotherapists to save them years of study.

Butler hated his bossy clergyman father, and the feeling was mutual. So severe, critical, stern, and punitive was Butler *père*, so rigid his method of raising children, that his son never forgave him for it, even as a grown man. Awed by his dictatorial parent even after the man was dead, Butler did not dare to take his revenge while he himself was alive—his novel was published posthumously. In this curiously engaging book—imagine Dickens without the ruffles and the mawkishness—Butler recalls stultifying silent Sundays, endless, tedious homilies, and harsh punishments. Yet he puts this childhood oppression in context. Like his narrator, he had broken free of his familial shackles and built himself an eventful, self-directed, well-savored life. He urges his readers to follow his example and not to dwell on their early misfortunes at the hands of those who warped them. "A man at five and thirty should no more regret not having had a happier childhood than he should regret not having been born a prince of the blood," he writes.

A more recent contender for the most overcontrolling parent in literature goes to the self-mythologizing title character of Christina Stead's *The Man Who Loved Children*. Sam Pollit, the blithely cruel father in this 1940 novel, builds a cult of personality around himself, using intellectual games, forced high spirits, and favoritism to make his seven children vie for his attention like members of opposing sports teams—while assuring that ultimately every victory goes to himself. Christina Stead's crystal-sharp voice chillingly conveys the far-reaching sadism in Sam Pollit's power games and offers a useful corrective to anyone who's a little too drunk on his or her own dominion. If you're given this novel by someone else, you'll know that includes you.

See also: Anally retentive, being • Dictator, being a • Give up halfway through, refusal to • Organized, being too • Reverence of books, excessive • Workaholism

CONTROL, OUT OF

See: Adolescence • Alcoholism • Carelessness • Drugs, doing too many • Rails, going off the • Risks, taking too many

August

GERARD WOODWARD

COPE, INABILITY TO

There are variations in the intensity of one's inability to cope. At one end of the spectrum, there's not being able to deal with the confusion of one particular moment—the laundry, the cat poo, the baby. At the other end our coping mechanism—perhaps depleted further by hormones, exhaustion, insomnia, or sickness—is so compromised by the volume of demands that it seizes up completely. Here we prescribe for the mild form of the ailment, somewhere between spilled milk and spilled blood. (If your inability to cope is more extreme, see: Stress; Depression. And if you suffer from just being too busy but are in fact juggling it all rather well, stop complaining and get on with whatever it is you've got to do—and, while you're at it, see: Busy, being too.)

When we first meet Colette in Gerard Woodward's excellent debut novel, *August*, she seems imperturbable. A "funny, interesting wife" to Aldous, she's also a mother of four with a quirky, blithe spirit. It's the seventies, and they live together in a bohemian North London home. Each August they go camping at the same spot in Wales, a holiday that becomes the symbolic center of their lives. She is delighted by all that surrounds her—her children, her clothes, her ability to move "like a ballet dancer" in her job as a bus ticket collector. But it all starts going downhill when she discovers a new means of mental escape: glue sniffing.

Colette's glue-induced hallucinations are described in thrilling, tempting terms. On holiday, she watches the top of a nearby Welsh hill from her tent, normally a "blend of moss greens and lime greens," but this afternoon becoming, "slowly, a brilliant fluorescent orange, as though a spoonful of syrup had been tipped over it." But by the time they get back to London, things have become more disturbing, and Colette is scrabbling around her living room trying to catch miniature sheep.

Faced with Colette's bizarre behavior, her family is completely out of its depths. It isn't long before her children start to show signs that they, too, are having coping issues. But even while Colette's family disintegrates around her, there's warmth and love here too. For those hanging over the precipice, the pellucid prose of this sympathetic novel will help clear the clamor of your mind—at least you have your mental faculties intact. Use them to regroup and set some priorities. Deal with what's important first, and leave what isn't until later on. It won't be hard to feel more in control than Colette.

See also: **Christmas** • **Cry, in need of a good** • **Exhaustion** • **Fatherhood** • **Motherhood** • **Single parent, being a**

COWARD, BEING A

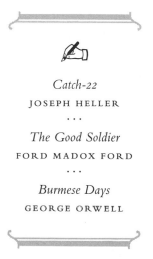

Catch-22
JOSEPH HELLER

• • •

The Good Soldier
FORD MADOX FORD

• • •

Burmese Days
GEORGE ORWELL

One of the twentieth century's best-known fictional cowards is Yossarian, the lily-livered bomber pilot at the center of Joseph Heller's *Catch-22*. Captain Yossarian has flown many successful missions but is completely terrified by his job. Malingering in the military hospital, he postpones returning to active duty for as long as he can because he has become obsessed by the idea that, as he explains to an officer named Clevinger, "They're trying to kill me." "No one's trying to kill you," Clevinger tells him. "Then why are they shooting at me?" Yossarian asks. "They're shooting at *everyone* . . . They're trying to kill everyone," Clevinger answers. "And what difference does that make?" Yossarian retorts. Joseph Heller's breathtakingly funny and sad tale of the violence and pointlessness of war demonstrates that just because a man is cowardly doesn't mean he's wrong to be afraid.

Despite his overt cowardice, Yossarian is one of the most rational of all the characters in Heller's novel. Before judging your failure of nerve too harshly, ask yourself if, like Yossarian, you're actually in the sort of dangerous circumstances that any normal person would want to evade. If the answer is yes, get help! If, however, after some self-examination you conclude that you face no life-threatening challenges and are actually just being a wimp, buck up and try to learn from the example of some of literature's whiners.

Think, for instance, of the doleful narrator John Dowell of Ford Madox Ford's *The Good Soldier*, who is too naive and weak-willed to acknowledge his wife's evasions. "I can't believe that that long, tranquil life, which was just stepping a minuet, vanished in four crashing days at the end of nine years and six weeks," he reflects, the precision of his dates hinting at a retrospective awareness of the exact length of his lapse. Dowell suffers enormously from his passivity. Let his experience embolden you to face up to disagreeable truths rather than prolong the agony of a poisoned relationship (see also: Confrontation, fear of).

While John Dowell is motivated (to an extent) by concern for others, the craven protagonist of George Orwell's *Burmese Days* has no such credit to his name. James Flory, a self-pitying English expat in Burma, indulges himself in the lazy sort of cowardice that hurts others while benefiting no one. Though Dr. Veraswami is Flory's best friend, someone he dines and hunts with, Flory refuses to endorse his membership to the exclusive European Club because it would be slightly awkward. "It is a disagreeable thing when one's close friend is not one's social equal; but it is a thing native to the very air of India," Flory self-servingly muses. He admits to himself that, "in all probability, if he had the courage" he could get Dr. Veraswami in. Even though he knows that "in common decency it was his duty to support the doctor," he does not do so. Flory does not have common decency. He's a coward—nobody's role model, but an excellent deterrent for anyone who knows that cowardliness can get in the way of doing the right thing.

See also: Risks, not taking enough · Seize the day, failure to · Superhero, wishing you were a

CRY, IN NEED OF A GOOD

Sometimes you just need to let the misery out, whether it's a broken heart, a broken heirloom, or out-of-control hormones. Take these novels with tissues and brandy.

See also: **Tired and emotional, being**

THE TEN BEST NOVELS TO MAKE YOU WEEP

A Lesson Before Dying .... ERNEST J. GAINES
The Fault in Our Stars .... JOHN GREEN
Tess of the D'Urbervilles .... THOMAS HARDY
One Day .... DAVID NICHOLLS
Doctor Zhivago .... BORIS PASTERNAK
Kiss of the Spider Woman .... MANUEL PUIG
The Notebook .... NICHOLAS SPARKS
Sophie's Choice .... WILLIAM STYRON
The Story of Lucy Gault .... WILLIAM TREVOR
My Dear, I Wanted to Tell You .... LOUISA YOUNG

CULT, BEING IN A

Amity and Sorrow
PEGGY RILEY
...
American Pastoral
PHILIP ROTH

"Join us, wear strange clothes, get castrated, and then drink poison." This was the message, if not the slogan, of the American cult Heaven's Gate, whose members were brainwashed into believing that by committing mass suicide they would escape the imminent "recycling" of planet Earth and transport themselves to a waiting alien spacecraft.

Being in a cult, it seems, may not give you the best chance of long-term happiness, or indeed survival. Should you ever find yourself receiving an unnervingly enthusiastic welcome by a previously unheard-of community with a single, charismatic leader; if your previous culture, community, or habits are roundly criticized and rejected by them; and if you are encouraged to break ties with family and friends and give all your resources away, a cult will have just made you one of its members. If it's already happened, we're too late. If it hasn't, vaccinate yourself immediately with Peggy Riley's luminous novel *Amity and Sorrow*, an account of the trap—and lure—of life in a cult. In this case, it's a fundamentalist, polygamous community in the far north of Idaho.

If you are not inclined to resist cult membership on your own account, consider the woe that your indoctrination will bring upon your family. Philip Roth's searing novel *American Pastoral* shows the destruction that a daughter brings to her family when she is brainwashed beyond recognition. Seymour "Swede" Levov rises from immigrant beginnings to become an all-American success story. But one day his daughter, Merry, who has grown to be an angry, sullen teenager, disappears. To his horror, Swede learns that she has joined a Jainist cult. Still worse, she has killed four people in a bombing, and doesn't regret it. Reeling in disbelief, Swede tells himself Merry is "in the power of something demented" and tracks her down, yearning to rescue his little girl. He cannot bear to admit to himself that the emaciated cultist freak who calls him Daddy can be his child. Altered beyond recognition, filthy and rank, she is utterly indifferent to her father's emotion. "No!" Swede bellows, grieving like an American Lear. "This will not do!" But "this" has already been done. After chanting, zombielike, "The truth is simple. Here is the truth. You must be done with craving and selfhood," Merry shuts her mouth and refuses to speak. Swede pries open her mouth as if he can find some real sense inside.

Reading of Swede's heartbreak and his daughter's ruin, even the surliest rebel may come to see that, appealing as it may seem to attach yourself to a passionate cause, joining a cult is not a prudent outlet for it.

See also: Bullied, being • Family, coping with • Family, coping without • Outsider, being an • Self-esteem, low

Zuleika Dobson
MAX BEERBOHM
. . .
The Rachel Papers
MARTIN AMIS
. . .
Elliot Allagash
SIMON RICH

Oscar Wilde once said that the cynic is a man who knows the price of everything, but the value of nothing. Cynicism is an attitude many of us outgrow as life lengthens, time shortens, and the satisfaction we once derived from attributing base motives to everyone else loses some of its spark. That said, there would be no tabloid magazines or stand-up comedians if the scathing, mocking power of cynicism did not serve some purpose.

Perhaps because this affliction is most acute during youth, the novels that best treat cynicism tend to be set at school. *Zuleika Dobson*, Max Beerbohm's elegantly scathing riff on Edwardian Oxford, is an early exemplar. Beerbohm wrote meanspiritedly about his heroine—Zuleika—portraying her as a heartless, vain young adventuress who takes pride in the fact that her beauty drives hundreds of love-struck college boys to kill themselves. What were Zuleika's sins? She was beautiful and alluring, and she knew it. She was also picky. Does that make her hateful? Beerbohm paints Zuleika as a cynical creature, but it's his starchily entertaining caricature of her that's truly drenched in cynicism. If a pretty woman doesn't return the love of every stranger who pines for her, does that make her loathsome? If you, like Beerbohm, have a tendency to ascribe bad motives to people who excel and stand out, reading *Zuleika Dobson* will prompt you to sheathe your barbs.

Martin Amis, writing *The Rachel Papers* decades later, also made his hero a heartless, vain young man. Charles Highway, a "chinless elitist and bratty whey-faced lordling" just turned twenty, keeps a cynical, detailed reckoning of his trysts with willing young women. Here he is recalling one energetic coupling: "During the long pre-copulative session I glanced downwards—and what should I see but Gloria, practicing the perversion known as fellatio." Isn't it romantic? But Amis saves Charles's most thorough, blow-by-blow chronicling for a girl named Rachel, for whom Charles belatedly comes to sense that he might actually have real, uncynical feelings. Telling his story from precocious retrospect, wondering at his patronizing attitude, Charles muses, "I suppose I was just moodier then, or more respectful of my moods, more inclined to think they were worth anything."

Emerging from his fog of self-absorption, Charles has begun to suspect that other people's moods deserve respect, too. Take note: this is the first step on the road out of cynicism and toward a more empathetic worldview.

And in America, in the last decade, a witty New York wunderkind, Simon Rich, wrote a delirious satire, *Elliot Allagash*, set in junior high school, in the *gotcha!* world of smug adolescent score keeping. Rich's Machiavellian title character, a phenomenally wealthy teen, arrives in eighth grade at a Manhattan private school and resolves "purely for sport" to transform a plump, goony nebbish named Seymour Herson into a big man on campus, and to get him into Harvard. Using every underhanded means he can muster (he has a dazzling arsenal), Elliot appears to succeed in his project. Seymour can't help being flattered by his Svengali's attention, and exhilarated by his star turn—for a while. Unlike Elliot, though, he has a conscience. As Elliot's lies and stratagems begin to hurt other people, Seymour loses his appetite for ruthless self-promotion—to Elliot's fury. He would rather be ordinary and decent than extraordinary and corrupt. If you have been cynically pondering a career in guile, reading *Elliot Allagash* will caution you against it.

See also: **Antisocial, being** • **Bitterness** • **Killjoy, being a** • **Misanthropy** • **Pessimism**

D

Emma

JANE AUSTEN

Being a daddy's girl never did anyone any favors. It's fine when you're the doted-upon darling who can't put a foot wrong. But when you grow up and discover that the rest of the world doesn't find your foibles as adorable as Daddy does, it will come as a bit of a shock. The new boyfriend won't be amused to discover he's barred from the number one spot in your heart. But maybe it doesn't matter, because he won't last very long anyway. Nobody's good enough for a daddy's girl, and Daddy will make sure this is known.

Emma, the eponymous heroine of Jane Austen's satire of nineteenth-century marriage, is the ultimate daddy's girl. To her nervous, frail, and foolish father—whose chief obsession in life is to protect himself from drafts and persuade his friends to eat a nourishing boiled egg—the beautiful, clever Emma is a model of goodness who deserves to have everything her way. It doesn't help Emma's skewed vision of herself that her parental triangle is completed by an absent (dead) mother and an overly devoted governess.

And so her hapless, hopeless father sends Emma, at twenty-one, out into the world with an overly high opinion of herself and a self-centeredness that can only bring her grief. When she competes in love with the equally accomplished yet impoverished Jane Fairfax and publically mocks Miss Bates, Jane's aunt, for being a chatterbox, Emma is not only being unkind but is breaking unspoken rules of social propriety regarding the treatment of one's social inferiors. For a while she risks losing the respect of everyone in her community—a calamity for someone in her position. And we blame her silly old dad. Because who better to correct a child of her faults than a parent who loves her unconditionally? Imagine the fairer, stronger person Emma might have become if she had been affectionately teased through the years.

Heed this cautionary tale. Daddies: don't do it to your daughters. And daughters: beware of having a doting Mr. Woodhouse for a dad. If you do, your best option is to stop playing the game and show him what a bad girl you can be. For some inspiration, see: Rails, going off the.

DEATH, FEAR OF

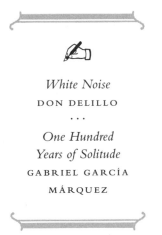

White Noise
DON DELILLO
...
*One Hundred
Years of Solitude*
GABRIEL GARCÍA
MÁRQUEZ

Do you ever wonder how anybody manages to function knowing they may be wiped out at any moment? Do you ever awake in the night in a cold sweat, pinned to your bed by the terrible knowledge that a looming eternity of nonexistence awaits you?

You're not alone. An awareness of death is what sets us apart from animals. And how we choose to deal with it—whether we opt to believe in God and an afterlife, reconcile ourselves to nonexistence, or simply repress all thoughts of it—is something that sets us apart from one another.

Jack Gladney, chair of Hitler studies in a midwestern college, suffers constantly from acute fear of death. Jack obsesses about when he will die, about whether he or his wife, Babette, will die first (he secretly hopes that she will), and about the size of "holes, abysses and gaps." One day he discovers that Babette fears death as much as he does. Until then, his blond and ample wife had stood between him and his fear, representing "daylight and dense life." The discovery shakes his soul—and the foundations of their otherwise happy marriage.

Jack explores all manner of arguments and philosophies to overcome his fear of death, from placing himself within the protective realm of a crowd to reincarnation ("How do you plan to spend your resurrection?" asks a friendly Jehovah's Witness, as though asking about a long weekend). His most successful method for soothing (and distracting) himself is to sit and watch his children sleep, an activity that makes him feel "devout, part of a spiritual system." For those lucky enough to have sleeping children at hand, this is a balm we heartily endorse not just for fear, but fears of all kinds.

Maybe one of Jack's mental arguments will work for you. If not, at least *White Noise* will help you laugh about your fear. DeLillo is a funny writer, and his description of Jack attempting to pronounce German words gets our vote for one of the funniest passages in literature. Reach for it in the night when your death terror hits, and witness the metamorphosis of fear into laughter.

The other cure to keep by your bed is *One Hundred Years of Solitude.* This novel about the Buendía family of Macondo can be read over and over, as the events occur in a sort of eternal cycle, and it's so densely written that you'll find new gems and revelations every time. As the novel spans a full century, death occurs often and matter-of-factly and the characters accept their part in the natural order of things—an attitude that, in time, may rub off on you.

If it doesn't, keep reading. Over and over again. And one night, perhaps, as you wearily reach the last page and begin again, you'll start to see the need for all good things, eventually, to come to an end.

See also: **Angst, existential**

DEATH OF A LOVED ONE

Of all the challenges we face in life, none, perhaps, is harder than this.

Whether it is a parent, spouse, sibling, or child we have lost, a lifelong friend, or someone we knew only briefly, the death of a loved one brings with it a bewildering slew of emotional states, all of which can be bracketed under the general heading of grief. It has helped many people to think of their grief in terms of the five stages that Elisabeth Kübler-Ross identified in the late six-

After You'd Gone
MAGGIE O'FARRELL
. . .
Incendiary
CHRIS CLEAVE
(continued)

ties: denial, anger, bargaining, depression, and acceptance. Not everybody goes through these five stages, and those who do don't necessarily experience them distinctly or in this order. But we hope that by borrowing these

*Extremely Loud and
Incredibly Close*
JONATHAN SAFRAN
FOER
. . .

What I Loved
SIRI HUSTVEDT
. . .

Here Is Where We Meet
JOHN BERGER

categories we might more clearly direct mourners to the novel most likely to offer you solace and comfort when you need it.

If you suspect you are in denial about your loss—which many see as the body's way of moderating the onslaught of grief, stalling its flood with numbness and shock—we offer Maggie O'Farrell's *After You'd Gone*. When we first meet Alice, she is on her way to visit her sisters in Edinburgh. But in the ladies' loo at the station she sees something so terrible, so unrepeatable, that she cannot process it—and immediately takes the train back to London. That night, her state of shock is made absolute when she is hit by a car, sustaining a head injury that puts her in a coma. It is from this dreamlike state of the protagonist's coma that we explore her life up to this point and discover a lurking and unprocessed grief. Let this novel give you permission to exist for a while in your own cocoon of shock. Don't worry if you can't seem to persuade yourself to come out of it; your body will shed the cocoon when it's ready.

If anger dominates, you need to let it out. There is no better model for this than *Incendiary*, Chris Cleave's heartrending cry of anguish and fury from a woman who has lost both her husband and small son in a fictional terrorist attack on Wembley Stadium. Written in the form of a letter to Osama bin Laden—who is thought to be behind the attack—the narrator hopes to make Osama understand and love her boy so that he won't ever kill again. "I'm going to write to you about the emptiness that was left when you took my boy away . . . so you can look into my empty life and see what a human boy really is from the shape of the hole he leaves behind," she writes. Her voice is as unforgettable as its message, for the rawness of her delivery— ungrammatical, full of crude colloquialisms and tabloid headline short-hands—shows a woman past caring about things that don't matter. Words "don't come natural for me," she tells Osama—but, oh, do they pack a punch.

Fearless and increasingly maddened by imagining her lost boy shouting for his mummy, she vents until she cracks, but we know, by the end, that this venting has been deeply necessary. Your anger may feel endless—and so it should, for it is the transmutation of your love. But it can dissipate only if you let it out. This stage cannot be rushed. Mourners experiencing grief in this way should also see: Rage.

It is not uncommon when suffering from acute grief for us to enter into a negotiation with ourselves, or with fate. If only we can find the right answer to X or Y, we believe, the pain will go away. Children are particularly prone to this—as illustrated by the search over New York undertaken by nine-year-old Oskar Schell in *Extremely Loud and Incredibly Close*. After his father, Thomas, is killed in the 9/11 terrorist attacks, Oskar finds a little key in an envelope at the bottom of a vase in his father's closet. The envelope has the word "Black" written on it. Oskar decides that if he can find the lock the key opens, he will understand something about what has happened to his father. So he embarks on a mission to visit all the Blacks in the telephone directory.

The search turns out to be a wild-goose chase, of course, but what Oskar finds in the process is more precious: an understanding of suffering and loss from the lives of his grandparents before he was born and, in a touch that will help to rewarm your heart, the desire for a grief-stricken but loving mother to help her son recover from his enormous loss.

The stage that everyone dreads the most, perhaps, is depression. There is no getting around it: some things cannot be made better, and it is vital that we allow ourselves, and others, to exist in this bleak, dark stage, in which attempts to cheer up are inappropriate and unhelpful, for as long as we need to. Siri Hustvedt's novel *What I Loved* is an unflinching exploration of this place. Narrator Leo Hertzberg and his friend Bill Wechsler are both in mourning. The lives of both men were once so full of promise, but now they are disintegrating. Both also mourn the past, their intellectual lives in New York, which they had somehow thought would last all their lives.

Hustvedt's characters, including the children, are an intelligent, thoughtful crew. What she shows is that our intelligence cannot save us from pain; sometimes, it actually makes it harder for us to find our way through. Pain is an unavoidable part of life, and experiencing yours in the company of these characters will help you inhabit its darkest corners—perhaps the most vital part of the process of grieving, if you have any hope of moving on.

Some people find their way to acceptance more easily than others. When the narrator of John Berger's *Here Is Where We Meet* encounters his mother—dead for many years—in a park in Lisbon, it's her walk he recognizes first. In the conversation that follows, he finds himself watching familiar, endearing gestures—licking her lower lip, as she always used to after applying lipstick—and being irritated, as he was as a child, by an outward show of sureness, which, to his eyes, seemed to conceal a complete lack of sureness underneath.

Berger's narrator travels from city to city, finding evidence of his dead. In Kraków he reencounters his mentor Ken, and as they observe a chess game together, he "suffers his death" as if for the first time—reminding us that grief is often experienced in waves, and at random, unpredictable moments throughout our lives. In Islington, London, he remeets his friend Hubert who is overwhelmed by the problem of sorting out the drawerfuls of sketches created by his dead wife, Gwen. "What am I to do?" he cries. "I keep on putting it off. And if I do nothing, they'll all be thrown out."

Walking in these places offers the narrator a way of remembering, and the conversations with the dead a way of assimilating his love of those he has lost. "I've learned a lot since my death," the narrator's mother tells him, referring afterward to "the eternal conundrum of making something out of nothing"—for she knows, finally, that this is what it is about. The narrator considers the question of what to leave at a graveside (one of his leather gloves, perhaps?) and notices how his dead take on new elements to their character—his mother, for instance, has a cheeky new impertinence about her, "sure now that she is beyond reach," and his father now claims to prefer swordfish to salmon. Thus Berger allows the dead to change and develop as the living do. Give your relationships with your dead the same new lease on life—you will find it more rewarding than leaving them locked and static.

So it is that, further along in our mourning process (though the process never ends), we come to see our lost loved ones as they really were, the good and the bad together. We can settle accounts, and we can also gather together the wonderful things about them, the things that we miss, and, perhaps, find a way to incorporate them into our lives in a different, magical way. Take a trip, with Berger, to the places where you spent time with your loved ones, do the things you used to do together, and relish and celebrate all that they gave you while they were alive—and continue to give you now.

See also: Anger · Appetite, loss of · Broken heart · Guilt · Insomnia · Loneliness · Nightmares · Sadness · Turmoil · Widowed, being · Yearning, general

DEATH OF A LOVED ONE

DEMONS, FACING YOUR

Beyond Black

HILARY MANTEL

We've all got a few demons on our backs. Some of us live with them so successfully that we're able to forget all about them until, one day, we catch sight of one in the mirror. Then there's hell to pay. Some of us, however, live with our demons in plain sight, rolling their eyeballs like marbles as they follow us down the street. Luckily, our friends can't always see them. We maintain that all demons should be faced and vanquished, sent back to the hell from which they crawled out. To help you purge, we prescribe the scourge of *Beyond Black* by Hilary Mantel.

Alison lives off her demons, unwillingly. A charming, friendly psychic, she indulges in a vast amount of comfort food to keep her complex past safely smothered (for more on psychological battles with weight, see: Obesity). After a demanding performance in front of an audience of hundreds on the outer edge of London, she wakes up in the early hours of the morning craving sandwiches, doughnuts, pizza. Alison's assistant, Colette, tries to put her boss on a diet. But this turns out to be as doomed as Alison's efforts to find out what really happened to her when the men that she still finds sprawled semi-clad around her living room—having now "passed into spirit"—first took her to the shed to "teach her a lesson" as a little girl. To bring this traumatic memory to the surface, Alison must quite literally confront them, led by her spirit guide, Morris. Was her father one of these men? she wonders. And if so, which one was he?

Alison first discovered her ability to communicate with "spirit" when, also as a girl, she was befriended by a little pink lady named Mrs. McGibbet in the attic, who faded back into the space behind the wall whenever her mother's heavy tread came up the stairs. Her powers don't come without pain. "When I work with the tarot, I generally feel as if the top of my head has been taken off with a tin opener," she tells us. But little by little, we begin to understand the references to what the dogs ate in the woodshed, and to what happened to the invisible Gloria, to whom Alison's mother speaks continually. The almost constant prickle of fear disappears only when the psychic meets her monsters head-on. Alison's final epiphany is an act of supreme psychic redemption. Take heart from her triumph, shake that demon off your back, and look it in the eye at last. The process may not be painless, but you will, like Alison, find it less terrifying than you think.

See also: **Haunted, being** • **Scars, emotional**

DEPENDENCY

See: **Alcoholism** • **Coffee, can't find a decent cup of** • **Cold turkey, going** • **Drugs, doing too many** • **Gambling** • **Internet addiction** • **Neediness** • **Shopaholism** • **Smoking, giving up**

READING AILMENT   *Depletion of library through lending*

CURE   *Label your books*

Yes, you want to tell everyone about the book you've just read, and you want everyone you love to share the experience too. This is how news of a good book gets about, and we are all for spreading the word. But what about the lurking anxiety that you won't get the book back? The gradual depletion of a library of its most beloved tomes is a woeful thing. To protect your treasured books, design your own "Ex Libris" label to stick inside each book as you lend it out—complete with careful instructions as to how to return the book once read and a warning about the consequences of late or nonreturn. (Be imaginative about this. We find the threat of a curse to be effective.)

For extreme cases—if your books have a tendency to fly off your shelves faster than you can buy new ones—we recommend keeping a library-style catalog. Check books out, and then in, and set up an alarm on your digital calendar to alert you to overdues. Then see: Control freak, being a; and Friend, falling out with your best.

DEPRESSION, ECONOMIC

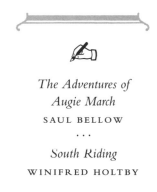

The Adventures of Augie March

SAUL BELLOW

...

South Riding

WINIFRED HOLTBY

In these times of austerity, when moneymaking opportunities are thin on the ground and a flexible approach to one's métier is called for, what better companion to have at one's side than Augie March, an everyman struggling to make good in his own hard times of the Great Depression. Raised on the rough west side of Chicago, Augie is a man who lives by "luck and pluck," going at things "free-style." Never quite managing to get himself a formal education, Augie moves from job to job—and girl to girl—as he searches for what he was meant to be.

The litany of lives he tries on for size makes for an eclectic list of job ideas and as such is an excellent resource for anyone in search of a novel way to spin a dime. For your convenience, we list them here: distributor of handbills at a movie theater; newspaper boy; stock unpacker at Woolworth's; Christmas elf; funeral wreath maker for a flower shop with a gangster clientele; butler, secretary, deputy, agent, companion, right-hand man (plus arms and legs) to a wheelchair-bound real estate dealer; assistant manager to a heavyweight boxer; robber; salesman of shoes, hunting gear, and paint; driver of illegal immigrants over the border; pampered dog trainer, washer, and manicurist; book racketeer; house surveyor; trade union organizer; hunter (with trained eagle); researcher for wannabe author; merchant marine.

If you're out of work and have plenty of time, read this charming, picaresque novel and stumble on the jobs yourself. You'll see that a life that takes in so many different roles—not all of them entirely honest—ends up a somewhat shapeless thing, to which Saul Bellow's baggy narrative testifies. But its go-with-the-flow opportunism, its eye for a laugh, its shrug, its easygoing all-American swagger are precious commodities in these highly competitive, pared-down days, and Augie's winding trajectory will help free you up when mapping your own path.

Apart from forcing us all to tighten our belts (which for some might be no bad thing; see Extravagance), one of the first casualties of economic depression is the funding of public services: health, education, the arts. For a sobering reminder of the hard-won advances we are in danger of seeing slip away, read Winifred Holtby's *South Riding*, set in the north of England just before the formation of the welfare state. It tells the story of local schoolmistress Sarah, a feisty redhead swimming with ideals who falls in love with tortured, married landowner Robert Carne, whose wife is mentally ill. Part socialist idealist meets conservative traditionalist, the tale shows how the members of a rural community work with and against one another with varying degrees of selflessness. One of the characters, Joe Astell, knows he is dying of tuberculosis, but becomes an alderman—an elected member of the local council—in the hope of rescuing the town from being the "wastepaper basket of the South Riding." Perhaps Holtby modeled him on herself, for she, too, was dying as she wrote this fervently political book.

As public funding dwindles, values and individuals are trampled underfoot. Let Holtby remind you that, in times of austerity, we must strive not just for ourselves but for the collective good.

See also: **Broke, being** • **Job, losing your** • **Unemployment**

DEPRESSION, GENERAL

The Unbearable Lightness of Being
MILAN KUNDERA
• • •
The Bell Jar
SYLVIA PLATH
• • •
Mr. Chartwell
REBECCA HUNT
• • •
The Marriage Plot
JEFFREY EUGENIDES

Depression is a sliding scale. At the mild end, where most of us dip in a toe from time to time, are those occasional days or periods when nothing goes right, it seems as if we don't have any friends, and we are plunged into a state of gloom (see: Failure, feeling like a; Left out, feeling; Sadness; Grumpiness; Pointlessness). At these times, we need a novel that shifts our perception of the world, reminding us that it can be a place of sun and laughter too. See our list of the Ten Best Novels to Cheer You Up below for a positive pick-me-up read that will open the window and let in a blast of fresh air.

But at the other end of the scale, sufferers experience a heavy black cloud that descends without warning, for no particular reason, and from which they can't see any way out. This is clinical depression, a severe form of mental illness that is hard to treat and can recur. If you are unlucky enough to be prone to this kind of depression, your spirits are unlikely to be lifted by a light and breezy read. Such a novel may well make you feel worse—guilty that you can't muster a chuckle, irritated by anything that strikes you as naively optimistic, and hating yourself even more. It sounds counterintuitive at first, but at such times a novel that tells it like it is—with characters who feel as depressed as you do, or with an uncompromisingly bleak view of the world—is likely to hit home, encourage you to be gentler with yourself, and support you in a more appropriate way. If you're in this situation, you need a novel that can accompany you into your dark melancholic place, acknowledging and articulating it, so that you realize that others have been there too, and that you are not, after all, so different, or so dreadfully alone.

The mental torment and nightmares experienced by Tereza in Milan Kundera's novel *The Unbearable Lightness of Being* may help in this regard. Tereza's anguish is triggered by her lover Tomas's inveterate womanizing; having cut himself off from his failed marriage and young son, Tomas has chosen to embrace the life of a libertarian bachelor. But from the start we see that Tereza is weighed down by life: the heaviness to Tomas and his mistress Sabina's lightness. Kundera divides people into two camps: those who understand that life is meaningless, and therefore skim its surface, living in and for the moment; and those who cannot bear the idea that existence should come and go without meaning, and insist on reading significance into everything. When Tereza meets Tomas, she knows that she has no choice but to love him forever, and when she turns up in Prague to see him again, with her worldly goods in a suitcase, she also brings a copy of *Anna Karenina*—a novel that perhaps sums up more than any other the suffering that results when meaning breaks down. Much as he loves her, Tomas knows she will be a heavy presence in his life. When she is pushed to the brink of insanity by Tomas's refusal to give up other women, Tereza berates herself for her weakness at wanting Tomas to change. At her lowest ebb she tries to take an overdose. Whenever you have sunk to such depths that it seems impossible for anyone else to reach you, pick up this novel and let Tereza keep you company down there. She, too, wants to live and rise above her sadness—and she finds a way to do so in the end.

A disproportionate number of writers suffer from depression. Some say creative types are more vulnerable to it, others that writing about one's illness is cathartic. The American novelist Richard Yates would spend hours staring blankly at the wall in a state of catatonic depression. Ernest Hemingway, too, was increasingly plagued by depressive episodes, and drank heavily (if this is your choice of escape, see: Alcoholism). He lost his battle with depression in the end, as did Virginia Woolf, and Sylvia Plath, but not without leaving the invaluable gift of their experience behind. These gifts—novels about the experience of mental illness—are there for us to make use of, so that we can find solace where these writers did not.

Plath suffered from bipolar disorder, and in her powerful autobiographical novel *The Bell Jar*, she documents through her young heroine Esther Greenwood the bewildering mood swings that caused her to be searingly happy one moment—"lungs inflating" in a rush of delight to be alive—and unable to rise to any emotional reaction at all—"blank and stopped as a dead baby"—the next. Esther's voice is a great comfort for depressives. What makes this novel so readable is the lightness of Plath's prose, and the way that even in the most disturbing passages Esther's humanity and youthful zest shine through. Remember this when you can't imagine ever feeling happy—or even just plain "normal"—again. Others can see the potential for lightness in you, even when you can't.

Learning to perceive your depression as something separate from you—such as a big, black, smelly dog—may seem a bizarre notion, but it can be a useful way of distancing yourself from your illness so that it doesn't define who you are. Rebecca Hunt's bold first novel, *Mr. Chartwell*, will take you through the process. Mr. Chartwell is the manifestation of Winston Churchill's "black dog"—the depression that haunted the august politician for much of his life—and which also moves in with his temporary secretary, Esther Hammerhans. Visible only to his victims, Black Pat (as the dog is called) arrives on the second anniversary of Esther's husband's death by suicide, ostensibly answering her advertisement for a lodger. Soon he is making free with her house, crunching bones outside her bedroom door, and even doing his best to join her in bed. Black Pat may have revolting habits, but as only sufferers of depression will understand, he has a peculiar charm that is hard to resist and Esther receives him with a mixture of despair and fascination.

She is not the first of his victims—not only has Black Pat been visiting Churchill, but Esther deduces that he's lived in her own house before, unperceived by her. As she begins to understand more about her husband's illness, and therefore her own, her relationship with the shaggy mutt heads toward its resolution. You'll have to read the novel to find out if she overcomes her depression; we all know Churchill managed to hold down a job through it all. And when Esther and her elderly mentor first realize that they can both see the dog but are afraid to mention it—such is the taboo surrounding mental illness—Churchill's tactful circling around the giant black creature's malodorous presence and his rousing encouragement to Esther to "stand firm" is touching and reassuring to Esther and reader alike.

If you are not depressed yourself but are close to someone who is, you may identify with Madeleine, the heroine of Jeffrey Eugenides's novel *The Marriage Plot*, in which three college seniors at Brown University in the 1980s get caught up in a love triangle. Leonard, brainy, haughty, and erratic, has concealed his manic depression from Madeleine, his adoring, bluestocking girlfriend. And when a severe episode engulfs him, he ditches her rather than divulge his secret. But when Madeleine gets a phone call on graduation day informing her that Leonard is in a psych ward, she at last understands why he has been so mystifyingly, and upsettingly, hot and cold during the course of their romance. His moods are beyond his control: "The smarter you were, the worse it was," he thinks. "The sharper your brain, the more it cut you up." Seeing her boyfriend in the hospital, levelheaded Madeleine wishes she'd known about his manic depression before they'd got involved. But it's too late—Madeleine loves Leonard and will not give up on him. She succumbs to the trap Eugenides knowingly identifies: the desire to save him. If you find yourself struggling to cope with loved ones who suffer as Leonard does and who have perhaps pulled you into the vortex of their illness, this novel will help you stand back, understand what they're up against, and figure out if and how you can help them—and yourself, too.

In serious cases of depression, bibliotherapy is very unlikely to be enough. But we urge sufferers to make full and imaginative use of fiction as an accompaniment to medical treatment. Whether you require a novel to take you out of your funk or one that joins you in it, novels can often reach sufferers in a way that little else can, offering solace and companionship in a time of desperate need. Stand firm with Churchill, the two Esthers, and Tereza. Take reassurance from the fact that they—and the authors who created them—know something of what it's like to live with depression. And if their experience doesn't overlap with yours, maybe one of the others on our list of the Ten Best Novels for the Very Blue will (see below). You might not be able to see a gap in the clouds, but the knowledge that you're not the first to lose your way beneath them will keep you going as you wait for them to pass.

See also: **Antisocial, being · Anxiety · Appetite, loss of · Despair · Exhaustion · Hope, loss of · Indecision · Insomnia · Irritability · Lethargy · Libido, loss of · Nightmares · Paranoia · Pessimism · Self-esteem, low · Tired and emotional, being · Turmoil**

THE TEN BEST NOVELS TO CHEER YOU UP

Wake Up, Sir! .... JONATHAN AMES
Auntie Mame .... PATRICK DENNIS
Fried Green Tomatoes at the Whistle
Stop Café .... FANNIE FLAGG
Cold Comfort Farm .... STELLA GIBBONS
Fever Pitch .... NICK HORNBY
Absurdistan .... GARY SHTEYNGART
Major Pettigrew's Last Stand .... HELEN SIMONSON
I Capture the Castle .... DODIE SMITH
Miss Pettigrew Lives for a Day .... WINIFRED WATSON
The Family Fang .... KEVIN WILSON

THE TEN BEST NOVELS FOR THE VERY BLUE

Herzog .... SAUL BELLOW
Betty Blue .... PHILIPPE DJIAN
The Unbearable Lightness of Being .... MILAN KUNDERA
The Bluest Eye .... TONI MORRISON
The Bell Jar .... SYLVIA PLATH
Last Exit to Brooklyn .... HUBERT SELBY, JR.
By Grand Central Station I
Sat Down and Wept .... ELIZABETH SMART
Some Hope .... EDWARD ST. AUBYN
To the Lighthouse .... VIRGINIA WOOLF
Revolutionary Road .... RICHARD YATES

Alone in Berlin
HANS FALLADA

DESPAIR

One would never choose to live without hope (see: Hope, loss of). But sometimes one has no choice. Despair is to be found at the place where all hope is lost, and those in its grim grip need a cure that acknowledges what it is like to exist in this place. The author of *Alone in Berlin* understands it all too well, as do the characters that populate this sobering novel about life under the Third Reich. Let them be your companions as you acquaint yourself with your despair. Watch them and learn from them. As you will see, there are cracks of light to be found even in the darkest of places.

Berlin is a city in thrall to the Führer and his henchmen. Opponents of the regime—which include anyone failing to inform on anyone else deemed disloyal to the Führer—face violent intimidation and arrest, followed by summary execution or internment in one of the notorious concentration camps. When their only son is killed on the front line, uneducated factory worker Otto Quangel and his wife, Anna, begin their own, unique form of resistance: leaving postcards around Berlin urging their fellow citizens to stand up to the Nazis and fight back.

Unfortunately, the postcards backfire. Far from encouraging anti-Nazi sentiment, their postcards succeed only in engendering more fear and paranoia among the already cowed citizens of the city. This realization, when it comes, risks sending the couple deeper into despair. But the act of resisting has already saved them. It has given them the moral victory, and when they face their persecutors, it is the Quangels who have access to hope, light, and even joy. Their persecutors do not.

The Quangels are not the only ones who rescue themselves from despair in this way. Dr. Reichhardt, Otto's cellmate, does it by continuing to live as he has always lived: taking a walk each day (back and forth in his cell) and extending kindness and love to everyone he meets, good or bad. Eva Kluge, the ex-postwoman, does it by leaving the Nazi Party when she discovers that her adored son Karlemann has been photographed swinging a three-year-old Jewish boy by the leg and smashing his head against a car. In so doing Dr. Reichhardt and Eva Kluge put their lives at risk but keep their self-respect intact. As Eva says, this "will have been her attainment in life, keeping her self-respect."

It sounds like a small thing, but it is not. Our lives are nothing without it. And with it, our lives become notable, rich, meaningful. Despair cannot coexist with these things; certainly they bar the descent to depression. There may not be hope, but *Alone in Berlin* teaches us that sticking tenaciously, proudly, defiantly to our sense of what is right and true is enough—and the only fail-safe cure for despair that there is.

See also: **Broken spirit** • **Depression, general**

DETERMINEDLY CHASING AFTER A WOMAN EVEN THOUGH SHE'S A NUN

In the Skin of a Lion
MICHAEL ONDAATJE

If you are in the unfortunate position of having fallen in love with a nun,* Michael Ondaatje's *In the Skin of a Lion* is the novel for you.

First, because it features the best chance meeting between a man and a woman in literature, and if you're in a love with a nun, you'll need to engineer a good chance meeting. He, Nicolas Temelcoff, is a migrant manual laborer who happens to be dangling in a harness from a viaduct under construction in central Toronto. She is one of five nuns who have mistakenly walked onto the unfinished viaduct at night and are scattered by a sudden gust of wind. When she is blown over the edge, Temelcoff, hanging in midair, sees her fall, and reaches out an arm. The jolt of catching her rips his arm from its socket. Terrified and in shock, she stares at him, eyes wide. He, in excruciating pain and barely able to breathe, asks her, politely, to scream.

This unparalleled meeting (inspired by a real-life topple from a real-life viaduct) is especially serendipitous because it begins the process by which Temelcoff's nun decides she wants to kick the habit—which, obviously, at some point you'll need your nun to do too. Before the night is over, Temelcoff's nun has whipped off her wimple for him to use as a sling, allowed brandy to pass her lips for the first time, imagined what it's like to have a man run his hand over her hair, and renamed herself Alice, after a parrot. If your chance meeting does not have such a transformative effect, however, don't despair. Read on. Because *In the Skin of a Lion* features another man (Patrick Lewis) who is so in love with another woman (Clara, an actress) that even after a number of blunt rejections, even after she tries to pass him off onto her best friend, Alice (the ex-nun, in fact), and even after her boyfriend Ambrose Small sets him on fire with a Molotov cocktail, he still wants to sleep with her. And sleep with her he does.

In fact, Patrick Lewis ends up with the nun, but again that's beside the point. (If you're thinking this is a complicated novel, you're right.) Reading this novel will teach you determination. You'll get your nun. And

---

* While we assume that most readers will not question our categorization of this predicament as an ailment, we would like to suggest that those who do turn instead to: Common sense, lack of; and Love, unrequited. Only then, if the predicament still persists, should they return to this cure.

when you do, you'll be able to read to her passages from what is, in our view, one of the most lyrical and ingeniously constructed novels of the past half century.

See also: Mr./Mrs. Right, holding out for

DETERMINEDLY CHASING AFTER A WOMAN EVEN THOUGH SHE'S MARRIED

The English Patient
MICHAEL ONDAATJE

If you are in the unfortunate position of having fallen in love with a woman who is already married,* Michael Ondaatje is once again your man. (Ondaatje likes a challenge when it comes to love.)

The determined chaser is the English patient himself, who turns out not to be English at all but a Hungarian count named Almásy, although he is definitely a patient. When we meet him, he is lying in a ruined villa in Tuscany, burned beyond recognition after his plane crashed in the North African desert. It's the aftermath of the Second World War, and there are people dying from war-related injuries all around him, but it gradually transpires that the English patient's plane did not crash as a result of being gunned down by enemy fire, but as a result of . . . you've guessed it: him having fallen hopelessly in love with a married woman.

It is her voice he falls for, at first—reciting poetry around a campfire in the desert, with Almásy himself sitting just outside the fire's halo. "If a man leaned back a few inches he would disappear into darkness," Ondaatje tells us in prose that succeeds in inhabiting the metaphysical spaces of poetry. Before long Almásy and the freshly married Katharine Clifton are consumed by the sort of passion that hovers on the edge of violence.

We're not the sort to moralize, and Ondaatje isn't either. But sometimes literature finds it hard to resist. And one could argue that the price this pair of lovers pay for their adultery is their due comeuppance. But then again, maybe there is no moral message here and Almásy and Katharine are just the random victims of Ondaatje's cruel pen. Go ahead and chase your married

* If you do not see why this predicament is unfortunate, please turn first to: Adultery; Love, unrequited; and Optimism.

woman. Get her, for all we care. But think, now and then, about the cold, dark emptiness at your back, and the dangers of getting on the wrong side of husbands, especially very jealous ones with planes.

See also: Common sense, lack of • Mr./Mrs. Right, holding out for

DIARRHEA

Waste no sedentary moment. Select a novel from our list below, all of which are made up of fragments, vignettes, or very short chapters that won't suffer from being read in short snatches. Make a special shelf for them in the smallest room of the house.

THE TEN BEST NOVELS TO READ
IN THE BATHROOM

Company.. SAMUEL BECKETT
Women in a River Landscape........................HEINRICH BÖLL
Invisible Cities ....ITALO CALVINO
The Big Sleep................................... RAYMOND CHANDLER
Diary of a Bad Year ....J. M. COETZEE
Nowhere Man................................... ALEKSANDAR HEMON
The Collected Works of Billy the Kid........ MICHAEL ONDAATJE
Why Did I Ever.. MARY ROBISON
Shoplifting from American Apparel...........................TAO LIN
Cat's Cradle .... KURT VONNEGUT

DICTATOR, BEING A

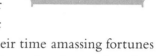

The Successor
ISMAIL KADARE
...
The Last Hundred Days
PATRICK MCGUINNESS

Your average dictator is more likely to sit down for an evening with a manual on how to rule the world and avoid being taken down than with a good novel. Which is a shame, because, given the right prescription of fiction, a dictator might improve his or her human rights record considerably. Instead, we address this ailment to the mini-tyrants who micromanage their companies and their households in a despotic manner. These more parochial dictators spend their time amassing fortunes instead of weapons, and tend to fire those who disappoint them rather than make them disappear. But their method of domination using fear and coercion as their tools is exactly the same and can cause plenty of misery in the little empire over which they rule. Look in the mirror. If you find one such tyrant staring back, make these novels your bedtime reading and prepare for a reshuffle of your realm.

The Successor by Albanian writer Ismail Kadare—himself an inhabitant of a once repressive regime—will show you why you don't have any close friends. The story opens with the sudden death of the nominated successor to a communist-style dictator in the Land of the Eagles (Albania). The death is not altogether surprising, as an alarming number of "suicides" seem to happen in this dictator's vicinity. People who get too close to him don't tend to live for very long. Chillingly, Kadare reveals the constant state of paranoia in which the dictator's friends and family live, as we glimpse the thoughts of those characters most at risk. Fear, paranoia, and a dreamlike sense of doom run rife—infecting, of course, none more than the dictator himself. Those of you who have a tendency to act as a dictator in the sphere of the domestic, take note: no one wants to live in a house that's more about hubris than home. Whether through envy or anger, an uprising will most likely bring about your downfall in the end.

And when that happens, there's no getting around it, dictator wannabes: a horrible death awaits. Nowhere is this inevitability more apparent than in Patrick McGuinness's novel *The Last Hundred Days*. Enjoyably depressing, it describes the deposing of the real-life tyrant Nicolae Ceausescu in Romania. While an unnamed young Englishman observes the events leading up to Ceausescu's execution, his friend Leo obsessively records the overnight disappearances of Bucharest's streets and buildings. Leo's book *The City of Lost Walks* was originally conceived as a guide to the city, but is fast becoming a book of yearning for places lost at the hands of the police state. The horrible denouement is brilliantly and powerfully drawn.

Despots large and small, read this and rue the day you chose to strike terror into the hearts of those around you, destroying your relationships, and instilling paranoia and distrust in your intimates. Whether you run a wartorn state, an international corporation, or a semidetached house inhabited by a family of five, you will surely see reason, abdicate in a hurry, and invite a democracy to be installed in your place.

See also: Bully, being a · Control freak, being a

DIFFERENT, BEING

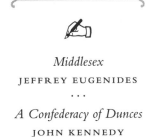

Middlesex
JEFFREY EUGENIDES
. . .
A Confederacy of Dunces
JOHN KENNEDY
TOOLE

It may be that some lucky, delusional solipsist somewhere on the planet has at all times been convinced she (or he) feels exactly like everybody else on the inside: completely, blessedly unremarkable and typical in every way. But as a rule, most people fall into one of two groups. They're either normal and don't know it, or abnormal and don't know it. This state of affairs is not permanent; it can turn on a dime. At one point or another everyone feels different. But different than *what*? That's the real question.

There may be no book that more richly and inventively handles the question of difference than Jeffrey Eugenides's Pulitzer Prize–winning novel *Middlesex*. In it, a girl in a warm and noisy Greek American family in Michigan discovers in adolescence that she is not a girl after all, but a boy. Her name is Calliope ("Cal") Stephanides, and she has a genetic anomaly that reveals itself only when she hits puberty. Cal's typical Michigan teenage life is completely overturned when the physiological changes start raining down on her—that is, him. You think *you* were weird at thirteen? Be glad you weren't Cal.

And yet, Cal's beautifully nuanced reflections are helpful to anyone who's ever felt out of place or eccentric. Eugenides's generous expression of Cal's character shows how full and uncontainable the human personality is, how much it exceeds commonly assumed boundaries. "Emotions, in my experience, aren't covered by single words. I don't believe in 'sadness,' 'joy,' or 'regret,'" Cal thinks. "I'd like to have at my disposal complicated hybrid emotions, Germanic train-car constructions like, say, 'the happiness that attends disaster.' Or: 'the disappointment of sleeping with one's fantasy.'" Eugenides will bring these to you through the panacea of his literary imagination, so you can celebrate whatever difference you may believe yourself (at the moment) to possess.

Then again, there's a more objective kind of difference that deserves consideration: the purely external difference you might call the grotesque, including extreme beauty, extreme hideousness, or extreme appearance and behavior generally—of the sort that either seeks or commands attention. This kind of difference appears in tabloids and on entertainment television in the form of people who court celebrity by bearing eight babies simultaneously, dressing like flesh-eating vampires, wearing loincloths in public, or singing, dancing, scoring goals, or winning elections. It is not unusual for those who self-consciously choose to be different to take pride in their aberration. Often, they write memoirs. But one of the more memorable fictional examples of this tendency is embodied in the oozing, corpulent form of Ignatius J. Reilly, the obese, unclean, arrogant, and effulgent hero of John Kennedy Toole's picaresque New Orleans novel *A Confederacy of Dunces*. The title of the book comes from Jonathan Swift's piercing remark: "When a true genius appears in the world, you may know him by this sign, that the dunces are all in confederacy against him." In his own opinion (and doubtless in Toole's) the revolting, cocky, garrulous Ignatius J. Reilly is such a genius. If you yearn to stand apart and excel in this manner, make him your blueprint.

See also: **Foreign, being** · **Hype, put off by** · **Left out, feeling** · **Outsider, being an**

DINNER PARTIES, FEAR OF

Cold sweat. Strange new rash. Sudden sickness. Facial tics. Inability to find anything clean to wear. Discovery of vital work to be done for tomorrow. Urge to sit and talk to the babysitter for an hour. These are the symptoms of the dinner party avoider. Partner of avoider, meanwhile, grits

There but for the
ALI SMITH

teeth and cajoles. They're about to leave at last when shrinking violet announces urgent need to go to the bathroom and locks self in there. At which point, exasperated partner slips *There but for the* under the door . . .

Our cure for a chronic fear of dinner parties tells the story of Miles, who leaves a dinner party (having first purloined a saltcellar) and locks himself in a spare room upstairs. He stays there for several weeks. Word spreads, and while the world observes him through a window from Greenwich Park, setting up camps to encourage his "protest," he becomes a minor celebrity.

At first the appalled hosts try to ignore what has happened. Then they begrudgingly slide flat packs of wafer-thin ham under Miles's door. Nine-year-old Brooke, however, the precocious daughter of some neighbors and chief observer in the local community, is the one to demonstrate what Miles should have done when struggling with the social event that started this off: learn to be curious and ask your fellow guests questions about themselves. And if all else fails, fall asleep at the table.

Emulate Brooke. You'll have a much better time at the party and get home sooner, too.

See also: **Antisocial, being** • **Misanthropy** • **Shyness**

Le Grand Meaulnes
ALAIN-FOURNIER

DISENCHANTMENT

The malady of disenchantment comes with being a grown-up. It's not surprising, really. We spend our childhoods dreaming of great adventures, our teens whipping them into intense, romantic fantasies, and our twenties (if we're lucky) making bold steps toward these new horizons. And then responsibility hits: work, mortgage, a routine. And suddenly we find that the world has gone from an enchanted place where anything could happen to a place of predictable, humdrum mundanity (see: Mundanity, oppressed by). Where, we can't help wondering, have all the dreams gone?

To answer this question, reacquaint yourself with the character in whom the romance and hopes of adolescence find their most intense expression: Le Grand Meaulnes. The mysterious seventeen-year-old arrives one Sunday in November at the schoolhouse home of narrator François in Sainte-Agathe.

François has heard his footsteps in advance in the attic—a step "very sure of itself." A moment later, Meaulnes impresses François by setting off fireworks on his doorstep. Two "great bouquets" of red and white stars shoot up with a hiss and, for a wondrous moment, François's mother opens the door to see her son and the tall stranger hand in hand, captured in the glow of this fantastical light.

To François and the other schoolboys at Sainte-Agathe, Meaulnes is everything they find compelling: fearless, a dreamer of impossible dreams, an adventurer who always has one eye on a distant horizon. He is bold in the way that only the young are bold, before doubt and cynicism and the possibility of failure set in (see: Cynicism; Failure, feeling like a). They christen him, with canny accuracy, Le Grand Meaulnes. Translators the world over have struggled to do justice to that seemingly simple word—*grand*—capturing as it does the physical meaning (big, tall) but expanding as the story progresses into something loftier, something great.

Le Grand Meaulnes will take you back to a world of heightened senses in which everything is more enigmatic, more lovely, and more intoxicating. Meaulnes's tragedy is that when he finds happiness he can't embrace it. His sense of identity is too firmly bound up with yearning, and he needs the dream to remain a dream. But we can live differently. Let Meaulnes remind you how to live a life of enchantment, then bring this enchantment into your every day.

See also: Innocence, loss of · Zestlessness

DISHONESTY
See: Lying

DISSATISFACTION

Cannery Row
JOHN STEINBECK

Many of us live to the accompaniment of a perpetual sense of dissatisfaction, a gnawing feeling that we have not quite achieved enough, don't quite have enough to show for our time of life. For some, it's not enough material things. For others, it's not enough time—an endless sense of scurrying through to-do lists before we finally achieve the space to think and breathe. And for still others, it's a sense of being emotionally, intellectually, or spiritually incomplete—we yearn for a better relationship or better job or better lifestyle that would make us feel we could, at last, begin our lives for real.

We hate to break it to you, but if you keep looking for the answers outside yourself, the dissatisfaction will stay. Clichéd it may be, but the answer lies within. And often the only way to see this is to stop chasing those butterflies and stand still for a while and take stock.

Mack and the boys know how to do this. In *Cannery Row*, John Steinbeck's ode to the ambition-free life of the bum, we meet them sitting on the discarded rusty pipes from the sardine canneries in a vacant lot. Mack, Eddie, Hazel, Hughie, and Jones are men with three things in common: no families, no money, and no ambitions. Yet this isn't entirely true. They themselves form a sort of family—along with the lovable Doc, who plays a fatherly role—and they realize ambition in making a home together.

To many they're a band of no-good thieves and bums. But to Doc they are life's success stories—healthy, "clean" men who are able to spend their days doing what they want. They live a hand-to-mouth existence, living on the cash earnings of whatever jobs they can get, but they are happy this way. While others race through life striving to achieve and accumulate and keep up in their endless search for more—forever falling short of their targets— Mack and the boys approach contentment "casually, quietly," and absorb it gently. "What can it profit a man to gain the whole world and to come to his property with a gastric ulcer, a blown prostate, and bifocals?" Steinbeck asks.

You might think this side of America doesn't exist anymore. But it does if you know where to look. Take a day out of your life to steep yourself in this tender, loving, idle world of men who are happy with little and whose hearts are in the right place—a place of nonstriving and acceptance. Then apply this casual, quiet approach to your own life, and watch the dissatisfaction flow softly away.

See also: Boredom · Grumpiness · Happiness, searching for · Mundanity, oppressed by · Querulousness

DIVORCE

Divorce may be common these days, but it's still one of the most traumatic experiences a person can go through—particularly if there are children involved—and if there's any chance of avoiding it, we urge you to take it. All marriages go through peaks and troughs, and even if you've been in a trough for a number of years, your problems may very well be more easily surmountable than you realize. If your marriage is on the rocks because either you or your partner is suffering from one of the many predicaments described in this book, first treat the problem at its root. Once cured, the strain in your relationship may disappear. If not, read on. Our remedy begins with two novels for those on the brink of divorce—be sure to read them before any knots are severed. And for those who have already gone through divorce, or who need encouragement to see it through, we offer a one-in-a-million novel of hope and inspiration about a woman who gets it right the third time around.

Intimacy
HANIF KUREISHI
. . .
The Sportswriter
RICHARD FORD
. . .
Their Eyes Were Watching God
ZORA NEALE HURSTON

Intimacy is the raw, and at times uncomfortably honest, first-person account of Jay, a man who has decided to leave his partner of six years, Susan. As he puts his two little boys to bed and sits down to a supper *à deux*, he is aware that this is the last night they will all spend as "an innocent, complete, ideal family." Inevitably, there's a tumult of conflicting emotions in his head—guilt, confusion, and terror at the damage he's about to inflict on the children, but also a desperate need to "live" again, to close the door on unhappiness and move on. When Susan, a successful publisher, comes home from work, we get a glimpse of what has gone wrong. As she casts him an infuriated gaze, he feels his body "shrink and contract." Clearly there has been a communication breakdown. And in the dialogue that ensues, we get a sense that their problems have never really been discussed. Read this as your wake-up call. If, like Jay, you haven't been open about your feelings with your partner, you may be giving up too easily. Take some responsibility for the failure. Initiate the conversation. Don't give up until you both understand—and agree—where you went wrong. Chances are, the return of honest communication will bring you closer again.

Certainly a mutual acceptance of the new reality will make life as a divorced couple easier—especially if you have children, since you will need to continue a relationship as parents for many years. Two years on from his divorce, Frank Bascombe—the sportswriter of Richard Ford's *The Sportswriter*—is beginning to realize that if he were to live his life again, he might not choose to get divorced. He and X, as he calls his ex, still live near each other in the suburb of Haddam, New Jersey, so that their two kids, Paul and Clarissa, can move between homes. They talk at least twice a week on the phone and often bump into each other. It was X who initiated the divorce, but Frank is reconciled to it—living alone has helped him to know himself better. X, too, is moving on, for she is finally pursuing the promising golf career she gave up when she married. But complicating the couple's divorce is that it is overshadowed by grief over the loss of a third child. While Frank denies the tragedy was the cause of the breakup, a sense of exhaustion and failure hangs heavily over the novel. As Frank discovers—along with some help from the other men at the Divorced Men's Club in Haddam—life as a divorcé isn't all about sex and liberation.

If, however, you have already admitted defeat and are looking to the freedom that divorce can provide, pick up *Their Eyes Were Watching God*, Zora Neale Hurston's tale of love in the Deep South. For Janie, certainly, turning her back on a rushed marriage to dull farmer Logan Killicks turns out to be a good thing. Her grandmother, an ex-slave, is determined that Janie will marry well and not be left for men to go "usin' yo' body to wipe his foots on." There's little joy to be had with Logan, though, whom she can't bring herself to love. And when Jody Starks, an energetic and entrepreneurial man with a plan, comes through, his hat set at an angle, Janie doesn't think twice. They elope and settle in an emerging all-black town in Florida and live a comfortable, respectable life for many years. It's not quite a match made in heaven, though, and eventually the ever feisty Janie feels stifled.

As luck would have it, she gets a third bite of the apple, and this time it's the real thing. If you think your romantic life is over, take note of Janie—at forty, still swaggering down the street with her true love, Tea Cake. This is a life-affirming novel, poetic, profound, and wise. Stay openhearted. Give your marriage every chance it's got, but if you must let go, be generous. Move on with a lighter step. The world is made new every day; you never know who may yet come your way.

See also: **Anger** · **Breaking up** · **Broken heart** · **Falling out of love with love** · **Murderous thoughts** · **Sadness** · **Single parent, being a** · **Turmoil**

DIY

Caribou Island
DAVID VANN

You are balancing on a stool with a screwdriver between your teeth, a custom lightbulb in one hand, a fistful of ill-matched screws in the other, and a hammer under your arm. It is imperative that you mend this light fixture today, as tonight you're having a much anticipated dinner party. As you accidentally touch two wires together with your screwdriver, you are thrown across the room by a compelling force. And no, it's not your partner's rage.

Getting injured in the home is extremely common, and invariably the cause is do-it-yourself projects. Fingers are severed, roofs cave in, shelves come tumbling down with hapless victims sprawled beneath them. If you are feeling an irresistible urge to build that lean-to, customize your Ikea unit, or sand down your patio, make sure a copy of *Caribou Island* is sitting just inside your tool kit. After you read this, the utter folly of attempting home improvement projects on your own will become indisputable. Here we are not only saving you hours of pain, but also your marriage, your other intimate relationships, and quite possibly even your life.

In this magnificently grim novel, Irene observes her husband, Gary, make one last, superhuman effort to either save or destroy their marriage by building a log cabin on the other side of Skilak Lake. They already live in the wilderness of Alaska, but Gary has always dreamed of a haven for their retirement that is more remote still. Even before it gets under way, the project is doomed: "They were going to build their cabin from scratch. No foundation, even. And no plans, no experience, no permits, no advice welcome."

We watch Gary as the rain drives into his eyeballs like "pinpricks" and, inevitably, he puts the door on the wrong way. He leaves vital implements at home, across the soon to be frozen lake. Irene halfheartedly attempts to help, realizing more and more profoundly that her husband's dream of his log cabin has never actually involved her. While Gary rages against the rain (in Anglo-Saxon, no less), Irene, feeling abandoned by all humanity, huddles in a tent, longing for home.

And then, a part of her she never knew existed is awakened: her inner Diana, huntress to whom mere dwellings are irrelevant. As this civilized woman is taken over, Irene becomes magnificent, irresistible, a force more impressive than the elements. The superb conclusion of this novel will have you rushing straight to the yellow pages for a handyman.

See also: Divorce · Pain, being in

DIZZINESS

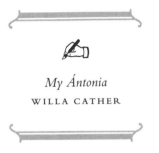

My Ántonia
WILLA CATHER

Whether it is a physical dizziness from which you suffer—seeing stars before folding, puppet-jointed, to the floor—or an emotional giddiness in which you lurch from pillar to post, you'll need to stop the world from spinning by holding on to something solid and firm. Perhaps you're pregnant (see: Pregnancy) or in pain (see: Pain, being in), jet-lagged or sleep deprived (see: Exhaustion), or coming down with something (see: Cold, common; Man flu). If none of these are the culprit, we suggest a no-nonsense dose of *My Ántonia*.

When ten-year-old Jimmy Burden loses both his parents in the space of a year, he is sent to live with his grandparents in Nebraska. On his way there, riding the train, he remarks, "The only thing very noticeable about Nebraska was that it was still, all day long, Nebraska." Once at the end of the line, he and an immigrant bohemian family, who will become his closest neighbors, are driven by wagon through the night. At one point Jimmy peeps out from under the buffalo hide and sees nothing—"no fences, no creeks or trees, no hills or fields . . . nothing but land." He has the feeling that he has left the world behind, and as the wagon jolts on, he allows himself to submit to its rhythm, to offer himself up to destiny. While in Nebraska, he meets Ántonia, the daughter of the immigrant family. He teaches her to speak English and in return learns about the importance of grit and hard work in order to survive. Their friendship turns out to be one of the most instructive in his life.

Read *My Ántonia* and inhale its waft of smelling salts. Emulate Jimmy's submission to fate and his connection to the grounded Ántonia. If your body is loose, and you submit to what will be, you won't hurt yourself when you fall.

DREAD, NAMELESS

*Something Wicked
This Way Comes*
RAY BRADBURY

You slide the CD into the car stereo, with, well, considerable dread. With a title like that, how could you not? Besides, rods of October rain are coming down hard against the windshield, heavier by the minute, and you have a long journey ahead.

Five hours later, you are still pummeling down the highway through rain, wipers flashing back and forth across your vision. But inside your head you are crouched behind a bookshelf in the library of Green Town, Illinois. Beside you are Will and Jim—both just turned thirteen—and the "Illustrated Man" is drawing inexorably closer. He knows exactly who he is looking for, for the boys' faces are tattooed on the palms of his hands. He wants them for his sinister circus. As this predator from the Pandemonium Show makes his way along the bookshelves, muttering to himself—"B for Boys? A for Adventure? H for Hidden. S for Secret. T for Terrified?"—your windshield suddenly fogs up. No matter how much you wipe the windows from the inside, it doesn't seem to make any difference. Your breathing comes hard and fast. It is as if your eyes are being sewn shut by the witch who travels with the circus, cruising in a black balloon, muttering spells at anyone who thwarts the circus's progress: "Darning-needle dragonfly, sew up those eyes so they cannot see!" You pull over and turn the audiobook off, pale and shaking.

But it is too late: you are hooked. You have to *know*. You wind down the windows to let in the air, not caring about the rain and, cautiously, you press "play." After a while you resume the journey, windows wide open.

It's a close thing. You are almost swallowed up by mist, feeling yourself beginning to turn to wax as Will and Jim so nearly do. But when a powerful secret in the novel is divulged, your dread, quite suddenly, disappears. And it does not come back.

By the time you arrive at your destination, you are cackling with glee. And as you pull up outside the house, you notice that it is the sort of house that would previously have filled you with a nameless dread . . . But this time you are armed.

See also: **Angst, existential · Anxiety**

DREAD OF MONDAY MORNING

See: Monday morning feeling

DREAMS, BAD

See: Nightmares

DREAMS, BROKEN

See: Broken dreams

DRUGS, DOING TOO MANY

Trainspotting
IRVINE WELSH
. . .
Brave New World
ALDOUS HUXLEY
. . .
Less Than Zero
BRET EASTON ELLIS

For Sherlock Holmes, the use of cocaine three times a day in a 7 percent solution was "transcendently stimulating and clarifying to the mind." But Watson was appalled by Holmes's habit, noting his punctured forearm with dismay. Sir Arthur Conan Doyle was ahead of his times in realizing there might be an addictive and dangerous side to the use of, for example, laudanum,* heroin,† and cocaine.‡ In any era there are substances that creep up on us with their addictive qualities, whose negative properties are not at first understood. And there are the drugs we might consider "recreational" until they become, for some, more than just a diversion. What are the signs that an experimental or occasional habit is becoming something more sinister and life-threatening? When does dabbling becomes depending? Read the following to help identify your symptoms and cut your supplies off before it's too late.

A far cry from Baker Street, where the syringe came in a leather-bound case and the user lay back on a velvet armchair, are the users and abusers of *Trainspotting*, Irvine Welsh's journey into modern-day heroin hell. Here the highs and the horrors of heroin addiction are spelled out blow by blow, from

---

* Used as a teething balm for babies.

† A popular cough suppressant.

‡ Known for its benefits in dental surgery.

the death of baby Dawn, who asphyxiates while her parents are out cold, to the amputation of a needle-infected leg, and the disintegration of friendships, family, and, it seems, the entire run-down district of Edinburgh in which the novel is set. "It's all okay, it's all beautiful; but ah fear that this internal sea is gaunnae subside soon, leaving this poisonous shite washed up, stranded up in ma body," reports Sick Boy, predicting the horror after the high. Because even while he shoots up, he knows that it is a "short-term sea" and a "long-term poison." Welsh's novel makes for gruesome reading and offers a compelling case for going cold turkey—or steering well clear in the first place.

The alarm bells truly ring out when we become so addicted that we can't recognize the need for help. In Huxley's dystopian *Brave New World*, the entire framework of society is dependent upon *soma*—a drug described as "like Christianity without the tears" by the "science monitors" who legislate this world in which babies are made in hatcheries and raised in factories. Taking *soma*—a mild hallucinogenic that leaves the taker on a blissed-out high—is mandatory: two grams on weekdays, six on Saturdays. When Lenina and Bernard meet John, the "Savage," who lives on a reservation where *soma* is unknown, their dependence on the drug appalls him. He urges them to throw away their poison and be freed. But they are too far gone to hear him. Be chilled by their example: they've reached the point of no return.

Bret Easton Ellis's *Less Than Zero* reveals the pivotal role drugs play in a generation characterized by nihilistic popular culture. Clay is the dispassionate and deadpan observer of his classmates, all in their late teens, who have turned to hedonism, drugs, and meaningless sexual encounters to spice up their lives. Ignored by their parents, dropping out of their colleges, they lack direction and conviction. "You have everything," Clay says to a friend who is heading down the road to self-destruction. "No. I don't," replies Rip. "I don't have anything to lose." And with that he returns to the distraction of having sex with a barely conscious eleven-year-old girl. Could a scene like this do anything other than drive the last nail in the coffin for those tending toward excess?

See also: **Broken dreams** • **Cold turkey, going** • **Concentrate, inability to** • **Insomnia** • **Irritability** • **Nightmares** • **Paranoia** • **Rails, going off the**

DUMPED, GETTING

See: Anger • Appetite, loss of • Breaking up • Broken heart • Cry, in need of a
good • Insomnia • Lovesickness • Murderous thoughts • Sadness

DYING

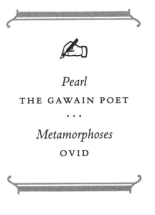

Pearl
THE GAWAIN POET
• • •
Metamorphoses
OVID

Death cannot be deferred forever, and when the time comes, we need to be ready. In the West, we have a tendency to avoid thoughts or conversations about death, yet it is essential to live in the presence of this unpleasant inevitability—at least so that we may always be fully alive. To prepare ourselves and maintain a healthy acknowledgment of death, we must look to some appropriate literary companions—works that console and still, while gently encouraging acceptance. The following, written in language that rises above the ordinary, have a timeless serenity and great beauty that will achieve both these things, whether read in silence or aloud to an ailing family member or friend.

Pearl is one of the most exquisite poems in the English language, thought to be written by the fourteenth-century poet who penned *Sir Gawain and the Green Knight*. *Pearl* describes the loss of a "pearl of great price," which many critics believe represents the two-year-old daughter of the poet, while others maintain it to be entirely allegorical, representing the loss of the soul. This ambiguity is what makes the poem so rich and irresistible. The agony of loss, the purity of love, the beauty of the pearl—all are wrought intricately into a remarkably complex poem. Don't be alarmed by the *olde* English—you will soon get your tongue around it, and you can read it in a modern translation if you prefer. Composed of 101 stanzas of twelve lines each, link words cleverly tie verse to verse, and thematic links create a connection between the two ends of the poem, producing a structure that is itself circular—much like the cycle of life and death.

Believers and nonbelievers alike can take comfort from the concept of transformation at the time of death. For even if we believe that death is the end, we can still see that, in some sense, death is merely a change in form.

To help you feel part of the eternal wheel of life, read Ovid's great work *Metamorphoses*, and see how one thing becomes another, ad infinitum. There is all of life within these pages, from the myths of creation to the lives of the philosophers, from Chaos to Eros, from the coming of the gods to the trials of Hercules and Prometheus. But Ovid's central theme is love: the power that transforms all things. Because of his desire, Zeus transforms himself into a swan, a bull, a shower of light. By his attempts on their honor, his victims become trees, water nymphs, birds, or beasts. Diana turns Actaeon into a stag because he fatally spied her naked. Narcissus metamorphoses into a flower out of his own self-love. And Echo lives forever as a repetitive sound, having pined away from lovesickness. Arachne is turned into a spider because she loved to weave.

In these mesmerizing myths of love and loss, we see that we abide in wildflowers, olive trees, streams, our lives flowing from one form to another in never-ceasing metamorphoses. Everything is mutable, nothing remains static, all beings pass from one state into another—not dying, but becoming.

E

Second Star to the Right
DEBORAH HAUTZIG

. . .

Life-Size
JENEFER SHUTE

ating disorders come in many forms. Self-starvation (anorexia nervosa) and bingeing and purging (bulimia) are the most common. Lesser-known but no less damaging disorders include orthorexia nervosa (an obsession with ingesting only the purest foods) and pica (an obsession with chewing and eating nonfood items). The jury's out on what causes these obsessive behaviors. Some can perhaps be traced back to a root cause of abuse, neglect, or trauma. And, of course, many people point the finger at the pervasive media culture of toothpick-thin catwalk models. A need to feel in control is likely another major cause. Whatever the trigger, literature has solace, comfort, and wisdom for both the victim and those with the painful, frightening task of watching, and trying to help, from the sidelines.

Leslie, the talented fourteen-year-old in Deborah Hautzig's *Second Star to the Right*, has a happy home life in New York with a mother who loves her "to the moon and back." But when she begins to diet because she feels too fat, she becomes addicted to the thrill of losing weight and ends up hospitalized. As the novel spans the whole of her adolescence, we follow her desire to reach her goal weight of seventy-five pounds amid a recognizable teen world of boyfriends, clothes, and uncomprehending grown-ups. Her loyal, intelligent best friend, Cavett, supports her unquestioningly throughout her illness.

The title comes from Peter Pan's instruction to Wendy that Neverland is "second to the right and straight on till morning." But the phrase resonates on a more complex, shocking level too. For it refers also to Leslie's mother's cousin, Margolee, who died as a teenager in Auschwitz along with her own mother. Given the choice of going "to the right" and living, or "to the left" to die in the gas chamber along with her mother, Margolee chose to go to the left. The tragedies of their deaths echo through the novel and provide a profoundly moving backdrop to the plot.

Despite the seemingly selfish solipsism of the anorexic, the question of whether Leslie herself chooses to go to the right or left—for it is, in the end, a choice—captures our sympathy absolutely. *Second Star to the Right* explores the immense psychological complexities of anorexia with clarity and compassion—and may offer hope for a way out.

Our second cure, *Life-Size*, is meant for friends and caregivers, taking as it does a character even further down the road of self-harm. In this disturbing novel, a young woman named Josie—described as a "starving organism"—does almost nothing but lie supine, occupying space. In the final stages of anorexia, she maneuvers her skeletal frame out of bed when nobody's looking and runs on the spot in a frantic attempt to burn calories. She feels that her brain is "closer to the surface" now, that she's able to see colors and experience smells more vividly than when everything was coated in "a thick aspic of fat"—as if she has attained "the self in its minimal form." As she rages against the hospital "despots" who try to make her eat, she recites the number of calories in everything from a piece of bubble gum to a slice of cucumber, and reveals her obsessive fascination with food through the imaginary recipes and menus she concocts. We become aware of the extraordinary costs of her triumphing over her appetite. When a new path opens up for Josie, a genuine hope is planted in the reader. A grueling but important read, you'll glean new insights into the powerful psychologies at play in eating disorders, and come away with the sense that there is light at the end of the tunnel, even in very serious cases.

See also: **Appetite, loss of** • **Hunger** • **Self-esteem, low**

EGG ON YOUR FACE

See: Blushing • Idiot, feeling like an • Regret • Shame

EGG ON YOUR TIE

Restoration
ROSE TREMAIN

For once, you're on time. You've got your best suit on and your notes in your hands. You climb the podium and look down to adjust the microphone. As you do, you notice a dribble of bright yellow egg yolk snaking down your shirt.

Sound familiar? If so, make the acquaintance of Robert Merivel, the hero of Rose Tremain's *Restoration*, set in the debauched court of King Charles II. Merivel is a glutton for the bawdy pleasures of seventeenth-century life. He's generally to be found with his stockings around his ankles enjoying a tumble with a juicy wench, or laughing so hard he sends a mouthful of raisin pudding across the table at a banquet. When Merivel is given a rare audience with the king, he messes it up so atrociously that it seems he has squandered his one opportunity for bettering himself. But then he gets a second chance. And it's on this occasion, just as he's being offered the illustrious position of court physician to His Majesty's dogs, that Merivel notices the egg stain on his breeches.

It matters not a bit. The king is delighted by Merivel, by his appetite for life and his ability to fart on demand, and goes on to bestow a string of favors on his feckless new friend. It doesn't last forever, but the message remains: being a little messy in life can work to your advantage, given the right context.

See also: Failure, feeling like a • Idiot, feeling like an

EGOTISM

See: Arrogance • Confidence, too much • Dictator, being a • Misanthropy • Selfishness • Vanity

EIGHTYSOMETHING, BEING

THE TEN BEST NOVELS FOR EIGHTYSOMETHINGS

EMBARRASSMENT

See: Egg on your tie • Idiot, feeling like an • Regret • Shame • Shame, reading associated

EMOTIONS, INABILITY TO EXPRESS

Like Water for Chocolate
LAURA ESQUIVEL
. . .
As I Lay Dying
WILLIAM FAULKNER

Those who find it difficult to express their emotions—or who share their life with someone who does—should bear in mind that a) an inability to express emotion doesn't necessarily mean that emotions are absent, and b) there are alternative forms of expression not involving words or gestures that may be (and may be being) used instead.

In Laura Esquivel's popular novel *Like Water for Chocolate*, Tita is forbidden from marrying her childhood sweetheart, Pedro, because tradition requires her, as the youngest daughter, to remain single and devote herself to looking after her tyrannical mother instead. And so Tita pours the love she's not supposed to feel for Pedro into the sumptuous food she prepares. Into the cake for Pedro's wedding—for Pedro marries Tita's sister Rosaura in order to stay close to Tita—she whisks martyrdom and bitterness. Into the meringue icing goes her longing. In the way we have come to expect from the Latin American magical realists, the guests digest the emotions along with the wedding cake and are all overcome by grief for the lost loves of their pasts. Tita's quail in rose petal sauce, infused as it is with her sensuous passion for Pedro, turns her virginal sister Gertrudis into such a frenzy of sexual excitement that she strips off her clothes and runs naked through the streets—to be duly carried off on the back of a horse by an equally horny rebel soldier. If you, too, find it difficult to say "I love you," try saying it with food. And partners who don't get to hear those words, look out for the sentiment expressed in other ways.

You may have to look quite hard. Of the five Bundren siblings watching their mother, Addie, die in William Faulkner's *As I Lay Dying*, Darl is the most articulate, Jewel the most demonstrative, and Cash—though the eldest—is the one who struggles most to express his love for his mother. He does it by building her a coffin, right under her window. His brother Jewel watches his meticulous, careful sawing of "the long hot sad yellow days" into planks and puts his act of intense and complex devotion into words for him: "See. See what a good one I am making for you."

And the coffin *is* good. Cash makes it into the shape of a grandfather clock, "with every joint and seam beveled and scrubbed with the plane, tight as a drum and neat as a sewing basket," so that they can lay her in it without crushing her dress. The young man funnels all his grief and desire to please into the making of this coffin, and his inarticulacy is deeply touching—especially in the chapter that consists of a list of reasons for making the coffin "on the bevel."

Embrace your—or your loved one's—inability to express in conventional ways. Employ—and allow—a wider repertoire.

See also: **Stiff upper lip, having a**

The Stranger
ALBERT CAMUS
. . .
The Heart of the Matter
GRAHAM GREENE

What is it that makes so many of us want to read about heartless bastards? Is it because, frustrated by our own sensitivity, we long to be tougher, more selfish, and more Teflon-coated ourselves? Do we take perverse pleasure in reading about people (men nearly always, let's admit) who give a damn about nothing but their own moods and desires because we wish we could be similarly self-indulgent? It's not a question that can be answered easily, but it's a question that can be weighed in the company of countless novels, for it clearly preys on the minds of authors too.

Who can forget Meursault, the young, unemotional narrator of Camus's *The Stranger*? The day after his mother's funeral, the nonchalant and detached Meursault goes swimming, hooks up with a pretty young woman, has a lot of sex, and goes to see a comic film. Over the next few days, he gets into a fight with a man who provokes him, and shoots him dead. In the aftermath, he's put on trial for murder. The jury, aware of the pleasure spree Meursault embarked upon after his mother's death, wants to convict him. He's definitely guilty of callousness. But does that mean he's guilty of murder? Judge your own empathy levels by how much you empathize with Meursault—and his victim.

In Graham Greene's *The Heart of the Matter*, a self-pitying white man in Africa named Scobie believes he teems with tortured Christian pity for Louise, his wife, but Greene makes sure that Scobie's hollow solace never tricks the reader. When Louise, her hair matted and stringy with sweat, looking vacant and as "out" as a "dog or cat," rises from her pillow under the mosquito netting to greet Scobie, "he had the impression of a joint under a meat-cover. But pity trod on the heels of the cruel image and hustled it away." Right . . . hustled it away onto the page, for all of us to savor, drawn by the coldness of the author's eye.

For those in your life who are plagued by a lack of empathy, we recommend you give them one of these novels to read. If they get the hint that you think they can relate to these cold customers, well, perhaps they'll show a tad more empathy with *you*. If you're the one suffering from a lack of empathy, then ask yourself if you felt anything for Meursault's victim or Scobie's wife. Are you shocked at the cold veil in which their emotions are wrapped? If not, you need to read every novel we recommend in this book, for scientific studies have shown that reading fiction is the number one best cure for lack of empathy.

See also: **Emotions, inability to express** • **Selfishness**

EMPTY-NEST SYNDROME

The Woman Who Went to Bed for a Year
SUE TOWNSEND

It can be embarrassing to admit to, but many parents feel lost when their children leave home. What on earth are they to do with themselves without all those packed lunches to make, dirty rugby shirts to load into the washing machine, and teenagers to chauffeur on Friday nights? Get a life, of course. Except it's not so easy when you're out of the habit. Now, thankfully, it's a "syndrome," and you can diagnose yourself with it, as Eva Beaver does in Sue Townsend's novel, *The Woman Who Went to Bed for a Year.* And with this typically Townsendian cure, you can have a laugh at the funny side, for there's no better way to take the air out of a syndrome than to affectionately mock it.

To anyone familiar with the seemingly endless chores that go along with being a mother and housewife (see: Cope, inability to; Housewife, being a; and Motherhood), going to bed for a year seems a completely sensible—and enviable—thing to do. But Eva is not only tired; she doesn't know who she is anymore. After twenty-five years of seeing to the needs of others and making, as she now sees it, a "pig's ear" out of bringing her children up, she retreats from the world in order to relearn how to be in it. Kicking her husband, Brian, out of the bedroom, she looks back over her marriage and reflects on the things she gave up (reading, among them) when her twins, Brian Junior and Brianne, were born. She suddenly feels a crushing sense of disappointment. When Brian moves into the shed with his long-term mistress, Titania, and Brian Junior and Brianne learn how to live away from home, Eva starts to make friends with various passersby—including the handyman—while she gets to the bottom of her grief.

As a strategy for recovering and recharging—and opening the doors to new friends, new careers, and new domestic arrangements—we recommend it heartily, though we think a year is a tad too long. If you start to test the patience of your loved ones, see: Bed, inability to get out of, for a countercure.

See also: **Children, not having • Loneliness • Yearning, general**

ENGLISH, BEING VERY
See: **Stiff upper lip, having a**

ENVY
See: Jealousy

Zorba the Greek
NIKOS KAZANTZAKIS

EXHAUSTION

Physical exhaustion can be a fantastic feeling, if brought on by arduous exercise—swimming in a lake, scaling a peak, galloping on a horse along a beach. But when brought on by standing on your feet for ten hours, plucking chickens, or digging a ditch in the rain, there's little pleasure in the pain. Mental exhaustion can be even more depleting still, causing stress (see: Stress) and an ill-functioning brain (see: Memory loss). Exhaustion through lack of sleep is particularly miserable, and can be remedied only by an uninterrupted eight hours in bed (at least). Truth be told, sleep is a pretty good cure for exhaustion all around, but if you're exhausted and want to find a way to keep going, read on.

Meet Zorba, a man of many soups and stories, with bright, piercing eyes, a weather-beaten face, and a gift for expressing himself through dance. Zorba uses dance to tell stories, to define who he is, to explain the world, and to revitalize his spirits when they flag. Our narrator is a young Greek intellectual, interested in Buddhism and books. But when he meets Zorba, with his irrepressible lust for life, he knows he's met a man with a spiritual secret. When the nimble-footed wanderer accepts his offer to become foreman of the lignite mine he has recently acquired on the island of Crete, he's delighted. The two take to drinking wine late into the night, discussing philosophy, with frequent musical accompaniment by Zorba's *santuri*. During these sessions Zorba often laments that if only he could express his friend's philosophical conundrums in dance, they could take the conversations even further.

And one day Zorba really does teach his young friend to dance—impetuously, defiantly, ecstatically. Soon they are both telling tales with their gravity-defying bodies. Zorba, we realize, is a man of great wisdom through natural understanding who can reach in "one bound" spiritual heights that would take others years to attain. What we love most about this archetype of energy is his apparently limitless ability to throw himself wholeheartedly into the next project, frequently picking himself up off the floor (when by all rights he should sleep for a week) and dancing himself back to life.

Become a student of Zorba yourself. When exhaustion hits, don't flop. Take to your feet, play some music, and find a dance within you. In years to come, wouldn't you rather say, with Zorba: "I've done heaps and heaps of things in my life, but I still did not do enough. Men like me ought to live for a thousand years!"?

See also: **Bed, inability to get out of** · **Busy, being too** · **Busy to read, being too** · **Libido, loss of** · **Tired and emotional, being**

EXISTENTIAL ANGST
See: **Angst, existential**

EXTRAVAGANCE

Extravagance—as in spending money on things you can't afford and don't really need—is a habit borne in times of abundance and profligacy. In times of austerity (see: Depression, economic), it needs to be stemmed. If not, you'll find yourself broke (see: Broke, being; and Tax return, fear of doing), working round the clock to pay off your credit card debts (see: Workaholism), and tempted to live your life in unprincipled and

Kingfishers Catch Fire
RUMER GODDEN
. . .
Breakfast at Tiffany's
TRUMAN CAPOTE

character-defiling ways (see: Rails, going off the). "He that is extravagant will soon become poor, and poverty will enforce dependence, and invite corruption," Samuel Johnson has already beaten us to saying.

Extravagant people tend to be dreamers and romantics. One way to curb an extravagant nature is to decide to romanticize frugality. This is very much what single mother of two Sophie does in Rumer Godden's *Kingfishers Catch Fire*. An expat wife estranged from her husband, Denzil, Sophie has until now been someone who spent money "extravagantly, carelessly . . . selfishly." Yet the deeply flawed Sophie falls in love with the beauty and simplicity she sees around her in rural Kashmir, where the women fetch water, pound grain, and spin their own flax and wool. For the peasants themselves, who have no choice, it's a tough existence. But to Sophie, it's picturesque and charming. She, too, wants to pick her "toothbrushes off a tree." Much to the anguish of her daughter Teresa, who longs to put down roots and live in a "proper" house back in England, she moves them into Dilkhush, a semi-ruin with no electricity. "We shall be poor and frugal," she tells her children. "We shall toil." And toil she does. She also gives up cigarettes, alcohol, and coffee, and works so hard that she almost dies from pneumonia. But she doesn't give up.

It helps, of course, that by opting to be poor among people who are even poorer than she is, Sophie makes herself, by comparison, rich. But whether or not she embarks on her frugal life with realistic eyes, Sophie does discover the pleasures of it, and so do her children. Teresa and little Moo spend their days climbing trees, sailing walnut shell boats in a stream, and tending to their animals. Sophie, meanwhile, with only a few books to entertain her in the long, lonely evenings, soon finds she is reading in a new way. "Every word impressed her, and what she read in the evening she pondered over the next day. She felt her mind stretch and deepen, grow rich; sometimes an evening had passed before she had noticed."

If the austerity fantasy doesn't do it for you, take a cue from Holly Golightly, the slender will-o'-the-wisp at the heart of Truman Capote's *Breakfast at Tiffany's*. Holly hails from the dirt-poor Texas sticks, where she's the child bride of an old widowed turkey farmer with a brood of children, but she escapes this dead-end life and sets herself up in Manhattan as if she were an heiress for whom money is no object. At eighteen, she becomes the toast of New York's café society, letting rich men pay for her meals, clothes, and jewels, and gaily conducting a whirligig existence. If she can't buy herself a diamond solitaire at Tiffany's, she can still go there and inhale its heady aura of luxury. "It calms me down right away, the quietness and the proud look of it; nothing very bad could happen to you there, not with those kind men in their nice suits, and that lovely smell of silver and alligator wallets," she rhapsodizes. Holly never expects the fantasy to last: "It's better to look at the sky than live there," she explains to one of the men who adore her. She can't perch at the pinnacle forever, and before long a drug scandal she swans into shakes her flagpole. But she'll stay up there, aloft and glittering, as long as she can keep a dainty foothold.

An extravagance habit is hard to kick completely. Even Rumer Godden's Sophie doesn't manage to lose it. She buys too many flowers from the flower boats, keeps animals for pets rather than food, and cannot resist buying a Persian rug with money she does not have, so entranced is she by its exquisite rose design. Sophie believes that sometimes, particularly when one is afraid, one should do something rash in order to reinforce one's sense of self—in her case, as a lover of fine things. Clearly, extravagance on a daily basis is a disaster. Spend what you have wisely to make it go far, and paint alluring visions of monkish austerity if it helps. But if the joy begins to go out of life, indulge once in a while. Like Sophie, buy the rug with the roses on it, and when you are hungry, the extravagance of color will feed your soul. Or like Holly, live the dream while cleverly eluding the bills.

See also: **Book buyer, being a compulsive** • **Common sense, lack of** • **Greed** • **Shopaholism**

F

The History of Mr. Polly

H. G. WELLS

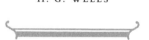

FAILURE, FEELING LIKE A

Your past is littered with abandoned enter-
prises. Everything you touch turns to lead.
Your very anticipation of failure is self-fulfilling—
although your fear of failure means that sometimes you don't even begin. You walk with your
head hung low, your shoulders slumping. You're
the embodiment of nonsuccess.

If we've just painted a picture of you, it's time to meet H. G. Wells's most
charming creation, the unsuccessful Mr. Polly.

When we first meet Mr. Polly, he's sitting on a stile near his home in fictional Fishbourne, Kent, complaining that he is stuck in an "'Ole!"—a
"Beastly Silly Wheeze of a Hole." Prone to mixing up his words ("See?
I'm going to absquatulate, see? Hey Presto right away"), which is part of
his charm, Mr. Polly lives in a permanent state of indigestion caused as much
by his negative self-image as by his dubious diet. Having succumbed to
the "zealacious commerciality" of keeping a drapery shop for the past fifteen years, he's now forty and has grown fat and balding. Realizing he has
spent his life so far "in apathetic and feebly hostile and critical company,
ugly in detail and mean in scope"—and that company includes his wife—he
is disconsolate enough to set up a life insurance policy that will ensure his
wife is comfortably catered for. Then he plans to kill himself (see: Midlife
crisis).

As luck would have it, his suicide attempt goes so splendidly wrong that he finds himself feeling—no, not a failure—more alive than ever before. Realizing that Fishbourne is not, after all, "the world," he sets off onto the open road, heading vaguely toward the sea. Walking for eight or nine hours a day, sleeping in countryside inns and the occasional moonlit field, Mr. Polly comes at last to Potwell Inn. Nestling under the trees at a bend in the river surrounded by hollyhocks, a picnic table out front and a buttercup meadow behind, the inn appears as a vision of perfection. All the more so because it's inhabited by the "plump lady," so wondrously "firm and pink and wholesome" that she seems filled with infinite confidence and kindliness. The two realize almost at once that they are "each other's sort." And so Mr. Polly finds his kingdom—or would have, if it weren't for one obstacle in his way.

Read the novel to find out if Mr. Polly completes his transformation from failure to success story. Our guess is that, by the end, your sense of the inevitability of failure, for yourself and for Mr. Polly, will have absquatulated into thin air. Align yourself to Mr. Polly. Turn your supposed failures on their head. Stand tall. Then stride off in search of your own Potwell Inn.*

See also: Give up halfway through, tendency to · Self-esteem, low

FAILURE TO SEIZE THE DAY

See: Seize the day, failure to

---

* Do not, however, align yourself with Mr. Polly so much as to attempt your own suicide and insurance scam. Mr. Polly survives only by chance, and such eventualities are unlikely to happen more than once, whether in fiction or reality.

FAITH, LOSS OF

For some people, having faith means believing in God; for others, it means believing there's a point to life (see: Pointlessness), and for others still it means having faith that there's goodness in the world. Whatever faith means for you, to lose it can mean that the light goes out of your life. At such times, we need novels that return us to the tenets we need to uphold if we are to go forward with joy and confidence. Our cures cover three different approaches to faith; take the one best suited to you.

If you see faith as the triumph of personal conviction over science, then make *Salmon Fishing in the Yemen* your bible. When Fred Jones, a civil servant in charge of the National Centre for Fisheries Excellence, receives a letter asking for his help in introducing salmon, and salmon fishing, into the Yemen, he does what any self-respecting scientist would do: he says no. It is "nonsensical," "risible" to attempt to defy the laws of nature for the whim of a sheikh with too much money and no education. But that is before he has met Sheikh Muhammad and discovered the power of one man's determination. Because Sheikh Muhammad is a visionary, and, as Dr. Jones soon realizes, this is not so much about fly-fishing as about faith. This feel-good novel will restore your belief in the power of faith to move mountains.

If your belief in God has been shaken, *The Exorcist* will send a powerful shiver up your spine that might just have you reconsidering. In this chilling novel—perhaps the most terrifying we know—we witness a mother's dawning realization that her daughter, Regan, is possessed. In desperation, she calls in Father Karras. Karras is himself currently questioning his belief in God, but the palpably hellish horror that he witnesses in Regan so clearly testifies to the existence of the devil that it brings his belief in the ultimate presence of good and evil in the world rushing back. It may have the same effect on you.

If you've lost a sense of the point of it all—and whether it matters if you're good or bad—we have a much gentler cure. Harold Fry is a dispirited gray retiree who barely exchanges formalities with his wife and has lost

Salmon Fishing in the Yemen
PAUL TORDAY
. . .

The Exorcist
WILLIAM PETER
BLATTY
. . .

The Unlikely Pilgrimage of Harold Fry
RACHEL JOYCE

touch with his grown-up son. When he receives a letter from his old friend Queenie telling him she's dying of cancer, he writes her a postcard and sets off immediately to post it. On the way, a chance conversation with a gas station attendant (the "garage-girl") lodges in his mind, and when he gets to the mailbox, instead of sending his letter, he keeps on walking—all the way from Devon to Berwick-upon-Tweed, in fact, where Queenie lives—beset with an increasing conviction that, while he walks there, she will stay alive.

Harold's conviction is tested many times on his journey. But he places his trust in providence, never taking more than he needs, sleeping in the open air rather than in people's homes, and becoming more and more like a pilgrim from another age. Eventually the press hears of him and he is soon being referred to as "that pilgrim," someone who everyone wants to touch and be touched by. The spread of faith, it seems, is infectious. His wife, Maureen, begins to fall back in love with him from afar, and Queenie . . . well, you'll just have to read it to find out.

At times of bleakness, when you've lost faith in life, God, love, someone else, or yourself, use these novels to bring yourself back to some fundamental truths. Because the garage-girl is right: "If you have faith, you can do anything."

See also: Hope, loss of

FALLING HEAD OVER HEELS IN LOVE

See: Appetite, loss of • Concentrate, inability to • Dizziness • Infatuation • Insomnia • Lovesickness • Lust • Obsession • Optimism • Romantic, hopeless

1Q84

HARUKI MURAKAMI

FALLING OUT OF LOVE WITH LOVE

True love. Moonlight. Roses. Eternal devotion. *The one.*

Get real, we hear you say.

Some of us reach the end of the road with love. We feel that our capacity to love has been used up, that our ability to inspire love has faded. That the time for romance in our lives is over.

We have no time for such jaded attitudes. We hereby pledge to pluck you from skepticism and reawaken you to the never-ending ability of love to return, again and again. The novel with which we'll do it is Haruki Murakami's epic *1Q84*.

To say that *1Q84* is a complex novel is an understatement. It is remarkably long, and takes place in two different worlds. But it is deeply, fundamentally romantic. The kernel of the romance rests in the pasts of the two main characters. When they were both eleven years old, they held hands for one very long moment in their classroom at school. The moment—silent, charged with meaning, quite unexpected for Tengo, planned but inexplicable at the time to Aomame—has continued to haunt them both ever since. Aomame knew that she was leaving, and Tengo had always been kind to her. She imprinted her essence on the palm of his hand, and his soul was altered forever.

Now, more than twenty years later, we follow Tengo and Aomame as they lead their separate, solitary lives. Neither has developed a grown-up relationship. Tengo now teaches at a math "cram school" and is writing a novel; Aomame lives a disciplined life teaching self-defense while moonlighting as a kind of hit woman. But then they both become embroiled with a religious cult, Sakigake, which soon has them on the run, separately, becoming slowly aware of each other's continued relevance to their lives.

One of the novel's preoccupations is the idea of becoming irretrievably lost—whether it's morally, or between two parallel worlds, or simply lost to love. While Tengo visits his dying father in a home, he reads him a story about the "Town of Cats," a place where people can find themselves beyond the reaches of love. Tengo thinks about the Town of Cats, this place of ultimate lovelessness, a lot. And when, in contrast, things start happening that reach beyond realism—an inexplicable pregnancy, two people finding each other against all odds, love coming to those who gave up on it long ago—it seems that love has proved itself to be the strongest force. Take this epic journey with Tengo. Fall with him back in love with love.*

See also: **Disenchantment** • **Hope, loss of** • **Mr./Mrs. Wrong, ending up with**

---

* But don't fall too hard. If you do, see: Romantic, hopeless.

FALLING OUT OF THE WINDOW
See: Alcoholism • DIY • Drugs, doing too many • Hospital, being in the

FALLING OUT WITH YOUR BEST FRIEND
See: Friend, falling out with your best

A Suitable Boy
VIKRAM SETH

FAMILY, COPING WITH

When we are with our families we have the best of times and the worst of times, if we may misquote Dickens. Certainly it's within the family unit that we seem to have our biggest conflicts—be they out in the open or swept under the carpet. Whoever it is that gets your goat the most—your tyrannical toddler, your squabbling siblings, your pressuring parents, your critical in-laws, your adolescent out-laws, your crepuscular cat, or that one particular member of the family who consistently fails to do his or her share of the dishes—we offer you Vikram Seth's *A Suitable Boy*, a hefty tome that explores the jockeying for power that goes on in families.

It tells a familiar story: Mrs. Rupa Mehra wants to choose the man that her youngest daughter, Lata, will marry, but Lata has other ideas. "I do know what is best," Mrs. Mehra tells Lata, and "I am doing it all for you." We don't need to be Indian to have heard these words before. For nearly fifteen hundred pages, Lata ricochets between Haresh, the "suitable boy" of her mother's choosing, "solid as a pair of Goodyear Welted shoes"; Kabir, the fellow amateur actor she falls in love with; and Amit, the friendly dilettante poet pushed forward by his sisters.

Lata is surrounded by people seeking to influence her. But whose life is she living anyway? She knows that ultimately she must make the choice herself—not as an act of rebellion or to win approval, but freely. The length of the novel testifies to the difficulty of her task.

The choice Lata makes shows that although we may fight our families for the freedom to be ourselves, we are also part and parcel of them—steeped in their culture, traditions, and values. We may turn our backs on them, but they have made us what we are. Battle it out with your family, but know that ultimately you are battling it out with yourself.

See also: **Aging parents** • **Christmas** • **Mother-in-law, having a** • **Sibling rivalry**

FAMILY, COPING WITHOUT

I Am Legend
RICHARD MATHESON

Far away from your family, physically or emotionally, you feel conflicting emotions. On the one hand relieved and freed, on the other lonely and bereft. Whether your distance is self-imposed or involuntary, keep this novel in your backpack to remind you that you can cope on your own—as long as you're not the last man on Earth.

Matheson's genre-creating vampire novel begins with an unforgettable scene. Robert Neville sits in his barricaded house, drinking beer and listening to a symphony called *The Year of the Plague* on his record player. This is, partly, to drown out the eerie calls of "Neville! Neville!" coming from outside his house.

We soon realize that his wife and daughter have both been lost to vampirism. Neville goes outside during the daylight hours only, grimly attempting to kill his predators as they sleep in their daytime comas. Not that this is a gore fest—we see little of the vampires and their unpleasant deaths at Neville's hands. Instead, it's Neville's solitude that comes to the fore, his efforts to understand the new world order, and his increasingly desperate attempts to find an ally. His sincere endeavor to befriend a dog apparently unaffected by the virus is one of the most tragic moments in the story. A likable chap to whom driving stakes through hearts has become routine, his metamorphosis into a creature of nightmare goes completely unnoticed by the reader—and therein lies the genius of the novel.

Neville's resilience is impressive. Staying alive in this vampire-infested world depends on keeping the generator going and foraging for tinned goods from ghostly supermarkets. Keeping his spirits up by listening to Schoenberg and attempting to find a cure for the disease that wants to claim him, he does his best to live in the moment and cling to glimmers of hope for a different future.

If living far from your family leaves you feeling lost and alone, this book will give you solace: at least you're not forced to go around killing off vampires on a daily basis or strewing garlic necklaces and mirrors around your house to keep them out. Instead you'll be so gripped by this story that you'll forget your isolation—or discover that yours isn't nearly as bad. And if you become *too* comfortable without your family, the final revelation will sort you out.

See also: **Empty-nest syndrome** • **Loneliness**

FATHERHOOD

The Road
CORMAC MCCARTHY
. . .
I'm the King of the Castle
SUSAN HILL

At its best, being a dad is a chance to be a kid all over again—while precipitating you into a new phase of maturity, both as a father and as a partner. It gives you the opportunity to pass on your passions and all that you've learned. But it also brings with it enormous responsibilities and can change your relationship with your partner in ways you don't like. Sometimes, this resentment gets let out on the child. If the mantle of fatherhood does not sit on your shoulders easily, or you wish to strengthen a father-child bond that has perhaps been blemished by this sort of emotional transferal, we offer you the fictional equivalent of a father-son how-to manual: Cormac McCarthy's harrowing, but astonishing, *The Road*.

Its premise is grimmer than the reality of any of our lives—we hope—will ever be: following a cataclysmic event, the exact nature of which the survivors can only guess at, America—and perhaps the wider world—has been devastated. Ash blocks out the sun. The cities have burned and trees have died. Through this "barren, silent, godless" land, a man and his son—known to us only as "the man" and "the boy," as befits a world without color and with scant humanity—follow the road south, where they hope to find warmth and increase their chances of survival. Along the way they try to sleep through nights that are long and dark and "cold beyond anything they'd yet encountered," they scavenge what food they can—from wild mushrooms to occasional cans—and they're under constant threat from the "bad guys," filthy, terrifying men who travel in packs wearing masks and hazard suits, carrying clubs and lengths of pipe, plundering and killing like animals.

It's as shorn of beauty as a world can get. The boy is frequently so sick with fear that he can't run when his father commands it. Half starved and yearning for his mother, the possibility of playmates—let alone any of the normal pleasures of childhood—is unknown to him. At one point, the father finds a can of Coca-Cola in a vending machine that's been opened with a crowbar and tells the boy to drink it all, slowly. "It's because I won't ever get to drink another one, isn't it?" says the boy. And so, through a can of Coca-Cola, we feel the full thud of the loss of a world that will never return.

But in emotional terms, his world is rich. For here, with everything else taken away, the extraordinary love that exists between a father and a son is revealed in its purest, most primal form, in which the only thing that matters is making sure the boy is "all right." If the boy dies, the man knows that he will want to die too. For what is the essence of fatherhood if not the hope for the next generation?

The novel leaves us on this note of hope. Celebrate your fatherhood, then, and along the way pick up the habit of absolute honesty that exists between these two characters. Observe the trust between them, the son's need for reassurance that they're the "good guys," that they "carry the fire"; his need to see that his father will never break a promise, never leave him, and will always tell him the truth if he asks—except, perhaps, if they're dying. If honesty is there, and love, a firm set of moral principles and a dependable presence, you can't go wrong.

And if you do, well, you can't go as horribly wrong as Joseph Hooper does when he brings Helena Kingshaw and her son, Charles, to live in his house. We smell a parenting rat straightaway, as Joseph never loved the ugly house he inherited from his own father, along with the collection of moths that made the old man a celebrity in his dusty field. And he clearly has not earned the respect of his son, Edmund, either. If only he were older, Joseph muses, and he could blame adolescence for the boy's recalcitrance . . . But he had left all the child rearing up to his late wife. It is a mark of his desperation that he has asked Helena to come live with them as a housekeeper. Her son is almost the same age as Edmund, and both adults assume the boys will grow to love each other as brothers.

They do not count on the deep-rooted dagger of ice that has already established itself in Edmund's chest. From the moment "Kingshaw" steps foot in his house, Edmund does his absolute best to cow him, scaring him with ghost stories and undermining him in every way he can. When the boys spend a night lost together in the woods, the tables seem to turn, as Kingshaw is more at home in the natural element, able to light a fire and reassure Edmund when he is scared of the dark. Edmund seems appreciative of this undeserved consideration, but the moment they are rescued, he reverts to type. "It was Kingshaw, it was Kingshaw, he pushed me in the water," he accuses. Kingshaw defends himself, but his mother takes her host's side; she has marital designs on Mr. Hooper and doesn't want to jeopardize things by suggesting his son's a liar.

Mrs. Kingshaw, unforgivably, lacks motherly intuition and indeed wisdom of any sort—failing even to notice when her son is locked in a concrete shed for several hours. But we lay the ultimate blame for the chilling events that follow at Joseph's door. By neglecting his son after the death of his wife, he has created the monster that Edmund, by sheer lack of love and attention, has become, and we hereby hold Joseph Hooper up as one of the worst fathers in literature. Anyone unfortunate enough to be in possession of such a father—or indeed a mother like Mrs. Kingshaw—should urgently consult our cure for Abandonment.

As this agonizing novel speeds toward its terrible finale, let it teach you not to be too hard on yourself. The path of parenthood is already strewn with guilt; don't let self-criticism trip you up along the way. Women are often reassured that there's "perfect" and "good enough"—and "good enough" is often preferable. It's time men heard the message too. Even if you occasionally burn the beans, forget the gym kit, or catch your child experimenting with the contents of the medicine cabinet, allow yourself a pat on the back every so often for not being a Mr. Hooper. And remember that how-to manual, *The Road*. Keep it simple: love and honest communication are all you need.

See also: **Children requiring attention, too many** • **Single parent, being a** • **Trapped by children**

Birdsong
SEBASTIAN FAULKS

FATHERHOOD, AVOIDING

No more late nights drinking. No more lazy Sundays with the newspaper and coffee till noon. No more undivided devotion of girlfriend/wife/partner/dog/mother. No more being able to say, without guilt, "Just off for a weekend with the boys. See you on Sunday night."

It's easier for women. As soon as they're pregnant, they start to be changed not just physically but emotionally by the new life that's growing inside them. This is what happens to Isabelle in *Birdsong*, Sebastian Faulks's tearjerking World War I epic. She realizes she is carrying Stephen's child soon after they run away together from Isabelle's unhappy marriage and almost immediately discovers a hitherto unnoticed "starving" desire for a child. But in her (perhaps hormonal) confusion, Isabelle decides not only not to tell Stephen about it, but she abandons him and runs to her sister Jeanne instead.

The next time we see Stephen—emotionally shut down and not having touched a woman for seven years—he is in charge of a platoon in the trenches of the Somme. As they struggle to cope with unimaginable daily horrors, and the possibility of death at any moment, the men send and receive letters from home. We become very aware of which of them have children and which do not as, rightly or wrongly, Faulks uses the existence of children in these men's lives to elicit our greater sympathy. There is Wilkinson, newly married and with a baby on the way, who dies a horrible frontline death. And there is the good-humored Jack Firebrace, who gets word from his wife that his son John is in the hospital dangerously ill with diphtheria. Jack asks his lieutenant—Stephen—whether he has children himself. "No," comes Stephen's reply. But we, of course, know that he does.

We may or may not approve of Faulks differentiating between one man and another in this way, but nevertheless a world opens up in this novel in which those with children differ from those without. And we cannot help feeling that Stephen, a father without knowing it, loses out desperately by his ignorance of his and Isabelle's child. If he were aware of being a father, how might he be different? He does not have Jack shot, but neither is he given hope in the dark days of war by the existence of his child in the way that others are. The novel ends with a birth, one that brings its father such a burst of unexpected joy that he rushes outside and hurls conkers into the air.

If you're an expectant father feeling nothing but bewilderment and a vague sense of dread at the apocalypse lying ahead, this novel's for you. If you're stepping crablike around the issue of commitment and marriage, this one's for you too. We know of many male partners who confess to feeling not a jot of fatherly love for the embryo they've sired while it's still in the womb, only to fall hopelessly in love the moment the child is born. Journey with Stephen and decide for yourself: a narrow escape, or a lost chance to experience an extra dimension to life?

See also: Commitment, fear of

FATHERHOOD, AVOIDING

FEAR OF BEING LEFT ON THE SHELF

See: Shelf, fear of being left on the

FEAR OF COMMITMENT

See: Commitment, fear of

FEAR OF CONFRONTATION

See: Confrontation, fear of

FEAR OF DINNER PARTIES

See: Dinner parties, fear of

FEAR OF DEATH

See: Death, fear of

FEAR OF DOING TAX RETURN

See: Tax return, fear of doing

FEAR OF FINISHING

See: Finishing, fear of

FEAR OF FLYING

See: Flying, fear of

FEAR OF SCI-FI

See: Sci-fi, fear of

FEAR OF STARTING

See: Starting, fear of

FEAR OF VIOLENCE

See: Violence, fear of

FIFTYSOMETHING, BEING

THE TEN BEST NOVELS FOR FIFTYSOMETHINGS

White Lightning .... JUSTIN CARTWRIGHT
Disgrace .... J. M. COETZEE
Spending .... MARY GORDON
The Diaries of Jane Somers .... DORIS LESSING
The Invisible Bridge .... JULIE ORRINGER
The Tenderness of Wolves .... STEF PENNEY
The Satanic Verses .... SALMAN RUSHDIE
The Stone Diaries .... CAROL SHIELDS
Dinner at the Homesick Restaurant .... ANNE TYLER
Young Hearts Crying .... RICHARD YATES

READING AILMENT *Find one of your books, inability to*

CURE *Create a library*

There are few more frustrating things in life than being possessed by the urge to read or refer to a particular book and
then not being able to find it. You know you own it. You can
picture it—the color of the spine, where you last spotted it on
your shelves. But it's not there anymore. What is the point of
owning books if you can never find the one you want?

We aren't going to *insist* that you alphabetize.* Some people
keep their books in a totally random arrangement and are still
able to home in on the required volume with the accuracy of a

(continued)

* This is the system of organizing books we espouse, although Susan Sontag's insis-
tence that to have Pynchon next to Plato "would set her teeth on edge" has definitely
given us pause. We also on occasion arrange according to geography.

guided missile. Others use a system that is discernible only to themselves. In her lovely book *Ex Libris: Confessions of a Common Reader*, Anne Fadiman makes a convincing case for sorting English literature chronologically (the better to "watch the broad sweep" of the centuries of literature play out) while arranging American literature alphabetically.

It doesn't matter what system you choose; just have a system. Take inspiration from Borges and designate one room in your house as the library. If rooms are scarce, hallways, landings, staircases, and downstairs bathrooms work well. Build shelves from floor to ceiling. Invest in a small stool on wheels or, even better, a ladder. Every so often, collect stray books and return them to their rightful place (wearing glasses perched on the end of your nose as you do so). Keep a lending diary. Consider a catalog or an app that stores your books on digital shelves. By giving books a respectful place and space in your house, you enable them to remind you of their presence, breathe their wisdom, and offer themselves up to you, like a long-lost lover, at exactly the right moment in your life.

READING AILMENT   *Finishing, fear of*

CURE   *Read around the book*

Y ou have been delighted by the book, befriended the characters in the book, wolfed down the book, dreamed about the book, missed the book, cried with the book, made love to the book, thrown the book across the room, been dead to the world

(continued)

outside the book—and now you are about to finish the book. We've all been there: it is a terrible, gutting moment.

But do not despair. You do not have to leave the world of the book behind. As soon as you've finished the book, read around the book—reviews, literary criticism, blogs, whatever you can find. Talk to other people who have read the book. Watch the film of the book. Read the book in another language, or in a different translation. And then, finally, reread the book. The best books, by the greatest authors, will stand up to being reread many times in a life, and indeed give back more on each rereading. In this way, you will never finish the book. You will become the book, and it will become a part of you. You have not reached the end. You are, in fact, just beginning.

FLU

Something that no medical doctor or scientific researcher has yet studied, or even noticed, is the following strange coincidence: the moment a flu patient begins to read an Agatha Christie novel marks the commencement of their recovery. Our favorite is *The Murder of Roger Ackroyd*, the Poirot mystery that confirmed Christie's genius as a writer of detective fiction.

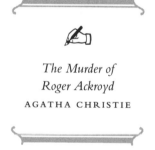

The Murder of Roger Ackroyd
AGATHA CHRISTIE

If the correlation is more than mere coincidence, we can only speculate as to what is, medically speaking, going on. Perhaps, like fish that cannot refuse the bait, our innate curiosity to find out whodunnit is stronger than the urge to wallow in our fluey misery.* Aches, chills, fever, sore throat, runny nose—all these are nothing compared with the determination to work out the guilty party *before* Poirot.† Perhaps the degree of brainpower

---

* Unless you have the much more serious strain known as man flu, in which case it's the other way around. See: Man flu.

† Forget it. You never do.

required to follow and attempt to solve an Agatha Christie is just the right amount to rally your sick gray cells without actually taxing them unduly—as if you've given them a light, healing massage as opposed to sending them out on a five-mile run.

Whatever the explanation, we prescribe Agatha Christie for your cure. Prop yourself up on your pillows. The masterwork of Hercule Poirot—that "detestable, bombastic, tiresome, egocentric little creep" (Christie's words)—has begun.*

See also: Appetite, loss of • Exhaustion • Headache • Nausea • Pain, being in • Sweating

FLYING, FEAR OF

Night Flight
ANTOINE DE SAINT-
EXUPÉRY

Our unconventional cure for this debilitating modern affliction is to slip into your carry-on luggage an account of a pilot struggling to wrest control of a flimsy two-seater aircraft caught in a cyclone on its way from Patagonia to Buenos Aires with the Europe-bound mail: Antoine de Saint-Exupéry's hair-raising *Night Flight*.

Fabien, the pilot of the mail plane, has been married only three weeks. As his wife gets up in the darkness of the small hours to kiss him good-bye, she admires him in his flying leathers and sees someone almost godlike: here is a man capable of waging war with the very elements. By the time ground control spots the storm heading off the Atlantic, it is too late. Somewhere over the Andes, Fabien is surrounded and can't turn back. With visibility reduced to nil, he has no choice but to tough it out from his tiny cockpit, the aircraft rolling and floundering in its vast sea of pitch. It takes all his strength to hold the controls steady so the cables don't snap. Behind him, the radio operator gets electric shocks in his fingers when he attempts to tap out a message. No one can hear them, no one can see them. The peaks of the Andes loom up like towering waves trying to pluck

---

* If this cure works, it proves that you didn't actually have the flu in the first place but just a bad cold (see: Cold, common). The search for a literary cure for the flu goes on.

them to their deaths. Any slackening of willpower, any weakening of his grip, and Fabien knows they are lost.

You, meanwhile—yes, you, reading *Night Flight* in the air-conditioned cabin of your Boeing 747 with a blanket on your knee, your gin and tonic neatly perched on your tray table, smiling flight attendants tripping down the aisle beside you, the mellow voice of the captain calmly announcing that you're leveling out at thirty-five thousand feet, lifting the window shade with your finger to admire the low orb of the sun . . . Terrified, did you say? *Terrified?* Really? How Fabien would smile at the thought!

If your heart insists on pounding, let it pound for Fabien and his radio-man, for the stricken wife waiting by her phone, for the pilot's boss, Rivière, holding his terrible vigil on the tarmac. Or, for that matter, let it pound for Saint-Exupéry himself, who disappeared while flying over North Africa in 1943. Peer out your window again. See anyone trying to shoot you down? Hmm. Didn't think so. Get back to your novel, chuck back that G&T, and pull yourself up by your cozy in-flight socks.

See also: Anxiety • Claustrophobia • Panic attack

THE TEN BEST NOVELS FOR PLANE JOURNEYS

So gripping you'll forget you're thirty-five thousand feet up in the air.

I'm Not Scared .... NICCOLÒ AMMANITI
The Count of Monte Cristo .... ALEXANDRE DUMAS
The Magus .... JOHN FOWLES
In the Woods .... TANA FRENCH
Carter Beats the Devil .... GLEN DAVID GOLD
The Woman in Black .... SUSAN HILL
The Girl with the Dragon Tattoo .... STIEG LARSSON
Labyrinth .... KATE MOSSE
The Lovely Bones .... ALICE SEBOLD
The Shadow of the Wind .... CARLOS RUIZ ZAFÓN

FOREIGN, BEING

Everything Is Illuminated
JONATHAN
SAFRAN FOER

If people dub you a foreigner and you do not dig this appellation very much, and it spleens you that they think you have shit between your brains just because you come from a different part of the globe, we suggest you make a feature of it, like Alex, the noncompetent narrator of *Everything Is Illuminated*. Then, even if you're not a particularly premium sort of person and not many girls want to be carnal with you, you can parrot him and at least make people dig you. Alex ensures his father, the owner of Heritage Touring, that he is fluent in English, and so he's dispatched to be a translator and guide for the novel's hero, Jonathan Safran Foer (we are meaning the character here, not the author, though you are right to be confused as they share many qualities, all of them premium), and together with Alex's weeping grandfather, once a farmer but now retarded, and a mentally deranged dog called Sammy Davis Junior, Junior (which we agree is not very flaccid to utter), they promenade in quest of a small Ukrainian shtetl dubbed Trachimbrod in the hope of dishing up the woman who may have saved Jonathan's grandfather from the Nazis. The history of Trachimbrod, told by Jonathan in interminable chapters, is an electrical one. But it's Alex's abnormal and memorizable voice—a potent result of his referencing a thesaurus rather than a dictionary—that is winning us. We suggest that if you are anticipating being foreign in the near future, or when you are less miniature, you go forth and disseminate some currency on a thesaurus or equivalent (we are cocksure that a cookbook or an automotive manual would deliver you) in the language in which you are incompletely fluent and you will not only illuminate yourself but make yourself very charming and oppressive in the process.

See also: **Different, being** · **Homesickness** · **Left out, feeling** · **Outsider, being an** · **Words, lost for**

FORTYSOMETHING, BEING

THE TEN BEST NOVELS FOR FORTYSOMETHINGS

FRIEND, FALLING OUT WITH YOUR BEST

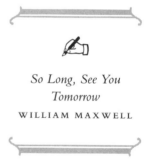

So Long, See You Tomorrow

WILLIAM MAXWELL

We hear a lot about the pain of failed romantic relationships, but what about the loss of a best friend of many years standing when, for whatever reason, you fall out irredeemably? Friends are meant to be forever, after all, and the pain of losing the one person in your life who has known you from your youth, seen you at your worst, and understands you inside out, is truly gutting. Not only must you face a future without that person by your side, but you will find yourself questioning whether you are, in fact, a good friend to others and, in turn, a good person.

This sorry state of affairs is captured in all its poignancy by William Maxwell in his exquisitely written novella *So Long, See You Tomorrow*. Clarence Smith and Lloyd Wilson are tenant farmers on adjacent properties in rural Illinois. They're marooned on the vast grasslands, and the only lights that can be seen from one house are the lights of the other. Over the years the two men come to depend on each other. When Lloyd has a sick calf, he calls Clarence before calling the vet. When the blades of Clarence's mower jam, Lloyd hears the sputtering engine from a quarter mile away and goes straight over to help out. Each man is the only friend the other has.

Fifty years on, the novel's elderly narrator—a man who grew up nearby and has an equally moving story of his own, which we won't go into here—looks back at the painful journey of Smith and Wilson and its tragic endgame. There is no judgment of either the betrayer or the betrayed, for each friend has his own side of the story, and the author shows compassion to both points of view. What is left is a weight of sadness that the narrator still finds difficult to bear. Maxwell's slow, elegiac prose, rising up like mist from the page, takes you beyond a simplistic "he said, she said" to a place concerned with the ineffability of grief, the terrible fact of shattered lives.

If it's not too late, do whatever you can to mend your friendship—new friends are hard to come by the older you get, and you can never replace all that shared history. If the hurt or resentment feels too great or you cannot win your friend's forgiveness, Maxwell's deeply understanding novel will help you feel your loss and grieve—and ensure that you'll never again treat a friend in a way you'll regret.

See also: Loneliness • Regret • Sadness

FRIENDS, IN NEED OF

See: Left out, feeling • Loneliness • Outsider, being an • Unpopular, being

G

GAMBLING

Grab some dice. Write down six actions you could take today. Think sublime. Think ridiculous. For example:

The Dice Man
LUKE RHINEHART

1. Shave off all your body hair.
2. Invite to dinner the next person that walks past you, regardless of age, sex, or species.
3. Blindly stick a pin in a world map and go wherever it lands.
4. Send this book to your boss, highlighting all the ailments he or she needs to cure.
5. Take a bucket and spade and walk all the way to the sea.
6. Read *The Dice Man* by Luke Rhinehart to cure you of your addiction to gambling.

Make a solemn promise that you will do whatever the die tells you. Now you know what to do.

See also: **Broke, being** • **Risks, taking too many**

GENIUS, BEING A

See: Brainy, being exceptionally

READING AILMENT   *Give up halfway through, refusal to*

CURE   *Adopt the fifty-page rule*

Some readers cannot bear to leave a novel unfinished. They'll plow on doggedly, joylessly, until they've reached the bitter end—either so that they can say, "I've read it," without blushing, or so that they aren't left with an unfinished story, however dull or irksome, dangling in their overdutiful head.

Life is too short. Read the first fifty pages of every novel you start, preferably in a maximum of two sittings. If, after that time, the book has failed to infiltrate your solar plexus, abandon it. As a reader it's important you learn to trust your judgment and your knowledge of your own literary taste: every book you read or try to read helps to map your future reading path (if you need help with this, see: Identity, unsure of your reading). Don't bludgeon yourself into taking routes that are not fruitful or enjoyable to you. Give every book you don't finish to someone who may like it better. This is a gesture of respect to the book and the effort the author put into writing it, and an insurance policy against ending up with a houseful of unfinished books staring at you balefully every time you walk past.

READING AILMENT *Give up halfway through, tendency to*

CURE *Read in longer stretches*

It may be that you are reading a terribly slow book. Although some have momentum from the very first line and others start slowly but reach full speed by the midway point, some are defiantly, or obliviously, slow for the duration. But if you notice a recurring tendency in yourself to launch in with great enthusiasm but slow to a dawdle, then grind to a halt; if your books are all studded with telltale bookmarks that never move, chances are the problem is not the books, but you.

The most likely diagnosis is that you don't give books a chance. You read in very short snatches—perhaps only five or ten minutes at a time—and therefore never get into the book. This is not fair to either book or author. Stories worth telling take time to tell: characters, like houses, must be built on firm foundations, and we need to care about them before we can be moved by what happens to them.

Do not attempt to begin a new book until you can devote at least forty-five minutes to the first and second sittings. Hopefully, by then the book will have wound itself around your innards and will keep you coming back for more. But if you're an inveterate giver-upper, try not to read for less than forty-five minutes *every* time you read. And if that still doesn't work, you've no option but to take a day off work, tie one of your limbs to the leg of your chair, and not release yourself until you've reached the end.

GIVING BIRTH

See: Childbirth

See: Give up halfway through, tendency to • Hope, loss of • Smoking, giving up

The Debt to Pleasure
JOHN LANCHESTER

GLUTTONY

Gluttony is an overindulgence in food, drink, or other consumables to the point of excess or waste. In other words, being a greedy pig. If gluttony is your malady, indulge in this juicy novel before you sit down to eat. (If it's a friend who's the pig, leave this novel on his or her plate and serve up supper two hours late.) The cure it effects will arrive in three courses, as follows.

For starters: This book is impossible to gulp down quickly and will delay the eating of your dinner, perhaps indefinitely. Tarquin, the narrator, expresses his thoughts so precisely, with such relish for the words themselves, that you'll want to read every paragraph twice, then copy it out in your reading journal to chew over as you would a morsel of calf's liver. Read not just before eating, but between courses too, to slow the meal down. You might even get up from the table to try out one of the recipes it contains (*blinis,* omelet, and salt marsh lamb, to name a few). For this novel, as with this part of your cure, is an almost eternal digression, using recipes as an excuse to reminisce, philosophize, and hint at where we are really going with this meandering yarn.

For your main course: The lingering delight that Tarquin takes in each ingredient will teach you how to savor, rather than scoff. Each edible you come across reveals a surprise. Peaches, for instance, remind Tarquin of his brother, Bartholomew—not just because they spent a summer gorging on this furry fruit in boyish delight, but because as a six-year-old our culinary enthusiast could not resist an early experiment in jam making, peach kernels and all, accidentally releasing the cyanide in the pits and causing a near fatal case of poisoning.

And for dessert: There is none, after all. Sorry. Because by now you will have the disconcerting sense that there is something sinister going on—and that you need to watch your waistline (see: Obesity).

This novel will teach you to relish more but eat less—and get to know the exact origin of every ingredient before it makes its way to your stomach.

See also: **Toothache**

GOODY-GOODY, BEING A

The Master and Margarita
MIKHAIL BULGAKOV

When the devil appears in a Moscow park one fine spring evening in the 1930s, he inserts himself between two bookish types deep in discussion on a bench. One is Berlioz, the bald, portly editor of a literary magazine. The other is Bezdomny, a young poet. The devil has no trouble seizing control of the conversation, which is about the existence or otherwise of Jesus Christ. For the devil—expensively dressed in a gray suit, "foreign" shoes, a gray beret cocked jauntily over one eye—has more charisma than both men put together. "Oh, how delightful!" he exclaims when his two new friends confirm they are atheists. The devil has an unpredictable, childlike mind, easily bored and always on the lookout for a joke—ideally at someone else's expense. One minute he's bursting into peals of laughter loud enough to "startle the sparrows out of the tree"; the next he is cruelly predicting Berlioz's death by decapitation under a tram. (It comes true.) And when Berlioz asks him where he's going to stay while in Moscow, he winks and says, "In your flat."

The devil has edge; he has wit. As in *Paradise Lost*, he has all the good lines and keeps everyone on their toes. When Bezdomny feels an urge for a cigarette, the devil—or Professor Woland, as it says on his calling card—reads his mind and whips out an impressive gold cigarette case with just the right brand inside. He and his bizarre retinue—which includes a large, crude, vodka-swigging cat named Behemoth—astonish the audience at the theater by causing a collection of Parisian haute couture—hats, dresses, handbags, makeup—to materialize onstage and then inviting all the ladies to strip and re-dress.

And, of course, the devil holds the best parties. Moscow has never seen the likes of it before or since: a midnight full-moon ball at which the guest of honor—Margarita—is washed in blood and roses. There's champagne in the fountains, scarlet-breasted parrots screeching "Ecstasy! Ecstasy!" and an orchestra conducted by Johann Strauss. This is the devil, though, and it's not all innocent fun and games. Apart from Margarita, the guests at the ball arrive in various states of decomposition, having come straight from hell.

We're not suggesting you renounce goodness and turn to evil. We're just saying liven up, get an edge. Don't go twisting off heads like Behemoth, but do throw scandalous parties. Keep a glint of mischief in your eye, a shard of wickedness up your sleeve. It will make you a lot more fun.

See also: Beans, temptation to spill the • Organized, being too • Risks, not taking enough • Teetotaler, being a

Union Atlantic
ADAM HASLETT
· · ·
The Pearl
JOHN STEINBECK
· · ·
The Colour
ROSE TREMAIN

GREED

G reed is good," the soulless moneyman Gordon Gekko declared in the movie *Wall Street* twenty-five years ago. For a while, this philosophy sounded not only defensible but exhilarating, as housing bubbles and things called "derivatives" and "credit default swaps" (which nobody understands) created fortunes far and wide. Ordinary people began to think they'd struck it rich as the value of their homes climbed up, up, up, year after year. Cars were bought. Summer homes were acquired. The occasional yacht set sail. And then the bubble popped, and all of us suddenly remembered. Untrammeled greed is bad for the soul—not to mention for the security and well-being of billions of people. Too late, we recognized the error of cheering on the unsavory speculators whose machinations inflated our retirement funds . . . then burst them.

Adam Haslett's urgent, fast-paced novel *Union Atlantic* (named for a reputable bank that turns rotten just before the 2007 crash) will cure you of any impulse you may have to become a Captain of the Universe dripping with ill-gotten gain. Under the management of a greedy money spinner named Doug Fanning, the bank "brazenly commenced acquisitions" that Doug knew were illegal but that he correctly anticipated would be approved—they were so profitable that rival banks were sure to start exploiting them too.

That's right: one of the worst things about greed is that it catches on. Once somebody visibly gets away with something, human nature makes everyone else try to join the gravy train. Only a pair of handcuffs can restrain Fanning's acquisitive zeal, and in his fall he brings down with him everyone who joined his hunt for undeserved reward.

But as we all know, greed can deform the psyche even when the stakes are far lower than what they were for the corrupt bankers of Union Atlantic. John Steinbeck demonstrates the power of greed to destroy a simple family in his allegorical tale *The Pearl*. Kino and Juana have what he portrays as the perfect life: they live in a shack by the sea, where Kino makes his living by diving for pearls. One day their infant son, Coyotito, is bitten by a scorpion and becomes dangerously ill. Unable to pay for medical treatment, Juana prays that Kino will find a pearl of great value so that their son can live. Miraculously, Kino finds exactly the pearl of their prayers. Not only can they now afford a doctor for Coyotito, but they can give their son an education. But no sooner is the pearl in Kino's possession than their world begins to unravel. Other people hear about the pearl and want it for themselves. Soon, Kino will do anything to protect the pearl. His wife immediately sees the potential for trouble and tries to persuade Kino to hurl the pearl back into the sea. But he won't let his dream of wealth go. Before long they are forced to leave their village—and will soon lose more than they know.

In Rose Tremain's *The Colour*, it's not the lure of gold that brings Joseph Blackstone to New Zealand. His motivation for upping sticks from his Norfolk origins and buying land in the New World for a pound an acre is to start a clean slate after past misdeeds threaten to catch up with him. But when the settler finds flecks of gold in the creek on his farm, his innocent dreams alchemize into something more. The modest rewards of farming suddenly seem small and petty compared with the wealth that gold would bring him, and he turns his attention to the search for "the colour."

Tremain vividly conveys the desperate lengths that men will go to in order to satiate their lust for gold—up to their necks in mud, sleeping in rat-infested tents, walking for days over treacherous terrain to find the longed-for virgin seam. When Joseph's wife, Harriet, turns up at the digging site, Joseph is horrified, viewing her as a potential thief of his meager findings. His awakened greed becomes the unholy twin of the evil deed that caused him to run away from England in the first place. But Harriet's reasons for joining him have nothing to do with greed at all—she has come looking for her husband's love.

Let Harriet and Juana be your mentors, the calm voices of reason in the face of temptation. If you allow greed to put down roots inside you, it will take over your life. No good comes of avarice, but plenty good comes from taking the moral high ground.

See also: Extravagance • Gluttony

GRIEF

See: Broken heart • Death of a loved one • Sadness • Widowed, being • Yearning, general

GRUMPINESS

The Island of Doctor Moreau

H. G. WELLS

If you are as grumpy as Doctor Moreau in H. G. Wells's antivivisection polemic of 1896, beware of the effect you are having on friends, colleagues, and cohabitants. Peevish demeanors are infectious—so much so that you'll soon find yourself surrounded by other truculent, ornery people, when they were previously sunny and light.

Moreau, in the privacy of his island in the Pacific, is attempting to turn various four-legged animals—hogs, hyenas, dogs, and leopards—into human beings, using a mixture of surgery and behavioral conditioning. Witness to his experiments is Edward Prendick, a shipwrecked Englishman who is rescued by Moreau only to find himself being held captive. At first Prendick misunderstands the project and fears for his life, believing Moreau's intention is to turn humans into beasts. Then he realizes it's the other way around. Moreau is only partially successful; his semihuman creations have a tendency to revert to their bestial natures, going down on all fours and chasing rabbits—hence his bad mood. And in the end, Prendick has nothing to fear from the Beast Folk. But by the time he has spent many months on this island, he's as crabby as Moreau, having been exposed for far too long to the scientist's grumps.

Don't bring everyone down with you. Keep your grumpiness to yourself.

Or, better yet, aim to lighten up and see our cures for: Irritability and Misanthropy.

See also: **Dissatisfaction** • **Querulousness**

GUILT

Crime and Punishment
FYODOR
DOSTOYEVSKY

Have you compromised your own standards of conduct, or violated a moral code? Or does your guilt spring from something you should have done but didn't?

Some people have an inability to feel guilt, and they are best avoided (psychopaths, babies, to name a few). For the rest of us, guilt and its little sister, shame (see: Shame), should perhaps be embraced, as these conditions are essential to the collective morality that binds society together. Our cure for this debilitating, if at times useful, affliction is the most radical and profound exploration of guilt in all of literature: Dostoyevsky's *Crime and Punishment*.

Written when Dostoyevsky was nearly destitute and deeply in debt, this book contains many autobiographical elements, and it's hard to shake the sense that the author must have felt many of the same things as his hero. Rodion Romanovich Raskolnikov is a former student in need of a job, living in a tiny garret on the top floor of a run-down apartment building in St. Petersburg. Bilious, dressed in tatters, and broke, he has an unnerving tendency to talk to himself, but he is, on the other hand, good looking, proud, and intelligent. From the start we learn that he is contemplating something desperate and dreadful: he has resolved to murder an old woman for her money, having persuaded himself that, being a pawnbroker, she is morally moribund, and her death therefore justifiable. He's caught in the act by the old woman's half sister and, in the heat of the moment, murders her too.

He steals from the old woman and hides his bounty under a rock. But almost immediately he is overcome with appalling remorse. A terrible liar, he wanders around the city racked with fever and raving. Meanwhile, another man confesses to the murders and it's clear that Raskolnikov could get away with his crime if he chose to—were it not for his conscience, and the intervention of his wise friend Sonya, who understands how his life cannot resume without a confession.

Dostoyevsky's portrayal of his young hero's torment is fascinating and painful to witness. It is mostly down to Sonya that Raskolnikov survives. If you don't have a Sonya in your life, borrow Raskolnikov's. Confess, pay your penance, expunge your guilt. Only then will you deserve the redemption and freedom that are the rewards for doing so.

See also: Guilt, reading associated · Regret

READING AILMENT   *Guilt, reading associated*

CURE   *Schedule reading time*

You have bought the latest talked-about novel. It winks at you seductively from the shelf next to your bed. You absolutely intend to read it. All your friends are reading it. But somehow you never seem to . . . actually read it. Sometimes it's a problem of overambition. You decide on a whim it's time to tackle *Infinite Jest*. Or to read all the winners of the Booker Prize since its inception. Unsurprisingly, you never begin.

The key is to schedule regular reading times into your week. Designate one lunchtime per week to reading—even if it's only half an hour in a café near your place of work. Block-book one evening a week as your reading evening, and announce it to whoever you live with. Fence off a part of the weekend—just an hour to start with, then two when your reading muscles are toned. Slowly, you will find yourself developing a good reading habit. And before long you'll have swapped your reading guilt for all sorts of other kinds of guilt: housework guilt, failure-to-walk-the-dog guilt . . . We would go on, but it's time for us to go and read.

H

The Little White Car

DANUTA DE RHODES

HANGOVER

Your forehead is a stage, thudding with the beat of thirty drummers. Your tongue is a piece of cooked bacon that's been sitting in the fridge for a week. And your mind is a washing machine on a fast spin cycle, with shreds of the events of last night whapping against the sides, revealing their colors for a brief, ghastly moment before sinking back into the foamy suds.

Yes, you have a hangover.

You get out of bed, or off the sofa, or wherever it was you passed out. You stumble toward the sink and fill a glass with cold water. You tip back your head (ouch!) and begin to gulp, the lovely cool liquid bringing back to life the . . . oh, God. That's when you remember. Worse than the pounding head. Worse than the confusion. The memory. Of what. Exactly. It was. You did. Last night.

At this point, reach for *The Little White Car* by Danuta de Rhodes. Because whatever it was you did, it wasn't as bad as what Veronique did, the spoiled twenty-two-year-old Parisian girl who emerged from her hangover to realize, with a plunge into a new ice age . . . Well, you'll have to read it and see.

Call in sick, then go back to bed. There you will read—in big, fat type that won't challenge your eyes and straightforward prose that won't befuddle your head—a lesson in how much worse it *could* have been.

Go on, indulge.*

See also: Anxiety • Bed, inability to get out of • Headache • Lethargy • Nausea • Pain, being in • Paranoia • Sweating

Fahrenheit 451
RAY BRADBURY

HAPPINESS, SEARCHING FOR

Happiness: the ultimate goal in life. Or is it? Many of us spend our lives searching for this transitory state in love, work, travel, and home life. As images of material wealth and blissful lifestyles taunt us from advertisements and television screens, we often feel like we just can't get enough—not enough luck, romance, possessions, or free time. It's a modern malaise. Or is it? Didn't Dickens's Fagin think he deserved a bigger piece of (someone else's) meat pie? Didn't Voltaire's Candide demonstrate the folly of thinking that "the best is yet to be"? And long before, then, weren't Milton's Adam and Eve told they'd be "happiest if ye seek no happier state"—advice that they, being human, ignored? Start raising your personal requirements for what it takes to be "happy" and you will open yourself up to all kinds of misery.

We're with Eastern philosophy on this one: the relentless pursuit of happiness is an ailment, and must be cured. Ray Bradbury knew this too. His prescient *Fahrenheit 451*, first published in 1953, came very close to showing us life as we now know it. In his dystopian future, nobody reads novels anymore. At first this is because people want their fiction in smaller and smaller doses, not having the attention span or patience to read a whole book. (Sound familiar? See: Give up halfway through, tendency to.) Then they start to think that books are their enemy, irresponsibly presenting different views and states of mind. Surely they'd all be happier living in an emotionless no-man's-land with no strong feelings at all?

* British author Dan Rhodes did—although he hid his shame at having used such a tasteless premise for this delightful trifle of a novel by passing it off as the work of one Danuta de Rhodes, an authoress several years his junior who works "in the fashion industry."

To counteract their emotional void, deprived of culture and deep thought as they are, people begin to live faster and faster, racing around the city at breakneck speeds—and killing whatever gets in their way. They almost never see their children, who go to school nine days out of ten. Having kids is a waste of time anyway; the women prefer to stay at home watching an endless interactive soap called *The Family*—the fate of which becomes more important to them than their own. (Brilliant as he was, Bradbury didn't quite make the leap into a time when women might want to work too.) Doped by these sagas, they go to bed with "shells" in their ears transmitting junky newsfeeds and more meaningless dramas all night long. Sleeping pills are popped like candy. Suicide is common, and attracts little remark.

When Montag, a fireman whose job it is to burn illegal books—and sometimes the people reading them too—meets a teenage girl who takes the time to look at the stars, smell the grass, and question the dandelions about love, he realizes that he is not as happy in his emotionally neutered state as he thought he was. He begins to wake up to a world of beauty and feeling, and wonders what the books that he burns might contain. One night he reads Matthew Arnold's poem "Dover Beach" to his wife's guests, interrupting an episode of *The Family* to do so, and the result of his reading is uncontrollable weeping and heartbreak: "Poetry and tears, poetry and suicide and crying and awful feelings, poetry and sickness; *all* that mush!" one distraught listener cries. Montag is forced to burn his own books—and his house with them—but he holds on to the belief that a future without the wisdom of books is an unbearable one. He would rather feel and suffer than live the comatose life that "civilization" considers the route to happiness.

Live to the full not by seeking happiness, but by embracing knowledge, literature, truth, and feeling of every sort. And in case Bradbury's vision becomes a reality, consider learning a novel by heart, as Montag does. You never know when you might need to pass it on to the rest of humanity.

See also: **Dissatisfaction** • **Mr./Mrs. Right, looking for**

The River Between

NGŨGĨ WA THIONG'O

· · ·

1984

GEORGE ORWELL

Hate is like a poisonous plant. Allow it to take root inside you and it will gradually consume you from within, contaminating everything you touch. Whether you hate another person, other drivers, semolina, hipster bloggers, or reality TV, it doesn't make much difference. Neither does it make it any better if the hate is justified and understandable, such as hating someone who has done you a grievous harm. The fact that you are nurturing this violent emotion in your heart will ultimately be a violence against yourself.*

In *The River Between*, Ngũgĩ wa Thiong'o shows very clearly how hatred can set in between two factions with opposed religious, political, or philosophical beliefs. Those consumed by hate would do well to read this fablelike retelling of *Romeo and Juliet*. As you read, ask yourself if you, too, are clinging too rigidly to a set of beliefs.

On either side of the river Honia (meaning "cure") lie two ridges. On one is the village of Kameno, and on the other Makuyu. Here the Gikuyu people of Kenya live undisturbed—until the white man arrives with his "clothes like butterflies," new ways, and new religion. Joshua, an elder of Kameno, is the first convert to Christianity. Soon he has the villagers turning away from their tribal customs. Trouble hits when his daughter Muthoni decides that she wants to be initiated into womanhood in the traditional "beautiful" way—circumcision—and dies following the procedure. She rapidly becomes a symbol for everything deemed barbaric and pagan about the old Gikuyu ways. The two villages pit themselves against each other, the old ways against the new. And when Waiyaki from Makuyu, with his beautiful "kinking" hair and eyes that "blaze," falls in love with Nyambura, Joshua's remaining daughter, the people are given a focus for their hate. This shared

* Because of this, neuroscientists have worked hard to investigate the neurobiology of hate. A few years ago they announced that they'd pinpointed the specific areas of our brains responsible for the venomous emotion. These areas included the middle frontal gyrus, the right putamen, the premotor cortex, and the frontal pole. We tell you this mostly because we wanted a reason to write "middle frontal gyrus" and "right putamen," but also because we find it amusing to point out that some of these areas of the brain—the putamen, for example—had previously been pinpointed by neuroscientists as the specific areas of our brains responsible for the feeling of love. Which either goes to show that love and hate are indeed closely related or shows nothing at all. Luckily, we have literature as a backup to science.

hatred gains momentum in the same way a herd of bullocks running downhill gains speed, and in the way of things that have lost control, it heads only one way: to mayhem and destruction.

Don't let yourself get swept up mindlessly by hate in this way. Instead, allow yourself to be lulled by Thiong'o's poetic, expansive prose, the importance he places on the land, and the concept of love as a guiding principle. Don't be a zealot. See things from another's point of view. Be open to compromise and embrace difference. This way you can turn your hate into love.

If letting go of hatred is just too hard, read George Orwell's *1984*. Start by studying "Hate Week"—seven days dedicated to rousing processions, speeches, banners, and films intended to whip the masses into a frenzy of hatred for the state's number one enemy, Eurasia. By day six, the crowd is in such a maddened delirium of hatred that if they could get their hands on individual Eurasians they'd tear them to pieces. But then, suddenly, the object of hatred is switched. Word goes around that the enemy is no longer Eurasia. It's Eastasia. Hurriedly, posters are ripped off walls, banners are trampled underfoot. The crowd barely misses a beat. Within a few moments, the "feral roars of rage" have been redirected to the Eastasians instead.

The apparent ease of this refocusing certainly gives one pause for thought. Does the feeling of hate have anything to do with the object of hate at all? Does it not perhaps have more to do with a determination to find *any* object on which to unleash one's ire? If this resonates, it's time to take a break from your hatred, and take a long, hard look within yourself.

See also: Anger • Bitterness • Judgmental, being • Murderous thoughts • Rage

HAUNTED, BEING

If you count yourself among the haunted, one of your problems will be getting others to take your tales of the haunting seriously. So give them *The Woman in Black* by Susan Hill. Set in Eel Marsh House, a lonely abode that is cut off by the tide twice a day, this novel recounts the story of Arthur Kipps, the solicitor called in to clear up the estate of the house's recently deceased mistress. He has no idea what the extremely bitter

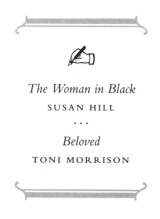

The Woman in Black
SUSAN HILL
. . .
Beloved
TONI MORRISON

spirits that haunt the place have in store for him—especially one particular ghost, a woman dressed all in black. The story cannot fail to send multiple chills down your spine, and while doing nothing to cure you of your own haunting, it will persuade your friends to listen to you a bit more closely.

For you, we prescribe Toni Morrison's Pulitzer Prize–winning *Beloved*. Sethe is an ex-slave living with her teenage daughter Denver—and the ghost of her dead baby. They have grown used to the presence of the spiteful spirit, which shatters mirrors, makes baby handprints in the icing of birthday cakes, and creates puddles of red misery in the doorway that visitors must wade through to come inside. Indeed, most people give the house and its occupants a wide berth. But when Sethe's old friend Paul D reappears after eighteen years, the ghost seems to go quiet. Until, that is, it returns in human form.

Beloved walks out of the river as a fully clothed adult. She spends a few days summoning up the energy to open her eyelids while her dress dries and her perfectly unlined skin grows accustomed to the sun. Her voice is peculiarly low, she is eternally thirsty, and she seems to possess superhuman strength, able to pick up her older sister with one hand. But Beloved is not a positive force. She drinks in her mother's love like the milk she never had enough of. She pushes Paul away from Sethe while forcing him, against his better judgment and desire, to "touch her on the inside part." She gorges on life like a blowfly. We know this cannot last. Sethe has within her the means to placate Beloved, but first she has a difficult truth to acknowledge to herself.

Hauntees, take heart. Whatever haunts you cannot only be faced, but spoken to, negotiated with, even loved. If your ghost wants to come and live with you for a while, spend all your money, and drive your loved ones away, so be it. Once it's got over itself, you can send it back to where it belongs.

See also: **Demons, facing your**

HAY FEVER

20,000 Leagues Under the Sea
JULES VERNE

Hay fever can ruin entire summers. When the itchy eyes, streaming nose, tight chest, and difficulty breathing get too bad, you long to plunge into a cool, clear pool—somewhere no pollen can reach you. Or, even better, to hitch a ride in a submarine and go live at the bottom of the ocean. Perhaps it was hay fever that drew Captain Nemo, the mysterious nautical traveler of the most famous of Verne's novels, to his peculiar underwater existence. The misanthropic captain shrugged off "that intolerable earthly yoke" and took to living in a "sea unicorn of colossal dimensions" (which naval observers at first took to be a giant narwhal), shunning everyone and everything apart from the sea creatures he studies (see also: Misanthropy). His ship, *Nautilus*, travels at incredible speeds and is capable of scientific wonders far beyond the technological know-how reached on land, since Nemo is both explorer and inventor. He dines off sea cucumber preserves that he believes even a Malaysian would declare to be unrivaled, sugar from the North Sea fucus plants, and marmalade of sea anemone. Nemo is not shy about his success as an underwater despot, calling himself "The Man of the Waters, the Spirit of the Seas," recognizing no superiors, and confident that he could pay off the ten-billion-franc national debt using the treasures he has found beneath the waves.

Whenever those pesky pollen motes threaten to invade your head, grab Jules Verne and escape to the airlessness of Captain Nemo's underwater kingdom. You never know—it might inspire you to strap an oxygen tank to your back and take to the depths yourself.

HEADACHE

Snow

MAXENCE FERMINE

Snow falls; flame-hair Snow steps light through air.
Bed of ice. Resting blind.
Mind pure.

See also: **Pain, being in**

HEMORRHOIDS

Downriver

IAIN SINCLAIR

If you suffer from hemorrhoids, it's unremitting agony. And we all know about those medical cures. Tie an elastic band around them till they drop off. Freeze them off. Have them amputated. Stuff them back into your arse. Ignore them. Walk around wanting to shove a cactus up your bum. Have colonic irrigation.

A more gentle cure is to read Iain Sinclair's novel *Downriver*. In twelve interwoven tales, stretching from the tragic sinking in the Thames of the *Princess Alice* in 1878, when 640 people drowned, to a near future in which the Thatcherite-style government policies of the "Widow" have inexorably destroyed life along London's river, Sinclair's enigmatic narrator takes us on a waterside tour. He travels mainly by foot—for Sinclair is the "walking author," renowned like Dickens for his London perambulations—and in the company of a motley collection of friends: actors, secondhand book dealers, tour guides. We visit a world of criminals and vagrants obsessed with the occult—a London that most of us know little about. His prose is dense and witty, sending your imagination ahead of your feet. Play it as an audiobook and walk as you listen. You'll be so well entertained that your mind will be taken off your bottom.

The Fit
PHILIP HENSHER

HICCUPS

Nobody knows what causes them, but we all have our own favorite method of curing them. John, the narrator of Philip Hensher's *The Fit* (in which a hiccup is designated by a "!"), has the hiccups for an entire month—starting the morning his wife, Janet, unexpectedly walks out.

He tries a litany of cures, from the classic (drinking a glass of water backward, holding his breath, drinking champagne) to the not so classic (smoking a cigarette, being tickled, kissing, snorting cocaine). Several shocks occur, quite by chance—including a German man with three rucksacks who turns up on his doorstep and announces he's in love with him. None of it works.

But then, finally, something does. You'll have to read to the end to find out what, but suffice it to say that, as with most literary afflictions, psychology has a lot to do with both cause and cure. And if this novel doesn't do the trick, we suggest you administer a short, sharp literary shock—the best of which are waiting to jump out at you from the pages of the novels below.

THE TEN BEST SHOCKING NOVELS

Guaranteed to deliver an ice cube down your back, these novels either accumulate shock as they go or pack a punch on a particular page. We're not telling which.

Señor Vivo and the Coca Lord................LOUIS DE BERNIÈRES
The Hunger Games.............................SUZANNE COLLINS
Gone Girl.................................... GILLIAN FLYNN
Schindler's Ark...................................THOMAS KENEALLY
The Painted Bird ....JERZY KOSINSKI
In One Person.......................................JOHN IRVING
Rosemary's Baby ....IRA LEVIN
The White Hotel ....D. M. THOMAS
Anna Karenina ....LEO TOLSTOY
Legend of a Suicide........................ DAVID VANN

HIGH BLOOD PRESSURE

Known to reduce anxiety, reading is a great habit to acquire if you've got high blood pressure—especially if you do it with a small furry animal curled up on your knee. Be careful what you choose, though—something too racy or nail-biting, and you'll be pumping the blood even harder than before. To slow you down, reduce anxiety, and encourage you to live in the moment, take your pick from our list of calming reads—novels that do not rush toward their resolutions, but luxuriate in nonevent and the virtues of the placid life. What they lack in pace they more than make up for in beauty and their ability to promote reflection.

See also: Stress · Workaholism

THE TEN BEST NOVELS TO
LOWER YOUR BLOOD PRESSURE

The Mezzanine...................................... NICHOLSON BAKER
A Closed Eye.. ANITA BROOKNER

HOMELESSNESS

Anywhere But Here
MONA SIMPSON
. . .
The House of Paper
CARLOS MARÍA
DOMÍNGUEZ
. . .
A House for Mr Biswas
V. S. NAIPAUL

If you're a vagabond at heart—or in reality—homelessness may at first have some appeal. Without being tied down to one particular place, you're free to go where the wind blows you; without rent or bills to pay, you can spend your time in non-laboring ways. But whatever its cause, the state of homelessness becomes exhausting after a while. Whether you are constantly on the road, living in a makeshift tepee exposed to the elements, or endeavoring to adapt to the habits of other people kind enough to take you in, the need for privacy, independence, and rootedness becomes impossible to ignore in the end.

For twelve-year-old Ann in Mona Simpson's spirited novel *Anywhere But Here*, homelessness brings with it a constant state of anxiety. After three short years of marriage, her mother, Adele, decides it's time to move on, and drives them both from Wisconsin to California on her abandoned husband's credit card—ostensibly so that Ann can "be a child star while [she is] still a child," but actually because being on the move is all Adele knows how to do. While they're waiting for their car to be fixed in Scottsdale, Arizona, Adele asks a real estate agent to show them a house. For a moment, Ann allows herself to believe her mother is serious, that this might be the place she can, at last, make her home. She starts to "breathe slower." But before she knows it they're back on the road again.

Ann understands far better than her mother that to develop and explore in normal adolescent ways, she needs stability and routine. If you spend all your energy looking for somewhere to sleep every night, how can you have energy for anything else?

Perhaps the answer is to build yourself a house. If you've got a big enough book collection, you could steal an idea from Carlos María Domínguez's novel *The House of Paper*. This delightful book about books begins at the scene of an accident: the narrator's friend Bluma has been hit by a car while engrossed in a volume of Emily Dickinson poems. While debate rages as to whether Bluma was killed by a car or by a poem, the narrator receives a mysterious parcel. Inside is a book encased in cement. It turns out to be a Joseph Conrad novel from the collection of an obsessive bibliophile named Carlos Brauer, who has lost his mind in the interstices between reality and fiction. (Beware his fate, readers—see: Read instead of live, tendency to.) Obsessed with the preservation of his twenty-thousand-strong collection, he decides to encase them in cement and build a book house.* Which all goes well—until he needs to find one of his books.

If you don't have enough books for such do-it-yourself measures, acquire *A House for Mr Biswas* by V. S. Naipaul instead. Set in the rich cultural melting pot of 1940s Trinidad, the story follows the young Mohun Biswas from cradle to grave as he searches for a place of his own. Biswas comes from a "family of nobodies," with no reason to hope for anything better than a life as an odd-job man. When, more by accident than design, he finds himself marrying into the vast and successful Hindi Tulsis family, he's guaranteed a roof over his head for the rest of his life. But in return, he has to contend with an entire extended network of in-laws at Hanuman House. Yet too sensitive to hold his own, he finds himself yearning for privacy and solitude.

Mr. Biswas gets his house in the end. His checkered journey will give you courage, and faith, that you too can find a roof of your own.

HOMESICKNESS

It's hard enough being homesick when you're away from home only temporarily. But what do you do when homesickness is your permanent state, and your native land lies at an enduring remove across the ocean?

Jhumpa Lahiri, born in England to Indian

The Namesake
JHUMPA LAHIRI
. . .
Brick Lane
MONICA ALI

---

* If you do the same, leave *The Novel Cure* out of it.

parents but raised in the United States, and Monica Ali, born in Bangladesh but raised in England, have written sensitive books dealing with this global longing. In Lahiri's *The Namesake*, the Ganguli family are the only Bengalis in their university town outside Boston. Being a foreigner, Mrs. Ganguli reflects, is "a sort of lifelong pregnancy—a perpetual wait, a constant burden, a continuous feeling out of sorts. It is an ongoing responsibility, a parenthesis in what had once been ordinary life, only to discover that that previous life has vanished, replaced by something more complicated and demanding." Her children will grow up to become unquestioningly American, but Mrs. Ganguli will always retain her hyphen.

In Ali's *Brick Lane*, Nazneen has left her village in Bangladesh for an arranged marriage in London to Chanu, an older Bangladeshi man with "a face like a frog." Though she misses her sister and her native land, Nazneen accepts her fate, having believed since childhood that "since nothing could be changed, everything had to be borne." But she doesn't find London terribly hard to bear; she adjusts, gives birth to two daughters, and gets used to her gossipy immigrant neighborhood. Only when Nazneen falls in love with a stranger does she think of returning to Bangladesh; and that is not because she wants to go "home"—she intuitively knows that "where she wanted to go was not a different place but a different time." Rather, she wants to escape the tumult of the love affair. It's Nazneen's husband, Chanu, whose nostalgia finally puts him on a plane back to Dhaka. He tells a London friend that Benglalis in England never really belong to their new country: "Their bodies are here but their hearts are back there," he proclaims. But Nazneen disagrees, and so do her daughters, for them, London is their true home. And that is the cure for homesickness that "Brick Lane" provides; the demostration of how, slowly, organically, even the most unfamiliar surroundings can evolve into the place where you belong. The cure for homesickness, in other words, is time.

See also: **Family, coping without** • **Foreign, being** • **Loneliness** • **Lost, being** • **Yearning, general**

HOMOPHOBIA

Maurice
E. M. FORSTER

Once, not so very long ago, homosexuality was seen as an aberration, a perversion, a sickness. Even though gay men and women enjoy greater acceptance and equality than ever before, homophobia is still very much alive—but the tables have turned: homophobia is now the sickness in need of correction. For those still harboring sexual prejudice—whether openly or in the dark recesses of their heart—we implore you to read *Maurice*, arguably the first modern novel dealing with homosexuality.

It is impossible not to be moved by this story of male love. From the first stirrings in Maurice's heart when he meets Clive Durham at Cambridge, to his initial refusal—both to himself and to Clive—of that love, any reader will recognize the tender connection and the gentle eroticism of their touch. Ultimately Maurice turns from inward self-loathing to outward fury at a world that won't allow him, and his deepest emotions, to be "normal." He finds himself increasingly surrounded by unenlightened, hateful souls—even Clive, who first enabled his love, but who becomes the worst oppressor of them all.

Share Maurice's sad joy at overcoming his own hypocrisy. Burn with his rage at the society in which he has to live with "the wrong words on his lips and the wrong desires in his heart." Ache with him at the devastating loneliness he's left with when Clive finally rejects him in disgust. And be thankful that we no longer live at a time when an author would not dare to publish this novel during his own lifetime. (It was published in 1913, after Forster's death.)

Maurice does not speak in euphemisms. If you are homophobic, you will have no choice but to confront your fears and prejudices and—hopefully—see that the characters are as human as us all.

See also: Hatred · Judgmental, being

HONEST, BEING TOO

See: Beans, temptation to spill the

HOPE, LOSS OF

Of Mice and Men
JOHN STEINBECK

We can cope with anything as long as we have hope. If you don't believe this, it's time for you to pick up Steinbeck's classic *Of Mice and Men*. George and Lennie are itinerant farm-hands. They arrive at a new ranch, "work up a stake," then go to town and blow it all. With no family, no home, nothing more to look forward to in life, they consider their kind to be the "loneliest guys in the world." Except that they are different—as George keeps telling Lennie. One day, he says, they will hit the jackpot and have enough money to buy themselves a little house and a few acres on which to keep a cow and some chickens and "live off the fatta the lan'." George loses his faith in this dream eventually, but continues to nurture it in Lennie. He knows life is easier with hope.

See also: **Broken dreams** • **Despair**

HORMONAL, BEING
See: **Adolescence** • **Cry, in need of a good** • **Menopause** • **PMS** • **Pregnancy** • **Teens, being in your** • **Tired and emotional, being**

HOSPITAL, BEING IN THE

When we're in the hospital, we desire the tender administrations of angels—or an escape to somewhere wild and woolly. Take your pick.

See also: **Boredom** • **Pain, being in**

THE TEN BEST NOVELS
TO READ IN THE HOSPITAL

ANGELS
Skellig .... DAVID ALMOND
Good Omens .... NEIL GAIMAN AND TERRY PRATCHETT

READING AILMENT   *Household chores, distracted by*

CURE   *Create a reading nook*

If there isn't a meal to cook, there's vacuuming to be done. And if the vacuuming's done, there's the bathroom to clean. If the bathroom is clean, there's the fridge to sort. And if the fridge has been sorted, it's probably time you went shopping. And when you come back, there'll be the laundry, the beds, the car washing, the garden, the recycling, the trash, and all the other myriad tasks that living in a house demands. What hope is there for one dreaming of a precious hour tucked away with a book?

Create a cozy reading nook—a dedicated space where you go to read. This should be in a small and enclosed corner of your house or garden—an alcove, a study, behind the curtains in a large bay window. The important thing is that when you are nestled inside it, you cannot see anything that needs your attention.

Make your nook deliciously warm and inviting. If you like to curl up on the floor, fill it with cushions and a furry rug. If you prefer to stretch out, treat yourself to an elegant chaise longue.

(continued)

You'll need good lighting in your nook, a soft blanket, socks or slippers, and a flat surface on which to put some books, your reading journal, a pencil, and a cup of tea. Keep earplugs in there, and a set of headphones for audiobooks. Hang a sign at the entrance to your nook gently dissuading others from visiting—unless they, too, want to crawl inside and read.

Once inside your nook, forget about the chores. Take your hour with your book. With luck, someone might see you in there and do the chores instead.

HOUSEWIFE, BEING A

Little Children
TOM PERROTTA

· · ·

House-Bound
WINIFRED PECK

· · ·

Diary of a Mad Housewife
SUE KAUFMAN

· · ·

The Stepford Wives
IRA LEVIN

· · ·

The Ten-Year Nap
MEG WOLITZER

On the surface, you're the perfect wife and mother—content to stay at home and look after your spouse and children. But are your cleaning products shelved in alphabetical order? Do you have unnaturally gleaming grapefruit spoons? Do you dress like a belly dancer to greet your husband at the door when he returns from work? If so, all is not well underneath. Perhaps you find you need to self-medicate with a shot of vodka before you pick up the kids in the afternoon. And that you are just a bit too obsessed with plumping your scatter cushions. You could be suffering from being a housewife in the clinical sense and need to draw from our Valu-Pak of cures to wrench yourself away from the kitchen sink.

For Sarah, a young mother (and grad school dropout) in the 1990s in Tom Perrotta's *Little Children*, being a stay-at-home mom fills her with anxiety. As she halfheartedly joins in the chatter with other mothers about their various levels of exhaustion and the eating habits of their offspring, she tries to transcend the tedium of her child-bound days by pretending inwardly that she's an anthropologist, the Margaret Mead of the modern American playground scene. "I'm a researcher studying the behavior of boring suburban women. I am not a boring suburban woman myself," she tells herself. Might this strategy work for you? Or does it hit too close to home?

To ponder the burdens of domesticity at a soothingly distant remove, pick up Winifred Peck's 1942 novel *House-Bound*. Rose, the privileged heroine, had "never washed a vegetable" in her life, until the Second World War brought a national shortage of servants. Lacking a scullery maid, Rose must learn to run the house herself. Chaos ensues. As she becomes increasingly enslaved by domestic duties, Rose comes to realize that we are all housebound, not just within our four walls, but "tethered inexorably to a collection of all the extinct memories like bits of domestic furniture, inspected and dusted daily." You might appreciate the freedom she eventually finds for herself, if not the means by which she comes by it.

Come the sexual revolution several decades on, the comparatively carefree Manhattan hausfrau Bettina "Tina" Balser, in *Diary of a Mad Housewife*, has a mental meltdown even if her life looks hunky-dory to outsiders. She has a maid, a handsome husband, and can float around all day drinking cocktails if she likes. But she's dissatisfied all the same, and takes to keeping a journal to vent her frustrations and stay sane. "What I really am and have been since midsummer is paralyzed," she writes. To fill the emptiness, Tina takes up a lover, the appalling George, an A-list celebrity. Meanwhile, her husband, Jonathan, is having a fling of his own, and things at his job are going down the tube. Like the cockroaches trapped inside the clock face in Bettina's kitchen, squeezed between the two hands, the couple seem doomed to a slow, suffocating marital death. Luckily, they realize what is happening in time.

Breaking free of the husband as well as the house is the only answer for the female inhabitants of *The Stepford Wives*. Ira Levin's 1972 novel is a terrifying exploration of what could happen if all the men in a small American town were to conspire to transform their spouses into their idea of the perfect wife. By chance, the characters have the necessary technical and practical expertise at their disposal to do just this. We all know what happens next—but it still makes for thrilling reading.

These days, it's the liberated women—more than their husbands—who are likely to impose wifely transformations on themselves. Meg Wolitzer's funny and poignant novel *The Ten-Year Nap* describes just such a woman. Amy Lamb has opted out of her law career to become an unimpeachable mom and housewife. She toys with the idea of going back to work—an idea her husband fully endorses—but the longer she stays out of the fray, the more she fears reentering it. When she finally snaps herself out of her domestic trance, she finds, to her relief, that "it was a pleasure, an honor, weirdly, just to be working." The old Amy hadn't gone away; it had just been buried under velveteen rabbits, mops, and coupons for a while.

So when the sippy cups become too much, do not fill them with booze and try to drink away your homebody blues. Remember that, unlike women of the past, you have a permanent ticket out of the nursery, and the children will be leaving it before long anyway. These novels will remind you that, once the children can dress themselves, you will be able to extricate the woman you once were from the mom and cutlery polisher you have become. Still, you may have to give yourself a gentle maternal nudge to be reminded to untie those apron strings.

See also: Boredom · Dissatisfaction · Household chores, distracted by

HUMILITY, LACK OF

See: Arrogance

HUMORLESSNESS

Everybody's funny bone requires a different trigger. Use this list to help find what sets you off.

See also: Grumpiness · Killjoy, being a · Querulousness

THE TEN BEST NOVELS TO MAKE YOU LAUGH

Lucky Jim	KINGSLEY AMIS
Bridget Jones's Diary	HELEN FIELDING
Tom Jones	HENRY FIELDING
Home Land	SAM LIPSYTE
Gentlemen Prefer Blondes	ANITA LOOS

HUNGER

Hunger
KNUT HAMSUN

In those days when you wander about hungry in a strange city that no one leaves before it sets its mark on him; when you consider, by force of habit, whether you have anything to look forward to today; when you realize you have not a single krone in your pocket, you must seek out Knut Hamsun and you will find yourself so energized by this novel that you will be able to see everything in sharp and perfect detail and have no question that the mere appetite of your body is necessary to satisfy, but that the nobility of your mind is incalculably more important. If only you might sit down and write a treatise on philosophy, a three-part article that you can sell to the paper for probably ten krone; if only you will sit and write it now on a park bench in the sun, then you will have the money to buy a decent meal. Or, alternatively, pawn your jacket, your waistcoat, for one krone fifty ore. Just make sure you don't leave your pencil in the pocket, like the unnamed hero of Hamsun's novel does, as then you will never be able to write your article, which will not only earn you money but will help the youth of the city to live in a better way. You're only pawning it, of course, because it is getting a bit tight for you, and you will pick it up again in a few days' time, when your article is published. Then you can give a few krone to the man on the street with the bundle in his hands who hasn't eaten for many, many days, and who made you cry because you could not give him a five-krone piece. Of course, you haven't eaten either, and your stomach will not hold down ordinary food anymore as it has been empty for too long. Though don't forget that you gave that ten-krone note that you felt was wrongly yours to the cake seller, you thrust it into her hands and she had no idea why, and perhaps you can go to her stall and demand some cakes that were paid for on account, so to speak. The police might pick you up as you are out in the early hours of the morning, lacking a place to stay—but, then, how could you wish for anything more than an excellent, clean, dry cell? The police believe, of course, that you are really a man of good character and principles, who has merely been locked out of his house and has plenty of money at home. You can use this experience and write all about it in your next article that you can sell to the paper, and it may even make fifteen krone; and, of course, there is your play, the one you just need to clinch that elusive last act of, and if this is published, you will never have to worry about money again. Before this, you will arrive at the joyful insanity hunger brings, and be empty and free of pain.

READING AILMENT *Hype, put off by*

CURE *Put the book in its place*

Sometimes a book generates so much buzz in the press—perhaps it has won a major award, or the author is particularly young or good looking—that you are bored of it by the time you get around to reading it. You've read so many reviews that you feel you know the book already. And you're too sullied by everyone else's opinion to have any hope of forming your own.

The best way to give such a book a chance is to store it in your garden shed, greenhouse, or garage. You might also like to re-cover it in a piece of leftover wallpaper, some Christmas wrapping paper, a brown paper bag, or silver foil. And when taking a break from watering the tomatoes one day, pick it up and start to read. The unexpected, unbookish surroundings will bring an air of humility to the book, counteracting the hype, and encourage you to come to it with a more generous and open mind.

HYPOCHONDRIA

The Secret Garden
FRANCES HODGSON
BURNETT

Reading *The Secret Garden* serves as a polite reminder that many of our ailments are, in fact, fictional.

Young Colin, confined to his bedroom since birth, is convinced there is a lump on his back that will, eventually, lead to an early demise. Of course, there is no lump, unless you count the vertebrae of his spine. His caregivers have encouraged him to believe he is deformed, doomed never to grow to adulthood, and that fresh air is poison to his blood. Mary, his spoiled cousin, just as capable of throwing tantrums and ordering others around as he is, will have none of it. The only person brave enough to tell Colin that there's nothing wrong with him, she matches his rage at his presumed fate with her own fury at his inertia. Only a fierce little girl hell-bent on bringing her secret garden to life can pierce the bubble of Colin's terror and show him the truth.

Mary's passion for the garden lures Colin out of his sick chamber into the world of buds and birds—a world also inhabited by freckled, irresistible Dickon, the quintessence of health. Let this novel lure you from your bed to find your own secret garden—maybe even your own Dickon—and a lusty return to tip-top health.

See also: **Anxiety** · **Cold, common** · **Dying** · **Man flu**

I

IDENTITY CRISIS

Who are you, reader? A parent, a professional, a student, a child? Are you always yourself, or do you have two selves: one you show only to certain people, one you show to everyone else? Or do you feel that the "real" you has never seen the light of day at all?

Literature is stuffed to the gills with people having identity crises, whether through memory loss, psychiatric breakdown, or more inexplicable processes. The narrator of *I'm Not Stiller*, by the Swiss postwar writer Max Frisch, persistently denies accusations that he is the missing sculptor Anatol Stiller. And indeed, according to his passport, his name is James White. But friends, acquaintances, and even his wife repeatedly identify

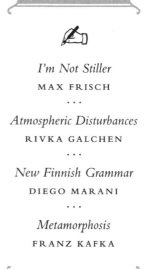

I'm Not Stiller
MAX FRISCH
. . .
Atmospheric Disturbances
RIVKA GALCHEN
. . .
New Finnish Grammar
DIEGO MARANI
. . .
Metamorphosis
FRANZ KAFKA

him as Stiller—a conundrum that confounds us as much as White (or should we say Stiller). As the truth gradually emerges, we are given a rare glimpse into the fragility of our relationship to ourselves.

Rivka Galchen's novel *Atmospheric Disturbances* flips Frisch's conceit. A psychiatrist in New York named Dr. Leo Liebenstein has convinced himself that his wife, Rema, has disappeared . . . and been replaced with an exact replica of herself. He doesn't think *he* has an identity crisis; he thinks *she* does. In other words, he makes his crisis hers. "It was a little uncanny, the feeling I had, looking at that look-alike," he muses. The "impostress," as he calls her, continues to come to Leo's home every day as if it were hers (which she maintains it is) and insists that she is the "missing" person. Leo refuses to believe her, even though she resembles his wife in every particular. She has the same "hayfeverishly fresh" shampoo, the "same baby blue coat with jumbo charcoal buttons, same tucking behind ears of dyed cornsilk blonde hair," Leo concedes. "Same everything, but it wasn't Rema. It was just a feeling, that's how I knew." Leo scours the streets of New York looking for the woman he believes has vanished, and when New York fails to produce her, he decides to journey to Argentina, her native land, and hunt for her in Patagonia. Galchen's story is Borgesian and intriguing: it hints at the constructed nature of identity. On some level, all of us must invent who we are. And if the results don't convince ourselves or others, we can labor to build a more satisfactory self.

If both of these novels suggest that it might be wise to carry more than a passport to identify yourself, Diego Marani's *New Finnish Grammar* certainly ups the urgency of doing so. A man is found clubbed nearly to death in Trieste during the Second World War. The Finnish name tag on his clothes proclaims him to be Sampo Karjalainen, but when the man regains consciousness, he has no memory of who he is—and no language. A Finnish doctor is among the passengers on the hospital ship where the man ends up, and he begins to rewire Finnish into the man's brain, complete with its fiendishly complicated grammar and consonant-rich words. But what if this man wasn't really Finnish in the first place? What will he become in a different language? What is it that makes him himself? In the end it's the new relationships that he forges on the boat that reveal his identity to himself.

But if you *are* ever unlucky enough to lose your identity completely, the best cure you can get your pincers around is *Metamorphosis* by Franz Kafka. Traveling salesman Gregor Samsa wakes up one morning to discover he has turned into a giant cockroach. He is disgusting not only to himself but to his entire family, and though Gregor tries to continue his life as it was before, it becomes increasingly difficult. Eating is challenging, communication impossible, basic hygiene ever more compromised. Gregor slowly sinks into an empty but peaceful, ruminative state as he starves to death.

Count your blessings that, even if you don't know who you are, you are at least human. Admire your fingers, toes, the tip of your nose. Revel in the use of your limbs. Read the last paragraph of Kafka's masterpiece aloud, and enjoy the fact that your voice is not the terrifying rasping of an insect. Celebrate your humanity—whoever it may belong to.

See also: **Identity, unsure of your reading**

READING AILMENT   *Identity, unsure of your reading*

CURE   *Create a favorites shelf*

If you feel you have forgotten—or perhaps you have never known—what sort of books are *your* sort of books, and as a result find yourself unable to choose what to read next, we suggest that you keep a favorites shelf. Select ten books that fill you with warmth, nostalgia, a flutter of nervous excitement. If some of these are favorites from your childhood, all the better. Make these, the ones that beckon you, your standard. Put them on a special shelf in the room in which you tend to do your reading or where you will pass them every day. If possible, reread them (or at least parts of them). They will remind you of what you love most in literature, and—if your reading life has been rich—of who you are. Next time you feel unsure of what to read next, use your favorites shelf as a guide and gentle nudge to your literary soul. It will tell you the answers to questions you didn't even know you had.

IDIOT, FEELING LIKE AN

The room goes quiet, and you find yourself the focus of a sea of faces. It dawns on you that you're the only one who doesn't understand what's wrong with what you've just said. Then someone starts to laugh, and one by one the others join in.

The Idiot
FYODOR
DOSTOYEVSKY

You feel a hot flush take over your face (see: Blushing), followed by a blood-draining sense of shame (see: Shame). They're not laughing with you, but *at* you.

We've all been there. Feeling like an idiot is almost as inevitable as falling in love. In fact, being an idiot is not necessarily a bad thing.* The gentle prince Lev Myshkin in Dostoyevsky's *The Idiot* is an idiot in a social rather than an intellectual sense, standing outside society because he has no comprehension of its mechanisms: money, status, small talk, the subtle intricacies of daily life are all obscure to him. But when we readers think about Prince Lev, it is not with any sense of disparagement, but with absolute fondness and love. Indeed, everyone who encounters the prince in the novel is both exasperated by him and deeply enamored of his profound understanding of a version of reality that most of us do not see.

Next time the room falls silent around you, remember the prince. Look everyone back in the eye, and anticipate affection instead. You'll probably get it.

See also: Failure, feeling like a

IGNORANCE
See: Homophobia • Idiot, feeling like an • Racism • Xenophobia

Indecision
BENJAMIN KUNKEL

INDECISION

Are you inclined to get yourself tied up in knots whenever you are called upon to make a decision? Do you see things from everybody else's point of view except your own? Do you drive yourself and your friends crazy as you bounce between a plethora of paths, unable to choose or commit to any one of them? If so, you

---

* While falling in love, with the wrong person at least, frequently is. See: Love, unrequited; and Love, doomed.

are not alone. You're suffering from the quintessential ailment of our age: indecisiveness. Because never before has there been more choice—and yet never have we been more paralyzed.

Dwight Wilmerding, the twenty-eight-year-old slacker hero of Ben Kunkel's novel *Indecision,* finds that he can't "think of the future until [he's] arrived there"—a quality shared by many indecisive types. Underemployed, halfhearted about his girlfriend Vaneetha, he makes decisions on whether or not to accept invitations by flipping a coin—the only way to ensure that his "whole easy nature" doesn't end up seeing him doing everybody else's bidding. Meanwhile, decisions continue to be made for him. His employers at the pharmaceutical company where he works give him the boot, and when his old school friend Natasha invites him—in a suggestive sort of way—to join her in Ecuador, he goes. And, unsurprisingly, when his friend Dan offers him a new trial drug, Abulinix, which promises to cure him of his indecision, he embraces the gemlike blue capsule. Only after gleefully ingesting it is he told that it has some interesting side effects: satyriasis, or an excessive desire in males to copulate, and potentiating alcohol, meaning that once in the bloodstream, one drink becomes two.

Perhaps because of the wonder drug, or perhaps not, things take quite a turn in Ecuador. Even better than Natasha, he finds the beautiful and highly politicized Brigid, who speaks in alluringly foreign tones. Whether it is the Abulinix or the psyche-altering hallucinogenic they take in the jungle—or, in fact, a fundamental shift of consciousness—Dwight begins to make proactive choices for the first time in his life.

Take this novel with you, go find your Abulinix and/or your Brigid and/or your jungle drug equivalent, and be prepared to wake up to a newly decisive life. Or, on the other hand, don't.

See also: **Starting, fear of** • **Vacation, not knowing what novels to take on**

INDIFFERENCE
See: Apathy

INFATUATION

Les Enfants Terribles

JEAN COCTEAU

There is nothing so heady, so sweet, or so intoxicating as being in the throes of a serious crush. Whoever your love object, to be lost in the admiration of a fellow being is one of the most absorbing and deliriously pleasurable ways to lose great chunks of your life. But for all the pleasure of this state, there is a price to pay. The love object may well not feel the same way, for one thing. And by its very nature, infatuation is blind to practicalities. It is an unreasoned, extravagant love, feeding off itself more than off the returned affections of the love recipient (see also: Love, unrequited). And though not as dangerous as obsession, it can be a precursor to this state, rendering the sufferer incapable of seeing his or her own folly and the inadequacies of his or her object.

Cocteau's enigmatic little novel is a paradigm of intoxication. It illustrates a perfectly puzzling love maze, in which a brother and sister score points by transferring their infatuation with each other to other young men and women, then back again. Paul and Elisabeth nurse their mother in a Parisian apartment with one huge room (rather like a stage). Eventually, they are left alone there, with their imaginations and neuroses to grow like hothouse flowers. At school, Paul had been infatuated with Dargelos, a beautiful boy who threw a snowball at him with a stone inside it. This sends the delicate Paul to bed for several weeks, where as an invalid enjoying the "sweet delights of sickness," he learns to love his sister a little too much. On recovery he meets Agathe (who closely resembles Dargelos), and Paul transfers his infatuation to her. Meanwhile, Paul and Elisabeth have perfected "the Game," a means of deepening their relationship by wounding each other in a series of circling conversational attacks. As their mutual infatuation becomes more extreme, they withdraw from the world into a make-believe existence where all that matters is the Game.

It cannot but end badly—it is all too heady, too intense, and prismatically refractive. And it's only a matter of time before we hear the shatter. If you are in the throes of a similarly intense infatuation, switch the object of your fascination from life to the page. Cocteau was known in artistic circles of his time (whose members included Picasso, Modigliani, Proust, and Gide) as the "frivolous prince," and inspired infatuation many times himself. His sensual prose and mercurial imagination are equally ravishing. He wrote *Les Enfants*

Terribles during a period of withdrawal from opium, and you can feel the call of the author's blood for the drug in each heightened sentence. "The world owes its enchantment to . . . curious creatures and their fancies," he muses. "Thistledown spirits, tragic, heartrending in their evanescence, they must go blowing headlong to perdition."

Don't let yourself be blown to perdition by currents of whimsical desire. The pleasure to be found in aesthetic heights will last forever; your mortal crush will not.

See also: **Disenchantment** • **Lovesickness** • **Lust** • **Obsession**

INNOCENCE, LOSS OF

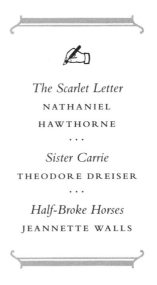

The Scarlet Letter
NATHANIEL
HAWTHORNE

· · ·

Sister Carrie
THEODORE DREISER

· · ·

Half-Broke Horses
JEANNETTE WALLS

Breathe a sigh of relief: Hester Prynne, the disgraced unmarried mother of Nathaniel Hawthorne's novel *The Scarlet Letter*, is dead. That is to say, she never existed, of course, being fictional. And the misfortune of being vilified as Hester was—for having a baby but no wedding ring—is much rarer today than it was when Hester's woeful story took place four centuries ago. The current age is, on the whole, a better moment for the cheeky "sadder but wiser" girl who is as good, or as bad, as she wants to be and doesn't spend much time worrying what church elders might think of her behavior.

Still, if you've been fretting remorsefully that you're naughtier than most or if you're pining for the simplicity of your younger, better-behaved years, read Theodore Dreiser's *Sister Carrie* to remind yourself why you shouldn't (necessarily) bemoan your experience or give too much thought to what others think of your conduct. Dreiser's flowing, disapproving sermon of a novel about a girl who leaves rural Wisconsin and goes to Chicago (and, later, New York) to make something of herself will likely make your blood boil, stirring you to defend assertive women and giving you strength to flout the opinion of moralizers who would pin your wings.

"When a girl leaves her home at eighteen, she does one of two things," Dreiser warns. "Either she falls into saving hands and becomes better, or she rapidly assumes the cosmopolitan standard of virtue and becomes worse." Oh, puh-*leeze*. Dreiser's writing is so beguiling and enveloping, and so fascinatingly evocative of a now vanished social world, that you will get sucked into his storytelling and want to read every page to see how Carrie's reinvention progresses. But unlike the author, you will likely applaud his heroine's transformation into a more interesting, audacious, fulfilled person. As a star of the New York stage rather than an unremarkable chaste drudge on a nameless farm, Carrie inarguably become less pure, but who can blame her?

For another take, read Jeannette Walls's gutsy and refreshingly pragmatic novel *Half-Broke Horses*. Rosemary escapes hardscrabble beginnings to become a teacher and daredevil horse racer on ranches in the American West. Her sister, Helen, is prettier but has less self-confidence. While struggling to make it as an actress in California, Helen succumbs to the wiles of a "series of cads." Worrying that her sister is headed down the wrong path, Rosemary writes letters to her, "warning her not to count on men to take care of her and to come up with a fallback plan." When, as Rosemary has foreseen, Helen gets pregnant, she runs to her sister's side, despairing at her ruined reputation. Watching her sister's tear-streaked face as she sleeps, Rosemary has no inclination to blame her for her lost innocence: she thinks she looks "like an angel, a slightly bloated, pregnant angel, but an angel nonetheless." Rosemary rejects the idea that loss of innocence is an irrecoverable tragedy; but Helen is much harder on herself, with tragic consequences. Reading about the attitudes of these sisters will show you the error of judging yourself or others too harshly for the messy missteps that we humans—male and female—so often make; simple accidents that don't deserve the brand of "shame."

INSANITY

See: Madness

INSOMNIA

Everyone suffers from insomnia occasionally. But if you suffer from it nightly, it can wreak havoc on your relationship, your career, and your ability to get through the day. It traps you in a vicious circle, the problem feeding on itself. As your level of exasperation rises with your accumulating fatigue, nothing is more likely to stop you from sleeping than the anxiety that you might not be able to sleep.

The House of Sleep
JONATHAN COE
. . .
The Book of Disquiet
FERNANDO PESSOA

Insomniacs often turn to reading as a way to endure those lonely wee hours. We heartily agree that there is no better way to spend this otherwise wasted time. Jonathan Coe's *The House of Sleep* is one invaluable tool for exploring your sleeplessness, but it should not be read at night unless you are prepared to accept that you will be up until dawn—despite its title, the novel is far from peaceful. Pick it up during the day, when you are wide awake and prepared for a thorough analysis of why you can't get to sleep.

The novel is divided into six parts, each representing the various stages of sleep, and follows four loosely connected characters who each have a different issue with sleep. Sarah is a narcoleptic whose dreams are so vivid that she can't tell the difference between them and real life. Terry, a budding film critic, sleeps a minimum of fourteen hours a day because he is addicted to dreams of such "near-paradisal loveliness." Gregory, Sarah's boyfriend, becomes a psychiatrist at a sleep clinic and begins self-experimenting with sleeplessness for scientific purposes, believing it to be a disease that must be conquered. Robert—at first seemingly the most normal of the four—becomes so obsessed with Sarah that he puts himself through a dramatic transformation in order to inveigle his way into her life, and bed. With lustrous technical detail sure to fascinate the sleep deprived, this novel may offer some ideas for practical cures as well.

The novel to reach for in those restless hours, on the other hand, is *The Book of Disquiet*, the plotless journal of Bernardo Soares, assistant accountant at Vasques and Co. on the Rua dos Douradores—a job "about as demanding as an afternoon nap." Soares both despairs and celebrates the monotony of his humdrum life because he recognizes that everything he thinks and feels exists only as a "negation of and flight from" his job. And what thoughts and feelings they are! Because Soares, a man in possession of a face so bland that it causes him terrible dismay when he sees it in an office photograph, is a dreamer, his attention always divided by what is actually going on and the flights of fancy in his head.

For his disappointment in himself, his dreaminess, his constantly breaking heart, it's impossible not to fall in love with Soares. Quiet, unobtrusive, plaintive, constantly drowsy, a man who, though prone to nostalgia and bouts of desolation, is not immune to joy, he is the perfect nighttime companion. Pondering whether life is in fact "the waking insomnia of [our] dreams," Soares thinks a lot about sleep—in fact, he barely discriminates between sleeping and wakefulness.

Besides all this, nowhere in literature are the rhythms of prose more attuned to the lumbering gait of the sleepless hours. If your eyelids start to droop as you read, Soares won't mind. You can pick up your conversation with him, wherever you left off, tomorrow night.

See also: Depression, general • Exhaustion • Irritability • Stress • Tired and emotional, being

INTERNET ADDICTION

Wolf Solent
JOHN COWPER POWYS

What have we become? We are a race that sits, by our millions, for hours and days and years on end, gazing in solitary rapture at our screens, lost to a netherworld of negligible reality. Even though we may get up from time to time to eat, sleep, make love, or have a cup of coffee, our computers and smartphones call to us like sirens to come back, interact, update, reload. Like moths drawn to brightness and warmth, we seem unable to resist—even though our eyes are strained, our backs are sore, and our ability to focus is shorn. Sometimes it can seem as if life is more compelling on our screens than off them.

Our cure for this most deplorable of modern ailments is one that will require you to turn your back on life for a few hours more: the mystical, delightfully eccentric John Cowper Powys novel *Wolf Solent*. Set in a West Country already familiar to fans of Thomas Hardy, it is a densely written—but worthwhile—tome. Once you discover JCP, as we shall call him, you'll want to chuck your monitor into the nearest Dumpster and go and live out the rest of your days among the birds and the bees.

Wolf Solent opens with the eponymous hero—an unprepossessing thirty-five-year-old with "goblinish" features—making an escape from London, where he's been chained to a dull teaching job for ten years. He's returning to the town of his childhood, where he will reconnect with his own "furtive inner life." At Wolf's core is what he calls his "personal mythology," a sort of mystical place he goes to connect with nature, and from the moment he catches his first whiff, from the train, of the smells of a Dorset spring morning—fresh green shoots, muddy ditches, primroses on a grassy bank—his "real life" begins again. He experiences what he describes as an "intoxicating enlargement of personality" that draws its power from nature itself.

It's heady stuff—and becomes more so. Soon after Wolf arrives and takes up his new job as researcher for the malicious squire Urquhart, he falls in love with two women at once: the "maddeningly desirable" Gerda, who can imitate the song of a blackbird, and Christie, who shares his passion for books. As Wolf struggles to find a way to love them both, he chases after the bodily sensations that make him feel alive. It's impossible to resist his raw, ecstatic response to the natural world, and through his eyes you will come to see the animal energy in other people. As a way of rediscovering how to live in the world again—sensually, sexually, with the full engagement of mind and body—it can't be beaten. And perhaps, like Wolf, being surrounded by all that vegetable efflorescence will soothe your eyes, strengthen your back, and, most crucially, return your fractured brain to full capacity.

See also: **Antisocial, being** • **Concentrate, inability to**

IRRITABILITY

The Blackwater Lightship
COLM TÓIBÍN

Where someone is being irritable, you can be sure there's another, unexpressed emotion lurking, iceberglike, beneath the surface.

In *The Blackwater Lightship*, Irish writer Colm Tóibín dissects the bitterness and hurt that have set in between three generations of narrator Helen's family—grandmother Mrs. Devereux, mother Lily, and daughter Helen—since Helen's father died many years earlier.

When Helen hears that her brother Declan is dying of AIDS, she has to break the news to their estranged mother, Lily. And when they decide to take Declan to their grandmother's house in Blackwater, Helen is thrust back into a world she had hoped never to revisit. The knives are out between Lily and Helen before they've even arrived, and once they are all shut up in the small, stuffy house, the barbed comments really start flying. Amid their petty accusations and bitter recollections, Declan lies dying, the catalyst of all their arguments, yet the only one not drawn in. Luckily, Declan's two loyal friends are present—the talkative Larry, the coolly direct Paul—who take the women aside, one by one, and encourage them to vent their feelings. By the end of the novel, all involved have a much clearer understanding of one another's grievances.

Don't wait for a crisis to force your irritability to the surface. If you or someone you know is prone to irritation, invite a couple of patient, understanding friends into the mix and talk your icebergs out of the water.

See also: Anger · Dissatisfaction · Grumpiness · Querulousness

IRRITABLE BOWEL SYNDROME

See: Constipation · Diarrhea · Nausea · Pain, being in

ITCHY FEET

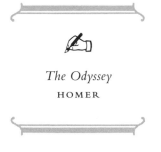

The Odyssey
HOMER

The urge to be constantly on the move is both virtue and folly. While we may gain insight and maturity from constant change and new experiences, we risk polluting our fragile environment and becoming a stone that has gathered no moss. For how do we build a life in multiple places? One needs to commit to a place in order to put down roots (see also: Commitment, fear of), fertilize relationships, and come into flower. To soothe and still your itchy feet, therefore, we recommend a chapter of *The Odyssey* every morning, taken after your shower and before your breakfast. It will invigorate your circulation and satiate your desire for travel.

Odysseus himself is an inveterate sufferer of itchy feet. King of Ithaca, he left his island home ten years before the action begins, in order to fight the Trojan War. Now he sets off back to Penelope, his wife, and his small but significant sovereignty. But it'll be another decade before he feels the soil of Ithaca under his well-worn sandals. He is held captive for years by the sea nymph Calypso. The Cyclops Polyphemus keeps him in a cave, along with his men and ovine herd, for some time before Odysseus cunningly blinds his jailer. He is regularly at the mercy of an enraged Poseidon, who sends storms that wash him and his crew up on the island of Circe, where they are all turned temporarily into pigs.

But, frankly, the gods alone cannot be blamed for all his meanderings. Many of his diversions are self-induced—such as when Odysseus foolishly shouts his name to Polyphemus, triggering Poseidon's pursuit of him in the first place. In the end, after twenty years of tardiness, Odysseus returns just in time to save his wife from an enforced remarriage.

Don't let your life go by in your absence. By the time you finish reading this ancient epic, meandering in its adventures but introspective in nature, you will have had enough vicarious travels to last a lifetime. Now get on with life in the place where you are.

See also: **Dissatisfaction** • **Happiness, searching for** • **Jump ship, desire to** • **Wanderlust**

ITCHY TEETH

If you've never even heard of this ailment, you've clearly never met the long-suffering hero of Saul Bellow's *Henderson the Rain King*. Because Gene Henderson—a fifty-five-year-old millionaire with big, "blustering" ways, a large nose, and more children than he can remember the names of—has had itchy teeth all his life. In fact, all his

Henderson the Rain King
SAUL BELLOW

pain, physical and emotional (and there's a lot of it), congregates in his teeth. When he's angry, his gums ache. When he's faced with heartbreaking beauty, his teeth itch. And when his wives, his girls, his children, his farm, his animals, his habits, his money, his violin lessons, his drunkenness, his brutality, his hemorrhoids, his fainting fits, his face, his soul, and—yes—his teeth all start giving him grief at once, he decides to gate-crash his friend Charlie's honeymoon in Africa, and from there go "in country," to find himself.

It doesn't work. What he finds is the same blustering fifty-five-year-old millionaire he left behind. And what's more, while he's away he breaks the bridge at the side of his mouth, ruining many dollars worth of complicated dentistry and leaving him spitting fragments of artificial molar into his hand.

Itchy teeth is a rare complaint, but it has its sufferers—and not just in Bellow novels. Those afflicted experience almost unbearable torment. The only thing that can drive a person madder than the itch of the teeth itself is having everyone else doubt their dental woes. This uproarious battering ram of a novel will elicit sympathy for those afflicted at last.

J

JAM, BEING IN A

Jams come in many flavors, hues, and consistencies, but they do not get any stickier than that of Pi Patel, who finds himself stranded on a lifeboat at sea with a zebra, a hyena, an orangutan, and a three-year-old Bengal tiger. The young hero of Yann Martel's Booker Prize–winning novel *Life of Pi* is under no delusions about how dangerous the tiger is (for soon it's just him and the tiger, the laws of natural selection swiftly dispatching the other three). And when he and the tiger first confront each other, the tiger with its eyes blazing, its ears "laid tight to its head," and its fangs and talons drawn, Pi's response is to throw himself back overboard and sweat it out in the sea.

Which is the correct response. As is building a raft alongside the lifeboat so that he and the 450-pound carnivore can occupy separate quarters. But it's what he does next that wins our admiration. Spotting the tiger's weakness—seasickness—he draws on the training skills he acquired by osmosis in his father's zoo and wages a battle of minds with the tiger that reduces the magnificent creature to a state of begrudging obedience. The face-off that clinches the boy's authority is the best staring contest in literature. Keep this novel at hand whenever you are attempting to find a way out of your own

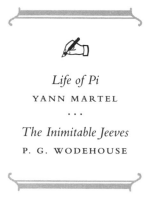

Life of Pi
YANN MARTEL
. . .

The Inimitable Jeeves
P. G. WODEHOUSE

(we hope, less sticky) jams. The potential for mastery in even so slight and hungry a boy as Pi is inspiring.

For those facing jams of the social variety—finding yourself backed into a corner from which there's no dignified escape, for example—we recommend a companion in the mold of Jeeves, the valet in the novels of P. G. Wodehouse. If you can't afford a real one, the fictional one will do. This smooth-tongued, eyebrow-raising valet, as well versed in Dostoyevsky as he is with the right way to wear a scarlet cummerbund,* is forever getting the hapless Bertie Wooster out of scrapes. Rich in status but poor in good sense and sound judgment, Wooster knows he wouldn't survive a day without Jeeves or his curative cups of tea—although he'd never admit it.

Whenever things get hairy, hit too many snags, or start to bubble too fast—be it with a tiger or something slightly more commonplace—imagine what Pi or Jeeves would do, and adjust the temperature accordingly.

See also: **Stuck in a rut**

JEALOUSY

Venus in Furs
LEOPOLD VON
SACHER-MASOCH

Unlike envy, which is the coveting of something another person has, jealousy is the tendency to torture oneself with the thought that someone else may take what you have. This results in an urge to cling ever more tightly to what you have, becoming needy and insecure and full of fury at the potential absconder. Blind to reason, it's a supremely destructive force, and if left unchecked will eat away at your self-esteem and ultimately prevent you from having a healthy relationship with the thing you guard with such desperation. Whether it's jealousy among siblings for parental attention (see: Sibling rivalry), jealousy over a promotion at work, or jealousy over a suspected rival in love, those in the grip of this affliction would do well to recognize that they are more likely to lose their love object than those free of its taint. Luckily, jealousy—of whatever sort—is self-inflicted, and the person who has created it also has the power to spirit it away.

* Don't.

Our cure, Leopold von Sacher-Masoch's *Venus in Furs*, shows very clearly the self-inflicted nature of jealousy. Unique for its time (the novel was published in 1870), *Venus in Furs* explores the lure of sexual subjugation. One afternoon after dozing off in front of a magnificent painting entitled *Venus in Furs*, the narrator and his friend Severin share a dream about this deity, and both admit to their predilection for beauty dressed in haughtiness. Our narrator picks up Severin's memoir, which we then read over his shoulder. It describes Severin's relationship to a woman named Wanda—Venus's mortal embodiment. Wanda is a cruel and beautiful tyrant of a woman who alternately loves Severin unreservedly—entertaining him, philosophizing with him, titillating him—and then abusing him, whipping him, locking him up, calling him her slave, and taunting him with her interest in other men.

Severin laps it all up. When she talks about another lover, Severin is seized with passion—a "sweet madness"—and when we realize that he gave up on a far more gentle relationship for this, we begin to see how unhealthy his love for Wanda is. He wants to be treated badly—the harsher, the better—and he obeys her edicts abjectly, his body trembling with resentment. And so begins a series of humiliations, ecstasies, and terrors, which at one point have him fearing for his life.

Only at the end of his "confession"—which constitutes most of the book—does Severin stand back and see the relationship for the self-torture it really was. "Whoever allows himself to be whipped, deserves to be whipped," is the moral he draws. It's no accident that Masoch gave us the word for this pleasure in pain: "masochism." Your jealousy is similarly masochistic—it comes from the lashes of your own crop. Bear witness to Severin's self-hate, then hang up your crop and walk free.

See also: Anger · Bitterness · Neediness · Paranoia

JET LAG

See: Dizziness · Exhaustion · Headache · Insomnia · Nausea

JOB, HATING YOUR

See: Bullied, being · Career, being in the wrong · Job, losing your · Monday morning feeling · Stuck in a rut

Bartleby the Scrivener
HERMAN MELVILLE
. . .
Lucky Jim
KINGSLEY AMIS

Losing your job can be a hideous blow, both to your pocket and to your ego. The best way to deal with it is to try to see it as an opportunity—a chance to take a break from the daily toil, reconsider your options, and perhaps expand into new territories. Rather than conclude that you were a bad fit for the job, decide that the job was a bad fit for you (see also: Career, being in the wrong). If you're not convinced, consider all the occasions on which, in your job, you did not want to do the things you were asked to do. Like Bartleby.

Herman Melville's Bartleby is a scrivener, and when he first arrives for duty at the narrator's law office, "pallidly neat" and "pitiably respectable," his employer thinks his sedate nature will have a calming influence on his other employees. And at first Bartleby does seem to be the model worker, industriously copying out letters in quadruplicate. But then he begins to rebel. When his employer asks him to check over his writing, Bartleby gives the response: "I would prefer not to." It soon becomes apparent that he will do nothing beyond the most basic elements of his job. If asked to do anything more, "I would prefer not to" comes the inflexible reply. A dire impasse develops in which his employer can't bring himself to fire the scrivener because he's so meek and seems to have no life whatsoever beyond his desk. And Bartleby will do only what he wants.

Be inspired by Bartleby's act of resistance. To what degree did your job entail compromising over what you really wanted to do? Bartleby's rebellion saw him refusing to leave his desk at all. You, however, now have a chance to move on and find pastures new.

Perhaps you can even begin to celebrate the demise of your job. When Jim Dixon is appointed lecturer in medieval English history at a nondescript university in *Lucky Jim*, he has no intention of messing things up. He duly accepts his boss Neddy Welch's invitation to attend an "arts weekend" in the country, realizing that he needs to keep "in" with Welch. But once there, he can't seem to avoid getting himself into trouble. Farcical scenes ensue, including burning bedsheets, drunken madrigal singing, and various sexual entanglements. It's when he gives his lecture about "Merrie England," however, that he blows things most spectacularly, delivering the final moments "punctuated by his own snorts of derision."

Have a much needed laugh, then start looking for a job that is even more suited to you. Because there is an unexpected denouement to Jim's very public disgrace. Seeing someone make a pig's dinner of his job—and still coming out on top—will boost your morale immeasurably.

See also: Anger • Broke, being • Failure, feeling like a • Unemployment

JUDGMENTAL, BEING

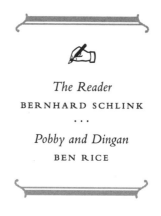

The Reader
BERNHARD SCHLINK
· · ·
Pobby and Dingan
BEN RICE

It is tempting, especially in youth, to go around forming instant and strong opinions about others. To judge, to pronounce, to label—such things can seem to an immature mind to be synonymous with strength and confidence. But having strong opinions must never become a mandate for being judgmental, which is the tendency to judge a thing or person based on one quality or attribute alone. A judgmental person will insist, for instance, that all criminals are terrible people, that all fussy eaters are bad in bed, and all teenagers are naive and judgmental.*

To stamp out your judgmental tendencies, we recommend you immerse yourself in the complex tale of Nazi guilt, personal shame, and retrospective horror that is Bernhard Schlink's *The Reader*, a novel that explores the question of how postwar generations should approach the Holocaust and those implicated in its tarry atrocities. Michael Berg is just fifteen when he begins a relationship with thirty-six-year-old tram conductress Hanna. Their assignations, which often involve bathing together—a hint at a Lady Macbeth–style need to scrub away past sins—also revolve around books, for Hanna likes Michael to read to her (*The Odyssey* in Greek, *War and Peace*), something we wholeheartedly approve of (see: Loneliness, reading induced; Non-reading partner, having a). Only later, when Michael is a law student sitting in on a war crimes trial, does he recognize one of the faces on the dock. His

---

* They are right about the last one.

first love was once an SS guard, complicit in the deaths of hundreds of women. And she has another secret of which she is even more ashamed.

Michael spends his whole life struggling to come to terms with what Hanna did—and what she has done to him. And while she suffers remorse, and even allows herself to be judged for shouldering more responsibility than she actually had, Michael's decision not to reply to her letters from prison causes her pain. Thus Schlink brings the reader into the ethical fray. Do you allow yourself to be moved by Hanna's suffering or continue to condemn her along with her crime? Herein lies your test. May this novel show you that holding strong opinions and being nonjudgmental do not by necessity cancel each other out.

If you lack the stomach for such heavy ethical questions, a gentler cure is available. If ever a novel—or novella—could trick you into dousing your judgmental fire, Ben Rice's slim debut *Pobby and Dingan* is it. Kellyanne, little sister to narrator Ashmol, has two imaginary friends: Pobby and Dingan. As one would expect from any self-respecting older brother— especially one raised in the hard-bitten opal mining community of Lightning Ridge, Australia—Ashmol has no time for such childish things. Would you, after years of being instructed to set places for Pobby and Dingan at the table and being told you can't come to the pool because, with Pobby and Dingan in the backseat, there's no space for you in the car?

By the end of the novel, yes. Because when Kellyanne announces that Pobby and Dingan have died, and is made so ill by her grief that she winds up in the hospital, Ashmol does a wonderful thing: he goes around town putting up signs offering a reward to anybody who can find his sister's friends ("Description: Imaginary. Quiet."). And from this moment you, too, will want to be on the side of those who buy in to the little girl's fantasy, not those who sniff and sneer.

Remain open. There is good, bad, mad, and sad in everyone, and you don't have to condone or believe in every element to be kind to the whole package. This also applies to yourself. If you tend to write yourself off as hopeless at everything (see: Self-esteem, low), start by practicing a nonjudgmental attitude toward yourself.

See also: **Antisocial, being**

JUMP SHIP, DESIRE TO

Rabbit, Run
JOHN UPDIKE

When you feel the urge to jump ship—from your relationship, your job, your life—we beg you not to do so until you have read *Rabbit, Run*. The urge to jump generally strikes when the ship we're on appears to be sinking—and it's more likely to feel this way if it started out high in the water. This is certainly the case for Harry "Rabbit" Angstrom (the nickname is a result of the nervous twitch beneath his "brief nose"). For Rabbit was once a teenage basketball star, a local if not national hero, who now, at twenty-seven, spends his days demonstrating the MagiPeel Kitchen Peeler, married with a son and another on the way, the best of his life behind him. Or so he feels. Coming home from work one day, Rabbit joins a scuffle of kids shooting balls in an empty lot. Exhilarated to find he still has his "touch," he decides in a moment of positivity to quit smoking and throw away his cigarettes. But when he gets home, the sight of his pregnant wife, Janice, slumped mindlessly in front of the TV, drinking, leaves him suddenly infuriated. As he later tells the local vicar Jack Eccles, he can't stand the fact that he was once first-rate and now—well, "that thing Janice and I had going, boy, it was really second-rate." And so he jumps—or, as Updike would have it, runs.

Almost immediately, Rabbit meets someone who knows that running away doesn't work—at least not without a definite plan. "The only way to get somewhere, you know, is to figure out where you're going before you go there," points out a gas station attendant when Rabbit admits he doesn't know where he's heading. And later—too late, because by this time tragedy has struck—Rabbit's old basketball coach, Tothero, struggling to formulate the words following a stroke, spells out one last lesson: "Right and wrong aren't dropped from the sky . . . We make them," he says. Then: "Invariably . . . misery follows their disobedience. Not our own." Rabbit hasn't so much as paused to think about the consequences his running might have on other people.

And he still doesn't now. Tothero's wisdom penetrates us, but it doesn't penetrate Rabbit. He just carries on hating Janice and running away. Sure, we feel sympathy for Rabbit, but we soon see that his problem is not so much that he's trapped by Janice as that he's trapped by ignorance, not knowing how to help Janice—or himself. Join in with Tothero and tell it to Rabbit, then to yourself: The thing is, Rabbit, it's better to stay on board that ship, do what you can to plug its holes, and redirect its course. Because if you jump, you jump into the sea. And if you are the one holding the tiller, you won't be the only one who'll drown.

See also: **Commitment, fear of** • **Itchy feet** • **Wanderlust**

K

KILLJOY, BEING A

Roxana
DANIEL DEFOE

If you happen to stumble on a party—or hear one going on next door—what do you tend to do? Grab a glass, concoct a cocktail, and leap into the fray? Or do you recoil in horror from the blaring music, complain about the folly of setting off fireworks, and frown at the mess and the drunkenness? Are you, in short, a party pooper, a sourpuss, a spoilsport—one of life's killjoys?

If so, it's time to awaken your inner Roxana and learn to be the life and soul of the party. Daniel Defoe's most controversial and psychologically complex novel follows the fortunes of a young woman who falls on hard times when her husband absconds with the family's accumulated wealth, leaving her with five children to feed. What, in those days, could a poor girl do but make use of her natural assets? Foxy, fluent in French, and a nimble dancer, Roxana has plenty of offers and—parting from her children "to avoid having to watch them perish"—becomes a paid mistress to various men. She soon becomes adept at seducing not only new lovers, but entire seventeenth-century ballrooms. Her moment of glory occurs when she appears in full Turkish dress at a ball, dazzling the masked guests so effectively that she's showered with money, attracts the attention of the king, and earns herself the exotic name by which we know her.

Roxana may be forced into her role of party girl, but her ability to bring a buzz to proceedings even when her chips are down makes her an ideal mentor. You don't have to be in a party mood to begin with; just be willing to plug in and give it your all. The mood will come. Like Roxana, you'll bring smiles to the faces of others—and may even catch the eye of some interesting new friends in high places.

See also: Antisocial, being • Goody-goody, being a • Humorlessness • Misanthropy • Nobody likes you • Teetotaler, being a

KNACKERED, BEING

See: Busy, being too • Busy to read, being too • Children requiring attention, too many • Exhaustion • Fatherhood • Motherhood • Pregnancy • Tired and emotional, being • Workaholism

KNOCKED UP, BEING

See: Pregnancy

L

LAID OFF, BEING

See: Anger • Bitterness • Broke, being • Failure, feeling like a • Job, losing your •
Unemployment

LAZINESS

See: Adolescence • Ambition, too little • Bed, inability to get out of • Lethargy •
Procrastination

LEFT OUT, FEELING

Sometimes it can feel as if we are being intentionally excluded, left out of the fun. If we'd chosen not to join in, then it would be all right—not all of us are party people. But when we want to join in yet somehow the welcome hasn't arrived, we can end up feeling extremely sorry for ourselves, and begrudging of those selfish, oblivious others who've failed to do anything about our distress. The natural response often takes one of two misguided paths: to force ourselves upon the group or to reject the group that has rejected us.

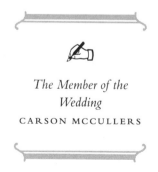

The Member of the Wedding
CARSON MCCULLERS

Neither strategy works. Twelve-year-old Frankie, the motherless heroine of *The Member of the Wedding*, one of Carson McCullers's odes to loners and oddballs set in the small-town American South, tries them both. It all starts going wrong when her best friend moves to Florida and her father asks who this "great big long-legged twelve-year-old blunderbuss" is who's still sleeping in his bed. She takes up some worrying habits after that—shooting her father's pistol in a vacant lot, stealing a knife from Sears and Roebuck, committing a "queer sin" with Barney MacKean in his family's garage. None of it stops her feeling "unjoined," and when the neighborhood kids have a party in the clubhouse, she listens from the alley behind.

At first she decides the answer is to become a "we" with her older brother, Jarvis, and his fiancée. She'll become a "member" of their wedding, and after the wedding she'll go out into the world with the two of them. When Jarvis and Janice fail to catch on to this idea, she decides to run away instead. But like most twelve-year-old runaways, she doesn't get very far.

The solution, when it appears, brings with it a "shock of happiness." *The Member of the Wedding* will strike a chord with all those who feel they're on life's sidelines. Read it and be reminded: Don't force things, and don't run away. Have patience. Your ticket to the party will come.

See also: **Different, being** • **Foreign, being** • **Loneliness** • **Nobody likes you** • **Outsider, being an** • **Shyness**

LETHARGY

The Sheltering Sky
PAUL BOWLES
. . .
Don Quixote
MIGUEL DE
CERVANTES
SAAVEDRA

You may have made it out of bed, but you have about as much bounce in your stride as a pregnant hippo. When you're overcome by physical or mental lethargy, dragging your heavy limbs and empty of motivation, it is notoriously hard to shift. To combat lethargy you need energy—but where does the initial injection of energy required to reverse the inertia come from?

Our two-part tonic begins by immersing yourself in the sort of stagnant environment in which lethargy thrives. Paul Bowles's inimitable *The Sheltering Sky*—subtle, grave, intense, and filled with a sense of doom— is such a place. Port, his wife, Kit, and their "astonishingly handsome" friend Tunner—Americans who have shunned their homeland yet have failed to find anything better—are drifting through the North African desert. A strangely featureless, restless group, they spend their days mostly in avoidance of one another, the local inhabitants, and any real engagement with life. An unspecified menace seems to exist between them and the Arabs they meet—dark figures that lurk and cannot be trusted. Stones are thrown from unseen hands, wallets are almost pinched. And so the trio move on with no particular destination in mind, an ominous wind at their backs and a "limpid, burning sky" overhead.

Kit is the most dysfunctional. Some days she is so filled with a prophetic sense of doom that she turns inward and can barely function. Tunner bores her, and she finds his morning greetings "offensively chipper." For Port, meanwhile, the only certainty is an "infinite sadness" at the core of his being—reassuring because of its familiarity. When Kit tells Port one day, "We've never managed, either one of us, to get all the way into life," she hits the nail on the head. Their lives are like petri dishes in which the bacteria of lethargy breeds: full of languor, uncertainty, miscommunication, and alienation. Take a good look at yourself and ask whether those petri dishes are present in your life too.

The second half of our cure must be taken as soon as you've turned the last page, as it will zap your body with the electric shock of contrast. Cervantes's lovable, excitable Don Quixote—who styles himself on the knights-errant in the courtly romances to which he is addicted and stays up all night to read—is everything the characters in *The Sheltering Sky* are not. He rises early, he dons his grandfather's spruced-up coat of armor, and he sallies forth in search of adventures—a damsel in distress to rescue and love, a rascal to run through with a lance. Could lethargy grow here? By sooth, we'd say not! While Bowles's disaffected Americans reduce the mystery and beauty of the desert to odd, untrustworthy parts so that it cannot hurt them—denying it the magnificence or epic resonance that would give them a place in history—Don Quixote turns plain roadside inns into castles with silver pinnacles, windmills into an army of giants. And all this with an irrepressibly jaunty, blithesome disposition, immune to the cautions of his trusty squire.

Take it neat, spilling from the pen of Cervantes with its breathless up-swing and cavalier call to arms, its romance and zest. For those who are sluggish and slow, it's the most electrifying tonic that literature has to offer this side of the law.

See also: Ambition, too little · Apathy · Bed, inability to get out of · Boredom

*In Praise of the
Stepmother*
MARIO VARGAS LLOSA

When your sex drive takes a nosedive, glean inspiration from this wicked little prank of a novel by the Peruvian author Mario Vargas Llosa. Each night, after his fastidious nighttime ablutions, Don Rigoberto takes his wife, Doña Lucrecia, into his arms and murmurs: "Aren't you going to ask me who I am?" Doña Lucrecia knows the game. "Who, who, my love?" she implores. And Don Rigoberto—a sensualist, a lover of art, a widower who cannot believe his luck at finding love again in midlife and a stepmother for his teenage son, Alfonso—begins to talk from the point of view of a character in a famous painting.

Because what turns him on is for him and his wife to inhabit the figures in these paintings in their fantasies. One night he is the King of Lydia in a work by the seventeenth-century Dutch master Jacob Jordaens, proudly extolling the virtues of his wife's voluminous buttocks. The next he is aroused and titillated by François Boucher's *Diana at the Bath*, imagining Lucrecia as the goddess of the hunt having her body rubbed with honey and her toes sucked one by one by her female lover. On a more complicated night, it's Francis Bacon's anguished and unprepossessing *Head I* that gets their juices flowing.

Possibly they take it too far. Cast as Venus in Titian's *Venus with Cupid and Music*, Doña Lucrecia is aroused so much by her husband's descriptions of Cupid tickling her with his wings and "roll[ing] about on the satiny geography of her body" that she finds herself entertaining dirty thoughts about her angelic stepson, Alfonso. Perched on the cusp of his nascent sexuality, the golden-haired boy is only too keen to egg her on.

There's nothing wrong, though, with borrowing a little inspiration from art and literature to fan the flame of desire in a tired conjugal bed. In the spirit of Don Rigoberto rather than Doña Lucrecia, we hope you may find something to steam up the windows in your home.

See also: **Orgasms, not enough** · **Sex, too little**

LIMB, LOSS OF

Peter Pan
J. M. BARRIE
. . .
The Third Policeman
FLANN O'BRIEN

The loss of a limb is an awful bind and will slow you down for a while, but as literature shows there are ways of using it to your advantage. Make a feature of your missing limb, like Captain Hook in J. M. Barrie's delightful (even for grown-ups) *Peter Pan*, and wear a hook or other surprising arm or leg replacement with pride. Not only will you stand out in a crowd, but people will know that your suffering has added depth to your personality. Captain Hook's inability to cope with the sight of his own blood and his terror of crocodiles makes him all the more human to us and Peter Pan.

The one-legged narrator of Flann O'Brien's daft romp *The Third Policeman* is saved from death by his affliction. A one-legged bandit is about to kill him when he notices their common asymmetry and decides to make friends instead.

Be cheered. Life may be different when you lose a limb, but it need not be less hearty, less active, or less full of friends.

READING AILMENT *Live instead of read, tendency to*

CURE *Read to live more deeply*

It's simply not good enough to say you're too busy getting on with the process of living to spend time reading. Because as Socrates was the first to point out, "an unexamined life is not worth living." Books offer a way of turning inward, reflecting, and analyzing the life that starts up again as soon as we emerge from the book. And besides, how much living can one person actually do?

(continued)

Books offer us the lives of a thousand others besides ourselves—and as we read we can live these lives vicariously, seeing what they see, feeling what they feel, smelling what they smell. You could argue that living without books is to live only one limited life, but with books we can live forever. Without books it is easy to lose direction in life, and to shrink to something small and mean and clichéd. Books develop our capacity to be empathetic and nonjudgmental, to accept and honor difference, to be brave, to extend ourselves and make the most of ourselves. And they remind us that beyond the minutiae of life, there is another realm of existence common to us all: the mystery of being alive, and what that means. One cannot live fully without spending time in that realm, and books are our ticket there.

LOCKED OUT, BEING

To pass the time while waiting for the locksmith, you surely need a great detective/crime/spy novel. Keep a stack in your garden shed (where—*ahem*—you should also consider keeping a spare key). You might pick up some ideas for how to break in.

THE TEN BEST NOVELS FOR WHEN YOU'RE LOCKED OUT

Burglars Can't Be Choosers .... LAWRENCE BLOCK
The Shape of Water .... ANDREA CAMILLERI
The Woman in White .... WILKIE COLLINS
Angels Flight .... MICHAEL CONNELLY
Live and Let Die .... IAN FLEMING
Break In .... DICK FRANCIS
Bad Chili .... JOE R. LANSDALE

LONELINESS

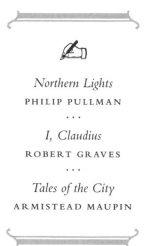

You need never be lonely with a roomful of novels—or even just the one you'd take with you to a desert island—and we all have our favorite literary friends. But there are inevitably times of literary drought when you may have no novels at hand at all, and for these times you must be sure to have prepopulated your brain with plenty of characters, ideas, and interesting conversations, gathered from fiction, to ensure your interior world can always be relied upon to keep you company.

Northern Lights
PHILIP PULLMAN
...
I, Claudius
ROBERT GRAVES
...
Tales of the City
ARMISTEAD MAUPIN

One of the best such antiloneliness vaccines is *Northern Lights* by Philip Pullman, as well as the other two novels that make up the His Dark Materials trilogy. Because in the fictional world that most closely resembles our own—Pullman has created many worlds within the world of these novels—the human characters all have a daemon, an animal companion that sits on their shoulders and keeps them company throughout their lives. Daemons are not just companions, though, but representations of a person's spirit. If a daemon strays too far from its human, both human and daemon feel physically compromised; if the daemon is in any way hurt, the human feels the pain too. A daemon is part best friend, part partner, part physical manifestation of one's very soul, and a human with a daemon is never alone.

Terror strikes in this compelling novel when the "Authority"—the religious organization ruling the land—decides to separate children from their daemons, supposedly for the good of their souls. Lyra, a feisty preadolescent, experiences terrible torture as she comes very close to losing her daemon, Pantalaimon, who appears mostly in the form of a pine marten (the form of one's daemon does not settle permanently until one's teens). As you are swept up in Lyra's quest to prevent this atrocity and rescue Roger and the other children from the "Gobblers" in the frozen North, you will be convinced of the absolute necessity of daemons—and surely will know what form your own would take.

It's hard to believe that Robert Graves was ever lonely, so heaving with intriguing characters are his large and populous novels. Living in an idyllic corner of Mallorca, he wrote his two most successful novels, *I, Claudius* and *Claudius the God,* as a means to fund his sociable lifestyle—because he not only hosted a garrulous community in his head, but also in his home. Many glamorous writers, artists, and film stars flocked to his house parties and took part in the theatrical performances he organized. Use his novels to keep the party going in your own head.

I, Claudius is the fictional autobiography of a nobleman who begins life as a stammering fool, derided and ignored by his odious family, only to rise above them all. The sycophants and schemers who surround him make for highly entertaining company, among them the wise Augustus and his conniving wife, Livia, sadistic Tiberius, and the frankly insane Caligula. With his family at constant war with itself and everyone trying to poison one another all the time, Claudius himself is always in a throng. It all adds up to a fascinating, bustling sense of what it must have been like to live in the Roman Empire in the first century AD. You might actually be quite glad about your solitude once you've put the novel down.

Sometimes when we don't have the energy for new friends, it's old, familiar friends we yearn for. In this case, let the residents of 28 Barbary Lane in Armistead Maupin's symphony to San Francisco back into your life. (And if you haven't already met them, it won't take you more than a few pages to feel part of the gang.) Creations of the late seventies and early eighties, Mary Ann Singleton, Mona Ramsey, Michael "Mouse" Tolliver, Brian Hawkins, and their marijuana-growing landlady Mrs. Madrigal are still surprisingly fresh. With its episodic form—the experience is as close to watching TV as literature gets—this novel and its seven sequels are for keeping in your kitchen along with your cookbooks. Don't eat alone, but with wisecracking Mona making you laugh as she flips you an egg, sunny-side up, Mouse brewing up some reassuringly strong coffee, and Mrs. Madrigal taking the mug from your hands and replacing it with pearls of wisdom and a joint. Who needs to go out on a Friday night when Maupin's tales of the city are at home?

See also: Loneliness, reading induced

READING AILMENT *Loneliness, reading induced*

CURE *Read in company*

We all enjoy the pleasure of being left alone with a good book. But sometimes after several hours of immersion we lift our heads and look around, suddenly struck by the quiet, the absence of others. The world outside—and perhaps the world of our book—teems with people interacting with one another. But we are all alone. Something plaintive has entered our soul: we are suffering from reading-induced loneliness.

For some, reading is a way of escaping loneliness in the first place (see: Loneliness); feeling perhaps that nobody understands us, we find great solace in the company of a like-minded book. Sometimes we turn to books to escape the people around us, for there can be loneliness within a crowd too. How contrary, then, that the very thing that first cured us of our loneliness has now delivered us into a different sort of isolation.

The solution is to read in the company of other reading people—whether in a public space such as a café or a library, or in your own home, with your reading friend or partner at the other end of the sofa. Next time you look up, you'll see someone else similarly engrossed, and you won't feel alone at all.

Reading can be sociable: if you're at home, try reading aloud with your friend or partner, either at length or just the bits you've underlined. Consider joining a reading group in which everybody takes turns reading aloud from a novel. Reading a book communally is a wonderful way to share an otherwise internal and solitary experience, and you're likely to come away with a greater insight into and understanding of the book from the reactions of others during and after. It's also a great way to make new reading friends. Maybe at some point one of them might occupy the space at the other end of your reading sofa.

The Road
CORMAC MCCARTHY

LONG-WINDED, BEING

An exemplary model of short-windedness, and to illustrate its effectiveness as a cure, we, having just reread it, will say no more.

LOSING HOPE

See: Hope, loss of

LOSING YOUR FAITH

See: Faith, loss of

LOSING YOUR JOB

See: Job, losing your

LOSING YOUR MARBLES

See: Drugs, doing too many • Madness • Senile, going

LOSING YOURSELF

See: Fatherhood • Identity crisis • Identity, unsure of your reading • Lost, being • Selling your soul • Trapped by children

Please Look After Mom
KYUNG-SOOK SHIN

LOST, BEING

To lose one parent, Mr. Worthing, may be regarded as a misfortune; to lose both looks like carelessness," Lady Bracknell says severely in *The Importance of Being Earnest*. For Oscar Wilde, her remark was a joke, but if you've ever gotten lost, you know that the experience is no joking matter. Maybe you've lost your compass, misread your maps, and found yourself at nightfall on a spooky, desolate mountainside that you've climbed in search of a ruin . . . not knowing that you would end up being the ruin. Perhaps you're standing, bewildered and hungry, among mazy alleyways lined with endangered species in cages, trying to decipher street names that look like hieroglyphs, and fuming that your partner refused to spend the holidays in Umbria, as you'd wanted. Or maybe you're at the mall with young children when you suddenly notice that they have disappeared. The sensation produces an adrenaline rush, cold sweats, and recriminations. It's tempting to make it somebody's fault, but often hard to pin down who deserves the blame.

Kyung-sook Shin's melodramatic, tear-jerking novel *Please Look After Mom* tells the cautionary tale of a selfless, rural South Korean mother, So-nyo Park, who gets lost during a visit to her grown children in Seoul. When she fails to follow her husband into a crowded subway car before the door closes, she gets stranded. Illiterate and ashamed of it, she doesn't know how to navigate the city. Why didn't one of her children pick their parents up at the station as usual?

Shin builds her story by alternating narrators—the children's accounts, as well as the father's and So-nyo's. And, along the way, we see that her children's dormant consciences slowly revive and come back to bite them. Beautifully told and rich in detail of South Korea's rural traditions, *Please Look After Mom* perceptively documents generational change, showing how the close, familial world that long characterized South Korea has given way to an anonymous, urbanized world. Mothers like So-nyo—familiar to any reader—seem to have lost their rootless children even as they are looking at them face-to-face.

LOVE, DOOMED

What is the cure for doomed love? We prescribe a wrenchingly good cry, provided by a vicarious wallow in the heartbreak of heroes and heroines whose suffering quite possibly (we hope) exceeds your own. Love born under a maligned star—like Tristan and Isolde's, Cathy and Heathcliff's, Tess and Angel Clare's—is terrible to watch. It is also terribly cathartic.

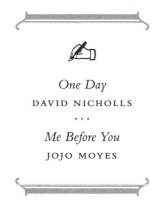

One Day
DAVID NICHOLLS
. . .
Me Before You
JOJO MOYES

If you're in the clutches of a hopeless passion, making a fool of yourself over someone who doesn't know you exist, or obsessing over a lover who behaves like the villain of a blues ballad, then it's time you gained some perspective. Dive into *One Day*, David Nicholls's delectable slow-burn novel about the long-deferred romance between the cocky, self-centered toff Dexter Mayhew and the goofy, unconfident Emma Morley. Emma and Dex hook up briefly and inconclusively as students, and remain in each other's orbit ever after, mostly unhappily. One of them, usually Dex, veers away just when they might get close. As you accompany the two of them through two decades of near misses, you can revisit the eighties and nineties in Nicholls's faultlessly conjured evocation, from shabby college rooms where "you were never more than six feet from a Nina Simone album" and every girl has a photo of Nelson Mandela on the wall "like some dreamy ideal boyfriend," to the coked-up London media parties of the nineties. When Dex is off his head (often), he finds himself thinking of Emma: "It's Emma that he wants to see the most. Why isn't she with him tonight?" he thinks. Answer: because he's a moron. Yet, somehow, they can't shake each other. Why? Because they're made for each other, don't you know. When will they figure it out? Will they? The suspense will make you tear your hair and forget, for the protracted, captivating moment of the novel, your own love woes. When Dex at last declares himself, Emma tells him, "It's too late." Luckily, it turns out not to have been, quite, and we can breathe a sigh of long-deferred relief. By the time they've woken up to the love they have wasted, they're battle scarred enough to appreciate what they have, while it lasts.

If you wish to submit to still more drenching floods of tears, take up Jojo Moyes's rending *Me Before You*, whose bright, matter-of-fact voice lures the reader into a lovelorn labyrinth that is all the more poignant because the lovers themselves remain unaware, for so long, of the emotions that have overtaken them. Louisa "Lou" Clark is a no-nonsense working-class girl who supports her parents, sister, nephew, and grandfather with her paycheck. When the café where Lou works closes, she finds a job as a caregiver to a man who has been paralyzed from the neck down in a motorcycle accident. That man, Will Traynor, is the thirty-five-year-old son of the most prominent family in Lou's little town. Before the accident, he had been a rich, arrogant businessman who traveled the world and had his choice of flawless, leggy, model-thin girlfriends. After the accident, he's furious at his straitened life, and annoyed by Lou's efforts to improve it.

Lou is as small, dark, and invisible as Jane Eyre, while Will is as irascible and rude as Mr. Rochester. Even though Will is trapped in a wheelchair, Lou is initially cowed by him. But her self-respect and her sensible nature give her the gumption to persevere, and when Will lashes out peevishly at her, she retorts, "I'm not employed by you. I'm employed by your mother." Then she declares she will continue to work for him no matter what: "Not because I particularly care about you, or like this stupid job, or want to change your life one way or another, but because I need the money. Okay? I really need the money." Her show of pique amuses and impresses him. For once, he's not being pandered to. He begins to make her a kind of pet project, leading her to read books, watch foreign films, and travel, nurturing her mind as she nurtures his spirits. As they grow closer, Lou's boring boyfriend, Patrick, quarrels with her, resenting her for giving so much attention to another man. But when she accuses him of being jealous, he denies it churlishly: "How could I be jealous of a cripple?" he says. But Patrick, Will's mother, and Will's main caregiver, Nathan, realize far earlier than Lou and Will how their relationship has changed and deepened. But how can such a doomed love end? Read it and weep.

See also: **Mr./Mrs. Wrong, ending up with** · **Wasting time on a dud relationship**

LOVE, FALLING HEAD OVER HEELS IN
See: **Appetite, loss of** · **Concentrate, inability to** · **Dizziness** · **Infatuation** · **Insomnia** · **Lovesickness** · **Lust** · **Obsession** · **Optimism** · **Romantic, hopeless**

LOVE, FALLING OUT OF LOVE WITH
See: **Falling out of love with love**

LOVE, LOOKING FOR
See: **Happiness, searching for** · **Mr./Mrs. Right, holding out for** · **Mr./Mrs. Right, looking for** · **Shelf, fear of being left on the**

LOVE, UNREQUITED

Unrequited love is a particular kind of love that can only ever go one way. To prove our point, we'll borrow Ann Patchett's definition of it in her novel *Bel Canto* (also one of our cures for: **Mr./Mrs. Right, looking for**). Trapped in adjacent seats

Bel Canto
ANN PATCHETT
(continued)

The Sorrows of Young Werther
JOHANN WOLFGANG
VON GOETHE
. . .

Far from the Madding Crowd
THOMAS HARDY
. . .

First Love
IVAN TURGENEV

on an eighteen-hour flight, the young Swedish accompanist to the famous soprano Roxane Coss blurts out a confession of undying adoration that makes the singer wince. Coming out of the blue and without any basis in mutual friendship or attraction, it is too much, too soon—and stinks of recklessness: "The kind of love that offers its life so easily, so stupidly, is always the love that is not returned," Patchett writes. How can the object of your love see someone worth loving in return when you are willing to throw yourself at his or her feet, exposed and bleeding like a piece of uncooked meat?

It's only a matter of time before the accompanist sacrifices himself literally, for the poor sot is well and truly lost to the masochistic destructiveness of his hopeless love. When the terrorists who have taken both the soprano and her audience hostage offer freedom to anyone needing medical help, the love-struck man keeps mum, even though he's a diabetic requiring regular injections of insulin to stay alive. Staying to "protect" Roxane will mean certain death. Well, thanks a lot, Swedish accompanist, for dumping the guilt of your death on my hands, Roxane would be within her rights to point out. You call that love?

Literature is teeming with similarly tormented foolish types, dying to die for the love of someone who never asked for it in the first place. And it's not a pretty sight. The worst of the bunch is Werther in Goethe's *The Sorrows of Young Werther*, the sensitive soul whose hopeless love of the peasant girl Lotte—already happily engaged to someone else when they meet—drives him to take his own life in despair. He even has the audacity to arrange for Lotte to send him the pistol that will be the instrument of his death. Following this novel's first publication in 1774, sensitive artistic types from Ostend to Naples began dressing in the signature outfit of young Werther; appallingly, some killed themselves in copycat suicides with a pistol and an open book. It became known as the Werther effect. Goethe was quick to denounce the overblown emotions of the Romantic movement—known as Sturm und Drang ("storm and stress")—from which his novel had sprung. We do too. If you suspect you're the type to revel in the tragedy of your own unrequited love, we instruct you to steer well clear of *The Sorrows*. Turn to *Far from the Madding Crowd* instead.

This Hardy stalwart, set in the Wessex he loved, is the best novel in the business for showing how to, and how not to, love. Everyone gets it wrong at the beginning. Gabriel Oak—though lovable from the very first line with his beaming smile that reaches to "within an unimportant distance of his ears"—is somewhat simplistic in his approach to courting. Bathsheba—pretty, marriageable, soon to be rich—is vain and full of herself. She's also a tease, and though this works for Gabriel—for a prize worth winning has to be a little hard to get—the Valentine's card she sends in a moment of impetuous silliness to her neighbor William Boldwood is an act of irresponsibility she lives to regret. Hitherto unaffected by the good looks of his neighbor, the card gives Boldwood the idea of loving her, and soon he has plunged headfirst into a Werther-esque rush of unrequited love, sacrificing himself quite unnecessarily in its depths.

Bathsheba's third suitor, Sergeant Troy, is essentially a good man, though he, too, thinks a little too much of his looks. But he has done something even more reprehensible than Bathsheba, having gotten a woman pregnant and left her in the lurch. Gabriel Oak is the only one who comes through, and he does it by standing firm, by being a loyal friend to Bathsheba throughout the whole messy business with the other two men, and by waiting for Bathsheba to see his worth—as well as to prove her own.

If you insist on reveling—just for a while—in the ecstasies and agonies of unrequited love, do it with Turgenev's *First Love*. In this sun-drenched novella, young Vladimir, sixteen, is besotted with twenty-one-year-old Zinaida. She has a whole deck of suitors at her disposal, and though she treats him as a young confidant, she does not take his advances remotely seriously. She plays with all her infatuated lovers—and it becomes apparent only at the end who the true object of her affection is. It all, of course, ends in tragedy. Have one last revel in your love along with Vladimir, but decide thereafter to keep your cards close to your chest. Only then will you start winning the suits.

If the love you feel is not returned, pause in your foolish gushing and ask yourself the following question: in your eagerness to love, have you made yourself unlovable, lacking in self-respect? If the answer is yes, you'll be incapable of inspiring more than a guilty no. Buck up. Look yourself in the eye and tot up your worth. Then demonstrate that worth with the sort of behavior that someone as wonderful as the person you love surely deserves in return.

See also: **Infatuation** • **Jealousy** • **Love, doomed** • **Mr./Mrs. Right, holding out for**

LOVESICKNESS

The Price of Salt
PATRICIA HIGHSMITH

Literary heroes and heroines have been pining away from lovesickness for ages. Case in point: Palamon in Chaucer's fourteenth-century "The Knight's Tale," who, having caught sight of fair Emily through the window of the tower where he is imprisoned, nearly wastes away from the effects of seeing, but not having, her. It is only in our less romantic era that psychiatrists are called in and drugs prescribed. Our drug-free cure is a bracing dose of love requited.

Highsmith's second novel was inspired by an incident in her own life, when she was working in a department store selling children's dolls, just like Therese in *The Price of Salt*. She was so bowled over by a customer who seemed to "give off light" and made her feel that she had seen a vision, that she went home and sketched out the story in two hours. The tale is one of unexpected passion between two women: Carol, in her thirties, with a daughter and a husband she's in the process of leaving; and Therese, nineteen, drifting from job to job but with a flair for set design. It is Therese, the shopgirl, who initiates their affair.

At first Therese is openly besotted, and Carol remains playfully aloof. Therese's boyfriend is disconcerted; she has made no attempt to hide her obsession from him. "It's worse than being lovesick," he tells her, "because it's so completely unreasonable," failing to believe in the possibility of same-sex love. But what is true love but the triumph of emotion over reason? When Carol and Therese take off on a road trip across the States, Carol opens up to Therese and they become fully entwined.

When the two suddenly find themselves apart—they believe forever—Therese experiences extreme lovesickness: total lassitude and despair. "How would the world come back to life? How would its salt come back?" Only Carol can save her from her lovesick state. And she does.

See also: **Appetite, loss of** · **Broken heart** · **Concentrate, inability to** · **Dizziness** · **Infatuation** · **Insomnia** · **Lust** · **Nausea** · **Obsession** · **Romantic, hopeless** · **Sentimental, being** · **Tired and emotional, being** · **Yearning, general**

LUST

Lust has its place, of course. We wouldn't feel alive without it. But when it comes to exercising judgment, let lust take a backseat. Human desire is immensely powerful, but it is also entirely unreasonable, irrational even, and should not be influencing our decision making.

Take a leaf from Griet, the considered, measured maid-cum-muse of Johannes Vermeer in Tracy Chevalier's *Girl with a Pearl Earring*, a reconjuring of the moment behind the painting from which this novel takes its name. The humble girl captures the painter's interest when he notices that she's arranged her chopped red cabbage and carrots in such a way that the colors do not "fight," realizing at once that she has an instinctive painterly eye. By the time she sits for him, they have come to respect each other, working peacefully in his studio side by side. Griet has begun to refer to him as "her master" and, more tellingly still, as an unnamed "he." Both have taught the other new ways to see. And there's been a highly charged touch: Vermeer places his hand over Griet's to show her how to use the muller stone, causing such a powerful sexual charge to pass through her that she drops it. By the time the painting is made, the lust—his, but also hers—is there for all to see, in the glinting whites of the eyes, the moist lips just falling apart, the gently twirled and hitched fabric of the headdress, and, of course, the shine from out of the shadowy neck of that incongruous, lustrous pearl.

Griet knows full well that in seventeenth-century Delft a girl from her background can't tangle with a man from Vermeer's class. This is highly dangerous territory, and with the sexual tension blistering on the page, we know Griet's future is on the line. Chevalier's careful, concise sentences model the restraint required by her characters. Will they keep their passions in check, or will lust break through?

O lusty reader, when your hormones threaten to prevail over your head, take yourself off to a quiet place with *Girl with a Pearl Earring*. Let those elegant, disciplined sentences temper your passions, rein in your lust. Pause, slow down, rethink. Is your attraction for someone with whom you can share your carrots and cabbages? If not, enjoy the arousal for what it is, then take a deep breath and move on.

See also: Infatuation • Lovesickness • Sex, too much

Atonement

IAN MCEWAN

L ies come in many colors. Apart from the white ones, which we use to protect others from unnecessary hurt, lies are generally spawned by baser motives. Do not underestimate the damage they can do.

Look at what happens to thirteen-year-old Briony in Ian McEwan's *Atonement*. Still blinded by her childhood crush on Robbie, the son of the family's housekeeper, who has been brought up and educated as one of them, she is shocked to catch him and her cousin Cecilia in flagrante delicto in the library. Later, when she stumbles on her distressed cousin Lola in the dark, having been knocked down and violated by a shadowy retreating figure, she considers only one culprit: the socially inferior Robbie, who now metamorphoses in her febrile imagination into a brute who must be punished.

Trapped in her own delusion, Briony spins a story from her own misreadings and imaginings that causes her to drown out the voice inside her that knows the truth. Instead, she chooses to shore up her position and expunge her doubt, all for the sake of sticking to her story. And so, when she is asked by the inspector whether she saw Robbie clearly, with her own eyes, she lies.

Her lie ruins not just Robbie and Cecilia's lives, but her own as well. As she seeks atonement for her crime, she goes over the details of it in an eternal loop, like "a rosary to be fingered for a lifetime." This novel should be read as a vaccination against the temptation to tell an untruth. Read it and let it hover in your mind as a constant reminder.

See also: **Trust, loss of**

M

MADNESS

The Comforters
MURIEL SPARK

Literature is fond of its lunatics—from Mr. Rochester's insane wife in *Jane Eyre*, who scurries around on all fours growling like a wild animal, to the eerie presence that haunts Wilkie Collins's *The Woman in White*. But while these two crazies are harmless, many evocations of mental derangement can be dangerous to the reader who feels that he or she is becoming unhinged. If you feel yourself to be touched in this way, steer clear of Margaret Atwood's *Surfacing*, which tracks the gradual descent into psychosis of its unnamed narrator. Together with her lover Joe and a couple of friends, this narrator travels north to a remote island in Quebec in an attempt to find out what happened to her father, who has gone missing. Perhaps it is grief for her father that undoes her; perhaps it's the emotional void between herself and Joe. Or perhaps it's whatever horrible thing it is that she sees at the bottom of the seabed. But whatever its cause, her increasingly fragmented and ungrammatical narrative does such a good job of conveying her unbalanced mental state that it may well make a few more screws in your head come loose. And despite its title, you will find no comfort in the pages of *The Comforts of Madness*, Paul Sayer's novel about a boy so traumatized by abuse that he makes a conscious decision, when his father dies in the bed they share, never to move again. As the boy grows into a man—still lying in bed—his interior monologue is mesmerizing, heartrending, and somehow dangerously seductive.

The best novel for those seeking to avoid the loony bin is Muriel Spark's *The Comforters*. Almost all the characters in this novel are mad—that is to say, way up there on the scale, although still functioning in society quite happily. You might feel right at home—and rather normal—in comparison.

Caroline Rose is renting a flat in Kensington and experiencing midcentury angst around issues of feminism and aesthetics when she becomes aware of the tapping of typewriter keys. The *tap-tap-tap* is accompanied by the dispassionate narration of her own thoughts and actions, as if a Greek chorus were intoning the banal drama of her life, offstage, while someone else was writing it down. At first the Typing Ghost, as she calls it, simply provides a third-person narrative of her day as she lives it. But then it begins to predict her future. Caroline attempts to cheat it: when the Typing Ghost predicts she will "fritter away the day" and be forced to travel to Sussex by car instead of train, Caroline makes a desperate attempt to take the train after all. But, farcically, she can't outwit it.

If Caroline's particular brand of madness doesn't resonate, you might identify more with the diamond-smuggling granny, the Belgian Congolese Baron, the zealous Catholic convert, or, of course, the Typing Ghost itself. All the characters are equally delightful—and equally mad. "We're all a little mad, Willi," Caroline confirms to the Baron. "That's what makes us so nice, dear." With its gentle and original humor, this novel certifies that there's nothing wrong with being a tad bit off your rocker—it happens to the best of us. Leave literature's serious crackpots for your friends and family to read, and stick to the deviationist fringe.

See also: **Paranoia** · **Turmoil**

MALAISE, TWENTY-FIRST CENTURY

*The Little Girl and
the Cigarette*
BENOÎT DUTEURTRE
. . .
*Super Sad True
Love Story*
GARY SHTEYNGART

The sense of discomfort one feels that is unique to this century comes from a discrepancy between one's desires for a contented, fulfilled, even adventurous life and the absurdity of society as we see it unfurling around us: bureaucracy, political correctness, safety legislation, the dysfunctionality of humans caused by an excessive use of technology . . . The list goes on.

No novel captures this modern malaise more deftly than Benoît Duteurtre's *The Little Girl and the Cigarette*. Désiré Johnson, on the verge of being executed for the murder of a policeman, requests that he have a last smoke. His plea throws the authorities into confusion. Désiré's invocation of Article 47 is entirely within his rights, but tobacco consumption is banned within the limits of the prison. The absurdity of his outmoded request, and the obstinacy with which he insists on it, is all too much for the functionaries' legal capabilities. They decide that only the Supreme Court can make the decision. Meanwhile, another man, a technical adviser for the General Services Department of "Administration City," is having a different cigarette-related crisis. One day, as he enjoys a quiet puff out the window of the bathroom, a five-year-old girl walks in on him with his trousers down. She tells everyone and soon the man is facing charges of child molestation. A nightmarish satire, Dutcurtre's inverted vision puts justice in the hands of children. As you share your frustration at a world gone mad, you'll see you're not the only one crying out for reason.

In Gary Shteyngart's *Super Sad True Love Story*, Lenny and Eunice live in a world not too distant from our own, in which a data stream constantly updates individuals on their credit scores and social network ranking, while offering up-to-the-minute shopping ideas and the very latest of their friends' gossip. Lenny is thirty-nine, a Jewish immigrant from Russia, who anachronistically still loves—and reads—books (particularly Tolstoy). The object of his desire, Eunice, is a young Korean student. Their story is told through alternating diary entries, Lenny's told the old-fashioned way, Eunice's through her Global-Teens account—a kind of all-encompassing Facebook—so that we have the fun of Eunice's "teening" to listen to. Eunices's entries reveal her own angst about the future, and the contentment she keeps finding, to her surprise, with the "darling little dork" Lenny. Meanwhile, New York is beginning to disintegrate around them, America is at war with Venezuela, and everyone is so in debt to China that the plug may be pulled on resources at any minute. Lenny fears for their future, as individuals and as a nation.

After Duteurtre's satire and this romp through a media-mad, postliterate world of immortality seekers who have to consult "EmotePads" held to their hearts to learn their true feelings, you will find yourself reaching for a "bound, printed, nonstreaming Media artifact"—even if it will bring down your "PERSONALITY rankings." Lenny Abramov, last reader on Earth, turns out to be right about a lot of things.

See also: City fatigue • Disenchantment • Dissatisfaction

MAN FLU

Les Misérables
VICTOR HUGO

Infinitely worse than regular flu, and not to be confused with the common cold (which is hard, as the symptoms are identical), man flu is a miserable illness not just for the victim but for all concerned. Bed rest is essential, and the patient—indeed, "victim" is probably more apt—will require a great deal of sympathy. The victim should be propped up on soft pillows and provided with mugs of tea, heating pads, meals on trays, the remote control, and messages of support and commiseration from family and friends brought to him* regularly. Visitors to his bedside must take great care when making conversation to stick to the subject of the victim and his suffering. Do not venture into matters pertaining to the outside world or indeed the domestic (household chores and responsibilities), as this will agitate the victim and prevent him from focusing on his suffering and so begin the long journey back to full health.

Our "cure" (term used loosely) is Victor Hugo's classic novel of human torment and suffering, *Les Misérables.* Your patient might consider himself too ill for the application of a novel cure—he may even urge you to turn to the entry in this book on dying. However, it is important to have a firm

---

* Scientists cannot explain why this ailment affects only men, but it does.

hand in administering it, despite his resistance. Within a few pages he will have lost himself completely in the woes of Jean Valjean and Fantine, Cosette and Monsieur Marius, Eponine and police inspector Javert, recognizing his own sufferings in theirs, and taking great comfort as a result.

Because of its great length, *Les Misérables* may on the surface seem like a punishment. In fact, it will help the victim to find the patience and stoicism to endure his enforced inactivity—the most pernicious cases of man flu have been known to incapacitate for up to a week. Those responsible for nursing the victim, a round-the-clock job, will find him to be less talkative while taking the cure, thus giving everybody a chance to recover and delve more deeply within themselves to find unending supplies of love and sympathy. In the most effective cases, the cure might even enable the sufferer to forget about his symptoms completely and bring about a return to good humor, vivacity, and pleasure in life—even interest in others—which will seem quite miraculous when it occurs.

If the patient does not finish his medication before recovering, do not panic. Those prone to man flu are likely to experience recurrences of the illness at regular intervals throughout their lives, and an unfinished dose of the medicine is useful to have at hand. Being familiar with the medicine will mean the patient is more likely to be receptive to it and will agree to taking it the instant symptoms appear.

See also: **Cold, common** • **Dying** • **Hypochondria**

MANNERS, BAD

What do good manners mean anymore, in an age in which thank-you notes are sent by e-mail (if at all) and even the most august occasions are interrupted by the flashes of smartphone cameras and the rat-a-tat-tatting of texting guests? Every day it gets harder to figure out which social conventions still matter. But that does not mean we cannot make serious faux pas, or that we do not agonize about the possibility of making them.

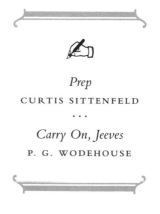

Prep
CURTIS SITTENFELD
• • •
Carry On, Jeeves
P. G. WODEHOUSE

In the meticulously well-observed novel *Prep*, by Curtis Sittenfeld, a precocious girl from the Midwest named Lee Fiora gets a scholarship to a prestigious East Coast boarding school. She arrives on the playing fields of Ault with no clue as to how to behave in her upscale new setting if she wants to avoid looking stupid or giving offense. "There was so much I didn't know," Lee reflects. "Most of it had to do with money (what a debutante was, how you pronounced Greenwich, Connecticut) or with sex (that a pearl necklace wasn't always a piece of jewelry), but sometimes it had to do with more general information about clothing, or food, or geography." Quickly, she learns to downplay her lack of knowledge and keep a low profile until she has a better sense of the contours of her new social landscape. Lee adopts a strategy that may help you, too, whenever you find yourself in situations in which you're not quite sure how to act. As she learns, manners don't exist in a vacuum; they're determined by where you are, what you're doing, and what sort of people you find yourself among. When it comes to manners, context is all.

Decoding this context, of course, is the tricky part. If only we all had a Jeeves, the brainy butler of P. G. Wodehouse's Jeeves and Wooster tales. Jeeves protects his employer, the rather blithering Bertie Wooster, from one blunder after another. In *Carry On, Jeeves*, Bertie is saved from his own boorish impulses on many an occasion (especially sartorial ones), and reading this book may offer you some advice to combat your own tendency to social clumsiness. More than just antiquated social formalities, good manners save you from your own worst impulses by prompting you to consider the sensitivities of others.

See also: Selfishness

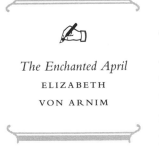

The Enchanted April
ELIZABETH
VON ARNIM

MARRIED, BEING

Being married? An ailment? If that was your first thought when you happened upon this entry, you probably don't need to read it. You've won life's biggest lottery and found yourself a mate you can live with effortlessly, peaceably, and productively. Congratulations.

If, on the other hand, you find that marriage sometimes involves a struggle to maintain your sense of self in the face of constant compromise, if your marriage is stuck in a rut, or if the passing of the years has somehow pushed you and your spouse apart rather than bring you closer, take a burst of luminous inspiration from *The Enchanted April* by Elizabeth von Arnim.

A neglected period piece from the 1920s, the novel tells the story of Mrs. Wilkins and Mrs. Arbuthnot, two married women who have become jaded and faded by their broken relationships. Both happen to spot the same advertisement in *The Times*: "To Those Who Appreciate Wistaria and Sunshine," it reads. "Small medieval Italian Castle on the shores of the Mediterranean to be let furnished for the month of April. Necessary servants remain." It calls to them both, and in a desperate bid for a gasp of happiness, the two women, though strangers, decide to take the castle together. They invite along a couple of feistier examples of their sex, who have relationship issues of their own—the impossibly proper Mrs. Fisher and the ethereally beautiful Lady Caroline, who is so sick of drooling attention from both men and women that she has become liberal with the icy put-downs.

Amid the purity of San Salvatore's bare white walls and stone floors, the women recover, and slowly begin to rediscover their sensuality and capacity for joy. With the help of juicy oranges, meadows of spring flowers, and the ever helpful gardener, Domenico, alchemical transformations occur. Faces puckered by fear and worry smooth out; hearts and minds that have been closed for years break open like buds in full sun. Love floods back in. "I was a stingy beast at home," declares Mrs. Wilkins, "and used to measure and count . . . I wouldn't love Mellersh unless he loved me back, exactly as much, absolute fairness. Did you ever. And as he didn't, neither did I, and the *aridity* of that house!"

We expect the women to find only themselves in their splendid isolation. But as it turns out, the husbands aren't forgotten. Marriages are saved and great loves reignited. If your marriage isn't what you'd hoped for, buy *The Enchanted April*. Then book a villa in Italy and read it on the journey out.

See also: **Children, under pressure to have** • **Jump ship, desire to** • **Orgasms, not enough** • **Querulousness** • **Sex, too little** • **Sex, too much** • **Snoring**

.

MEANING, LACK OF
See: **Pointlessness**

MELANCHOLY
See: **Sadness**

Remainder
TOM MCCARTHY

In comic television shows and films, amnesia is a condition that can be caused and cured . . . and caused again and cured again . . . by a bump on the head from a coconut. Should you have come by this traumatic condition in a less mirthful manner, you will doubtless be eager to restore your memory loss without recourse to a wind-whipped palm tree. Certainly, the services of a physician or psychiatrist ought to be engaged as a first step in the curative process, but you might also consider the recovery strategy pursued by the unnamed narrator of *Remainder*, Tom McCarthy's brainteaser of a novel.

McCarthy's hapless narrator has been wandering around, minding his own business, when he gets—you've guessed it—clonked on the head. But not by a coconut. "Technology. Parts, bits. That's it, really: all I can divulge. Not much, I know," he says. The company responsible for the whirling piece of something falling from the sky gives him a huge cash settlement, on the condition that he never discuss or in any way record the incident. Easy enough. As he tells his lawyer, "I never had any memory of it in the first place." The man's memory is entirely gone; his own past feels to him like fiction, and the word "you" sounds to him like somebody else. Simple acts like eating and walking seem unnatural. A physical therapist starts his recovery by making him "visualize things"—like raising a carrot to his mouth—to prompt his brain to create new neural pathways. The hope is that, once the brain can picture the activity, it will eventually remember how to make the limbs hop to it and execute it in real life.

Taking this medical advice to heart, the man uses his settlement money to employ legions of actors to enact banal scenes, over and over, to permit him to accumulate a kind of video library of lifelike occurrences. The more intricate these reconstructions become, and the more thoroughly the man engages in his new life, the more he worries that he has lost the capacity to be "real." "My movements are all fake. Second-hand," he tells a man named Greg, who was his friend before the incident. He feels as if he's always acting, as if he can no longer just authentically "be," he complains. Provocatively, Greg asks, "Do you think you could before?"

Is your spine tingling a little by now? *Remainder* toys with the philosophical question of what really makes us who we are. Our memories, this novel suggests, resemble fluid archival footage in our heads, which we change and reconstruct over the years into a story that usefully explains who we were and, more important, who we are now. We are constantly losing old memories and acquiring new ones. Identity may be memory, but if so, identity is also flux.

So if you have forgotten who you are, whether momentarily or more permanently, take comfort in knowing that this is, in some sense, the story of all human consciousness.

See also: Amnesia, reading associated

MENOPAUSE

The Summer Before the
Dark
DORIS LESSING
. . .
Miss Garnet's Angel
SALLEY VICKERS
. . .
The Private Lives of
Pippa Lee
REBECCA MILLER

It may be the end of your monthly cycles, but it doesn't need to be the end of you. In fact, for many women, reaching menopause triggers a desire to dig out the "you" that was buried or thrust aside by the distractions of the fertile years. Whether you had children early or late or not at all, the deposing of your ovaries from their throne allows you to throw off a certain motherly mantle and cloak yourself in something more exciting instead.

Take as your role model Kate in Doris Lessing's sixties classic of female self-discovery, *The Summer Before the Dark.* For a number of years, forty-five-year-old Kate has been holding back the tide—tinting her hair, keeping control of her weight, and "scaling herself down" in order to look and be the part of housewife and mother from her middle-class London suburb. But the youngest of her four children is now nineteen and ready to leave home, and though she is not yet menopausal, her family speaks about her as if she were. When a job comes her way—her first, as Kate chose to get married rather than have a career—she leaves her old clothes behind and buys sexy, sophisticated dresses that "would admit her, like a passport," to a life in which she's no longer Mrs. Brown, but Kate Ferreira.

Kate soon bores of this, though. The reason she's so good at her job, she realizes, is that she continues to play a diplomatic role—as if she were secreting some sort of "invisible fluid" that made "a whole of individuals who could have no other connection." In short, she's being everyone's mother. She continues to try on, then reject a series of other roles—and clothes—but finds them all variations on the mothering theme. This discovery sends her spiraling into a breakdown—although, in Lessing's world, breakdowns are always purgative. What shines through all the confusion is an epiphany she has halfway through her summer of change. Her future will not be a continuation of her immediate past, but will pick up where she left off as a child: the intelligent, feisty, and, yes, sexy Kate she used to be.

If you are past caring about sexiness, turn with relief to thoughts of art, self-education, spirituality, and self-discovery. In this, *Miss Garnet's Angel* should be your accomplice. A spinster of just past sixty, and still a virgin, Miss Garnet has occasional regrets that she has never been loved by anyone enough to marry. But now that her flatmate—"the only person she had ever eaten with"—has just died, all she wants is a little adventure somewhere exotic. Quite randomly, she decides on Venice. There, Miss Garnet opens herself to experiences in a way she never has before, making friends easily and being sucked into an intriguing art theft, as well as a near romance. Most important, though, she discovers the angel Raphael. Invigorating, wise, and refreshingly free of sex, Miss Garnet's late flowering will inspire you to higher things in life.

But if you're not done yet with the reckless adventures of youth, grab Rebecca Miller's *The Private Lives of Pippa Lee*. From the terrible tedium of a retirement community—albeit one for the filthy rich—where Pippa Lee looks doomed to spend her middle age with her more senior husband, Herb, who's eighty-one, we travel via memories of her troubled childhood and speed-crazed twenties into the arms of the younger Chris, a recovering Christian. Art and angels may have their place, but so, sometimes, does post-menopausal sex. Take this novel to bed—it's never too late for new love.

See also: **Fiftysomething, being** · **Headache** · **Insomnia** · **Libido, loss of** · **Sweating** · **Tired and emotional, being**

MIDLIFE CRISIS

Girl, 20
KINGSLEY AMIS
...
The Year of the Hare
ARTO PAASILINNA
...
The Art of Fielding
CHAD HARBACH

Are you trying to figure out how you can "bribe your own daughter to do camouflage duty so that you and your mistress can have an evening out against her boyfriend's wishes behind her stepmother's back?" If the answer is yes, and said mistress is seventeen, and you're three times her age, then congratulations. You have landed in an epic midlife crisis of the kind that Kingsley Amis commemorated in his 1971 novel *Girl, 20*. The book ages remarkably well. The freshly knighted violinist and conductor Sir Roy Vandervane has never been particularly faithful to his second wife, Kitty, but after ten years of marriage, Kitty senses "he's getting ready for another of his goes." She should know—after all, she was the one who pried him away from his first wife, during a pre-midlife crisis. Roy feels no regret. "I know all this makes me look a right shit, and probably be a right shit," he tells his go-between, Douglas Yandell, "but I am in love with this curious little creature, and perhaps that doesn't justify anything, but you can't imagine how it makes me look forward to each day."

If you're past the first bloom of youth and find yourself tempted to follow Sir Roy down a similarly destructive devil-may-care path, then take up *Girl, 20* and focus on Douglas's attempts to reform the randy Roy and soothe his betrayed wife. With luck, Douglas's hand-wringing will chasten you and bring you back to your senses.

If you're only on the verge, then seek preventive care for the midlife malady in the form of the gently humorous 1975 Finnish novel *The Year of the Hare* by Arto Paasilinna. A journalist named Vatanen has tired of his job and his wife in Helsinki, and sets off on a road trip with a friend. On the way, he adopts a wild hare, which they had injured on their drive and which becomes his traveling companion. He ends up, much refreshed, in a rustic cabin in Lapland. Slip this slim volume into your overnight case the next time you're on a business trip, and refer to it whenever that midlife crisis urge comes upon you. Better Lapland than lap dance.

For some, a midlife crisis is a chance to embrace the life they hadn't gotten around to living. In Chad Harbach's *The Art of Fielding*, we follow the taciturn stripling Henry Skrimshander from the cornfields of South Dakota to a small liberal arts college in Wisconsin called Westish. Skrimshander, silent and unremarkable in most respects, is a natural at baseball, an outfielder with a "transcendent talent" for fielding that enables him to catch the most elusive balls. Westish gives the boy a full ride so its baseball team can benefit from his magic arm. There, young Skrimshander meets the college's widower president, Guert Affenlight.

At the age of sixty, Affenlight falls hard for Skrimshander's roommate, the self-assured, breezy, brilliant Owen. Affenlight "didn't think of himself as gay," he reflects, as he sits on a love seat with Owen, reeling at what has just transpired between them. He hadn't even thought of himself as sexual, after a protracted dry spell. But at once he senses that this affair will be life changing. "From here on out," he thinks, "he'd be with Owen or no one. No one or Owen." His ecstatic transformation shakes him. Owen is comfortable in his own skin, but Affenlight definitely is not. As their relationship progresses, Owen recognizes that they must keep a low profile on campus but bristles at being hidden away like a shameful secret. "I know we can't just walk around holding hands," he complains to his august lover, but "what if we were in New York, or San Francisco, or even down the road in Door Country? What if you came to Tokyo with me? Would you walk down the street with me then?" Or, he adds, "Would that be too gay for you? Better to stay right here, in the heart of the problem, where your restrictions will protect you."

"You've been reading too much Foucault," Affenlight retorts. But love trumps literary criticism. There's no question that Affenlight's May-December affair with Owen wreaks havoc on his life. But it also lets him start living, at last. Sometimes, a midlife crisis can be a welcome wake-up call.

MISANTHROPY

The Holy Sinner
THOMAS MANN

If you are a hater of the human species, try living on a rock in the middle of a lake for seventeen years, like Gregory in *The Holy Sinner*. He has extremely good reasons for his own mistrust of human nature. He married his mother, killed his father, and is himself the offspring of a brother and sister. Then he decides he must atone for his (admittedly unintended) sins, and takes off to live on an island in the center of a lake. He shackles himself to a rock using a leg iron, just to make his penance more painful. On his limited diet—he suckles from the stone of Mother Earth—he shrinks to the size of a hedgehog.

Meanwhile, the last pope has died, and two bishops have had a vision of a bleeding lamb, which (somehow) makes them understand that the next pope is to be found on an island in the middle of a lake. With great distaste and confusion, the bishops bring the bristly homunculus back to dry land, where Gregory is miraculously restored to normal human size again and goes on to become one of the greatest popes of all time—admired for his clemency, wisdom, and understanding.

If, like Gregory, you tend to stand apart from humanity, despising what you see, consider whether your hatred isn't in fact hatred of yourself. Adopt, like Gregory, the expression *Absolvo te*—"I forgive you"—and turn it inward. Once you've learned to love yourself, you'll find it easier to forgive others' failings as well.

See also: **Antisocial, being** · **Cynicism** · **Dinner parties, fear of** · **Grumpiness** · **Killjoy, being a** · **Selfishness**

MISCARRIAGE

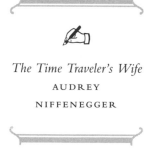

The Time Traveler's Wife
AUDREY
NIFFENEGGER

Miscarriage is miserable, bloody, and lonely. No matter the circumstances, it's hard for any woman to deal with the despair it brings on, especially with your hormones still raging and your womb aching. While you recover, read *The Time Traveler's Wife*.

Clare has loved the same man all her life. She first met him when she was only six and he thirty-five. Henry is not a pedophile but a time traveler, and he knows that in his future, and hers, they will be married. The strange, haunting tale of their love is both agonizing and wonderful to witness. Clare waits for Henry, rejecting suitors from the start. But she has no control over the romance: Henry cannot choose when he time travels—sometimes he leaves Clare for months or even years on end—even when they are happily married. Clare turns inward, coping with the solitude by channeling it into her art.

The real problems begin when they try to have a baby. Clare goes through five miscarriages before it dawns on them that the fetuses might be inheriting the time-traveling gene and leaving the womb prenatally. Each time it happens, there are blood-soaked sheets, sometimes a "tiny monster" in Clare's hand, hope and despair hot on each other's heels. Clare perseveres because she is desperate to have a child, and eventually they find a way around their unique predicament. But she suffers for each loss as you will have suffered, and to bear witness to her grief is deeply comforting. If you, too, are determined, keep trying, and may this life-embracing novel both console and inspire.

See also: Children, not having • Cry, in need of a good • Failure, feeling like a • Pain, being in • Sadness • Yearning, general

MISSING SOMEONE

See: Breaking up • Death of a loved one • Family, coping without • Homesickness • Lovesickness • Widowed, being • Yearning, general

MISSING YOUR CHILDREN

See: Empty-nest syndrome

Mrs. Dalloway
VIRGINIA WOOLF

MONDAY MORNING FEELING

If the thought of Monday morning fills you with doom, if you emerge into wakefulness with the weight of a mountain pressing on your chest, pep yourself up with *Mrs. Dalloway*. For with this masterpiece, Virginia Woolf invented a whole new way of writing, of capturing thoughts in constant flux and the vitality coursing through the veins of a woman experiencing, moment by moment, one day in June, in the London she loves after the war has ended. The day is not, in fact, a Monday, but a Wednesday, and Clarissa Dalloway is preparing for a party that night.

She decides to buy the flowers herself. You, too, might like to take re-sponsibility for a task—something pleasant, something sensual—that you would normally leave to someone else. The thought of this will help you out of bed. As you eat your breakfast, drink up Clarissa's exuberance, her cut-from-crystal thoughts—"What a lark! What a plunge!"—and run with the longer, meandering thought that follows, bending through time, and gather-ing up sounds: "For so it had always seemed to her when, with a squeak of the hinges, which she could hear now, she had burst open the French win-dows and plunged at Bourton into the open air." What a sentence! What an invitation! Can you not hear that squeak, feel the little shove as the doors give way? Can you not taste that clean, cold air?

Then receive, through your eyes and mind and into your body, Clarissa's appetite and love of life. Inhabit her neat and birdlike figure, light, springy, upright, as she stands on the curb preparing to cross. Notice the "particular hush," the "indescribable pause" before the tolling of Big Ben. Become aware, as she is aware, of the presence of death—that all these scurrying people will one day just be bones and dust—and carry this awareness with you into your day. Let it heighten your sense of being alive, this particular Monday. Let it help you make the most of your day. Your *Monday*.

Then step out. And . . . why not? Go and buy the flowers yourself.

See also: Bed, inability to get out of • Career, being in the wrong • Dissatisfaction

MONEY, NOT HAVING ANY

See: Broke, being • Tax return, fear of doing • Unemployment

MONEY, SPENDING TOO MUCH

See: Book buyer, being a compulsive • Extravagance • Shopaholism • Tax return, fear of doing

MORNING SICKNESS

See: Nausea • Pregnancy

Our Spoons Came from Woolworths
BARBARA COMYNS
. . .
I Don't Know How She Does It
ALLISON PEARSON

How I dislike the idea of being a Daddy and pushing a pram!' said George. So I said, 'I don't want to be a beastly Mummy either; I shall run away.' Then I remembered if I ran away the baby would come with me wherever I went. It was a most suffocating feeling and I started to cry." This excerpt from *Our Spoons Came from Woolworths*, a soufflé of a novel published in 1950, could be printed on packets of birth control pills as a reminder of the realities of having a baby. Once it's there, it's there all the time, and you're responsible for it, whether you like it or not.

Motherhood can't be cured, but it can be treated, and Barbara Comyns's self-deprecating and largely autobiographical novel is an excellent place to start. Sophia is the relentlessly optimistic heroine, who marries far too young, carries a newt called Great Warty around in her pocket, and is utterly ill equipped for the impending onslaught. She and her young painter husband are bohemians at heart, cut off from their families and living hand to mouth, barely employed. Sophia has two babies, and Charles's reluctance to make any concessions to fatherhood doesn't bode well for their harmony—he doesn't see, for example, why you can't keep a baby in a cupboard. Sophia's hideous experiences at the birthing hospital are enough to put many a prospective mother off, but her ability to bounce back after the most appalling setbacks—such as her mother-in-law first swearing not to come to the wedding at all, then turning up with swarms of relatives and expecting to be hosted in the new couple's dingy flat—makes her spirited and positive company. She goes from odd job to odd job, frequently supporting the entire family, while Charles continues to believe he is magnificently talented and should not allow fatherhood to get in his way.

It all adds up to an extreme version of what many new mothers experience, and the refreshingly offbeat humor, combined with Sophia's beguiling voice, will have mothers laughing along with her as she does her best to play house without any help from her spouse. If you're a new mother, you'll be well prepared by absorbing some of her survivalist attitude.

For a more modern take on motherhood, Allison Pearson's *I Don't Know How She Does It* is a hilarious dissection of the juggling skills required to hold down a top job, keep a lover, make some pretense at being married, and be a mother. The book begins with Kate Reddy, age thirty-five, up at 1:37 a.m. on the thirteenth of December, "distressing" store-bought mince pies to make them look homemade. She's determined to at least seem like a "proper mother," a "self-sacrificing baker of apple pies and well-scrubbed invigilator of the washtub" rather than the "other sort."

By day Kate is a fund manager in a City firm, where her boss stares at her breasts "as if they were on special offer" and she keeps long hours, her main entertainment being an e-mail romance with the too-good-to-be-true Jack Abelhammer. She constantly agonizes about missing her children's milestone moments—"Today is my son's first birthday and I am sitting in the sky over Heathrow"—and rages against the misogynist world that has put her in this position. Her marriage seems decidedly last century, too, as she bears the brunt of all child-related organization, domestic chores, and school runs, albeit by remote control.

Pearson writes with such humor that reading this will pose a challenge to your postbirth pelvic floor muscles. If you haven't yet entered the realm of motherhood but are curious about what goes on behind the fence, this novel will read as a warning against attempting to "have it all." But those already living on that side of the fence will take much roguish delight as Kate Reddy gears up for her next move—still joyfully juggling the balls of marriage, career, and kids.

See also: **Children requiring attention, too many • Housewife, being a • Mother-in-law, being a • Single parent, being a • Trapped by children**

MOTHER-IN-LAW, BEING A

Daughters-in-Law
JOANNA TROLLOPE

Ladies, please pause to consider. If you are a mother-in-law, do you at least attempt to defy the cliché?* Are you loving and supportive of your son- or daughter-in-law?† Have you accepted him or her, gracefully, as he or she is?‡ Do

---

* No one is good enough for your child, of course, but it's still a cliché.

† However little you actually like him or her.

‡ Though you would not have chosen him or her yourself.

you endeavor to see things from his or her point of view,* even if it contradicts your own offspring's,† knowing that in the end this will strengthen their marriage and, indirectly, help your precious child?

Of the three mothers-in-law (MILs) featured in Joanna Trollope's rigorous exploration of intergenerational in-law relationships, it's Rachel—the mother of three grown-up, married sons, and MIL to Sigrid, Petra, and Charlotte—who has the longest list of destructive behaviors to her credit. An energetic, efficient, protective "tiger" mother when her sons were growing up, she has become a forceful, interfering, invasive, controlling old cow now that they're putting their own partners first. Charlotte's mother, Marnie, appears on the surface to be benign—she's generous, and wants to help out the couple financially. But they soon realize there's a fine line between support and suffocation.

Of all the characters, it is Sigrid's mother who provides a role model for how to be a second mother to your extra children. She insists, calmly, that you can let your adult children go successfully only if you have interesting, absorbing work—or some other creative outlet—of your own, plus a strong enough relationship with your own partner, if you have one. This will prevent you from begging your children for the time and attention they should be giving their own families.

Be loving, supportive, generous, understanding, kind, and fun. But make sure you don't have the time to interfere.

See also: Control freak, being a

Daughters-in-Law
JOANNA TROLLOPE

MOTHER-IN-LAW, HAVING A

Ladies, we sympathize. MILs—mothers-in-law—can be forceful, interfering, invasive, controlling old cows who believe that no one will ever be good enough for their son or daughter, make no attempt to conceal how little they like you, always take their offspring's side, and assume, by default, that you're wrong.

---

* Albeit mistaken.

† Even though your darling is always in the right.

But this doesn't mean you're off the hook. Intergenerational in-law relationships have got to be worked at from both sides. Think about it from the point of view of Rachel, one of the MILs in Trollope's novel. Her identity as a woman is thrown off balance when her third son, Luke, gets married. Suddenly no one wants her to do the thing she's good at anymore. Left without agency or power, she panics—and when she panics, as she admits herself, she "barks." It's not that she doesn't like you; it's that she doesn't like this new person your arrival has forced her to be.

MILs need to be stood up to, and you must never be afraid to do this. The old family dynamic is obsolete and a new one must be built. But while it's happening, be the sort of second child your adjusting MIL might like to have: loving, supportive, generous, understanding, kind, and fun. And make time to interfere.

See also: Christmas · Divorce · Family, coping with · Murderous thoughts

MOVING

Heligoland
SHENA MACKAY

Consider the snail. His house is on his back, he can slither into it whenever he likes, and as long as no blundering oaf comes by with thoughtless feet, he's always got his home to hand (or, rather, proboscis). We, on the other hand, are not so adaptable. When we move, we require moving vans, checklists, a small forest's worth of cardboard boxes, packers, carriers, in-laws, nannies, dogsitters, and, afterward, therapists. It's one of the most demanding and stressful events we go through in life, and causes a range of side effects, including angst, hair loss, and conflict within your relationship. Not to mention it throws your bank balance seriously off-kilter. To avoid these side effects completely, climb inside a box with this small but perfectly formed novel by Shena Mackay.

Heligoland describes the residents of an unusual shell-shaped house called the Nautilus.* Gleaming "like a pearl" and with an anchor at its heart connecting it to the seabed of London, the house was built in the 1930s by Ce-

---

* The perceptive will notice that the house shares its name with Captain Nemo's submarine in Jules Verne's *20,000 Leagues Under the Sea.*

leste and her husband as a place to bring artists and writers together. Now an old woman, Celeste still lives in the Nautilus, though the echoing house is not the hubbub of artistic life it once was. Its current occupants—including a minor poet and an antiques dealer—are jaded has-beens, one way or another. But there is Rowena too, an orphan of Indian extraction who has come to be the new housekeeper.

Rowena is a lost soul, drawn to the Nautilus and its intriguing denizens because she craves a combination of the lonely life she shared with her aunt in the Scottish Highlands as a child and the communal existence of her old boarding school. As she begins to feel at home in the quirky spaces, Rowena's deep loneliness starts to abate. One day she shyly cooks up an Indian feast in the kitchen without telling anyone what she's doing. The fragrances lure them from their shells, and they all appear, dressed for dinner, just like in the house's heyday. Little by little, Rowena brings new life to the Nautilus, galvanizing the old crowd to throw a birthday party for her, to clear out the old swimming pool, and discover forgotten areas of the garden.

Mackay's prose, lustrous as the pearly shell she describes, is precise and calm and will declutter your mind as you read. And you'll be greatly inspired by Rowena's ability to re-create the idealized dream home she's imagined since her childhood, the Heligoland of the title: something between an island in unnavigable seas and a fairground merry-go-round. Catch her spirit of optimism as you, too, create your own dream home and start anew.

See also: **Broke, being** • **Exhaustion** • **Family, coping with** • **Friend, falling out with your best** • **Stress**

MR./MRS. RIGHT, HOLDING OUT FOR

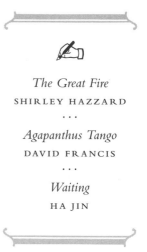

The Great Fire
SHIRLEY HAZZARD
...

Agapanthus Tango
DAVID FRANCIS
...

Waiting
HA JIN

Compromise is unavoidable once you're married, but those refusing to compromise *before* they're married are opting for a risky strategy. Whole lives can pass by in the waiting, and there's no guarantee that, at the end of it all, you'll find your hoped-for prize.

Those holding out need encouragement to keep their nerve, because the alternative is worse. (If you're in any doubt, see: Mr./Mrs. Wrong, ending up with.) Take heart from the story of Aldred Leith in Shirley Hazzard's magisterial *The Great Fire*. Thirty-two but feeling older, Leith is emotionally beached after the trauma of World War II and a dissolved "war marriage" to Moira. He expects nothing from life from here on out. But in the damp hills near Hiroshima, where he has come to write a government report, he meets two remarkable children: Helen Driscoll and her terminally ill brother, Ben. The fragile siblings have nothing in common with their oafish father and insincere mother, who represent everything that Leith despises. But together they have created a little haven of intellectualism, reading aloud to each other— "they live in literature and make free with it." Leith finds, almost to his embarrassment, that he has met his true love match in Helen. With her small breasts only just showing beneath her dress, he guesses she is no more than fifteen.

At first he puts it down to a need for comfort in an "entire world" that needs comforting, but they experience true happiness when they meet. Shirley Hazzard makes what might otherwise be an inappropriate pairing (see: Age gap between lovers) beautiful and real by the force of her zealously unsentimental prose. Leith and Helen wait for each other, spanning their separation with letters while also having to cope with the antipathy of Helen's parents and the transplantation of their relationship to a different country. But the certainty with which they recognize—and we, too, feel—their rightness for each other is inspiring to anyone holding out for the same. Their confidence is well placed, in the end.

If you believe you have already met your Mr. or Mrs. Right but are forced to hold out because *he or she* fails to see it, we urge you to read *Aga-*

panthus Tango, David Francis's gem of a novel set partly in the parched Australian outback and partly in the green fields of America's horse-racing country. We won't make any promises for a happy ending here, but Day's feelings for Callie are so evidently real, the two of them so clearly suited, that our hearts sit on a cliff edge as we watch the eighteen-year-old Australian boy being continually rebuffed by the untamed Callie.

Day has run away from home following his mother's death and lands himself a passage to America along with a thoroughbred racehorse. Offering himself as a stable hand to the horse's new owner there, he meets the sixteen-year-old Calliope Coates, another runaway. Unreachable, cocky, troubled, smelling of damp hay, and with a cruel streak in her that sees her whipping her horses, she is all that Day wants, from that moment on. Day, recognizing another damaged spirit, understands her and accepts her as she is, and simply doesn't give up. Is Day a fool to suffer the wounds and rejections and still hold out hope? Or does he exhibit real emotional bravery? Those finding themselves tempted to be rocklike for someone unavailable like Callie must read right to the end of this exquisitely written novel to find out whether such strength of spirit pays off.

In *Waiting* by Ha Jin, Lin, a doctor in the city, keeps his girlfriend, Manna, waiting for eighteen years because first he must divorce Shuyu, the illiterate village girl with bound feet his parents forced him to marry. Each year Shuyu agrees to a divorce, but each year he arrives at the courtroom only to find she has changed her mind. Manna, head nurse at the hospital where Lin works, wastes her thirties waiting for Lin, and her resentment turns to bitterness (see: Bitterness).

She's not the only one damaged by the years of waiting. Shuyu endures a hard, lonely life bringing up their daughter Hua in the countryside, and only belatedly does Lin realize what a poor father to Hua he has been. Eventually, Manna has waited so long for Lin that it becomes too late *not* to keep waiting. Yet by that time, Lin's romantic passion for Manna has faded and his own shilly-shallying has caused him to lose self-respect. "I know your type," Lin's roommate tells him. "You're always afraid that people will call you a bad man." Lin knows his weakness has ruined all their lives, and even when the waiting is over, there is more waiting on the horizon. Let this novel be a warning: don't let your whole life become one big wait.

See also: **Change, resistance to • Commitment, fear of • Indecision • Optimism • Procrastination • Risks, not taking enough • Romantic, hopeless • Wasting time on a dud relationship**

MR./MRS. RIGHT, LOOKING FOR

The Pursuit of Love
NANCY MITFORD

. . .

Emma
JANE AUSTEN

. . .

Pride and Prejudice
JANE AUSTEN

. . .

Joshua Spassky
GWENDOLINE RILEY

. . .

Bel Canto
ANN PATCHETT

Finding your ideal partner—best friend, lover, companion, bankroller, chef, artfully combined in one winsome package—is generally considered to be the jackpot in the great lottery of life, the best way to secure happiness, good health, and longevity. For many, it is the major obsession of early life, and, if the search fails, the primary cause of unhappiness in later life (see: Shelf, fear of being left on the; Mr./Mrs. Wrong, ending up with; Loneliness). Since the nineteenth century, novels have shared—or reflected, or fueled, depending on your take—this obsession. Hundreds of searches for Mr. and Mrs. Right have been presented for our entertainment and edification. But have two centuries' worth of reading about them made us any better at it? Have we, in fact, merely become such perfectionists that we are in danger of seeking an ideal that doesn't exist (see: Mr./Mrs. Right, holding out for; Happiness, searching for)?

It doesn't seem so. Many of us still follow the terrible example of Linda Radlett in Nancy Mitford's *The Pursuit of Love*, who, despite starting out with the conviction that true love comes only once in a lifetime, goes about it using the method by which she later buys clothes: trial and error. That is, she marries two Mr. Wrongs before she finds what she thinks is the real thing, at last, in the wealthy French duke Fabrice. Fabrice funds her shopping sprees and for a while makes her the happiest woman in the world—but not, alas, for long. Oh, that she had not been in such a rush and held out for "the one"!

Of course, we often *do* meet Mr. or Mrs. Right early on—sometimes staring us in the face, in fact—but we fail to recognize it, whether through our own failings or someone else's. The former is the case with Jane Austen's Emma, who takes the span of a whole novel to develop enough self-awareness to be struck by the arrow informing her, with absolute, wondrous certainty, that her Mr. Right is her neighbor Mr. Knightley. The latter is the case with Elizabeth Bennet in *Pride and Prejudice*, whose Mr. Darcy has a few character flaws to be ironed out before he can be a Mr. Right for her (see: Arrogance).

And both are true with the drink-befuddled, damaged pair in Gwendoline Riley's *Joshua Spassky*. After five years of on-and-off dating and failed sexual encounters, Natalie and Joshua take themselves off to Asheville, North Carolina, where they lie in a motel room and try to work out whether or not they're in love. If you *don't* find it maddening to watch them deliberate, and do feel a great sense of relief when the emotionally frozen Natalie finally announces that she feels like a bottle of milk "that's just been taken out of the fridge"—suggesting an emotional thaw is finally on its way— you're probably equally scared of commitment (see immediately: Commitment, fear of). Don't be too hasty to dismiss the friends in your immediate circle when you're looking for love; many of the happiest partnerships are between people who don't have to look far to find each other.

But sometimes Mr. or Mrs. Right is very far away indeed. This is the case for Mr. Hosokawa, the boss of a Japanese electronics company who would surely have gone on believing he could feel true love only for opera rather than another human being if he hadn't been thrown into unlikely circumstances: when he's taken hostage during a concert in his honor. In one of the best stories we know about love blossoming where it's least expected, Ann Patchett's brilliant *Bel Canto* sees the emergence of three true loves: Mr. Hosokawa with the beautiful soprano Roxane Coss; his highly educated interpreter, Gen, with a completely uneducated peasant-turned-terrorist; and the French diplomat Thibault, who until recently has taken his elegant wife, Edith, for granted. Transformed by the beauty of Coss's singing—Patchett writes tremendously about the almost painful, visceral capacity of music to move—and forced to live in the heightened moment by the constant threat of death, the extraordinary outcome for those in the cocoon of the vice president's mansion (where they are being held) is that everyone, hostages and terrorists alike, gravitate to culture and art—to singing, reading, learning, cooking, playing chess—and, of course, to love.

All of which is not to say, of course, that you should go get yourself taken hostage. The takeaway here may be to not look too far or try too hard, for your Mr. or Mrs. Right may just be closer to you than you think. Cultivate your passions, live your life, grow and develop in interesting ways, and enjoy it while you're at it. Then—who knows—maybe your Mr. or Mrs. Right will find *you*.

MR./MRS. WRONG, ENDING UP WITH

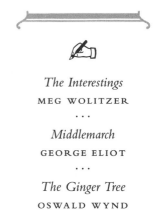

Before you slap your head with recognition, thinking to yourself, "Yes, yes, *that's* my problem—my partner has blighted my happiness!" read Meg Wolitzer's wise and generous novel *The Interestings*, in which a handful of couples fall in and out of love with their spouses, and in and out of fortune's favor. The main characters in the book meet as teenagers one summer in an arts camp; decades later, they still struggle to live up to their youthful high opinions of one another. Jules, who has married an unartistic, depressive, but supportive man named Dennis, often thinks she's married beneath her. "If you want to get out of this marriage, then just do it," Dennis tells her at one point, fed up with invidious comparison. But grown-up Jules is no barrel of laughs herself; she has long abandoned her comedy dreams and works as a therapist. When Dennis rebels against her unrealistic standards, defiantly proclaiming his "absolute lack of specialness," Jules realizes that he is, after all, special. And she needs him. "In a marriage, they both knew," Wolitzer writes, "sometimes there was a period in which one partner faltered, and the other partner held everything together. Maybe that was even a definition of marriage." *The Interestings* shows that maturity and understanding can turn Wrongs into Rights.

Then again, sometimes a mismatched couple is doomed from the start. George Eliot's masterful novel *Middlemarch* ruthlessly, unsentimentally examines the consequences that result from an obviously incompatible union. The misery the reader feels when the peerless Dorothea Brooke throws herself away on fusty old scholar Casaubon brings home the enormity of such a mistake. Although Dorothea doesn't think she's making a mistake, we know it's only a matter of time before she sees him for the dried-up pedant he is. The "large vistas and wide fresh air" she had dreamed of finding in her husband's mind, she ultimately sees, are in fact "anterooms and winding passages" leading nowhere.

Dorothea is saved from a lifetime of grim servitude when the Grim Reaper comes knocking for her husband. But the dashing young doctor Lydgate, Dorothea's friend, is not so lucky. He and Rosamond, drawn blindly to each other by romance, face a lifetime of torment when their actual personalities begin to emerge from beneath their facades. Rosamond's spending habits stymie Lydgate's ambitions, and when her motivation for marriage is exposed as having been little more than social advancement, bitterness corrodes their bond. Trapped in a loveless marriage, they might have avoided their fate if only they'd looked past superficialities and truly gotten to know each other before taking the plunge.

If it's too late for you, too, take heart from Mary, the feisty heroine of Oswald Wynd's *The Ginger Tree*. True, her Mr. Wrong abandons her when she has an affair with the Japanese count Kentaro (see: Adultery), but Mary has a habit of picking men who run off with her children as well, and loses two in the course of the story. Fortunately, this stoic young woman— marooned first in China by her cold, military attaché British husband, and then forced to flee to Japan—is keen to understand and adapt to the cultural differences around her in order to survive. Like the ginger tree of the title, which "remains the stubborn stranger" in the garden, she manages to maintain a strong sense of self within her alien culture, outcast or not, while doing so. Written in the form of journals and letters to her mother in Scotland and her friend Marie, this novel will have you shedding the tears Mary rarely sheds for herself. Be inspired by Mary to either grow in new directions, within the garden you find yourself in, or to find a door in the garden wall to let yourself out.

See also: **Dissatisfaction** • **Divorce** • **Murderous thoughts** • **Non-reading partner, having a** • **Regret** • **Stuck in a rut**

MUNDANITY, OPPRESSED BY

When the world seems awfully humdrum, you need to discover the transporting capacities of fantasy fiction. And we don't just mean Harry Potter—we love him too, but there's more to fantasy fiction than Hogwarts and Quidditch. Spread your wings with the list below. They will take you into the realm of the miraculous and the marvelous.

See also: **Boredom** • **Disenchantment** • **Dissatisfaction** • **Malaise, twenty-first century**

THE TEN BEST FANTASY NOVELS

MURDEROUS THOUGHTS

Thérèse Raquin
ÉMILE ZOLA

Everyone has them. Even kids. Even cats. So don't pretend you don't. You live with someone. They put their tea bags in the sink. They leave long, ginger hairs in the soap. They lean in a bit too close. They make sounds as they eat. And sometimes you want to kill them.

Most of us don't take it any further than a brief internal rant, followed by a period of secret brooding—at which point we come to our senses. However, some do take it one step beyond, and begin to plot. If you ever catch yourself doing this, Zola's *Thérèse Raquin* is your wake-up call. It describes the abject life of Thérèse and Camille, a married couple who live above their shop in the Passage du Pont Neuf along with Camille's mother. Zola lays on the desolation with a trowel; the winter light coming in through the arcade glass roof, for instance, throws "nothing but darkness on the sticky tiles—unclean and abominable gloom."

Indeed they are so miserable that we sympathize when Thérèse turns for some passion and excitement to another man, Laurent, gentleman painter and idle sponge. But when she and Laurent decide to kill Camille in order to clear the way for their love, our affinity with the heroine is challenged.

It's not that we feel any great affection for Camille—he's portrayed as a spineless, spoiled sop. But Thérèse and Laurent become progressively more detestable as the novel continues. We won't give away what happens, but the message is clear: this sort of solution will only lead to bad dreams, bad sex, and yet more homicidal thoughts. So stop your plotting. Breathe deeply. And again. Then see: Snoring; and Married, being.

See also: **Rage** • **Vengeance, seeking** • **Violence, fear of**

N

NAPOLEON COMPLEX

See: Short, being

NARCISSISM

See: Arrogance · Confidence, too much · Selfishness · Vanity

NAUSEA

There are few things worse. Excuse our vulgarity, but since recovery is impossible without letting it all come out . . . That's it. Go on. We won't look.

Brideshead Revisited
EVELYN WAUGH

Shivery, sweaty, shocked? Still a little queasy, perhaps? Go brush your teeth, then come back here and assume a horizontal position, wrapped in a blanket, propped up with pillows, a heating pad at your side, and your reeling head stilled by the perfectly balanced prose of Evelyn Waugh.

More than any other writer, Waugh can be trusted to put you back on level ground. To take you by the hand—gently, demurely—lift you up to your tiptoes, pause, then bring you down carefully again. Nobody does it better.

From the first paragraph of the first page of *Brideshead Revisited*, his paean to the privileged, observe how Waugh uses repetition to maintain a state of measured equilibrium: "I had reflected then" is balanced by "and I reflected now." A little farther down you'll find "a quarter of a mile" in one clause echoed in the next. Drop your eyes to the bottom of the page and watch alliteration and overlap take over, carrying us forward in precise dancer's steps: from "the camp stood" to "the farmhouse still stood" to "the ivy still supported." Semicolons act as brief, unobtrusive pauses—a moment's holding of a pleasing shape, sustaining the upward lift—while commas accommodate the fluency of flow and twirl thereafter. Not for a moment are we left in doubt as to the beat: "In half an hour we were ready to start and in an hour we started." Oh, the steadiness, the sureness, the settling of your tummy! This prose is a dance, and Waugh is the graceful, accomplished partner whisking us across the floor.

Whoops! Steady on. If you are afraid of the nausea returning, read on. For Charles, our narrator, whose "rooms" at Oxford are on the ground floor right next to the quad, forges the most intense relationship of his life because of vomit. Sebastian, the teddy bear–dependent younger son of the lord and lady of Brideshead Castle, "magically beautiful, with that epicene quality which . . . sings aloud for love," has had too much to drink. And, passing Charles's open window just before midnight, the young aristocrat leans into the room and throws up. Charles is generous enough to see "a kind of insane and endearing orderliness" about Sebastian's choice, in his moment of need, of an open window, but the roomful of flowers he finds on his return from lectures the next day, and the contrite invitation to "luncheon," charm him more. Soon he is cast into a world in which hard-boiled plovers' eggs are offered to guests—a world of beauty, intensity, and dysfunction that will set his youth aglow, then leave him to a lifetime of disappointment thereafter.

But life—and fiction—is made extraordinary by such friendships. If it weren't for Sebastian's nausea, he'd never have gone to Brideshead, or met Sebastian's "madly charming" sisters, or entered the "enclosed and enchanted garden" that gives him, at least for a spell, the happy childhood he never had.

Thanks, therefore, be to nausea, his and yours—and to Evelyn Waugh for making everything better.

NEEDINESS

True Grit
CHARLES PORTIS

Are you always asking for help? Unable to do anything on your own? Wanting someone to hold your hand at all times? Asking for help is, of course, a good thing, but complete dependence is not. There comes a time when you need to learn independence and rely on yourself and yourself alone. Like a slushy road, a dose of grit is your cure.

Set in America just after the Civil War, Charles Portis's novel *True Grit* describes the steely determination of Mattie, a fifteen-year-old girl seeking to bring her father's killer to justice. The killer is Tom Chaney, an employee of her father's, who pulled a gun on him in a fit of drunken pique. Mattie has come to Fort Smith ostensibly to fetch her father's body, but, unknown to her family back home, she has her own agenda.

The first thing Mattie has to do is recoup some money owed her father, then persuade the grittiest ranger she can find to track Chaney down and bring him to justice. Rooster Cogburn is as gritty as they come, but she is grittier. The next thing she has to do is persuade him to take her with him. Cogburn tries to give her the slip, but she won't be left behind, and as they plunge into the snowy landscape of Arkansas, Mattie endures hunger, gunfights, and the bitter cold without complaining even once.

Mattie's Presbyterian good sense verges on the pious. But her estimable pluck in the face of outlaws, knives, bullets, snakes, and corpses wins our admiration every time, and will encourage an immediate assumption of independence as you read. And although she uses the people around her to help her to achieve her goals, she relies on herself to see her plan through to its conclusion. It is an older Mattie, looking back on this formative chapter in her life, who tells this tale, and her adult self is very much the product of all this hardship and loss. Steel yourself, reader. Say farewell to mush, and welcome a handful of grit into your soul.

See also: **Coward, being a** • **Seize the day, failure to** • **Self-esteem, low**

If Nobody Speaks of
Remarkable Things
JON MCGREGOR
· · ·
Cloudstreet
TIM WINTON

If it's your parents who f★★k you up, it's your
neighbors who wind you up.

Unfortunately, neighbors can be neighbors
for a very long time. Fall out with them and it
can make your life a misery. Learn to live with
them—and even to like them—and you'll earn
yourself an on-the-spot social life. Plus eggs,
milk, and sugar whenever you need it. Sometimes
it's not so much that you've fallen out with your
neighbors, but that you've never actually met
them. People live cheek by jowl for decades with little more than a formal
nod. Our first cure, then, will have you sticking your head over the fence to
say hello. Our second will have you knocking the fence down.

In *If Nobody Speaks of Remarkable Things*, Jon McGregor's lyrical first
novel, we know the inhabitants of an entire street in a city in northern England, not by name but by the number on their door: "the young woman
from twenty-four," "the man with the carefully trimmed mustache from
number twenty." McGregor's narrative takes flashes of consciousness from
these myriad neighbors and builds them into a symphony of sound, a blur of
activity, a chaos of unlinked events. Except that they *are* linked. Like the
"quivering flutter of a moth's rain-sodden wings," each tiny happening
within this small geographical area conspires to bring remarkable life—and
death—to our consciousness. McGregor manages to capture the infinite
possibilities of neighborly interaction, from total indifference to selfless love
and sacrifice—all of which are available to us, and the people we live among.
Throw a street party right away, and enrich your life.

But what if, when we meet them, we can't stand them? Neighbors could
not have less in common than the Pickleses and the Lambs in Australian
author Tim Winton's lovable novel *Cloudstreet*. Which is bad luck for them,
or so it initially seems, as they share a "great continent of a house" in Perth.
Sam Pickles, a gambling man, can afford to install his family in the mon-
strosity he's inherited only if they rent half out. So they build a makeshift
fence from old tin signs down the middle of the yard, and Lester and Oriel
Lamb and their brood of six move in. Before long, Sam Pickles is looking on
in mild astonishment as the Lambs take to their knees on their side of the
yard planting vegetables and rearing chickens, and replace their living room

window with the shutter of a grocer's shop. Suddenly the house looks like an "old stroke survivor paralysed down one side": a maelstrom of activity on the hardworking Lambses' side and inert lifelessness on the Pickleses'.

As the linguistically inventive Winton moves between each of the main characters' points of view, the line between the two sides of the building starts to blur. Cloud Street becomes Cloudstreet—a single entity, and a symbol of teeming life. Though there is plenty for the two families to fight about—noise, religion, gambling—and the odd slipper is lobbed from one side to the other, they take a live-and-let-live attitude. And in the end, neighbors become relations.

Next time you're woken by next door's teenager playing the drums, think about how soulless it would be if they weren't there. Bring the fence down—metaphorically, if not literally—and feel the warm breeze blow through.

See also: City fatigue • Misanthropy • Noise, too much

NEIGHBORS, NOT HAVING
See: Loneliness

READING AILMENT   *New books, seduced by*

CURE   *Learn the art of rereading*

It's tempting to see books the way we see gadgets: that we need the very latest, most up-to-date version. But just because a novel is new doesn't mean it's any good; indeed, with a new novel being published every three minutes,* the chances that it's good are actually rather low. Far better to wait and see if a novel stands

* Except on Sundays.

(continued)

---

the test of time, and in the meantime read one that's already proved itself to be worth reading. Because the art of rereading is a neglected one, and arguably even more important than the act of reading the first time around.

Sometimes a novel operates only at the level of the story; in this case a second reading will be a watered-down experience of the first. But the best novels converse with the reader on many different levels, and in our rush to find out what happens we swim over things. A second reading nets those fish. No longer so blinded by the whats, we can appreciate the hows and the whys. We're more likely to notice the ominous foreshadowing of events before they happen, for instance, and smile with the author at how a character deceives himself or herself—and at how the author first deceived us. We're more likely to have a clearer taste of the philosophy underscoring the book by the end. And we'll certainly be more alert to the author's skill at steering the narrative—what was held back, what was told—and how language, dialogue, themes, and imagery were used to achieve the atmosphere, momentum, and tone.

The revisiting of an especially admired or loved book can become, perhaps, a five-year ritual, marking the passage of time in your life, helping you to see how you have changed, and how you have remained the same. Do not go always rushing after the new. Like the best friendships and wine, the best novels get better over the years.

NIGHTMARES

If you're prone to being disturbed by bad dreams in the lonesome early hours, a soothing novel will help to reset your psyche. Keep a stash of these river reads by your bed and drift back to sleep in their current.

THE TEN BEST NOVELS FOR AFTER A NIGHTMARE

NINETYSOMETHING, BEING

THE TEN BEST NOVELS FOR NINETYSOMETHINGS

NOBODY LIKES YOU

See: Unpopular, being

NOISE, TOO MUCH

When your surroundings are too noisy—maybe the TV is always on, or your fellow commuters are shouting into their phones, or the guy on the treadmill is grunting—seal yourself off in a world of your own with an audiobook and a good pair of headphones. You'll find that to be read to is a treat—and, with these readers, an unforgettable experience.

THE TEN BEST AUDIOBOOKS

Middlemarch..............................GEORGE ELIOT, READ BY JULIET STEVENSON

The Great Gatsby.................F. SCOTT FITZGERALD, READ BY FRANK MULLER

The Corrections........................ JONATHAN FRANZEN, READ BY DYLAN BAKER

The Return of the Native ....THOMAS HARDY, READ BY ALAN RICKMAN

The Old Man and the Sea.............................ERNEST HEMINGWAY, READ BY
DONALD SUTHERLAND

Ulysses .... JAMES JOYCE, READ BY JIM NORTON

Motherless Brooklyn ....JONATHAN LETHEM, READ BY STEVE BUSCEMI

Wolf Hall.....................................HILARY MANTEL, READ BY SIMON SLATER

His Dark Materials trilogy...............................PHILIP PULLMAN, READ BY
PHILIP PULLMAN AND OTHERS

Harry Potter and the Philosopher's Stone ....J. K. ROWLING, READ BY
STEPHEN FRY

READING AILMENT   *Non-reading partner, having a*

CURE   *Convert or desert*

If you live with someone who doesn't read books, it can be hard to carve out and protect reading time for yourself—especially if your partner prefers to watch TV, talk to you, or position him- or herself between you and your book when you're reading in bed. You have two choices: convert or desert.

To convert, browse this book for some ideas, then take your partner to a cozy bookshop and treat him or her to a new book. If you can't persuade your partner to read what you buy, try reading aloud to each other. This is a wonderful way to share the experience of a book together, and spend time strengthening your bond with books as the glue. See our lists of Ten Best Novels to Turn Your Partner On to Fiction (male and female) for ideas.

If that doesn't work, acquire some audiobooks to play on long car journeys or while you're involved in domestic chores together—something that both of you will enjoy (see our list of Ten Best Audiobooks, above). If your partner gets into a particular novelist, you can give him or her a physical copy of another book by the same author to follow up.

If your partner still refuses to join in, you'll need to set some parameters to protect your reading time. Decide how many hours you'd like to read per week, and negotiate when these hours will be—Saturday afternoons, perhaps, and the half hour before you go to sleep. Find a place in the house to read where you will not be disturbed—perhaps in your reading nook (see: Household chores, distracted by). If you read in bed, retire half an hour before your partner does. If your partner is lost without you (no one likes to be ignored), work out together what he or she could do while you're reading: Grow tomatoes? Learn to play the banjo? Make some bookshelves for you?

(continued)

If none of these things work, and you can see that life with your partner means a life without books, then you have no option. Desert him or her and find someone else. See: Mr./Mrs. Right, looking for.

THE TEN BEST NOVELS TO TURN YOUR PARTNER (MALE) ON TO FICTION

For mysterious reasons, men don't read as much fiction as women. If you're saddled with a man who hasn't touched a novel since school, give him one of these. (Tell him it's nonfiction in disguise.)

The Wasp Factory	IAIN BANKS
City of Thieves	DAVID BENIOFF
Any Human Heart	WILLIAM BOYD
The Amazing Adventures of Kavalier and Clay	MICHAEL CHABON
Microserfs	DOUGLAS COUPLAND
The Name of the Rose	UMBERTO ECO
Catch-22	JOSEPH HELLER
A Prayer for Owen Meany	JOHN IRVING
Galatea 2.2	RICHARD POWERS
Breath	TIM WINTON

THE TEN BEST NOVELS TO TURN YOUR PARTNER (FEMALE) ON TO FICTION

For equally mysterious reasons, some women don't read novels. If your partner lacks the fiction gene, seduce her with a really good story. Engrossing, engaging, entertaining, these are by some of the best storytellers of modern times.

NOSE, HATING YOUR

Perfume: The Story of a Murderer
PATRICK SÜSKIND

So you hate your nose.

All noses are pretty weird, if you gaze at them long enough. Some are big, some are dainty, some are ski jumps, some are craggy outcrops complete with craters—but none, we can probably agree, are particularly lovely. What dictates how others perceive our nose is our own opinion of it, and those with high self-esteem carry their noses off whatever shape and size they are. To learn to love your nose, start not with the organ, but with yourself. See: Self-esteem, low.

On the other hand, if you really do have an ugly honker—and, wow, have we seen some misshapen disasters*—bury it immediately in *Perfume: The Story of a Murderer* by Patrick Süskind. Within a page, you'll be plunged into a time (the eighteenth century) when there reigned in the streets a stench "barely conceivable" to us today—a noxious mix of manure, urine, and "spoiled cabbage," of "greasy sheets" and chamber pots, of blood, foul breath, and "tumorous disease." Here, in the most putrid corner of the stinkiest of cities (Paris), is born Jean-Baptiste Grenouille, on the hottest day of

---

* Yes, we are hypocrites.

the year, his mother squatting among the fish guts under a table on which she'd just been scaling a (stinking) fish. He's passed into the hands of a wet nurse, and thence to a cloister of monks—because, the wet nurse complains, the baby has no smell. There follows a description of how baby *should* smell— their feet are like "warm stone," or "curds," or "fresh butter," the wet nurse says, feeling her way; their bodies "like a pancake that's been soaked in milk," and the back of their heads, the little bald spot left by the cowlick, that bit smells "best of all . . . like caramel."

And so, within a few pages, we are vicariously exposed—because good writing succeeds in reproducing the whiffs themselves, or at least the reception of them in our brains—to smells at both ends of the olfactory repertoire. Jean-Baptiste himself, of course, though devoid of personal odor, has the most acute sense of smell in Paris and an indiscriminate, dangerous appetite for procuring new scents, especially those of young virgins. But, on the positive side, he earns a good living from his nose as a perfumer. And if, like him, you make full use of your nose, educating it with full-bodied red wines and freshly ground coffee beans, with subtle *parfums* and jasmine and a few drops of lemongrass essence on the sponge in your morning shower— if you fully appreciate its sensual input in your life—then, we guarantee, you'll learn to love and appreciate your nose.

Even if it really is grotesque.

See also: **Vanity**

O

OBESITY

For a beautifully simple cure for obesity, follow the advice of Mrs. Hawkins, the double-chinned heroine of Muriel Spark's mischievous satire of the publishing industry in postwar London. Mrs. Hawkins is liberal with her advice and doles it out on such far-ranging topics as finding a job, writing a book, improving your concentration, getting married, how to say no, where to go if you've had a lot of trouble,* and how to deal with too much casual correspondence. But her tip for losing weight is the best: eat half of what you would normally eat. "I offer this advice without fee," she says. "It is included in the price of this book." We bought her novel, and are now including the advice free in the price of ours.†

A Far Cry from Kensington
MURIEL SPARK
. . .
Pereira Maintains
ANTONIO TABUCCHI
. . .
The No. 1 Ladies' Detective Agency
ALEXANDER MCCALL SMITH

Obesity often has a psychological cause, however, and no amount of dieting will help if the psychological cause remains untreated. So it is with Antonio Tabucchi's Dr. Pereira, the portly, widowed editor of the culture page

---

* Paris.

† The novel also contains a more complicated cure for obesity, though this isn't included in the price of our book. You will have to read it and work it out for yourself.

of the *Lisboa*, Lisbon's evening rag. It's 1938, and under the shadow of war-torn, Fascist Spain, Lisbon "reeks of death." Nobody has the courage to print the real news, and Pereira fills his page with translations of nineteenth-century French literature instead. Each day he cheers himself up by talking to a photo of his dead wife and tucking into an *omelette aux fines herbes* and several glasses of lemonade at the Café Orquídea, washed down with coffee and a cigar.

That the omelets are having a deleterious effect on his waistline is clear to Pereira, but he finds himself unable to resist. It's only when he meets Dr. Cardoso at an out-of-town spa that he begins to understand his need for fatty foods and sugary drinks. General Franco is making a mockery of his job, and therefore of him. Salvation arrives in the form of a young couple he meets at the Café Orquídea, who, Pereira eventually realizes, are involved in underground activities. Here is a way to fight Franco, and recover the "chieftanship" of his soul. It's not long before Dr. Pereira is ordering seafood salads and mineral water instead.

If you're overweight because you're unhappy, don't padlock the fridge or put yourself on a rigid diet; the diet will fail and you'll only make yourself unhappier still. Try to discover why you are seeking consolation—this book may give you some ideas (for starters, try: Stuck in a rut, or Career, being in the wrong). Once you've ironed out your relationship with yourself, your relationship with food will self-correct.

And if you're large and you like it, embrace the big-is-beautiful world of "traditionally built" (size twenty-two, to be precise) Mma Precious Ramotswe, star of Alexander McCall Smith's famous detective series set in Botswana. Precious Ramotswe will show you how to be bold and break the rules, to carry your weight with dignity and aplomb, and win the heart of a good man (if you want one) just by being your witty and wise abundant self. They're best read in order, beginning with *The No. 1 Ladies' Detective Agency*.

See also: Gluttony · High blood pressure · Lethargy · Self-esteem, low · Snoring · Sweating

OBSESSION

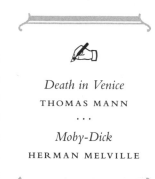

Death in Venice
THOMAS MANN
...
Moby-Dick
HERMAN MELVILLE

The truth is that the obsessed do not want to be cured. What they fear most is an end to their obsession, and to this heightened experience of life. For Aschenbach in *Death in Venice*, the three or four hours he spends each day sitting on the beach watching Tadzio at play—and then stalking the boy and his sisters through the increasingly fetid streets of cholera-ridden Venice—are "far too dear to him" to give up. He goes to bed at nine o'clock because, once Tadzio has left the scene, there's nothing to stay awake for; indeed he can no longer imagine life without this gray-eyed boy with his captivating smile. He knows that the responsible thing to do would be to warn Tadzio's mother about the "sickness" invading Venice, then lay his hand for the first and last time on Tadzio's head and say good-bye. For by not warning her, he is risking Tadzio's death from the cholera epidemic, as well as his own. But he knows that such an act would break the spell, "restore him" to himself, the reasonable Aschenbach of old. And he will not do it.

Part of what keeps the obsession alive is that Tadzio is Polish and Aschenbach can't understand anything he says. So that what might be the "sheerest commonplace" is elevated, in Aschenbach's ear, to the realms of music. When Tadzio emerges from the sea, his wet curls lit by the sun, nothing that he shouts out to his siblings on the beach can ruin it. In Aschenbach's eyes he's the real thing: a "tender young god."

Moby-Dick assumes mythological proportions too. The crew have heard the rumors and seen how the whale possesses their own tormented Captain Ahab for a long time before they encounter the great Leviathan himself. When they finally glimpse him, they see only parts—a hump or a tail, a hot jet of vapor blasted into the sky—while the "full terrors" of his vast, shadowy bulk remain submerged. Moby-Dick's inscrutability gives him power over the crew of the *Pequod*, and Ahab's inscrutability gives him power over them too. Ishmael doesn't even set eyes on the captain until several days into the voyage, and even then it's a "moody stricken Ahab" he sees, so caught up in his own interior claims as to be unapproachable. But how else other than with sheer charisma could Ahab persuade his crew to pursue Moby-Dick, even when the boat was full to capacity with blubber—enough to make them all rich—and when to carry on meant almost certain death? For they are compelled by one that is himself compelled; such is the power of obsession.

To the reader of *Death in Venice*, Tadzio is just a boy. But Moby-Dick is never just a whale, and Captain Ahab is never just a man. When Ahab and Moby-Dick disappear together beneath the "great shroud" of the sea, their mutual charisma doesn't die—something vast, tantalizing, terrible still remains, just out of reach. And so the power to obsess is transferred from the whale to the novel. Because perhaps more than any other novel in literary history, *Moby-Dick* has the ability to hook readers in a way that keeps them coming back throughout their lives. If Aschenbach had been able to know Tadzio, if Ahab had been able to know his whale, if the crew of the *Pequod* had been able to know Ahab, if the reader of *Moby-Dick* were able to *know* Moby-Dick, if Herman Melville . . .

Oh, what's the use? You don't want to know how to overcome an obsession. Being obsessed, you don't want to be cured.

See also: **Control freak, being a** • **Infatuation** • **Loneliness, reading induced** • **Love, unrequited** • **Read instead of live, tendency to** • **Reverence of books, excessive** • **Sci-fi, stuck on**

OLD AGE, HORROR OF

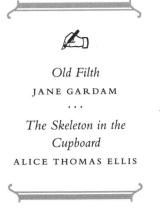

Old Filth
JANE GARDAM
. . .
The Skeleton in the Cupboard
ALICE THOMAS ELLIS

"Old age has its pleasures, which, though different, are not less than the pleasures of youth." So said wise old Somerset Maugham, who enjoyed his latter years so much he clung on into his nineties. But most of us can't quite see the appeal, even as we're forced to let old age creep slowly up. In order to inspire you to embrace the swan song years that lie ahead in a more positive way, we prescribe two novels to show you that just because you're on in years doesn't mean you're past it.

Judge Feathers in Jane Gardam's *Old Filth* is a supremely dignified and still strikingly handsome man with a powerful presence. And despite being given the nickname of the title, he's also very clean—ostentatiously so. His shoes shine "like conkers" and his clothes have a 1920s elegance, complete with a silk handkerchief in his pocket and yellow socks from Harrods. There is no smell of old age in his house—he is rich and long used to having "staff" do things for him. It is not for any lack of personal or domestic hygiene, then, that Judge Feathers is known as Filth, but because, in a phrase he self-deprecatingly coined himself, he "Failed in London, Tried Hong Kong."

He and his wife, Betty, indeed tried Hong Kong, and were spectacularly successful there. And everyone assumed they would stay. But assumptions made about Old Filth tend to be wide of the mark, for secrets lurk in his life, and underneath them, fueled by the traumas of his past, is an entirely different man. Beneath the surface, we discover a diorama of projected journeys, a host of people he plans to visit, dreams of redemptive rendezvous—and he's more than capable of making them happen.

The elderly Mrs. Monro in *The Skeleton in the Cupboard* also casts old age in a refreshing light. This sharp, witty narrator is merciless in her observations of her nearest and dearest. All she desires is to see her son Syl settled and married before she dies, and indeed the wedding day is imminent. Her reflections on her mean but loving son, her dead and faithless husband, and her inappropriately young and self-denying prospective daughter-in-law make for a wonderfully unsentimental drama. What's more, the wicked Mrs. Monro actively looks forward to death, experiencing a burst of "unimaginable joy" when she glimpses the point at which the temporal meets the eternal, where "eagles might clash with angels and the ice-bright light, shattered like gems, would scatter and dissipate." As a vision of the afterlife it's certainly more interesting than most.

As these old cranks will teach you, don't be horrified by old age—it is just a different take on the same story.

See also: **Aging, horror of** • **Amnesia, reading associated** • **Baldness** • **Memory loss** • **Senile, going**

ONE HUNDRED, BEING OVER

THE TEN BEST NOVELS FOR
THE OVER ONE HUNDREDS

OPTIMISM

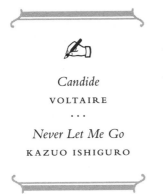

Candide
VOLTAIRE
. . .
Never Let Me Go
KAZUO ISHIGURO

Incurable optimists sometimes need to bite the maggot in their apple in order to temper their expectant orifice with a taste of reality. While we embrace optimists in our hearts, we also feel the need to warn them of being *too* blithely cheery in the face of the inevitable injustice and pain in the world; one cannot always assume the best motives. Between optimism and naïveté, sometimes, lies a lot of unnecessary strife.

Candide is a case in point. Brought up in an idyllic Eden with Pangloss as his teacher, Candide has been taught that "everything is for the best in the best of all possible worlds." So when he has his first taste of the world beyond his childhood walls, he is in for a bit of a shock. The illegitimate nephew of a baron, he falls heavily in love with the baron's daughter Cunégonde. But the baron has other plans for Cunégonde, and when he catches them kissing, he expels Candide from his castle.

Even worse, Candide finds himself forcibly conscripted into the Bulgar army, and he witnesses a horrific battle. Then, after wandering off from camp for a walk, he is brutally flogged as a deserter. The trials and tribulations continue, but through them all the young man resolutely maintains his optimistic outlook. Only toward the end does his optimism begin to waver—and by then, he's been robbed of his fortune and lives with a much altered Cunégonde, and his beloved Pangloss has been hanged, dissected, and beaten to a pulp (and that is not even the end of his story). You, too, will surely see the folly of grinning glibly as the catastrophes rain down.

If not, then *Never Let Me Go* by Kazuo Ishiguro is guaranteed to blast your optimism out of its foundations. Growing up in the mysterious Hailsham House, Kathy, Tommy, and Ruth are encouraged to express their imaginations, create art, and develop relationships. But at the same time they are curiously repressed and separate from the world. We won't give any more away. Suffice it to say, we're so sure this cure will work we'll give our right arms if you still believe in the best of all possible worlds by the end.

ORGANIZED, BEING TOO

On the Road
JACK KEROUAC

An unfortunate side effect of a busy life is that we can become so adept at organizing our time, dividing up our days into half-hour segments allocated to a particular use—work, sleep, exercise, mealtimes, errands, shopping, social—that we forget to allot any portions to those aspects of living that won't fit neatly under a heading. Just sitting around? Taking off in a random direction without a plan? Bumping into someone on the street? If you want to avoid the realization, on your deathbed, that you ticked off everything on your list but never actually just stepped out your door and let life come to *you*, spend some time in the company of Sal Paradise and the "great amorous soul" of Dean Moriarty in Jack Kerouac's hymn to the generation that knew how to hang, *On the Road*.

Nobody in *On the Road* does anything more than make a very vague plan. And when they go, they go fast, jumping on a bus or onto the back of a flatbed truck, hearing a "new call," an "ode from the Plains" in the general direction of the West. They don't take much with them—just a few things in a canvas bag, plus a sheer, Benzedrine-fueled exuberance and a love of life's infinite possibilities. Because Sal and Dean and Dean's new "beautiful little sharp chick" Marylou are on a wave, a "wild yea-saying overburst of American joy" that sweeps them across the country in a spirit of reckless excitement, improvising to the beat of bebop, yelling and talking all the time. They are people that "like everything," who want to get caught up in "the whole mad swirl" of whatever it is they find, and when they get to

Denver, or Chicago, or New Orleans, or wherever it is they're going, they'll do whatever it is that people do in those places. Why? "Hell, we don't know. Who cares?" They'll find out soon enough.

Take it from these boys. Being organized, planning ahead, deciding things in advance—these are not the holy grail of existence. If you want some carefree exuberance to balance out your sensible, predictable life, give yourself a shot of *On the Road* at the start of each day, and let the beat play out.

See also: Anally retentive, being · Control freak, being a · Goody-goody, being a · Read instead of live, tendency to · Risks, not taking enough · Seize the day, failure to

ORGANIZED, NOT BEING ENOUGH

See: Carelessness · Cope, inability to · Find one of your books, inability to · Overwhelmed by the number of books in your house · Risks, taking too many

ORGASMS, NOT ENOUGH

Flowers in the Attic
VIRGINIA ANDREWS
. . .
Fanny Hill
JOHN CLELAND
. . .
Lady Chatterley's Lover
D. H. LAWRENCE
. . .
Gravity's Rainbow
THOMAS PYNCHON
. . .
Ulysses
JAMES JOYCE
(continued)

Can one ever have enough? One might well ask. It used to be thought that having too many orgasms drained one's chi and shortened one's life span, but now experts seem to think that the more you come, the more you'll keep on coming—in every sense. For some, though, an inability to reach orgasm with ease—or at all— can mar an otherwise happy intimate relationship. Known as anorgasmia, the condition is more common among women than men, and though science is unsure of the cause, repression stemming from a lingering belief that female sexual expression is somehow "wrong"—a holdover from Victorian days—is often mooted. We suggest, therefore, that those afflicted should moderate their literary diet accordingly: no more euphemistic or avoidant Victorians (we name no

Doing It
MELVIN BURGESS
...

The Butcher
ALINA REYES
...

The Idea of Perfection
KATE GRENVILLE
...

*The Private Lives of
Pippa Lee*
REBECCA MILLER
...

The Bride Stripped Bare
NIKKI GEMMELL
...

The Story of O
PAULINE RÉAGE
...

Venus in Furs
LEOPOLD VON
SACHER-MASOCH
...

*The Swimming Pool
Library*
ALAN HOLLINGHURST
...

A Boy's Own Story
EDMUND WHITE
...

Our Lady of the Flowers
JEAN GENET
...

Fingersmith
SARAH WATERS

names*). Instead, loosen yourself up with novelists who tend toward the explicit.

For many of today's adolescents, it's vampire novels with their dark, unrealized yearnings that bring newly sexual beings to their first literary climax. Virginia Andrews's incestuous captives in the *Flowers in the Attic* saga still continue to fascinate, with more explicit sexual encounters offered by the likes of Ellen Hopkins. Adults get their rocks off in literature in so many different ways that we can barely moisten the tip of our finger before feeling the need to insert a long and varied list, both of novels that suggest ways of achieving orgasm and of novels that are so erotically compelling that you may need no more than the text itself, mulled over at your own pleasure. But we'll limit ourselves to a choice few.

John Cleland's 1748 novel *Fanny Hill*—generally considered to be the first pornographic novel in English—will surprise you with its young female prostitutes indulging in mutual masturbation, discussion of penis size, and sexual romps that last several days at a time. In the twentieth century, *Lady Chatterley's Lover* led the way—for those who could get their hands on a copy—with a brazen, earthy sensuality and overt references to male and female genitalia that had not laced the pages of literature for a hundred years. Once it became widely available, in the 1960s, the floodgates opened and everybody joined in. *Gravity's Rainbow* by Thomas Pynchon sports an actual orgy on board the *Anubis*—outlandishly erotic, with its nautical setting adding to the hilarity; a public spanking culminates with all those on board climaxing simultaneously. Bloom's masturbatory fantasies in *Ulysses* may do it for the boys, while for the girls we have Molly's reminiscences

* Dickens.

about how her afternoon of sex with Boylan made her "feel all fire inside." In *Doing It* by Melvin Burgess, we get the chance to relive the complicated and fraught sexual fumblings of teenagers, while Alina Reyes's *The Butcher* describes one summer an adolescent girl spends working in a butcher shop and is drawn into an exploration of flesh that is not just about offal. (What is it with butchers and sex scenes? Kate Grenville also could not resist their siren call in *The Idea of Perfection*, which has more sweaty couplings in butcher's overalls.) The heroine of *The Private Lives of Pippa Lee* by Rebecca Miller precociously achieves orgasm in her teens by doing the breaststroke (of the swimming variety), and Nikki Gemmell's anonymously published *The Bride Stripped Bare* has its heroine taking time out from her recent marriage to explore her inner whore and dominatrix. Pauline Réage's *The Story of O* unleashes a sadomasochistic fantasy about a sex slave that harks back to the inaugural work of this genre, the late nineteenth-century *Venus in Furs* (for more on which, see: Jealousy)—have whips at the ready for these two. Meanwhile, lesbian and gay literature has been making up for years of repression with fulsome abandon: Alan Hollinghurst's *The Swimming Pool Library* is a rich source of gay male erotica—happily brandished hard-ons are the order of the day here. Emerging homosexuality is explored in Edmund White's *A Boy's Own Story*, a paean to young gay male love, while a more agonized male-on-male take explodes with floral metaphors in *Our Lady of the Flowers* by Jean Genet. Girls can add costume drama to their repertoire with *Fingersmith* by Sarah Waters, queen of lesbian erotica. Sufferers of situational or complete anorgasmia should keep these novels by their bedsides, applying their suggestions alone, or with a friend.

See also: **Dissatisfaction** • **Married, being** • **Seduction skills, lack of** • **Sex, too little**

ORGASMS, TOO MANY

See: Sex, too much

OUTSIDER, BEING AN

Oscar and Lucinda
PETER CAREY

The outsider is one who doesn't belong. He or she is not left out (see: Left out, feeling), because he or she was never in in the first place. And though certainly different (see: Different, being), he or she is also transplanted. Because the outsider has left the world of others behind, roaming the world as the perennial observer, looking in, but always staying just outside. If this describes you, you will cheer at the eventual meeting of outsiders extraordinaire Oscar and Lucinda in Peter Carey's 1988 Booker Prize winner.

Oscar Hopkins is such an outsider that he doesn't even know there is an inside. He's brought up in the tiny Devon village of Hennacombe with his botanist father, who, though loving, is a member of an evangelical sect called the Plymouth Brethren, who interpret the Bible literally, "as if it were a report compiled by a conscientious naturalist." He begins to sense that they are different when the servant Fanny Drabble makes him a Christmas pudding and his father, being against Christian feasting, calls it "fruit of Satan" and makes him drink salt water until he brings it back up. But he does not question his father's beliefs or realize how much of an oddity his upbringing has made him until he's at Oxford and his "ignorance" becomes a talking point.

When fellow student Wardley-Fish—a member of the "fast set"—bangs on Oscar's door looking for somebody else, he invites Oscar to the races even though Oscar is known as "the Odd Bod." Oscar joins him and, winning his first bet nine to one, develops a pathological relationship to gambling that threatens constantly to uncollar him later on, once he's become the Reverend Hopkins. But when, on board a boat to New South Wales, he meets Lucinda Leplastrier, an heiress and owner of a glass factory, it becomes a cause for celebration—for Lucinda is just as much an outsider as Oscar, and happens to share his addiction. Coming to him for confession, she tells him in a voice so tiny "you could fit it in a thimble" of her seemingly unquenchable thirst for a game of dice or poker—or even a cockfight. Oscar can hardly believe his ears. Holy thoughts soon shoved aside, he knows he has met his match.

What Lucinda and Oscar do with their bond is for those of us who've read it to know and those of you who haven't to find out. The healing is there in the scene on board the ship when Lucinda looks into Oscar's eyes and sees herself "mirrored" in them. The outsiders have found each other, but as long as they are together, outsiders they are no more.

See also: Foreign, being • Loneliness • Shyness

READING AILMENT   *Overwhelmed by the number of books in the world*

CURE   *See a bibliotherapist*

The fact is, one simply cannot hope to read every book that exists. Or even every good book. If thinking about the size of the reading mountain out there sends you into a blind panic, breathe deep. Extreme selectivity is the only solution. Reading time is hard to come by, and you don't want to waste any of it on even a mediocre book. Reach for excellence every time.

The Novel Cure is a good place to start when picking a more discerning path through the literary jungle. Consider also booking a consultation with a bibliotherapist, who will analyze your reading tastes, habits, and yearnings, as well as where you're at in your personal and professional life, then create a reading list tailored especially for you.

For optimal health, happiness, and book satisfaction, see your bibliotherapist at least once a year, or whenever you feel the need for an overhaul. A good book, read at the right moment, should leave you uplifted, inspired, energized, and eager for more. With so many books to choose from, what's the point of reading even one more that leaves you cold?

READING AILMENT   *Overwhelmed by the number of books in your house*

CURE   *Cull your library*

Sometimes the sheer volume of books in your house can get out of hand. Not only have books taken over your walls, but they are piled by your bed and on the end of each stair. There's a stack in the bathroom, and they're filling up the windowsills, the boot rack, the bed. Sometimes you have to remove them from the sink before you can wash the dishes.

Reader, cull your books. Do it every six months, and aim to cut your library by at least 10 percent each time. Give away any books you failed to finish—or forced yourself to finish (see: Give up halfway through, refusal to). Take to a charity shop those books that disappointed you. Keep only books that fit into the following categories: books you love, books that are beautiful objects in themselves, books you consider to be important, edifying, or otherwise necessary, books you might return to one day, and books to keep for your children. Everything else is just bits of paper taking up space.* This way, you will keep your library fresh and make room for new additions.

OVERWORK

See: Busy, being too • Busy to read, being too • Career, being in the wrong • Cope, inability to • Exhaustion • Insomnia • Nightmares • Stress • Tired and emotional, being • Workaholism

---

* As Susan Hill says in her lovely *Howards End Is on the Landing*, "You don't have to pay its rent just because it is a book."

P

PAIN, BEING A

See: Adolescence · Antisocial, being · Cynicism · Daddy's girl, being a
Grumpiness · Humorlessness · Hypochondria · Killjoy, being a · Lovesickness ·
Man flu · Misanthropy · Neediness · Querulousness · Teens, being in your ·
Teetotaler, being a · Vegetarianism

PAIN, BEING IN

The Death of a Beekeeper
LARS GUSTAFSSON

No life is free of it. And though modern medicine offers various ways to numb it, and literature can help you to escape it (see our list of Ten Best Escapist Novels, below), it is harder to find suggestions on how to bear it and live with it.

The Death of a Beekeeper does. Through the experience of Lars Westin, a divorced exschoolteacher who lives in the beautiful, remote countryside of Västmanland in Sweden with his dog and his bees, we explore the world of physical pain—its various pitches, frequencies, and decibel counts—and what it is like to endure pain without drugs. Lars's pain is from cancer. As winter begins to thaw, he discovers that he will likely not live to see the fall, and decides not to go to the hospital in the city but to stay where he is—because this is his life and he wants to live it. And so, taking his dog, he goes on long walks through the gray February landscape with its bare trees and boarded-up summer houses, and learns to live with pain.

At first, he is aware of the pain mostly at night, dreaming of it before it wakes him, and in his dreams he finds he is trying, literally, to turn his head away from it. The pain makes him more aware of his body—that he *is* a body. But he also projects the pain outward. On his walks, the landscape sometimes assumes his pain for him—a tree becomes the tree where his back really hurt; at a fence post where he strikes his hand when passing, he tries to somehow leave it "hanging on the fence" and walk on without it.

But as the pain gets worse, conjuring memories from his marriage and childhood, he enters a stage where the pain is so "absolutely foreign, white hot and totally overpowering," that he struggles to cope. And this is when he realizes that the art of bearing pain is just that: an art, like music or poetry or eroticism or architecture, except that its "level of difficulty is so high that no one exists who can practice it." Somehow, though, he does—as others do, every day.

If you are unlucky enough to experience pain at this level, think of yourself as an artist practicing something so demanding, so challenging that you are elevated to a master by the act of your endurance. And let the beekeeper accompany you there. For as he discovers, blaming others for your pain, or even grumbling about it to others, doesn't help. With the beekeeper, you will discover a terrible but wonderful truth: that pain makes you feel more alive.

THE TEN BEST ESCAPIST NOVELS

When you need to forget the pain in your head, heart, or body, when you're waiting for a bus that never comes, when you want to press "eject" on the daily grind, decamp with one of these.

Corelli's Mandolin .... LOUIS DE BERNIÈRES

Jamrach's Menagerie .... CAROL BIRCH

The Savage Detectives .... ROBERTO BOLAÑO

A Passage to India .... E. M. FORSTER

Even Cowgirls Get the Blues .... TOM ROBBINS

Mating .... NORMAN RUSH

A Town Like Alice .... NEVIL SHUTE

The Map of Love .... AHDAF SOUEIF

Dreams of Leaving .... RUPERT THOMSON

The Story of Edgar Sawtelle .... DAVID WROBLEWSKI

PANIC ATTACK

Shane

JACK SCHAEFER

There is only one thing more frightening than thinking you might be about to have a panic attack, and that is having the panic attack. Knowing this makes the possibility of having the panic attack even more likely. Those caught up in this chicken-and-egg situation need to keep a flask of literary tranquillity at hand and take a long, slow draft—either by reading or quietly reciting passages committed to memory—whenever you feel a panic attack coming on. Practice it often, and in time just the title alone will have your heart rate abating. The novel for the job is *Shane*.

Shane rides into the valley dressed in black. When he politely asks for water for himself and his horse, all three members of the Starrett family are drawn to him—he exudes something powerful and mysterious. They persuade him to stay with them, offering him work as a temporary farmhand, even though it is clear that farming is not his trade. It becomes rapidly apparent that Shane is the essence of calm. A man of few words, he has a strong sense of justice, and although his strength and power could easily overwhelm another man, he clearly holds no truck with aggression. He keeps his gun under his pillow rather than, as other men do, on his belt.

The first thing Shane does when he goes to live with the Starrett family is to take an ax to the ironwood stump in the yard that has been niggling at Joe Starrett ever since he first cleared the land. The stump is big—big enough to feed dinner on to a family twice their size—but, as Shane cuts it, the clear ringing sound of steel on wood strikes young Bob as no sound ever has before, filling him with warmth. At that moment Shane becomes the hero that Bob needs in order to grow up "straight inside, as a boy should." For Bob needs an example from outside his family unit—someone he can emulate. Determined, graceful, just, with sorrows we know nothing of, and a man will always do the right thing, Shane is that mentor—and not just for Bob, but also for his father, Joe.

Install this fierce, hard gem of a man in your heart. Your blood will pump as steadily and calmly as that clear ringing ax on the obstinate stump. Let panic be the tree stump you know you can conquer.

See also: Anxiety

PARANOIA

The Crying of Lot 49
THOMAS PYNCHON

This novel is all about you. You'll find your name in it. Try page forty-nine.*

PARENT, BEING A

See: Children requiring attention, too many • Fatherhood • Motherhood • Mother-in-law, being a • Single parent, being a • Trapped by children

PARENTS, AGING

See: Aging parents

PERFECTIONISM

See: Anally retentive, being • Control freak, being a • Organized, being too • Reverence of books, excessive • Risks, not taking enough

PESSIMISM

Robinson Crusoe
DANIEL DEFOE

A man's fate is his character," said Heraclitus, many years ago. Society in the West took a grand detour from this idea, believing in medieval times that God, or fate, held the reigns and the individual was a mere pawn. If an individual couldn't shape his or her own destiny, what did personality matter? But then, suddenly, God (or

---

* Actually, it's about something far more interesting than you. It's about perpetual motion, entropy, LSD, an underground postal system, and an era in American cultural history that we wish we could have experienced ourselves. But read on. Because we will cure you of your paranoia by proving to you, during the act of reading this novel, that if you look hard enough for something, you will find it. Rather than look for the conspiracy theories you want to find, therefore, let Pynchon's fantastically complex and curious worldview take you on a journey into the curious mind of Oedipa Maas as she investigates her own conspiracies. By the time you've run around San Narciso with this maiden in search of a knight of deliverance, you'll be hooked on her story rather than your own false terrors, and looking out, instead of within.

fate) took a backseat. A successful life depended on an individual's ability to make it so—and, hey, *presto*, the novel was born.*

Robinson Crusoe was the first demonstration in literature of the power of optimism to turn a life around. At first, Crusoe's situation looks unremittingly bleak. The sole survivor of a shipwreck, he finds himself on a barren, uninhabited island with nothing but a knife, a pipe, and a little tobacco in a box. In "terrible agonies" of mind, he runs around like a madman, convinced he's about to be eaten by a ravenous beast.

As we all know, it's hard to achieve anything when you're in such a state (see: Broken heart; Depression, general). What saves Crusoe is forcing himself to think positively. He plunders what remains on board the ship before it sinks, finds a pen and paper among the booty, and sets down "the good against the evil" of his situation—in other words, he writes a good old list of pros and cons. By doing this, he discovers something simple but life changing: that the pros cancel out the cons, and because he can't imagine anything worse than his predicament, he concludes that there's "scarce any condition in the world so miserable but there was something . . . positive to be thankful for in it." Hurrah to that!

And so, buoyed by looking on the bright side, Crusoe does all the things necessary to survive: he hunts, rears goats, plants crops, adopts a parrot, makes pots, and does his own handiwork (and is good at it, but if he wasn't, we'd direct him to: DIY). He goes on to become a self-sufficiency expert on the island for twenty-eight years.

A successful life is about finding your inner resources—never more so than when times are hard. If you refuse, in your darkest moments, to give in to pessimism and despair, but instead dig up some optimism and a cheery outlook, you'll not only have discovered the best in yourself, but you'll also become your own best friend. We'll go as far as saying that, with optimism at hand, it almost doesn't matter what happens. Bring on the shipwrecks. Keep Crusoe by your side. As Heraclitus might have put it if he'd thought of it first: choose optimism over pessimism and you'll have a much nicer life.†

See also: **Cynicism** • **Despair** • **Faith, loss of** • **Hope, loss of** • **Pointlessness** • **Trust, loss of**

---

* Following this line of argument, the novel was born (with *Robinson Crusoe*) in 1719. On other days, though, we follow other lines of argument.

† But don't take it too far. See: Optimism.

PHOBIA

See: Agoraphobia · Claustrophobia · Homophobia · Xenophobia

PMS

Your legs ache. You've got the chills. You don't want to move very fast. Anything too challenging may reduce you to tears. Cozy up under the duvet with a heating pad and a good girly read: an all-enveloping analgesic.

See also: Bed, inability to get out of · Cry, in need of a good · Headache · Irritability · Pain, being in · Tired and emotional, being

THE TEN BEST NOVELS FOR DUVET DAYS

Life: A User's Manual
GEORGES PEREC

POINTLESSNESS

We know what you're thinking. What's the point of prescribing a cure for pointlessness? In fact, what is the point of prescribing anything for anything? It's all meaningless, devoid of purpose, right? Not once you've read Georges Perec's novel* *Life: A User's Manual.*

The novel opens with an apartment block in Paris, frozen in time just before eight p.m. on June 23, 1975, seconds after the death of one of its inhabitants, Bartlebooth. Another resident, Serge Valène, has set himself the task of painting the entire apartment block "in elevation"—with the facade removed—revealing all the inhabitants, and their possessions, in perfect detail.†

It transpires that the recently deceased Bartlebooth, a wealthy Englishman, had devised a (pointless) plan to dispose of his immense fortune, and thus occupy the rest of his life. The plan was for the painter Serge Valène to teach him to paint and for Bartlebooth to then embark, with his servant Smautf (another inhabitant of the block), on a decadelong trip around the world, painting a watercolor every two weeks, with the ultimate aim of creating five hundred paintings. Each painting would be sent back to France, where the paper would be glued to a support and cut into a jigsaw puzzle by another resident of the apartment block, Gaspard Winckler. On his return, Bartlebooth would solve the puzzles, re-creating the scene that he himself had painted. Each completed puzzle would then be sealed back together and removed from its backing to leave the scene intact. Precisely twenty years to the day after each painting was made, it would be sent back to the same place where it had been painted, at one of hundreds of places around the globe, then placed by an assistant stationed there in a special solution that would extract all color from the paper, then returned by post, blank, to Bartlebooth.

A pointless task, some would say. And to make it even more so, Bartlebooth goes blind during the process, so that it's increasingly difficult to finish the puzzles. And in the end, when he lies dead at his puzzle with one space in the shape of a W still to fill, and in his hand a piece in the shape of an X, we cannot help wondering what has been the point of it all.

And yet, the journey to this point in the novel has been remarkably rich. Perec has provided us with a wealth of stories, ideas, and opportunities for laughter—and herein lies the clue to the point of pointlessness. Pointlessness

---

* In fact, it is perhaps a series of novels, or even—you've guessed it—a very manual for existence. Perec liked games—mathematical ones, circular ones, unanswerable ones. *Life* is full of them (which is one of the points of the novel). A member of the group Oulipo, from the French *Ouvroir de littérature potentielle* (roughly translated as Workshop of Potential Literature), he and the other members gave themselves deliberate constraints, which they then followed when writing. See if you can work out the constraints Perec placed upon himself in writing *Life*. We will give you a small clue: there are ninety-nine chapters in the book, which describes an apartment block in which there are ten floors, ten rooms on each floor, and the narrative structure of the novel is dictated by the "knight's tour," which sees the novel as a chessboard.

† The point of this is never made clear.

itself can be a source of great joy, if we cease to worry about its pointlessness, reveling in the life, the quirks, the marvelous minutiae, the sheer excuse for stories, that this very pointlessness offers. And this is precisely the point—or one of its many points.* But its ultimate point is that the point of existence is simply that, despite its pointlessness—despite the fact that the last piece of your last puzzle does not fit—the journey toward that wrongly shaped hole is full of fascination and delight.

See also: **Cynicism** · **Despair** · **Happiness, searching for** · **Pessimism**

PREGNANCY

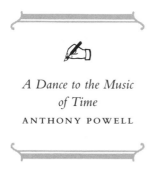

A Dance to the Music of Time

ANTHONY POWELL

Girls, it's one mother of a journey. One minute you're a happy-go-lucky solo player with ordinary things to worry about—what color to dye your hair, whether to go to Mongolia or Milan for your next trip, and whether to wax or shave—then the next thing you know you are ballooning out a pair of stretchy jeans, having to sleep with a pillow between your knees, and reading books which tell you to shove cabbage leaves into your bra cups.

While your ligaments soften and stretch, and while blood is being diverted to various complex tasks of internal creation, we suggest you make the most of your brain before full-on "mummification" sets in. Ignore the siren calls of your house to be redecorated. Milk your state by seizing this moment to read. Because pregnancy is a real chance to take on something long and engrossing, something that, in years to come, will define this expectant period of your life. And what better, as you contemplate your own current steps in the dance of time, than the twelve-novel cycle of Anthony Powell's *A Dance to the Music of Time.*

Inspired by Nicolas Poussin's painting of the same name, Powell's saga follows its narrator, Nicholas Jenkins, from his school days during the First World War right up to the 1970s, so that as well as running the gamut of a life, it is a portrait of a century. Marriage, infidelity, voyeurism, and even

* There are points all over the place in this masterpiece; it makes more points in more ways than almost any novel we have read.

necrophilia are in the mix, but creativity is the unifying theme—as More-land composes, Barnby paints, and Trapnel and the narrator write. Stack the twelve novels by your bed and devour them one by one as you nourish the burgeoning life inside you. You will delight in being lost to this bohemian world in the company of stylish people, and you'll be ready to begin a new dance yourself.

See also: **Bed, inability to get out of** • **Childbirth** • **Hemorrhoids** • **Motherhood** • **Nausea** • **Tired and emotional, being**

PRETENTIOUSNESS

See: **Arrogance** • **Brainy, being exceptionally** • **Confidence, too much** • **Extravagance** • **Vanity** • **Well-read, desire to seem**

PROCRASTINATION

The Remains of the Day
KAZUO ISHIGURO

Why do today what can be left undone until tomorrow? Because every day that you leave a task undone it grows bigger and the motivation for doing it gets smaller.

Procrastination, or the art of avoidance, has nothing whatsoever to do with laziness, or even busyness. Its causes are emotional. Quite simply (and, one could argue, quite sensibly), the procrastinator avoids those tasks which, consciously or subconsciously, he or she associates with uncomfortable emotions, such as boredom (see: Boredom), anxiety (see: Anxiety), or fear of failure. The problem with allowing an uncomfortable emotion to stand in your way is that, once avoided, tasks that were probably quite achievable to begin with grow larger both in our imaginations—and, often, in actuality—until they loom over us in such an oppressive way that they become worth procrastinating about. And while we're busy procrastinating and avoiding those uncomfortable emotions, untold opportunities for happiness and success—whole lives, in fact—pass by. It is this sense of a life half lived, and the intense regret that follows, that we should be trying to avoid—not just a few unpleasant emotions that will in any case quickly pass. What procrastinators need, therefore, is a lesson on the catastrophic consequences of running away whenever an unpleasant emotion threatens to ruffle our ponds. And who better to provide us with this than the very English, buttoned-up butler of Darlington Hall in Kazuo Ishiguro's *The Remains of the Day*.

Mr. Stevens is an arch avoider of emotions—*all* emotions. As such, he has the perfect job. Because he believes that what separates a great butler from a merely competent butler is the ability to repress one's real self and inhabit a purely professional front at all times—holding up as an example the butler who "failed to panic" on discovering a tiger under the dining table (see: Stiff upper lip, having a). His repression thus justified and protected, he spends his life focusing only on being the best butler he can be, even when it is clear that his boss, Lord Darlington, is a Nazi sympathizer, and even when his own father is dying. So it is that when his father wants to say his final good-bye, all Mr. Stevens can think of is hurrying back upstairs to serve the port. And when Miss Kenton, the housekeeper, tries to show her interest in him, he rebuffs her with coolness and distance from behind the fortress of his butler self.

It takes him twenty years to realize what he has missed. By failing to act on those "turning points" in his relationship to Miss Kenton as they presented themselves—those precious moments in which, had he been brave enough to make himself vulnerable, he might have let down a drawbridge into his fortress and allowed himself to feel his feelings—he has lost the chance of a happy married life, for both of them. Instead he has lived as if he had before him "a never-ending number of days, months, years in which to sort out the vagaries of [his] relationship with Miss Kenton." Now, of course, it's too late. He is left with the poor scraps of what remains of his day. Even someone with a lip as stiff as Mr. Stevens has a heart that can break when he realizes this.

Procrastinator: you do not have a never-ending number of days in which to accomplish the tasks you are so intent on avoiding. By procrastinating, you are allowing your negative emotions to become obstacles to an otherwise productive and forward-flowing life. Whether it's anxiety or fear that accompanies the contemplation of the task at hand, put out that hand and greet your emotions one by one. Invite them to come in and sit down, and make themselves comfortable. Then begin your task in their company. Once you begin, you'll find they don't hang around very long; in fact, they'll probably get up and leave immediately. And when you're close to finishing, you'll look up and discover far more pleasant emotional companions sitting in their place, waiting to celebrate with you when you're done.

See also: Indecision • Seize the day, failure to • Starting, fear of

Q

QUEASINESS

See: Nausea

QUERULOUSNESS

There are plenty of things to complain about in life. If you agree with this statement, you're one of them. Because you are one of those annoying people who suffer from querulousness, or a constant urge to grumble and complain, which is not only self-perpetuating—a determination to see the world in black and white being the surest way to bleach it of color—but it also precludes you from noticing life's bounty in the first place.

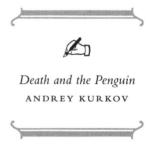

Death and the Penguin
ANDREY KURKOV

Viktor, the would-be novelist in Andrey Kurkov's *Death and the Penguin*—written with the deadpan concision of an obituary itself—has plenty of things to complain about. His girlfriend left him a year ago, he's trapped in "a rut between journalism and meager scraps of prose," he has just come home to a power outage, and his only friend is his pet penguin, Misha, who is himself depressed. And yet Viktor doesn't complain. He receives his lot with a sort of dumb acceptance that makes it unlikely that anything will ever get better.

But then it does. The editor in chief of *Capital News* offers him three hundred dollars a month for creating an index of "obelisk jobs," or obituaries, while the subjects are still alive. Viktor's first reaction is alarm—it sounds like real work. But once he begins, he finds he enjoys it. Soon, however, he becomes aware of the downside: that after a hundred obelisks, he hasn't yet had the pleasure of seeing his work in print. His subjects are all, stubbornly, still alive. When a contact of the editor's—a man who shares the name of Viktor's penguin, Misha, and so becomes known as Misha-non-penguin—pays him a visit, the urge to moan about this gets the better of him: "Here I am, writing and writing, but nobody sees what I write," he can't help protesting out loud.

That's when the VIPs start to die.

Don't grumble to anyone else. You might receive the wrong sort of help—and you'll certainly bring others down. But also, don't grumble to yourself. After the deaths start happening, Viktor's life improves in many ways, but by then the habit of accepting what life has given him is gone and he's querulous about the good things instead. Those who catch the habit of querulousness and find themselves constantly peeved about life may, like Viktor, fail to spot happiness even when it's delivered to them on a plate.

See also: **Dissatisfaction** • **Irritability**

R

RACISM

Invisible Man
RALPH ELLISON

Anyone on the receiving end of racist attitudes or behavior—or those still inclined to lay the blame for racial tensions at the door of the beleaguered minority—would do well to read Ralph Ellison's extraordinary and radical *Invisible Man*. The writing and publishing of this novel was a feat of heroism on the author's part, and when it exploded onto the literary scene in 1952, America was still a country bound by segregation and fraught with racial prejudice. Rosa Parks had yet to refuse to give up her seat on a bus. Martin Luther King, Jr., had yet to give his speech. Suddenly, here was a novel that offered a whole new black aesthetic: elegantly written in an ironically laid-back voice—the novel quickly acquired the label "the literary extension of the blues"—but opening with an act of shocking black-on-white violence that yet did not throw down a gauntlet. Because here we had a highly educated black narrator for whom the tendency of other people not to notice him is sometimes convenient (he uses it to live rent-free in the basement of a building reserved for whites) and sometimes, in a wry understatement typical of his voice, "wearing on the nerves." When a tall man with blue eyes and blond hair bumps into him and then insults him in the street, the Invisible Man grabs him by the lapels, brings the man's chin down sharp against his head, then kicks him repeatedly, demanding an apology. He refuses—to us—to take responsibility for the man's near murder. "I won't buy it . . . *He* bumped *me, he* insulted *me.* Shouldn't he, for his own personal safety, have recognized my hysteria, my 'danger potential'?" And so we are shown the geyser of rage that exists inside him, built up over the years, handed down from preceding generations.

Attitudes—and laws—have improved since 1952, both in America and elsewhere. But de facto segregation still persists far and wide, and statistics suggest vast inequalities in wealth, education, opportunities, and the treatment of racial minorities. Those experiencing racism will find Ralph Ellison's courageous, groundbreaking novel to be a bracing tonic—both as a literary achievement in its own right and as a nonpolemical examination of one man's struggle to define himself in relation to a disrespecting world. Those who know that racism resides in their hearts will, we hope, find a way to see themselves for what they are—and others for who they are. And whatever your race or color of your skin, know that it is an act of cowardice (see: Coward, being a) and shame (see: Shame) *not* to join the fight against racism whenever you glimpse its presence in the world.

See also: Hatred · Judgmental, being · Xenophobia

Cry, the Beloved Country
ALAN PATON

RAGE

Rage consumes. It's the hottest, fieriest emotion there is. Your vision turns red and you cannot think logically. You become a tsunami, wreaking havoc on everything around you. You don't care what you destroy.

The problem with giving vent to your rage is that you not only might hurt yourself or someone else, or break something valuable to you (in the event of which, see: Broken china), but your rage will frighten those who witness it and may make those who love you feel unsafe. Moreover, rage is deeply exhausting and wounding to the soul. Repeated outbursts will deplete you, leaving you a little more broken, a little less noble in heart, than before. It should be nipped in the bud at its first appearance, and before it becomes a habit.

Our cure, *Cry, the Beloved Country*, is a novel about a man who has more reason to rage against the world than any in literature, and it is told in language that soothes and calms. It shows by example that, even when confronted with the most appalling calamity, it is possible to contain your rage and choose a different way. "There is a lovely road that runs from Ixopo into the hills. These hills are grass-covered and rolling, and they are lovely beyond any singing of it . . ." So, with beguiling lyricism inspired by the language patterns of Zulu, begins this deeply moving account of a country parson's search for his errant son, Absalom, in Johannesburg. It is 1946, and Johannesburg is a frightening place for Stephen Kumalo. Unlike in his native village, Ndotsheni, where "every bus is the right bus," there are countless ways to lose oneself, both morally and physically. Following one word-of-mouth sighting after another, the gentle *umfundisi* (parson) and his wise friend and colleague Msimangu discover that Absalom, like countless other vulnerable, discriminated-against young black men in South Africa during Apartheid, has been swallowed up in a criminal underworld, and by the time they find him, it is too late. The boy has shot and killed a white man—a man who, to complicate matters, had devoted his life to campaigning for the rights of the black underclass. The *umfundisi* is forced to watch his only son stand trial for the murder of a widely admired and respected man, and we in turn must watch Kumalo become more and more bowed and frail as his heart breaks under the enormity of his grief.

There is no happy ending for Kumalo. Instead, what Alan Paton gives us is an extraordinary evocation of one man's endurance through suffering. Kumalo thinks and acts slowly, in the "slow tribal rhythm" into which he was born, and Paton monitors the old man's emotions as he struggles against his rage and grief with each new assault. Sometimes his rage wins out—for Paton's characters are nothing if not human—and Kumalo submits to the desire to wound with words, but he is always quick to back down, and later to go back and apologize.

Cry, the Beloved Country is a novel about having the courage to say what needs to be said, about apologizing when rage wins out, and about how hard and bitter words do not lead to resolution but to more anger and hurt. Kumalo's sufferings will put your own in perspective. Paton's language will quiet your raging soul. And the wisdom of Paton and his cast of suffering characters will show you how it is possible to live with your pain—and, even, to laugh again.

See also: **Anger** • **Road rage** • **Turmoil** • **Vengeance, seeking** • **Violence, fear of**

Goodnight, Nebraska
TOM MCNEAL

Though it occurs most often in adolescence, vulnerable people can go off the rails in their twenties, thirties, or even older. If someone you know is heading that way now, it can be hard to know how to help; he or she is likely to present you a toughened, prickly facade and push away the hand you reach out. And if you're heading off the rails yourself, how do you stop careering toward destruction? You fall in love with one of literature's wayward souls is how, and Randall Hunsacker is your boy.

When Randall, at thirteen, loses his father in a horrific accident at home (see: DIY), the loss is more than he can bear. He is shy and awkward, and his fragile relationships with his mother and sister nosedive further when his mother takes up with a new man, Lenny. And when Randall discovers Lenny enjoying a compromising moment with his sister, he finds a vent for the hatred he's been nursing ever since his father's death. Randall careers off the rails in spectacular fashion, involving a gun, a stolen Le Mans, two severed fingers, and juvenile hall. It's his football coach who comes to the rescue, dispatching him to a new life in the small town of Goodnight, Nebraska. Here, hurting and alone, he intimidates the locals with his "obstinate sullenness" and alarms his peers at school with his recklessness on the football field.

To disclose that he catches the eye of a popular local girl, Macy, suggests a Hollywood plain-sail ending, but McNeal is a braver writer than that. He takes Randall, and us, on a realistically bumpy—and moving—journey in which nothing turns out as you expect. Whether you're concerned about someone else going off the rails or think you might be heading that way yourself, this novel will help you to see the sensitive, wounded person beneath the angry exterior. Just because someone acts tough doesn't mean he or she doesn't, deep down, want to be rescued. A fall from grace generally begins with a loss, an absence, or a neglect; hitherto healthy human beings become disaffected when there's no one to catch them when they fall. Be there for your tumblers. Catch them and hold them. And if it's you who's falling, take heart from Randall's story. Someone will be brave enough to see who you are beneath that hardened skin. Let that someone in and, like Randall, you'll find your way back.

See also: Adolescence • Alcoholism • Drugs, doing too many • Rage • Risks, taking too many

---

READING AILMENT	*Read instead of live, tendency to*
CURE	*Live to read more deeply*

"The regular resource of people who don't go enough into the world to live a novel is to write one." So said Thomas Hardy of his fellow authors in *A Pair of Blue Eyes*. If you would rather read than live, you are in danger of missing out on the real McCoy. Actual experience is necessary if you've any hope of understanding and doing justice to your books. How can you feel the pain of Anna Karenina if you've never taken a risk, then found the ground whipped out from beneath your feet?

A good way to tell whether you've got the balance right is never to spend more hours of your spare time reading than living. Go forth and put some of the life lessons you've learned from novels into practice. Go and see someone instead of posting them a letter—like Harold Fry in *The Unlikely Pilgrimage of Harold Fry*. Take a trip on a camel, like Aunt Dot in *The Towers of Trebizond*. Throw caution to the wind like Pop Larkin in *The Darling Buds of May*. Read to live, don't live to read.

RECKLESSNESS

See: Adolescence • Alcoholism • Carelessness • Drugs, doing too many • Gambling • Rails, going off the • Risks, taking too many • Selfishness • Twentysomething, being

Bright Lights, Big City
JAY MCINERNEY
. . .
These Is My Words: The Diary of Sarah Agnes Prine
NANCY TURNER

If only.

Beware these two little words. They may sound innocent enough, but give them half a chance and they'll stick their steely hooks into you, winch you off your feet, and leave you swinging—ineffectually, miserably—for years. Because regret derails; it paralyzes and prevents. And what's more, it's often misdirected. For who's to say that we would have been better off if the thing that we wish hadn't happened *hadn't* happened, and the thing we wish *had* happened *did* happen after all? If you feel regret over things you never got around to doing, see: Procrastination. But if you feel regret for things you did get around to doing and wish you hadn't, read on.

The protagonist of Jay McInerney's *Bright Lights, Big City*—which is, actually, *you**—certainly seems to be setting himself—or, rather, you—up for regret. You mess up your job, you make absolutely sure to cut off all avenues back to it, then you stand up the only decent woman who's approached you in years. None of which does anything to slow your stride as you and your notorious friend Tad pursue your mission of having "more fun than anyone else in New York City." You still manage to end up in bed with a lovely girl.

Some would say the novel is amoral; others would counter that life is just endlessly available. You may have abused your twenties, screwed up in your thirties, and spent your forties on the psychoanalyst's couch—but no matter. Regret? Pah! There are more things ahead, this novel tells us, so just keep going.

That said, few in literature have more cause for regret than Sarah Agnes Prine, the narrator of *These Is My Words*. Having upped sticks once and traveled the Oregon Trail out west, Sarah's papa decides to sell up a second time and head to greener pastures still, in New Mexico Territory. It is a disastrous decision. Not only does the youngest son, Clover—"a top notch fellow after he got out of diapers"—die from a rattlesnake bite on the way, but they are attacked by Comanche Indians, who steal their entire herd of horses. Sarah,

---

* Conveniently for our purposes, the novel is written in the second person.

not yet eighteen, witnesses gruesome deaths among the families traveling with them (Mr. Hoover takes an arrow "plum" in the throat), watches the multiple rape of a friend, and has the blood of two white men and five Indians on her own hands. Meanwhile, her older brother Ernest loses a leg. By the time they get to their promised land, they find there's nothing for them there—it's hot and scorched, "deader" than where they have come from. And then, within a week of arriving, Papa himself dies from a gunshot wound, and Mama promptly loses her marbles.

"Couldn't we turn back and go home?" Sarah asks her papa, understandably enough, while they are still on the road. But Papa puts his hand on her arm and says, "Girl, there's never any turning back in life." Mr. Prine—may he rest in peace—is right. Turning back won't bring Clover back, nor Ernest's leg, nor eradicate the traumas from their minds, and the only thing that can bring Mama back to her senses is the passage of time. Instead, one has to allow oneself to be made stronger by one's experiences, and then move on. Readers of this novel will see clearly how Sarah is transformed by her sorrows and hardships. And without the pluck and resilience of character she acquires, would Captain Elliot, the droopy-mustached cavalry soldier, have noticed her?

Take heart from this novel. We can either spend our time looking back mournfully at the door that just closed behind us, or we can emerge from that door tougher for it. The wisdom and strength we've gained will help us through the door that comes next. At least this way we won't make the same mistakes twice. And what awaits us through the next door may very well be better than what we wish we'd never left behind.

See also: **Bitterness** • **Guilt** • **Shame**

RELATIONSHIP ISSUES

See: **Adultery** • **Age gap between lovers** • **Commitment, fear of** • **Jealousy** • **Love, doomed** • **Married, being** • **Mr./Mrs. Wrong, ending up with** • **Non-reading partner, having a** • **Wasting time on a dud relationship**

RESENTMENT

See: **Anger** • **Bitterness** • **Cynicism** • **Dissatisfaction** • **Hatred** • **Jealousy** • **Rage** • **Regret**

RESTLESSNESS

See: Anxiety • Claustrophobia • Itchy feet • Jump ship, desire to • Skim, tendency
to • Wanderlust

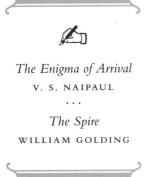

The Enigma of Arrival
V. S. NAIPAUL
. . .
The Spire
WILLIAM GOLDING

RETIREMENT

For many, the moment of hanging up your hatchet is a terrifying one—if not for you, then for your loved ones. What will you get up to in the next few decades? Set off on a round-the-world adventure, build your own folly, learn Sanskrit, or get under the feet of your family and neighbors by being constantly, annoyingly, *there*?

Retirement offers the first opportunity for reflection that you'll have had in a long time, and to start you off, read *The Enigma of Arrival*, V. S. Naipaul's fictionalized meditation on his own life—how he came to leave his native Trinidad and live his latter years in England. Naipaul studied at Oxford University as a young man, then traveled the world repeatedly and extensively, exploring Africa, India, America, and the Muslim world. Naipaul now turns his outsider eyes on the ancient heart of olde England, a place where he was "truly an alien," yet where he finds he's been given a second chance—a chance for "a new life, richer and fuller than any I had had anywhere else." For the first time, he is "in tune with a landscape": the hips and hawthorns of England suit his temperament better than the lush tropical vegetation of Trinidad. It's a surprising and inspiring discovery for someone at this stage in life. Have you, too, yet to find the landscape with which you most resonate and belong?

Bucolic and tranquil, *The Enigma of Arrival* will encourage you to take stock of your life and enjoy the unfolding of new possibilities. Try focusing, as Naipaul does so beautifully, on the minutiae of life—such as when he notices that the grass on the mown path through an orchard has been mown in two directions, "one swathe up, one swathe down . . . the two swathes showing as two distinct colors." Just because you're retired doesn't mean you can't learn to see the world in new ways—especially now that you have the time.

Sometimes the change from working to not working can be too fast and sudden, leaving you feeling you're in freefall or that there's no meaning to your days (see: Dizziness; Pointlessness). Perhaps, you think, retiring was a mistake. Perhaps you weren't quite ready to quit. If you find yourself tempted to jump back into the fray, we urge you to hesitate long enough to read *The Spire* by William Golding. Dean Jocelin will not rest until he has built a four-hundred-foot spire for the local cathedral, an act of religious and personal hubris. The fulfillment of his vision exhausts everybody, except him, and his blinkered determination to see the job completed against all odds leads to terrible suffering for others. It's an excuse for some brilliant writing about the desire for beauty in the world: "Everywhere, fine dust gave these rods and trunks of light the importance of a dimension. He blinked at them again, seeing, near at hand, how individual grains of dust turned over each other, or bounced all together, like mayfly in a breath of wind." But by the end, the folly of the endeavor is all too apparent. Think twice before embracing work once more—especially if it's to leave a last monument to posterity. Realize how lucky you are to be away from all that stress. Sign up for a literature course instead.

See also: Boredom

REVENGE, SEEKING
See: Bitterness • Hatred • Vengeance, seeking

READING AILMENT *Reverence for books, excessive*

CURE *Personalize your books*

Some people won't dog-ear the pages. Others won't place the book facedown, pages splayed. Some won't dare make a mark in the margin.

(continued)

Get over it. Books exist to impart their worlds to you, not to be beautiful objects to save for some other day. We implore you to fold, crack, and scribble on your books whenever the desire takes you. Underline the good bits, exclaim "YES!" and "NO!" in the margins. Invite others to inscribe and date the frontispiece. Draw pictures, jot down phone numbers and Web addresses, make journal entries, draft letters to friends or world leaders. Scribble down ideas for a novel of your own, sketch bridges you want to build, dresses you want to design. Stick postcards and pressed flowers between the pages.

When next you open the book, you'll be able to find the bits that made you think, laugh, and cry the first time around. And you'll remember that you picked up that coffee stain in the café where you also picked up the handsome waiter. Favorite books should be naked, faded, torn, their pages spilling out. Love them like a friend, or at least a favorite toy. Let them wrinkle and age along with you.

RISKS, NOT TAKING ENOUGH

The Sense of an Ending
JULIAN BARNES

It's one thing to steer clear of bungee jumping, wrestling alligators, or playing mumblety-peg. Risks like those are best left to thrill-seeking daredevils who thirst to expose themselves to needless danger. But if you are someone whose pathological timidity and fear of embarrassment lead you to dodge such everyday tests of mettle as asking for a raise, leaving a job you don't like, moving homes or to a new city, or pursuing the person you love, your risk averseness will maroon you in a sad half-life of missed opportunities. If you find this thought consoling rather than distressing, you are in need of a radical reading cure. It comes in the form of Julian Barnes's compact and powerful novel *The Sense of an Ending*, which is drenched in regrets for an underlived life.

Throughout his adulthood, narrator Tony Webster successfully endeavored to keep "passion and danger, ecstasy and despair" at bay. He began this campaign of excessive caution in college, when he kept the heat low on a love affair—which could have been a raging *grande passion*—to protect himself from "an overwhelming closeness I couldn't handle." Now sixty, he has been divorced for twenty years from a woman he'd had tepid, manageable feelings for. "We thought we were being mature when we were only being safe," he thinks. "We imagined we were being responsible but were only being cowardly." Of late, Tony has stopped taking satisfaction in his long career of repression. Looking back, he reflects that he had "wanted life not to bother me too much, and had succeeded." As he sits alone in his poky, aging bachelor lair, he occupies his idle hours with meaningless tasks: "I restrung my blind, descaled the kettle, mended the split in an old pair of jeans." Too late, he finds himself "in revolt against my own . . . what? Conventionality, lack of imagination, expectation of disappointment?" At least, he comforts himself, "I still have my own teeth."

Stirred by an uncharacteristic impulse to show romantic initiative, Tony musters the courage to attempt a rapprochement with his college flame, but when the two of them meet up, she puts him off with annoyance. "You just don't get it . . . You never did, and you never will," she says. Tony, feeling "foolish and humiliated" after this rare exercise of bravery, needs no further excuse to retreat back to the kettle and linoleum of his solitary kitchen.

Don't let Tony's regrets become yours. Live, love, risk, dare . . . not once, but many times. And with luck, you will end up having more than your teeth to keep you company when you sit nodding by the fire in your autumn years, with "time enough to ask the question: what else have I done wrong?"

See also: Coward, being a · Goody-goody, being a · Organized, being too · Procrastination · Seize the day, failure to

Breath
TIM WINTON
. . .
*Notes from the
Underground*
FYODOR
DOSTOYEVSKY

If you are a natural daredevil, prone to giving your nearest and dearest the heebie-jeebies by skiing off piste with yaks, crossing undulating rope bridges in a Zorbing ball, or white-water rafting through military war zones, you need to temper these tendencies with some daring, yet ultimately sensible, literature.

Start with *Breath* by Tim Winton. A novel about the desire of adolescent boys to push their limits, this takes the friendship of two young men as its focus. As teenagers, Bruce Pike (Pikelet) and his friend Loonie have the habit of diving into the local river, competing to see who can stay under the longest, and enjoying the panic this generates in anyone watching. Then one day they meet Sando, an older man whose obsession is surfing. "How strange it was to see men do something beautiful," muses Pikelet, who is drawn to the grace of the surfers as a direct antithesis to his fisherman father's inability to swim. The boys take up surfing too, with Sando egging the boys on to greater and greater feats of daring. "In time we surfed to fool with death—but for me there was still the outlaw feeling of doing something graceful, as if dancing on water was the best and bravest thing a man could do."

One day Pikelet pushes himself out on his board into a terrifying riptide, with no one around to rescue him. He knows he is not ready for it, but is powerless to resist the urge. Surviving his ocean baptism, he befriends Sando's wife. An ex-surfer herself with a permanent injury, she plays her own games with him, flirting with other alarming activities as a substitute for the thrill of the waves. It's a novel that will vicariously fulfill your desire to push your limits. With several near-death experiences, let it serve as a warning about what happens when you go too far.

Fyodor Dostoyevsky's tragicomic *Notes from the Underground* illustrates the consequences of a man's radical denial of his own natural drive. In this novel, short in length but huge in its implications for world literature (containing as it does the seeds of *Crime and Punishment*), Dostoyevsky inhabits the disintegrating mind of a man who has deliberately chosen to do nothing with his life at all.

Writing from his present existence as a bitter and misanthropic fortysomething, the unnamed narrator looks back at his younger self, when an encounter with a prostitute named Liza could have changed everything. "I used to imagine adventures for myself, I invented a life, so that I could at least exist somehow," he writes. But he is a man who thinks instead of living and who "consequently does nothing." A purveyor of paradoxes, he puts forward a convincing argument for the pointlessness of taking any action at all, let alone risks (see also: Pointlessness). We're not suggesting that you follow his example and reject a life of action altogether, but rather seek to achieve a halfway point between your audacious leanings and complete inertia.

Between the extremes these two novels represent there lies a middle path; you can walk this path without fear.

See also: **Carelessness** • **Confidence, too much** • **Gambling** • **Optimism** • **Regret** • **Selfishness**

ROAD RAGE

Instead of jumping out to assault the incompetent driver blocking the lane in front of you, stick one of these novels in your stereo. Some are angry, exhilarated, loud, to dissipate and divert your fury; others invite quiet meditation and reflection.

See also: **Anger** • **Rage** • **Violence, fear of**

THE TEN BEST AUDIOBOOKS FOR ROAD RAGE

Crash .... J. G. BALLARD, READ BY ALASTAIR SILL
2001: A Space Odyssey .... ARTHUR C. CLARKE, READ BY DICK HILL
Heart of Darkness .... JOSEPH CONRAD, READ BY KENNETH BRANAGH
Hopscotch .... JULIO CORTÁZAR, READ BY KEVIN J. ANDERSON
The Revised Fundamentals of Caregiving .... JONATHAN EVISON,
 READ BY JEFF WOODMAN
On the Road .... JACK KEROUAC, READ BY MATT DILLON
Zen and the Art of Motorcycle Maintenance .... ROBERT M. PIRSIG,
 READ BY JAMES PUREFOY

ROLLING STONE, BEING A

See: Wanderlust

The Go-Between

L. P. HARTLEY

ROMANTIC, HOPELESS

Do you scatter rose petals on your bed every night, expect your suitors to climb up to your balcony bearing chocolates, and leave love notes inside your partner's fridge? Would you travel thousands of miles to pick the first alpine strawberry of the season to present to your soul mate for breakfast? And expect him or her to do the same for you?

If the answer to any of these questions is yes, then you are indeed a hopeless romantic. We applaud you and lament you in equal measure. And though we love a hopeless romantic, we fear for your heart and hope it will not be too frequently broken (see: Broken heart). As a first defense against the inevitable heartache that will come your way, we urge you to turn to *The Go-Between*. Read at the beginning of spring each year—when romance is most likely to blossom—it will protect you from complete heartbreak by preshattering it just enough to prevent full-scale wreckage later on.

In the novel's prologue, we meet Leo Colston as an old man, stumbling upon a diary he wrote in 1900, when he was twelve. The little book triggers a terrible sense in Leo that he has wasted his life, as something that happened to him during the year of his Zodiac-decorated diary has marred his ability to have a happy relationship forever after. And so the story unfolds. Leo, an only child, is invited to stay with his school friend Marcus Maudsley for a few weeks during the summer holidays. When he arrives at Brandham Hall, he is ill equipped for the aristocratic milieu in which he finds himself, and his clothes are too hot, itchy, and tight. But he slowly adapts to his new environment—helped by his hosts, who buy him a new, lightweight suit. Over the course of his stay, he is drawn in to the relationship Marcus's older sister Marian is having with local farmer Ted Burgess, becoming their go-between, delivering letters from one to the other that help them meet up. Leo, in his naïveté, is completely unaware of the social consequences of this affair of the heart until he is too enmeshed in the web. The deadly nightshade in the woodshed that so fascinates and repels him is a symbol of the secrets at the heart of the novel, lurking in the dark and working their poisonous magic on their unwitting satellite.

We know from the prologue that Leo will be at least partially destroyed by the events of this stifling summer. But we discover only at the end that he is still, at his core, a hopeless romantic. Rather than scaring him off romance for life, he continues to idolize and worship the idea, treating the players in the story like the gods of the Zodiac, with himself as Mercury the messenger. This is why his life has not worked out. He is like the driver of a car with a shattered windshield, unable to see where he is. Don't make the same mistake. Bury those romantic ideals along with your diaries. Take a hammer to the glass and move on.

See also: Sentimental, being

RUT, STUCK IN A

See: Stuck in a rut

S

SACKED, BEING

See: Bitterness • Broke, being • Job, losing your • Murderous thoughts • Rage • Unemployment

SADNESS

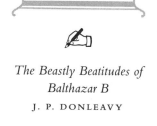

The Beastly Beatitudes of Balthazar B

J. P. DONLEAVY

When we are sad, our bodies move toward our bookshelves with the same irresistible, invisible force by which the tides are drawn by the moon or migrating birds are lured back home. To land with inexorable precision on *The Beastly Beatitudes of Balthazar B.* A novel so steeped in sadness, so embodying its lilting melodies, that the emotion seems to seep from the page by osmosis and mingle with our own, providing comfort in the inescapable knowledge that, in this world, deep sadness exists. Because no one understands this better than the Irish American writer J. P. Donleavy. Who drops his pronouns and active verbs as naturally as the melancholy drop their false cheer when they come inside and close the door. Who poses questions without question marks, and observes the subtle changes in the light with exquisite brevity ("And this evening a fresh green darkness over Paris"). If you are sad, immerse yourself in the warm, tender humor of this novel. To begin the long, slow uplift out of sadness that it effects.

Born into wealth in "the big house off Avenue Foch" in Paris, Balthazar B is a famously shy, elegant young man whose life is littered with loss and an endless search for love. His father dies, leaving him to his neglectful mother (see: Abandonment) and a "reservoir of riches." And so he attaches himself to "Nannie," her cheeks round and smiling, and Uncle Edouard, mad balloonist and adventurer, who regales the wide-eyed boy with tales of narrow escapes from bears and how he once persuaded a hot-air balloon to go up by venting his bowels over the sixteenth arrondissement. Dispatched in his white stockings and buckled shoes to a heinous English boarding school, where boys rise shivering "clutching towels" in the mornings and where his blue stuffed elephant Tillie is torn to shreds before his eyes, Balthazar finds solace in the carrot-headed Beefy, his only friend. Beefy stitches Tillie together and comforts Balthazar with thoughts of margarine and marmite for breakfast, and how they'll put salt in the masters' coffee, and how they will survive the beastliness of life by doing, whenever possible, the *in*decent thing. And then Beefy is expelled, and Balthazar is alone again.

There are wondrous joys along the way, but it is the ever present, ever gentle humor that keeps us going, including Uncle Edouard's advice on how to live—"lighthearted on the boulevard, gay in the café, a good shot at the shoot," with a flower in the buttonhole every day and the "roar of a lion" with every morning bowel motion. Keep this novel on a shelf by your bed and dip into its well of sadness whenever your own is threatening to overflow. By mingling your sadness with that of the emotion's grand master, you will come to know it, as he knows it, as a painful but tender and sometimes funny thing.

See also: **Cry, in need of a good**

Tender Is the Night
F. SCOTT FITZGERALD
. . .
Bound
ANTONYA NELSON

SCARS, EMOTIONAL

No author has written more perceptively and sensitively about the emotional scars of the human heart than F. Scott Fitzgerald in *Tender Is the Night*, his novel about the difficult marriage of the mentally fragile heiress Nicole Warren and her psychologist husband, Dick Diver. In addition to grieving over his wife's frequent breakdowns, Dick is burdened by guilt for his inability to cure her.

After one of Nicole's collapses, following the birth of their second child, Dick "harden[s] himself about her, making a cleavage between Nicole sick and Nicole well." He does this in order to protect their marriage by keeping his love for Nicole's healthy self intact. Though Dick's intentions are good, he worries that, in neglecting the damaged part of his wife's psyche, he's fostering "an emptiness" that depletes her. And when Nicole has yet another breakdown, Dick worries that his professional detachment has made him callous. It hasn't, of course; if anything, he feels too much—not too little—even though he doesn't want to admit it to himself. He muses: "One writes of scars healed, a loose parallel to the pathology of the skin, but there is no such thing in the life of an individual. There are open wounds, shrunk sometimes to the size of a pin-prick, but wounds still."

We all have them. What varies is how deep they run and how well you keep them hidden—both from yourself and others. And what is the best thing to do with your wounds, anyway? To air them at every opportunity so as to speed the healing process and keep the scars from forming in the first place? Or to lick your wounds in private and keep them buried, to protect the sanctity of your suffering?

Cattie Mueller, one of the protagonists of *Bound*, by Kansas-born Antonya Nelson, chooses the latter option. She would hate to be pitied. As the novel opens, Cattie's mother, Misty, has died in a car crash, but Cattie doesn't yet know it. A rebellious teen, she's on the run from a boarding school out east when her mother dies. The news catches up with her days later, when she at last checks her cell phone; she and her mother had been playing a game of telephone tag just before the accident, neither of them wanting to be the one who felt the need to call—or "loser caught caring," as Cattie puts it. "Proud, stubborn, superficially tough, secretly tender: these were the traits shared by mother and daughter," Nelson writes. "They'd rather throw a punch than shed a tear, burn bridges than mend fences."

Antonya Nelson's novels and short stories focus on men and women in the American West and Southwest who carry a lot of emotional baggage, which they either hide or flaunt like a badge of honor. Her scapegrace characters have messed-up love lives and work lives, but they move forward with a scavenger's instinctive, opportunistic persistence, like coyotes along the highway—coyotes who self-medicate with Jack Daniel's. Absorbing Cattie's edgy reserve in this American story of wounds and resilience will fill you with respect for those who bear their suffering bravely, and will help you medicate your own wounds not with whiskey, but with the author's healing insights.

See also: **Demons, facing your** • **Haunted, being**

SCARS, PHYSICAL

Skin Tight
CARL HIAASEN

If you're unlucky enough to have a serious scar on your body, you may spend time fretting over how to conceal it. Vitamin E cream, cover-up cosmetics, temporary or permanent tattoos, even plastic surgery may be options you have considered. Fret no more. Artful positioning of a novel—tipped nonchalantly, for instance, over that unsightly flaw on your chin—will either hide or steal all the attention away from your scar, especially if the title is intriguing enough. Observers will be far more interested in seeing what you are reading than in the underlying blemish.*

However, we digress. Our novel approach to healing your scar is Carl Hiaasen's *Skin Tight*. Like all Hiaasen's novels, it's set in Florida among the tourists and criminals of the Everglades. The antihero is Chemo, a man whose skin has erupted into horrific Rice Krispie puffs after an unlucky electrolysis incident. Chemo enters into a bargain with a plastic surgeon: facial reconstruction in return for the disposal of an inconvenient witness to the accidental death of one of the surgeon's other unfortunate patients.

At six foot nine Chemo is not the most discreet of hit men. He's also not gifted with enormous intelligence. To make matters worse, Rudy Graveline, the unorthodox plastic surgeon without a certificate to his name, has a backlog of mysteriously unfinished, dead, or otherwise unsatisfied patients. There is one woman, however, whose anatomy even the unscrupulous Rudy Graveline won't tamper with: the actress Heather Chappell, whose body is as

---

* The following titles are particularly good at distracting your interlocutors from your scars (this strategy, sadly, will not work with e-books): *I Still Miss My Man but My Aim Is Getting Better* (Sarah Shankman); *The Perks of Being a Wallflower* (Stephen Chbosky); *John Dies at the End* (David Wong); *The Hundred-Year-Old Man Who Climbed Out of the Window and Disappeared* (Jonas Jonasson); *Gun, with Occasional Music* (Jonathan Lethem); *Wait Until Spring, Bandini* (John Fante); *Do Androids Dream of Electric Sheep* (Philip K. Dick).

perfect as bodies get. Heather does not think so, however, and wants a boob job, a tummy tuck, rhinoplasty, and a chin implant. Her desperation to improve her nonexistent faults serves as a reminder that we often see flaws where observers do not.

A hilarious black comedy involving the gruesome and unlikely disposal of bodies and socially challenged evildoers getting their just deserts, this novel is guaranteed to keep you safely away from the surgeon's knife. Learn to love your scars. They are a part of your history and the narrative that lives on your skin.

SCHADENFREUDE

The Tiger's Wife
TÉA OBREHT

Schadenfreude is a cruelly mirthful German expression that means "delight in the misfortunes of others." Now . . . why would you want to do that? We hope you don't. But if you are susceptible to this sniggering affliction—if, perchance, you peruse Gawker or the tabloids with wicked relish—we suggest that you read the haunting, lyrical novel *The Tiger's Wife* to reset your moral bearings.

Its author, the gifted young Téa Obreht, who was born in Belgrade in 1985 but now lives in the United States, sets her novel in the aftermath of the various Balkan wars of the 1990s but reaches much further back, to World War II and beyond, to the violent battles in the region that have pitted Muslim against Christian, German against Slav, human against animal, man against wife since records were kept.

Natalia was a sweet little girl in the 1980s, fond of walking with her doctor grandfather to the zoo. Her grandfather would tell her stories from Rudyard Kipling, mingling them with stories that she assumed were made-up fables, about his boyhood life in a mountain village during the impoverished years of the Second World War. He particularly admired the tiger in the Belgrade zoo, inspiring him to share with her the "mythic" tale of a previous tiger in the zoo, which had fled in terror from the bombs of the war and sought refuge in the mountains of his village. A battered mute woman, the wife of the town's angry butcher, secretly tended to the beast.

But as she grows up in Belgrade during a new wartime, Natalia loses her taste for her grandfather's company and becomes a jaded teenager. Kids her age at school joke about the war, joke about the bombs, joke about the destruction—charged with gleeful adolescent schadenfreude. Now in the early millennium, Natalia, who has become a doctor like her grandfather, visits border towns in Croatia to treat sick orphans whose parents were killed by the bombs and soldiers she and her school friends had smirked about. Schadenfreude no longer seems as funny as it used to.

In *The Tiger's Wife*, Obreht seamlessly weaves together myths of the past and myths of the present, showing with disconcerting power how these myths pervade real life, and teaching you what not to mock.

See also: **Misanthropy**

READING AILMENT *Sci-fi, fear of*

CURE *Rethink the genre*

One of the most common absences in the reading galaxy of an otherwise well-rounded reader is that cluster of novels that falls under the banner of science fiction. For reasons that are not entirely clear, the term has the capacity to send a chill down the spine. Perhaps it conjures images of aliens, spaceships, and intergalactic warfare—with no human hearts in the throng. Perhaps the non-sci-fi reader is unable to see how unreal worlds could possibly relate to the world outside their own door.

Or perhaps readers are put off by an umbrella term that fails to communicate the range and quality of the genre. Instead of science fiction, think of it as "speculative fiction," as Margaret Atwood puts it—fiction that explores the possible directions in which the human race could go. Writers of speculative fiction have famously predicted our present: Ray Bradbury, Arthur C. Clarke, and John Brunner all envisaged the gadgets of today fifty years ago. The writers of such fiction now will predict, and in

(continued)

some ways shape, our tomorrow—and continue to serve as an early warning system. Think, for instance, about how literature has pointed up the dangers of genetic engineering (Margaret Atwood's *Oryx and Crake*), bioengineering (John Wyndham's *The Day of the Triffids*), and social engineering (George Orwell's *1984*). If, as readers, we consider ourselves students of what it is to be human, shouldn't we be as interested in our future selves as we are in our selves of the past?

In many ways sci-fi is a natural progression from the magical worlds we inhabited as children.* Speculative fiction opens up parallel universes to which we can escape and exercise our love for all things beyond our ken. Close off these speculative worlds at your peril.

THE TEN BEST NOVELS FOR SCI-FI BEGINNERS

Transcending the bounds of their genre, these books have run AWOL to classic status. Almost without realizing it, you will be converted to brave new worlds—within yourself as well as in fiction.

The Hitchhiker's Guide to the Galaxy .... DOUGLAS ADAMS
The Year of the Flood .... MARGARET ATWOOD
The Drowned World .... J. G. BALLARD
Neuromancer .... WILLIAM GIBSON
Brave New World .... ALDOUS HUXLEY
Never Let Me Go .... KAZUO ISHIGURO
A Wrinkle in Time .... MADELEINE L'ENGLE
The Left Hand of Darkness .... URSULA K. LE GUIN
The War of the Worlds .... H. G. WELLS
The Chrysalids .... JOHN WYNDHAM

* Many of us have, in fact, been reading and enjoying speculative fiction for years, without even realizing it. Remember that novel about a man who could time travel and the effect it had on his wife? If the publishers had chosen to package Audrey Niffenegger as a sci-fi author, many thousands of enchanted readers wouldn't have touched her with a lightsaber.

READING AILMENT   *Sci-fi, stuck on*

CURE   *Discover planet Earth*

Y ou only ever read sci-fi. There is not a single book jacket in your house that doesn't glitter with an alien glow. Sci-fi has become a reading black hole, and you have fallen in. While we applaud your imagination and your ability to take mental leaps with the laws of physics, we urge you to apply such well-exercised minds to artistic representations of the planet outside your front door. Because there are other literary universes out there. We suggest you take a tour of this unchartered territory.

Begin with Tolstoy's *War and Peace*, the great Russian epic that, like *Dune* by Frank Herbert, spans three generations of war and politics while never losing sight of the individuals caught up in the spokes of the wheels. Move on to *The Glass Bead Game* by Hermann Hesse, a novel reassuringly set in the twenty-fifth century but concerning itself with philosophical and spiritual matters. Next read Michel Faber's *Under the Skin*, a genre-crossing novel that will suck you in, then zap you with a powerful shock. Allow *The Infernal Desire Machines of Doctor Hoffman*, Angela Carter's exuberant magic-realist extravaganza, to introduce you to reality-distorting machines that mess with your mind. And Jeanette Winterson's genre-defying *The Passion* will leave you probing the underbelly of site-specific fiction. From here it's only a short step to all those other novels set in unfamiliar parts of our own planet. Now work your way through our list of Ten Best Novels to Cure Wanderlust (see: Wanderlust). By the end you'll be officially cured of your space-lust.

SEDUCTION SKILLS, LACK OF

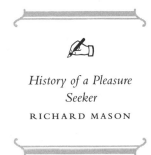

History of a Pleasure Seeker

RICHARD MASON

Of all life's skills, those pertaining to the gentle art of seduction are perhaps the hardest to come by, while also, surely, being some of the most crucial for a happy and satisfying life. But where do we turn to acquire them? We observe our parents with horror, our friends with amusement, and Hollywood movies with disbelief. Can literature come to our bedside rescue?

The answer is yes, of course, for seduction has been explored from Ovid to E. L. James by way of Anaïs Nin and *Les Liaisons Dangereuses*. But you have to pick and choose with care, as not all of the ardent lovers in these novels use strategies we'd care to encourage. For the best all-around handbook, offering a skill set that poses the least risk to oneself and others, we suggest *History of a Pleasure Seeker*, Richard Mason's racy tale of sexual and social conquest.

Piet Barol has many natural, physical advantages that make him attractive to women—and, in fact, to many men (and this arch-seducer is not one to let gender mess with his mojo). He's unafraid to use them, too, but he doesn't rely on looks alone. From his earliest youth, his mother, a singing teacher, taught him to read the emotions and thoughts of others. As he accompanied her students on the piano, he used the lessons to practice these silent skills, holding the gaze of the prettiest pupils while they sang.

In fact, much of Piet's seductive charm comes from his knowledge of music. Although not a great pianist himself, he knows when to choose a flirtatious Bizet over an abstract Bach, and when he applies for the job of tutor to young Egbert at the house of Jacobina Vermeulen-Sickerts, he remembers his mother telling him that the "only key for love is E flat major." And so his seduction of Jacobina begins.

Piet has ample opportunity to flex his skills, for there are two daughters in the household, as well as Jacobina, who has not been touched by her husband for a decade. His impressive draftsmanship, his ready wit, his awareness of the nuances of manners and clothing all stand him in very good stead. Even a fellow staff member, Didier, becomes enslaved. Neither does he restrict himself to the Vermeulen-Sickerts household. On an impulse, he emigrates to South Africa on the lavishly appointed *Eugénie*, where he encounters even more opportunities to seduce.

Throughout the novel, there is a recurring motif of a man on a tightrope, balancing precariously. It's perfect, for seduction is a high-risk art, and one is always close to falling. Take lessons from Piet: use your natural advantages, step boldly where others (husbands, for example) fear to tread, and know when it's time to (gracefully) retreat. Oh, and, like Piet, you'll need complete conviction in your own irresistibility.

See also: Orgasms, not enough • Self-esteem, low • Sex, too little • Shyness

SEIZE THE DAY, FAILURE TO

A Month in the Country
J. L. CARR
· · ·
The Hundred-Year-Old Man Who Climbed Out of the Window and Disappeared
JONAS JONASSON

We live only a limited number of days. And the number of days within that precious time span on which something or someone special comes along are few. Hesitate, or lack the courage, to grab what fate has offered, and we may live to regret it forever.

We know of no novel in which the hero—and in a superlative act of osmosis, the reader too—is more haunted by the ache of knowing that he failed to seize the day than J. L. Carr's eighties classic *A Month in the Country*. It is the immediate aftermath of World War I, and, carrying with him a terrible stammer and a twitch picked up at Passchendaele, Tom Birkin arrives in the village of Oxgodby in full anticipation of a "marvelous" recuperative summer. He has been contracted to excavate a medieval fresco on the ceiling of the village church, living in the bell chamber while he does it. The experience is every bit as healing as he hopes, for in this "haven of calm" he spends his days in blissful solitude at the top of his ladder, living off bully beef and Mrs. Ellerbeck's currant tea cakes, making friends with fellow frontline survivor Charles Moon—and falling in love with Alice Keach, the vicar's lovely young wife.

He doesn't expect anything to come of it. Alice visits regularly, but so does young Kathy Ellerbeek, and somehow it all seems part and parcel of the gift of the summer that he wishes could go on forever. One day, up in the bell tower, as the two lean together and Tom shows her the meadow where

Charles is digging, her breasts press against him. He knows it's now or never. What stops him? A certain habit of unhappiness he's acquired in the last few years, perhaps. English propriety. An assumption he makes about Alice. One leaves this novel a sadder person—unless, of course, you turn it into a commitment never to let the same thing happen to you.

If, like Tom, you have a tendency to be more of a passenger than a pilot in your life, you might need a lesson from the geriatric hero of Jonas Jonasson's *The Hundred-Year-Old Man Who Climbed Out of the Window and Disappeared*. Allan has always lived his life lightly, with more curiosity than conviction, yet has somehow been instrumental in many of the key events of the twentieth century. On the eve of his one hundredth birthday party in the Malmköping Old People's Home, to which the press, the mayor, and varied guests have been invited, Allan decides that the home won't, after all, be his last residence on earth, and that he will die "some other time, in some other place." He is not only blithe, but lucky—one of the first things he does after escaping is land a suitcase full of money.

What follows is a retrospective romp through Allan's life, from his birth in 1905 to his new beginnings, at age one hundred and one, in Bali, with a younger woman (eighty-five) at his side. Over the course of his many years, we watch him help create the atom bomb and advise world leaders such as Winston Churchill and Mao Tse-tung. His adventures continue in the present, taking him and his suitcase, via several accidental murders (Allan doesn't have much cop with morality), to many glorious places.

Jonasson's message is clear. If you find yourself asking "Should I?" the answer is: "Yes, you should."

See also: Apathy · Coward, being a · Indecision · Procrastination · Risks, not taking enough

SELF-ESTEEM, LOW

The Shipping News
ANNIE PROULX
(continued)

It's not surprising that Quoyle, the hero of *The Shipping News*, has low self-esteem. He spends his childhood being told he's a failure by his dad, his favored older brother Dick beats him up, he's fat and has a freakishly enormous chin, his wife can't stand him and sleeps around, he's underpaid by his employers, his parents get cancer and

A Kestrel for a Knave
BARRY HINES
...
Rebecca
DAPHNE DU MAURIER

kill themselves, his wife leaves him and takes their two daughters (who, by the way, are named Bunny and Sunshine, which can't help), he gets the sack, his wife is killed in a car crash—oh, hang on, maybe that's a positive bit. Anyway, you get the gist. Number of reasons to feel good about himself by the end of the first few chapters (yes, this all happens at the beginning): frankly, zero.

And so, "brimming with grief and thwarted love," Quoyle decides to follow his aunt's advice and start a new life in the somewhat unpromising environs of Newfoundland, where his father was born. This he does, with the aunt and two requisitioned, delinquent daughters in tow, and what follows is surely one of the most remarkable comebacks in literature. Those low in self-esteem should read this novel not just as a literary and curative experience in and of itself, but as a how-to manual. Do as Quoyle does, step-by-step. If you do not possess the relevant passport or visa requirements to live in Newfoundland, substitute with another inhospitable and inaccessible location, such as Iceland, the Outer Hebrides, or Northern Siberia. After acquiring a generous life insurance policy, arrange for the death in a car crash of the partner who torments you and—

Just kidding. But we do suggest that you at least go and stay for a while in the place your family comes from, however much you hate it, or them. While you're there, research your ancestors. You may, like Quoyle, uncover less than pretty facts about your lousy forebears—the crimes and wounds that, passed down from one generation to another, brought down your own self-esteem in the first place. With luck you'll be able to break the hereditary cycle, as Quoyle does, and move on.

Of course, it's not always the fault of dead relatives. Sometimes it's the fault of relatives who are still, unfortunately, alive. In what remains one of the most devastating social critiques of its generation, *A Kestrel for a Knave* (1968) by Barry Hines shines an unflinching light on the way a community can demoralize and stunt a youthful spirit by depriving him of love, trust, stability, encouragement, and praise. Not to mention breakfast.

Growing up in a bleak, depressed Yorkshire mining town, Billy has to fight his elder brother, Jud, for everything from space in the bed to their mother's scant affection. No one sees any promise in him—except Mr. Farthing at school, who hears Billy talk about the kestrel—a type of falcon—he keeps in the garden shed. Through Kes, Billy discovers a quality that no one else has shown him, for the beautiful wild bird "just seems proud to be itself." Kes means everything to Billy, and when he takes the bird out to fly it—using a lure to control its sweeps and loops, watching it eat a sparrow, receiving its weight on his gauntlet when it lands—Billy becomes transformed from a boy with no future except to go "down the pit" like his brother into an eloquent, confident lad full of promise and passion.

The lesson for those needing to escape their limitations is to find your own kestrel equivalent—it doesn't matter what you are an expert in, just so long as you can cultivate a passion that will build your self-esteem and, hopefully, draw the attention of others who will help you build a better life.

Sometimes, of course, you've got no one to blame but yourself. If you subject yourself to constant criticism, undermining your belief in yourself and your own opinions, you'll recognize a kindred spirit in the nameless narrator of Daphne du Maurier's *Rebecca*. From the minute she assumes her role as the second Mrs. de Winter, mistress of Manderley—the beautiful country estate owned by her older and more sophisticated husband, Maxim— she becomes gauche in the extreme, forever dropping her gloves, knocking over glasses, and stepping on dogs, blushing and apologizing as she tiptoes around, biting her nails and wondering whether she's being laughed at by the servants. Inadequately dressed and coiffed—and knowing it—she is clueless as to how to run a country estate and does nothing to help herself learn. She naively hands over her authority to the housekeeper, Mrs. Danvers, a spiteful specter of a woman who "adored" the first Mrs. de Winter and is only too happy to encourage the young woman's self-sabotage. "Second-rate," "odd," "unsatisfactory"—these are all ways in which, directly or indirectly, she describes herself. When Mrs. Danvers suggests she throw herself from the bedroom window, she very nearly agrees to do it.

Watching Mrs. de Winter put herself down and compare herself unfavorably to the elegant, clever, beautiful Rebecca, her husband's first wife, becomes hard to stomach after a while. If you're similarly self-critical, you'll blush in guilty recognition as you read, and swear to put an end to such self-destructive behavior once and for all.

See also: **Failure, feeling like a** • **Neediness** • **Shyness**

*One Flew over the
Cuckoo's Nest*

KEN KESEY

Selfishness, it seems, has become a positive personality trait these days. Look after your own needs first, the self-help books exhort. Make sure it's you who gets to the top. Putting yourself first may well bring you lots of money and land you a CEO's swivel chair, but it's never going to make you friends—or, at least, not the sort of friends you'd want. Nor will it make you happy.

It's time to take inspiration from one of our favorite characters in literature: Randle Patrick McMurphy, the bold and brassy Irishman in *One Flew over the Cuckoo's Nest*, Ken Kesey's 1962 exposé of psychiatric institutions, EST, and lobotomies. With his "big wide-open laugh" and absolute refusal to be cowed, McMurphy storms into the lives of the Acutes and the Chronics of the loony bin—damaged men, abandoned by the society that created them—and changes them forever.

McMurphy is not selfless in the tedious way of saints and martyrs, and he's probably feigning psychosis just to get out of doing chores on the "work farm" where he was previously held. Primarily, McMurphy is after a good time. But McMurphy's irrepressible spirit soon starts having an effect on the other patients. McMurphy knows that in this place of intimidation and fear, where the tyrannical Nurse Ratched rules, none of the men are going to get better. "Man, when you lose your laugh you lose your *footing*," he says.

And so, subtly and perhaps only half consciously, McMurphy begins to build his fellow patients up, winking and joking in group therapy meetings, persuading the doctor to let them play basketball in the corridors, listening to the others explain why they feel small. When one day he takes a group of them out on a deep-sea fishing trip with a couple of "aunts" (aka hookers), he rewards them for their courage by teaching them how a bit of bravado can help them keep their heads up, even if they have to pretend. It's a glorious, laugh-filled, heartbreaking day in which the men are reminded of what they could be.

McMurphy doesn't have to take any of them out with him on the boat. He doesn't have to share his spirit. He doesn't have to bring one of the hookers, Candy, to the party, and he certainly doesn't have to delay his escape so that the young, stuttering Billy Bibbit could spend his first night with a woman. He pays a terrible price.

But that's the thing with selflessness. It's not about you. It's about everyone else. So how do you want to be known: as bringing joy and generosity to others, or for just making sure everything's dandy in your own life? Maybe it's time to forget about number one and pay more attention to those you care about.

See also: Empathy, lack of • Greed • Manners, bad

SELF-SATISFIED, BEING
See: Arrogance • Confidence, too much

SELLING YOUR SOUL

Doctor Faustus
THOMAS MANN

Those who barter their literary souls tend to do so in return for eternal youth, knowledge, wealth, or power. In real life, this translates as losing your artistic integrity, preferring pots of money to having time to breathe, and turning your back on old friends. But the outcome is the same: you lose yourself. And what's the point of living if you're only half there?

Arch-consumer John Self in Martin Amis's *Money* believes himself to be a big shot in the film world. But he has signed his life away—not to the literal devil, but to debtors. Kurtz in Conrad's *Heart of Darkness* is less interested in the trappings of Western civilization than in power and control; he has sold his soul for sovereignty over his fellow men and, in doing so, reduced himself to an animal. But the best template for the glory and catastrophe of selling your soul remains Thomas Mann's masterpiece *Doctor Faustus*. In this version of the Faustus myth, it's a composer the devil ensnares. In return for twenty-four years of unparalleled artistic achievement, his soul will belong forever to Mephistopheles.

It is not the first time Adrian Leverkuhn has resorted to drastic measures. Before meeting the embodiment of devilishness, he deliberately contracts a case of syphilis with the idea that the madness it will bring him will deepen his artistic sensibilities. It's during a bout of syphilitic derangement that a vision of Mephistopheles appears. The devil warns him that he shouldn't assume he is hallucinating.

Unsure and terrified, Leverkühn returns to his work—and immediately starts creating masterpieces. He "invents" the radical twelve-tone system, is hailed a genius, and becomes the most celebrated musician of his generation. But there is something disconcerting about him, something cold that friends and audiences notice, which they can describe only as an absence, as if one's feeling toward him "dropped soundless and without trace."

Hold on to your soul. You may get your four and twenty years of fame, or whatever earthly riches you so desire. But what's the use if it means letting go of the most fundamental part of your being?

SENILE, GOING

The Hearing Trumpet
LEONORA
CARRINGTON

At the start of this surreal, wonderful novel, ninety-two-year-old Marian, "a drooling sack of decomposing flesh," is living happily with her son Galahad. She is in perfect bliss, in fact, feeding her cat on the bed, living largely off chocolate and soup, and regularly meeting up with her best friend, Carmella, to discuss plans for their trip to Lapland. But when her relatives can no longer bear her toothless exclamations and cat-fur-covered clothing, she is moved to an "extremely sinister" institution known as the Well of Light Brotherhood. Carmella gave her a hearing trumpet shortly before her move, and this gift transforms Marian from a victim of mild deafness to the heroine of a brilliant, if slightly fantastic, drama. Unfettered by her age to the point that she thinks nothing of scaling the roof of a house if it's the only way to listen in on what's going on inside, she clearly hasn't lost any sense of limitless possibility. The hearing trumpet simply enables her to engage with the world once more—so much so that she masterminds a nine-day-long hunger strike in which the ancient residents of the home subsist on nothing but chocolate biscuits smuggled in by Carmella (who is only too happy to come to the rescue).

With this group of nonagenarians, anything could happen. Indeed, a new and more positive world order seems to be taking over by the end. Read it and you will be skipping into your golden years with ear trumpet in hand.

See also: Aging, horror of • Amnesia, reading associated • Memory loss • Old age, horror of

SENTIMENTAL, BEING

A High Wind in Jamaica
RICHARD HUGHES

Once upon a time, being sentimental simply meant being in touch with your emotions, and, thus, perhaps more sensitive to the delights of literature, music, and art. But today the cold, hard world distrusts sentimentality for its shallowness and easy vulnerability. We, too, support a deeper, more subtle, more deliberate relationship with our emotions. If you are easy prey to sentimentality, we recommend a self-administered dose of *A High Wind in Jamaica,* Richard Hughes's searing tale of piracy, kidnap, and death.

This bracing tonic opens with five expat British children leading an idyllic existence in Jamaica. After surviving a minor earthquake and a major hurricane, Emily and John, the neglected offspring of emotionally absent parents, are shipped off to the mother country for a bit of education. On the way, their boat is seized by pirates. The siblings become embroiled in the pirates' way of life and before long are more attached to the pirates than to their stiff English family. As the story unfolds, they become ever more unfazed by the sometimes shocking events around them.

The children's total lack of sentimentality is a striking, if at times disconcerting, aspect of the tale. When a fellow child disappears at one point, for instance, the others forget about him almost at once. And eventually, the pirates fear the children more than the reverse—rightly so, the reader feels. Perhaps even too disillusioning in its portrayal of the loss of childhood innocence, the novel will nevertheless be the perfect counterbalance to your gooey nature. Something tells us this will do the trick.

See also: Romantic, hopeless

SEVENTYSOMETHING, BEING

THE TEN BEST NOVELS FOR SEVENTYSOMETHINGS

SEX DRIVE, LOW

See: Libido, loss of

SEX LIFE, ISSUES WITH

See: Libido, loss of • Orgasms, not enough • Seduction skills, lack of • Sex, too little • Sex, too much

SEX ON THE BRAIN

See: Lust

*The Thousand Autumns
of Jacob de Zoet*
DAVID MITCHELL

SEX, TOO LITTLE

If you're not seeing enough action in the bed-room, we urge you to compare your suffering with those of the monks and nuns in David Mitchell's multistranded *The Thousand Autumns of Jacob de Zoet*. Set on an island off Japan on the cusp of the nineteenth century, it tells of two single-sex communities so sexually deprived that they invent strange and disturbing rituals to alleviate their distress. You'll be so relieved you're not living *that* life that you'll embrace your own with more equanimity. If you're single, brush up on your seduction skills (see: Seduction skills, lack of) and hotfoot it to your local library to see what—and who—else you can pick up.

See also: **Libido, loss of** • **Married, being** • **Orgasms, not enough**

SEX, TOO MUCH

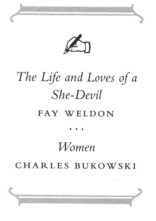

The Life and Loves of a
She-Devil
FAY WELDON
• • •
Women
CHARLES BUKOWSKI

Yes, it is possible to be oversexed.

Men who feel they are unduly fixated should pour a bucket of cold water over themselves in the form of Fay Weldon's *The Life and Loves of a She-Devil*. When Ruth's good-looking husband, Bobbo, leaves her for petite, dainty Mary Fisher—a cliché of femininity straight out of the bestselling romances Fisher herself pens—Ruth decides to embrace her inner devil (see: Vengeance, seeking). She sleeps around until sex means nothing to her, then uses it to get what she wants: ripping Bobbo's and Mary's lives apart with devastating aplomb. If you're married and tempted to stray, this novel will make you gulp and think twice. Married or not, you'll find Ruth's conclusion that pretty women use sex to control their menfolk sobering stuff. A good, long celibate stint will start to look as enticing as a wink after this.

Women in need of a turnoff will find it in the pages of Charles Bukowski's voracious *Women*. The narrator, Henry Chinaski—based more or less on the author himself—is a randy fifty-year-old whose craving for sex never lets up. A pint of whiskey, a vomit before breakfast, and he's latched on to the next pair of tight blue jeans, kissing and fighting—then wondering if his stomach is too upset for oral sex. There's soul here, and a crude and vulgar beauty that'll fascinate some, particularly if you have an ear for rhythmic prose. But you'll definitely leave your sexy underwear safely in its drawer.

See also: **Exhaustion** • **Pain, being in**

The Help
KATHRYN STOCKETT

hame is one of the earliest emotions to erupt in innocent, carefree hearts. The shamed feel an instinctive need to run away and hide—deep in the laundry basket, or to another country—where no one can find them. Take our cure into the laundry basket with you, and by the time you emerge, you'll see the wisdom and necessity of facing the music.

Set in Jackson, Mississippi, in the sixties, just as the civil rights movement is getting under way, *The Help* describes the very public shaming of generations of wealthy white families who used and abused cheap black labor in the form of maids, or "the help." The catalyst and facilitator of the shaming is a young white woman, a daughter of one such wealthy family.

Eugenia—Skeeter, as she is known—has high ambitions of becoming a writer, but is unsure of her material. "Write about what disturbs you, particularly if it bothers no one else," advises the New York editor who mentors her through her first journalistic attempts. It is a brilliant piece of advice. For just beginning to emerge within twenty-three-year-old Skeeter's chest is a vague sense of unease about Constantine, the black maid who raised her, and then disappeared abruptly from her family's home. She realizes that the story of Constantine and countless others—told for the first time, in their own words—would make for fascinating reading. Of course, she is met with terror and suspicion. Because who will hire these maids once they've betrayed their former, or current, employers?

In the end she gets more than she's bargained for. Aibileen, who has raised seventeen white children but lost her own son in an accident at work, and the outspoken Minny are brave enough to get the ball rolling. And so, jeopardizing the fragile balance of a society built on injustice and racism, Skeeter opens up a Pandora's box.

Revenge is not always the best medicine (see: Vengeance, seeking), but when the guilty fail to own up to their deeds, there's nothing wrong with a little tit for tat. The punishment meted out on Hilly Holbrook—instigator of an initiative to enforce separate bathrooms for blacks and whites—is impeccable in its justice. And when Minny joins in by giving her appalling employer her just deserts, Hilly gets something far worse than humble pie. Boosted by the bravery of these characters—and by the humiliation of those exposed—you'll be provoked to face up to your shame on your own. And as with feelings of guilt, you won't be able to move on until you do.

See also: Guilt • Shame, reading associated

READING AILMENT *Shame, reading associated*

CURE *Conceal the cover*

Caught red-handed reading *Flowers in the Attic* while waiting at the school gate? Shy of being seen sniffing over *One Day* while on your security-guard night shift? Embarrassed to pull out Proust while under the dryer? And what if your students spot their bluestocking lit professor gawking over a vampire novel on the bus? Go digital. Discretion is the e-reader's gift. Either that, or crochet a book cover. Nobody need know the source of the words causing your mouth to drop open, your eyes to shine. Your novels are your pleasure and yours alone.

SHELF, FEAR OF BEING LEFT ON THE

The fact that Douglas Cheeseman and Harley Savage get together in the course of Kate Grenville's *The Idea of Perfection* gives hope to anyone who fears failing to find a partner with whom to share life. Douglas has zero confidence and a face that makes him "look stupid." Harley is convinced from her third husband's suicide that she's not only a dud but actually dangerous to be with. Both are in middle age and dragging a deadweight of emotional baggage behind them.

The Idea of Perfection
KATE GRENVILLE

But get together they do. And in a novel that's all about learning to accept imperfections—first in oneself and then in others—their experience helpfully points out a possible way in which you might be sabotaging your chances beyond that first date. Be sure to keep the novel's epigraph, from Leonardo da Vinci, in your mind: "An arch is two weaknesses which together make a strength."

See also: **Mr./Mrs. Right, looking for**

SHOPAHOLISM

Tender Is the Night
F. SCOTT FITZGERALD
. . .
American Psycho
BRET EASTON ELLIS

The modern compulsion to spend, spend, spend has seen many an overexcited acquirer of nice things go under, credit card gripped between their teeth. Either we end up in debt (see: Broke, being) or strapped to the hamster wheel of earn, earn, earn in order to stay afloat (see: Workaholism).

One of our favorite shoppers is the beautiful, damaged Nicole in F. Scott Fitzgerald's *Tender Is the Night*, whose ability to spend—wantonly, guiltlessly—cannot but be admired. And while we are the first to admit that the sheer act of purchasing can give a high, it's not hard to see that if women such as Nicole were less dependent on looks and dresses for a sense of their own worth, they might not need to spend quite so recklessly (see: Self-esteem, low).

The profusion of designer labels splattering the pages of *American Psycho*, Bret Easton Ellis's groundbreaking and nerve-shattering foray into the head of a mass-murdering psychopath, is presented as an early warning sign of a world that has lost its values. And, indeed, if you are brave enough to tough this one out, it will put you off designer goods forever.

Patrick Bateman is a stickler for the rules. You have to be manicured, coiffed, perma-tanned, hard muscled, and wearing the right clothes. You have to eat—that is, be seen eating—at only the hottest restaurants. You have to own the nicest things. So it doesn't strike us as obvious that Pat Bateman is telling the truth when he mutters to his girlfriend that, far from being the "boy next door," as she likes to call him, he is in fact a "fucking evil psychopath." But once we start to witness this for ourselves, with random killings, mutilations, and torturings, we see it as a chillingly convincing extension of the contemptuous, controlling, inhumane facade we have seen in him all along.

At one point, Bateman makes a list of things he intends to buy as Christmas gifts for his Wall Street colleagues—and if you're anything like us, you won't be able to look at a silver-plated wine carafe, or anything else from this lunatic's list, in the same light again. We're not, of course, suggesting your buying habits make you a psychopath too. But do watch that spending. Don't fix your gaze so much on the starry labels that you lose sight of what really matters. One last warning: the scenes in this book are truly horrific and will stay with you for a lifetime; perhaps the association of obsessive consumerism with these grisly images alone will be enough to cure you of your shopaholic ways.

See also: Book buyer, being a compulsive · Extravagance · Greed · Tax return, fear of doing

SHORT, BEING

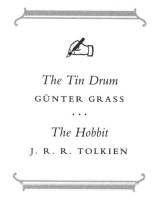

The Tin Drum
GÜNTER GRASS
· · ·
The Hobbit
J. R. R. TOLKIEN

For the vertically challenged, it's endlessly gratifying to read about characters who are powerful, immensely charismatic, and *short*. Here, we give you two such heroes, whose stories will thoroughly weaken any hang-ups you may have about your succinct stature.

Oskar Matzerath is a bundle of compressed energy, a man who makes up for his curtailed growth by becoming a galvanic force of myth creation. His subject is himself, and he narrates Günther Grass's *The Tin Drum* from within a mental asylum, where he has been incarcerated for the murder of Sister Dorothea. He is, we quickly realize, an unreliable narrator, claiming as he does that he was fully cognizant at his own birth. On his third birthday, he tells us, three pivotal things occurred: he deliberately ceased to grow; he was given a tin drum, from which he henceforth refused to be parted; and he stopped speaking, communicating now only by drum.

This drum becomes Oskar's voice for the next twenty-seven years, and although he is a character with many faults, he gives off an energy as compelling as a jazz solo. But it's his mastery over his physical destiny that really sets him apart. His self-willed shortness stands as a symbol of strength—and defiance.

The quiet, dignified essence of Bilbo Baggins in *The Hobbit* could not be more different. Bilbo belongs to a race of creatures about half the size of your average human, with big, hairy feet and soles so thick they make footwear redundant. Hobbits love comfort, warmth, and at least six meals a day, and they much prefer the predictability of staying at home. Bilbo, however, is destined for an epic adventure. When thirteen dwarves come to his door and ask him to help them in their quest to regain their rightful treasure from the dragon Smaug, something awakens in Bilbo's breast, something mad and magical handed down from his ancestors.

Take heart, O ye of little loftiness, and consider these sturdy heroes. They may be scant of skeleton, but they are huge in heroism and influence. Never let it be said that to be short is to be slight.

See also: Self-esteem, low

SHYNESS

The Dud Avocado
ELAINE DUNDY

Being shy can be paralyzing. School, work, social occasions, even running errands can fill sufferers with dread. While we wholeheartedly encourage the obsessive reading of novels as a general rule, we are also aware that burying your nose in a book may not be the best way to break free of shyness—it may in fact be more symptom than cure. So restrict your reading hours, then, and use novels to prepare yourself to get out more. One character who will nudge you into the realm of the extroverts is the *jolie* heroine of *The Dud Avocado*, Elaine Dundy's fifties classic.

A woman who has an orgasm in a café in Paris while holding the hand of a man she barely knows can hardly be accused of being shy. Sally Jay Gorce is a champagne cork of a woman who flies through life with a gush of bubbles in her wake. At twenty-one, she has gone to Paris just after the Second World War, having made a deal with her uncle Roger, who told her to go and discover herself, then come back and tell him all about it. She makes the most of her journey by dying her hair a rainbow of colors, becoming a mistress to Teddy, working as an extra on a film set, posing nude for an artist, and losing her passport in circumstances that lead her to discover that she can't trust all the menfolk in her life.

Her voice is sassy, knowing, and cool; she is a woman on her own in the world's most beautiful city. And she is clear about a thing or two: that she's here to fulfill her childhood dreams ("staying out late and eating what she likes"), that she'll meet people all on her own, that she'll live in a house "without a single grown-up," that when she walks around Paris no one will be keeping tabs on her, that her goal is to get to a point where she can "guess right about people."

With her sardonic tone and disdain of convention, Sally Jay is simply fabulous company for the shy. After spending three hundred pages with her, you may just find yourself adopting her breezy attitude toward life. *À l'enfer* with what *tout le monde* thinks of you. Learn to believe in *toi-même*.

See also: **Blushing** • **Dinner parties, fear of** • **Loneliness, reading induced** • **Seduction skills, lack of** • **Self-esteem, low** • **Words, lost for**

SIBLING RIVALRY

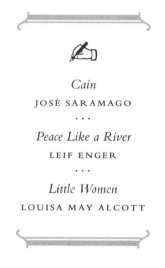

Cain
JOSÉ SARAMAGO
• • •
Peace Like a River
LEIF ENGER
• • •
Little Women
LOUISA MAY ALCOTT

Literature heaves with squabbling siblings, young and old. Little siblings in unrequited adoration of big siblings, siblings competing for parental attention, siblings who abuse, siblings who betray, siblings who love too much, siblings who are annoying just because they're siblings.

A little bit of competition between siblings is par for the course, but beware the example of Cain, who let it go too far. We know this archetypal tale of fratricide from the Bible, but in José Saramago's *Cain* we are given a fuller picture. The brothers start out the best of friends, but the competitiveness reaches dangerous heights when they are grown men. One day they make offerings to God—Abel the flesh of a lamb, Cain a bunch of vegetables. The Lord doesn't think much of the vegetables, and shows it. Cain experiences such intense jealousy that he takes the jawbone of a donkey and slays his brother in a cave. He immediately feels terrible remorse—and blames God for not intervening. (Frankly, we think he has a point.) For the rest of the novel, Cain seeks revenge on God by meddling with the Almighty's plans, sticking a wrench in the works of the Old Testament stories, from Sodom and Gomorrah to the flood. The results are delightfully entertaining.

Literary siblings seem to get along better when they're united in battle against someone or something—and when it's not a parent they're fighting, it's usually poverty or bullies. The siblings in Leif Enger's *Peace Like a River* are bonded together by hardship, hunger, and small-town suspicion in Roofing, Minnesota. Abandoned by their mother when their father downgrades from doctor to janitor (unimpressed, she leaves), these siblings show unquestioned love toward one another, perhaps because they feel they must stick together in solidarity. When eight-year-old Swede makes Christmas cookies using ingredients including frozen peas and macaroni, elder brother Davy crunches right through one, managing a "flawless display of gladness and enjoyment." And Davy goes a bit far in defending his siblings when he shoots the two town bullies, making an outlaw of himself. They might not always get things right, but their hearts are in the right place.

If any siblings had reason to wonder how they could possibly have come from the same gene pool, it's the March sisters in Louisa May Alcott's *Little Women*. Responsible Meg, tomboy Jo, goody-goody Beth, and spoiled Amy could not be less alike. But rather than despise one another for their differences, these sisters develop a genuine understanding and appreciation of the others' strengths. If you can stomach the old-fashioned girliness of it all (and you should; it's part of the novel's charm), this absorbing story has much to instruct any siblings facing rivalries of their own.

See also: **Christmas** • **Family, coping with** • **Jealousy**

SINGLE-MINDEDNESS

The Hunters
JAMES SALTER

We used to be in favor of single-mindedness. In fact, you could go as far as saying we were single-minded in our belief in single-mindedness. We believed that single-mindedness was a useful trait because it got things done. We have, in the past, been single-minded in our pursuit of various things, many of which we achieved, which surely had something to do with us having been single-minded about them in the first place.

But then we read *The Hunters*, and found that our approach had been, well, somewhat single-minded. *The Hunters* is about the single-mindedness of fighter pilots, and how the only thing they care about is becoming an ace.

One has to shoot down five enemy planes in order to become an ace, so naturally one runs a great risk of being killed in the single-minded pursuit of becoming an ace. Ergo: sometimes single-mindedness can kill you.

But that's not the only reason our faith in single-mindedness was shaken. While on leave from his single-minded pursuit of becoming an ace, Cleve Connell—thirty-one years old, a man of few words, honest, intelligent, brave; in other words, someone we wanted to see fall in love and live happily ever after—meets the daughter of a Japanese artist who was an old friend of his father's. The girl is only nineteen but has extraordinary poise. We could see immediately that she was good enough for Cleve. We also saw that if Cleve were to survive the war, he would come back to find her and then they would live happily ever after.

But in order to survive the war, Cleve would have to swap one single-minded pursuit for another. He'd have to swap the single-minded pursuit of becoming an ace with the single-minded pursuit of *staying alive*. Because one cannot pursue two single-minded objectives in direct conflict with each other. The problem is that to swap one single-minded pursuit for another, one has to be open-minded. And one cannot be open-minded when one is already single-minded. And so the happy-ever-after eludes him . . .

The crux of the issue, then, is that single-mindedness is the opposite of open-mindedness. And we had long ago sworn allegiance to open-mindedness in our lives, as open-mindedness allows us to grow, to learn, to experience new things, to allow for the unexpected. To let in open-mindedness, therefore, we had to give up on single-mindedness. And on this, we were of one mind.

See also: **Anally retentive, being** · **Change, resistance to** · **Obsession**

SINGLE PARENT, BEING A

No one said it would be easy. And unless you can afford not to work, or have a live-in nanny or a hands-on granny, trying to be there for your offspring emotionally and physically while simultaneously earning a living, running a house, and having a sniff at a social life is challenging even to the most stoic human being. Literature has a great and disproportionate appetite

The Sound of One Hand Clapping
RICHARD FLANAGAN
(continued)

Legend of a Suicide
DAVID VANN
· · ·
How I Live Now
MEG ROSOFF
· · ·
The Last Samurai
HELEN DEWITT
· · ·
Silas Marner
GEORGE ELIOT
· · ·
To Kill a Mockingbird
HARPER LEE

for single parents, and there is a lot to be learned from the range of parenting strategies on display.

At one end are the botch jobs, providing you with an excellent list of don'ts: The abandoned, alcoholic Bojan in Richard Flanagan's *The Sound of One Hand Clapping* belongs on this list, although he does get a chance to redeem himself as a grand-dad; while the father in David Vann's *Legend of a Suicide* wins top spot for the worst divorced dad in the business. As for single mothers, literature seems to argue that the more alternative the ap-proach, the better—see, for example, Aunt Penn in Meg Rosoff's *How I Live Now*. Though not strictly a single mother, she may as well be; and her hands-off parenting techniques may be attrac-tive to single moms attempting to juggle a fam-ily with a globally vital peacekeeping career: her fourteen-year-old, Edmond, might smoke and drive the family car, but he displays the sort of maturity and sensitivity that every mother dreams about kindling in her boys.

Our standout favorite single mom, though, is Sibylla in *The Last Samurai*. Mother to the super intelligent Ludo, she doesn't have enough money to heat the house, so they regularly spend whole days riding the Circle Line in a continuous loop to keep themselves warm. But Sibylla doesn't let poverty come between her and high achievement. Choosing to home educate, Si-bylla teaches Ludo to read by the age of two, and by three he is tackling Homer—in Greek.

No stranger to genius herself, Sibylla is undaunted by Ludo's lust for lan-guages, and in the next few years Hebrew, Japanese, Old Norse, and Inuit are added to his repertoire. The one thing she will not do is introduce him to his father, opting to depend on the classic Kurosawa film *Seven Samurai* for role models instead. This doesn't stop Ludo from embarking on a search for his real dad himself—but will any of the contenders compare with the sam-urai? It's a brilliant conceit, and the conclusion will bring a silent cheer to the heart of any single mom struggling to raise children in the absence of a com-mitted dad.

Usually it's women left holding the baby, but sometimes men find them-selves in this character-building predicament too, as we can see in George

Eliot's *Silas Marner*. Embittered and lonely, shunned by the other inhabitants of Raveloe, Silas Marner has nothing to live for except his accumulating gold, which he hoards beneath the floorboards. One day he finds a mysterious child asleep at his hearth side. Gradually, Eppie melts his heart, teaching him how to love and bridging the gap between Silas and the locals. If single parenthood wasn't something you planned and you're struggling to adjust, this novel will give you great heart.

Atticus Finch in Harper Lee's *To Kill a Mockingbird* gets our vote for the best single father in the business. For how to treat your children with respect, for how to give them freedom to play and discover the world for themselves, for how to show them the importance of standing up for what you believe is right and having the courage to take action against wrong, look no further. Build a house with a porch and put a rocking chair on it. Sit there with this gem between your hands. Read it once a year, first to yourself, and then out loud to your kids. Take heart. Be there for your children. The rest will come.

See also: **Busy, being too** • **Busy to read, being too** • **Cope, inability to** • **Fatherhood** • **Motherhood**

SIXTYSOMETHING, BEING

THE TEN BEST NOVELS FOR SIXTYSOMETHINGS

Things Fall Apart .... CHINUA ACHEBE
The Sense of an Ending .... JULIAN BARNES
The Unlikely Pilgrimage of Harold Fry .... RACHEL JOYCE
The Diviners .... MARGARET LAURENCE
Out Stealing Horses .... PER PETTERSON
American Pastoral .... PHILIP ROTH
Nobody's Fool .... RICHARD RUSSO
Last Orders .... GRAHAM SWIFT
Fathers and Sons .... IVAN TURGENEV
A Curious Earth .... GERARD WOODWARD

If your eyes are apt to skip ahead, scanning for dialogue or drama, sex or scandal, leaping rudely over passages of description, it may be that you are reading a bad novel. In which case, use this book to guide you to a better one. But it may be that your capacity to delay gratification has been eroded and you need to retrain your brain to slow down and digest.

Your therapy is to read a novel one page at a time—no more, no less. A page before you go to sleep, a page when you wake in the morning, a page as you eat your lunch. The best novel for the purpose is one in which every page glistens with intelligent insight; Robert Musil's *The Man Without Qualities* is ideal, but you can take your pick. The point is to allow whatever you read to trigger your thoughts, and then to spend time with these thoughts, penetrating to deeper and deeper seams within yourself. We agree that finding out what happens next is important. (And so are sex and scandal.) But do you want to live your life on the surface, just picking the icing off the cake? Sometimes chewing on a piece of really good bread is the most satisfying part of the meal. It's certainly the part that will fuel you through the rest of your day.

SLEEP, TOO LITTLE

See: Busy, being too • Depression, general • Exhaustion • Insomnia • Nightmares • Pregnancy • Sex, too much • Snoring • Stress • Tired and emotional, being • Workaholism

SLEEP, TOO MUCH

See: Adolescence • Ambition, too little • Apathy • Bed, inability to get out of • Depression, general • Lethargy • Seize the day, failure to • Unemployment

SLEEPWALKING

The Sleepwalkers
HERMANN BROCH

When we dream, the brain imagines all sorts of vivid wanderings. For most of us, the wires transmitting the intention to move from brain to body are blocked by sleep—we lie still, with no outward manifestations of our inner journey other than, perhaps, a twitch, a sob, or a squeak. In children and the elderly, plus a few odd bods in between, the wires malfunction every now and then, letting the intentions of the brain loose on the body and transforming a dreamer into a meandering somnambulist who will scare the living daylights out of any other members of the household who happen to be passing on the landing. Eyes glassy, somnambulists are completely unaware they are padding around barefoot—and if you wake them to tell them, you're likely to scare the living daylights out of them too.

We advise you to reconsider your use of the term "sleepwalker." From now on, begin to see it metaphorically, as does Hermann Broch in *The Sleepwalkers*. In this great experimental modernist epic—in fact three distinct novels, each written in a different style—Broch uses the term to represent those caught between two sets of ethical values, old and new, as the nineteenth century turns to the twentieth.

In the first of the trilogy we have Joachim von Pasenow (the romantic), a highly codified Prussian aristocrat who ardently espouses traditional values—so much so that he enters into a suitable but loveless marriage with the emotionally distant Elisabeth. But Pasenow is also passionately involved with the sensual Ruzena, a bohemian prostitute with whom he's ashamed to be seen in public. In the second, there is August Esch (the anarchist), a steady, responsible accountant who gives it all up to go work as a manager of a circus—only to find that that doesn't suit him either. And finally, in the third novel, in which Pasenow and Esch return, we have Huguenau (the opportunist), a man who cheats, murders, and rapes to get what he wants, without receiving any comeuppance.

No matter what era we live in, we are trapped, philosophically speaking, between different ways of living—like somnambulists, who are neither quite asleep nor quite awake. Are we living our lives deliberately, guided by a set of principles, or are we chasing after whatever false god we happen to favor in any given moment, with an eye only for the object and no consideration of the consequences? In other words, how should we live?

So, somnambulists, while you wrestle with the philosophical, psychological, existential, grammatical, transcendental, translational (we could go on) questions evoked by the metaphorical condition of sleepwalking, one of three things will have happened. Either you will have discovered an inner conflict of your own, the resolution of which will curb your nighttime wanderings forever. Or you will have so exhausted your brain by reading this dense trilogy that you will slumber in the deepest part of the sleep cycle with no possibility for sleepwalking. Or you will have fallen asleep midsentence, this doorstopper of a tome still weighing on your chest, where it will have you pinned to your bed till morning.

SMOKING, GIVING UP

Still Life with Woodpecker
TOM ROBBINS
. . .
Asylum
PATRICK MCGRATH

Shorn at last of its final glimmer of glamour, smoking is now bad for you in every conceivable way. But that doesn't make it any easier to give up. A good novel can be as effective as a nicotine patch for injecting a buzz—see our list of Ten Best Novels for Going Cold Turkey. But don't attempt to quit the ciggies without the help of the following two novels. The first allows you to revel in the accessories of smoking without actually inhaling. The second delivers a short, sharp punch to the thorax that will put you off destroying your lungs forever.

In *Still Life with Woodpecker*, the redheaded Princess Leigh-Cheri meditates on the iconic pyramids and palm trees of her pack of Camels for countless hours while her outlaw boyfriend Bernard Mickey "The Woodpecker" Wrangle is in prison, his only company also being a pack of Camels, identical to hers. As she feels the psychic connection, facilitated by their shared icon, she decides she can't actually smoke them, because to open the pack would be to destroy her imaginary world. "A successful external reality depends upon an internal vision that is left intact," she muses. Through her meditation, the reader gleans fascinating insights about pyramids, redheads, the purpose of the moon—you get the picture. When our two heroes find themselves trapped inside a genuine, newly built pyramid, believing they are entombed forever with nothing to eat but wedding cake and champagne, they make creative use of their practical and hallucinatory talents, plunging them into yet another pack of Camel cigarettes. In short, this novel is tons more fun than actually smoking a cigarette.

Asylum is a novel that will catch your breath, compress your lungs, and constrict your throat at a moment of unbearable horror. If you haven't quite managed to quit the habit yet, this will convince you that it's time. It's 1959 and Stella Raphael is isolated and depressed. With her forensic psychiatrist husband spending long days at a maximum security asylum, Stella becomes intrigued by one of the inmates. Once embarked on a misbegotten affair with the charming but erratic artist Edgar Stark, Stella is drawn deeper and deeper into his dark interior world. To cope, she smokes almost constantly, punctuating her days with long, deep pulls on her cigarettes.

When on a school trip with her son, Charlie, something appalling and preventable happens, but Stella looks away deliberately, her attention focused entirely on her cigarette. "With one hand she clutched her elbow as her arm rose straight and rigid to her mouth. She turned her head to the side and again brought the cigarette to her lips and inhaled, each movement tight, separate and controlled."

It is this moment, with its terrible chill, that will have you extinguishing your last cigarette by vigorously crushing it into the ground.

See also: **Anxiety** • **Cold turkey, going** • **Grumpiness** • **Hunger** • **Irritability**

SNORING

Sleeping with someone who snores can be a nightly torment. To save your sanity and your relationship—if not your partner's life—invest in a set of headphones and keep a stack of soothing audiobooks by the bed. Mellifluously read, tranquil in tone, these books are guaranteed to drown out your partner's snores while not interfering with your sleep. Play all night if need be, drifting in and out.

See also: **Divorce** • **Insomnia** • **Noise, too much**

THE TEN BEST NOVELS TO DROWN OUT SNORING

Vanity Fair
WILLIAM MAKEPEACE
THACKERAY
. . .
Rules of Civility
AMOR TOWLES

SOCIAL CLIMBING

There are two cures for social climbing. One is to fail so spectacularly or repeatedly that you're left to abandon your pursuit. The other is to succeed, through your superior social wits and graces. If you pull this off, you may soon find others making use of *you* as they scramble up the greasy pole—a fitting punishment, you devious arriviste.

To cure yourself, or simply acquaint yourself, with the manifestations of this guileful but sometimes beneficial failing, turn first to Thackeray's *Vanity Fair*, whose shamelessly self-promoting antiheroine, Becky Sharp, has come to symbolize the affliction at its most virulent. Just as a stubborn idealist is called a "Quixote," a stubborn social climber is called a "Becky Sharp."

Miss Sharp, lacking fortune or title but possessed of verve and an arsenal of wiles, springs from Miss Pinkerton's Academy for Young Ladies with her talons out and at the ready. She pounces first on her best friend Amelia's brother, Joseph Sedley, who is oafish, vain, and unconfident, but very rich. Joseph is warned off in time, but her next prey, Rawdon Crawley, the son of a baron, is not so lucky. He's caught and quickly hitched. From then on Becky's rise is meteoric. She sucks up to the source of the family's cash, Rawdon's spinster aunt, makes a profit out of Joseph when he panics over the looming Napoleonic Wars, considers absconding with Amelia's husband, then claws her way up in Paris and London until she's cavorting with a marquis—and then a prince—at the top. And for what? You'll just have to find out for yourself. But we'll say this much: it may be fun at the top, but there's not much room, and plenty of other contenders are eager to knock you off your spot.

Amor Towles's champagne revel of a novel *Rules of Civility*, set in New York City in 1938, tells the story of two girls with gumption who manage to make their rise seem purely evolutionary. Katey, the clever, literary-minded daughter of Russian immigrants and the "hottest bookworm you'll ever meet," deploys her brainpower to land a prestigious publishing job, and quickly is absorbed into the swell set. Her roommate, Eve, a gorgeous, impetuous heiress from the Midwest, catches the eye of the biggest catches, but also rebuffs whomever she wishes, only heightening her allure. Her eye, at any rate, looks to Hollywood. Both women are intrigued by a handsome young man named Tinker Gray, who projects an old-money air, though his money has in truth evaporated.

Towles sets his bright young things amid the nostalgia of ascendant prewar New York. Not only are Towles's characters all climbing, so is their city—and so is their country. Some rise, some fall, but the expanding and contracting of the era makes it hard, in the end, to tell who's who.

See also: **Ambition, too much**

SPEECH IMPEDIMENT

Black Swan Green
DAVID MITCHELL

David Mitchell's *Black Swan Green* offers a truly insightful exploration of the trials and tribulations of having a speech impediment. Thirteen-year-old Jason thinks a lot, and intelligently, about his stammer. The "Hangman," as he calls it, struck him when he was eight—around the time his parents' marriage began to fall apart. As tensions rise at home and his stammer worsens, the dreaded bullying begins (see: Bullied, being). It starts off mild but crescendos to excruciating heights, and we share Jason's pain as we watch him cling to his tattered reputation.

And then something magical happens: Jason discovers poetry. With the help of Mrs. de Roo, his speech therapist, and the eccentric Madame

Crommelynck, who makes sure his anonymous submissions to the parish magazine appear in print, he begins a new relationship with words, learning to love them and harness them to tell his truth. As Jason's narrative becomes increasingly studded with lyricism—an impressive sleight of hand by Mitchell—he begins his metamorphosis from someone filled with envy and shame to someone for whom words are, at last, a beautiful tool.

Jason's cure may not be your cure, as all speech impediments are different. But watching him reach the point where he can create an "appalled silence" in class by delivering a shocking riposte with metronome-slick timing will bring a glow to your heart. Anyone whose tongue gets in similar tangles must take two things at least from this novel: You, like Jason, will be the more mature for having had this extra battle to fight. And—again like Jason—blunted in one direction, you'll probably find you flower in another.

See also: Different, being · Self-esteem, low · Shyness · Words, lost for

SPEECHLESSNESS
See: Words, lost for

SPINELESSNESS
See: Coward, being a · Selfishness

SPOUSE, HATING YOUR
See: Adultery · Divorce · DIY · Midlife crisis · Mr./Mrs. Wrong, ending up with · Murderous thoughts · Snoring

The Blue Flower
PENELOPE
FITZGERALD

STAGNATION, MENTAL

Like the rest of our bodies, brains require regular exercise in order to stay in tip-top shape. If yours has fallen into a stagnant state from lack of use—or from being too much in the company of other stagnant brains—we suggest you shock it back to life with a mental defibrillator in the form of *The Blue Flower* by Penelope Fitzgerald.

The Blue Flower tells the story of the incandescently brilliant real-life German poet Friedrich von Hardenberg—later known as Novalis—and his adoration of Sophie von Kühn, a twelve-year-old girl with an unmistakably mediocre brain. Being in the company of the von Hardenbergs is constantly amusing, with Fritz's eccentric siblings delivering line after line of crisp, dry wit. But the main reason to read *The Blue Flower* is to experience the author's own brain writ large. It's partly what she puts in—making observations with devastating clarity, then moving on as lightly as a fly—and partly what she leaves out. She'll make geographic or spatial leaps between one sentence and the next that would have most novelists passing out in a panic. She'll give a character a simple tilt of the chin that contains a lifetime's dignified concealment of a broken heart. So much that's important remains unsaid, and our minds are kept mightily busy filling in the gaps. By the end your synapses will be thrumming and your mental acuity restored. Reread whenever you need an intellectual tune-up.

See also: **Boredom** · **Career, being in the wrong** · **Housewife, being a**

READING AILMENT   *Starting, fear of*

CURE   *Dive in at random*

You have a brand-new novel in your hands. You have read the reviews, it has been recommended by people you trust, you are sure you are going to love it. You may have been saving it for just this moment, knowing that you now have uninterrupted hours ahead of you to read, perhaps in the bath or on a train. But you hesitate. You've read and loved books by this author before—what if this one does not live up to his or her last? Are you committed enough to give it a chance? Can you be the reader this book needs you to be?

(continued)

Do not be shy. Open the novel at random and read whatever sentence catches your eye. Intrigued? Flick ahead and read two more paragraphs. Then close your eyes, karate chop the book, and where it falls open, read a page. Finally, throw the novel on the floor (gently, if it's a nice edition), then pick it up with a thumb inside. Read the page your thumb caresses, and turn over and read the next. By now you have opened several windows onto the book. You have glimpsed its interior and know a few of its secrets. Curious to know more? (In case you haven't noticed, you've already started. Now go back and start at the beginning.)

STIFF UPPER LIP, HAVING A

Where Angels Fear to Tread

E. M. FORSTER

Stiff upper lips—a peculiarly English facial modification—are caused by the repression and withholding of emotions. One's lip remains rigid as cardboard in the face of all calamities, from heartbreak and death of pet dogs to the caving in of ceilings. Those of this stern persuasion will dust the debris off their hair, make a relevant quip, and suggest a good strong cup of tea amid the devastation of their kitchen, rather than give any clue as to what they might be feeling. And though we admire such self-control, though we know that keeping calm and carrying on is the definition of Britishness, and though we know it's gotten us through centuries of tragedy and hardships, many would say that the famous British *froideur* is on the wane.*

Forster's beautiful but tragic *Where Angels Fear to Tread*—written at a time when the stiff upper lip was in its heyday—illustrates just how dangerous the lip can be to the lives of others, especially if they don't share it. Lilia, the widow of Charles Herriton, is a trifle too flighty for the tastes of her in-laws,

---

* Indeed some say it died forever, with Lady Di.

and they have encouraged her to travel to Italy as a means of distracting her from a new and inappropriate liaison. Supplying her with a suitably sober and spinsterish traveling companion, Caroline Abbott, they wave her off with every hope that the experience will prove ameliorative. As her brother-in-law Philip Herriton condescendingly remarks, "Italy really purifies and ennobles all who visit her."

But purification, in Herriton terms, eludes her. Because almost immediately Lilia falls head over heels in love with Gino, a beautiful, passionate, feckless Italian devoid of any title. "A dentist in fairyland!" exclaims Philip, who loves all things Italian—except passion (and dentists). The Herriton rescue party is dispatched once again, but arrives too late. Lilia has already married Gino, and they soon have a son.

For reasons that cannot be divulged, Philip and his sister Harriet eventually find themselves face-to-face with Gino. And in the confrontation that ensues—the expressive Italian unafraid to be vulnerable and show his feelings, in particular his love for his son—we can see that the restrained English way, all buttoned up and disregarding, is terribly flawed. For a moment Philip sees the lure of the Mediterranean way, and wavers. But Harriet, her lip kept very stiff indeed, brushes it off as sentimentality and forces everyone's hands. It leads them all to a place of irrevocable damage.

Let those lips wobble, let them tremble, let them open wide. And let those big, wet, messy emotions spill right out.

See also: **Emotions, inability to express**

STRESS

Your heart is pounding. Your breath comes fast and shallow. Your fists are clenched and your eyes and ears are straining for information that may save your life.

No, you haven't just come face-to-face with a bear. You're waiting for the train to work, or making toast, or deciding which toilet paper to buy—just some ordinary, everyday thing. Except that you're suffering from one of the most debilitating epidemics of the modern age: stress.

The Man Who Planted Trees
JEAN GIONO

We prescribe a novel that is so slim and undaunting that we guarantee it will not add to your stress.* *The Man Who Planted Trees* will soon have your soul slipping into a state of serenity. It is a simple tale. A shepherd lives in a stone house in a desolate part of France. He is surrounded by what he needs and no more. One day it strikes him that this part of the country is dying for lack of trees, and "having nothing much else to do he decide[s] to put things right." So he spends his evenings sorting acorns, good from bad, and his days planting them in the ground.

The lush forests of oak—then beech, then birch—that spring up around him transform the region into one that can support, nourish, and bring joy to thousands of people. But it's not the results of his labors that brings tranquillity of mind to the shepherd. It's the labor itself—the walking, digging, planting, watching, and waiting.

It's more or less impossible not to feel peaceful in the company of the shepherd. And when you've finished and chuckled at the postscript, put it down and step outside. What you need now is a good, long walk. Put a trowel in your pocket and set out for the fields.

See also: **Anxiety** · **Busy, being too** · **Busy to read, being too** · **Concentrate, inability to** · **Cope, inability to** · **Headache** · **High blood pressure** · **Insomnia** · **Libido, loss of** · **Nightmares** · **Workaholism**

STUBBED TOE

A Portrait of the Artist as a Young Man
JAMES JOYCE

The agony of a stubbed toe has to be endured; nothing can cure it. Thankfully, like a blow to the nose, the pain is short-lived. Expletives are usually one's only resort.

To prevent public outrage and embarrassment, we strongly suggest you arm yourself with the literary equivalent of a venting expletive: a quote that comes easily to the lips, something staccato, memorable, alliterative, musical, evocative, distracting—that is, the first paragraph of this most approachable of Joyce's novels, *A Portrait of the Artist*

---

* In fact, if we're honest, it's barely a novel at all. But, being stressed, you don't need to know this.

as a Young Man. We will here supply only the opening words, for if it is a novel that is not already in your possession, you must get hold of a copy immediately and commit to memory the first seven lines. Then, when you next stub your toe, be ready to exclaim: "Once upon a time and a very good time it was there was a moocow coming down along the road and this moocow that was coming down along the road met a nicens little boy named baby tuckoo . . ." and so on until "lemon platt."

Then read the rest of this edifying novel, wising up with Stephen on how best to avoid life's obstacles and find your wings.

STUBBORN, BEING

See: Single-mindedness

STUCK IN A RELATIONSHIP

See: Mr./Mrs. Wrong, ending up with

STUCK IN A RUT

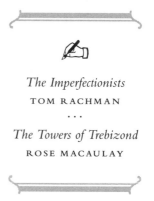

The Imperfectionists
TOM RACHMAN
. . .
The Towers of Trebizond
ROSE MACAULAY

It was probably Hemingway who invented the romance of the battered news hack, trapped in an endless cycle of deadlines, living from paycheck to paycheck, and squandering his meager earnings on drink as he valiantly avoids such moss as a family, a house, or a dental plan. But the experience isn't so romantic when you're the hack in the trap.

If you're stuck in a rut, professionally or personally, snap yourself out of it by reading Tom Rachman's bleakly funny and original novel *The Imperfectionists*, a collection of linked portraits of a dozen sad-eyed newshounds across the globe, all of them working, or sort of working, at the foreign offices of an international newspaper. Rachman's hacks should have jumped ship long ago and carved out independent careers, but, naturally, being stuck in a rut, they didn't.

Lloyd Burko, the paper's Paris correspondent, complains to his grown son, "I must have done, what, an article a day since I was twenty-two. And now I can't rustle up a single new idea. Not a one." Arthur Gopal, an obituary writer based in Rome, leads a life (if you can call it that) of lusterless tedium. When he interviews a curmudgeonly Austrian feminist scientist to get a jump start on her obit, she exclaims, "You're a bit of a dud," and he readily agrees. Gopal is going nowhere, and doesn't mind. He actually prefers to stay late at work, however little he accomplishes, cherishing his nearness to the supply closet and his even greater proximity to the watercooler—a "consolation" for his marooned state. Long before you've reached the travails of Winston Cheung, the paper's barely competent, barely employed Cairo stringer, you will find yourself resolving to avoid their fate, unstick yourself, and get a move on.

What you'll need, then, is to pull out the beguilingly daft *The Towers of Trebizond* by Rose Macaulay, which is spirited and loopy enough to wake the most paralyzed hack from a torpor. "Take my camel, dear," it begins—an invitation from the eccentric, aristocratic Aunt Dot to her niece Laurie, whom her aunt has brought to show her that "travel is the chief end of life." When Aunt Dot disappears into Russia with an opinionated old reverend halfway through their trip, bequeathing the camel to Laurie, the novel turns from semifarcical travelogue to soul-searching soliloquy. For Laurie, a proper young woman, has been having an affair with a married man, a relationship she cannot reconcile with her Anglican faith. She opens her heart to us and, with the camel as a catalyst, soon becomes as eccentric as her aunt, indulging her passion for fly-fishing at every opportunity and acquiring an ape that she teaches to play her at chess.

Let Laurie and Aunt Dot and their infectious whimsy inspire you to live life as a true eccentric. You will never find yourself anywhere near a rut again.

See also: Career, being in the wrong • Change, resistance to • Jam, being in a • Mr./Mrs. Wrong, ending up with

SUPERHERO, WISHING YOU WERE A

*The Amazing Adventures
of Kavalier and Clay*
MICHAEL CHABON
. . .

*This Book Will Save
Your Life*
A. M. HOMES

Wait—don't tell us. You imagine the red and blue Lycra. You wonder which superpower you'd choose. Just a bit of you still believes in Superman's gravity-defying flying prowess, the Hulk's incredible strength, and Wonder Woman's powers of telepathy. You don't completely write off the possibility that you might one day own something similar, if not identical, to Batman's Batmobile. And occasionally, as you go about your daily life, you imagine, in little bubbles over your head, the words *Woosh! Bam! Kaboom! Pzzow!*

Well, that's okay. Some children grow out of it; you didn't.

You'll have already read and adored *The Amazing Adventures of Kavalier and Clay*, Michael Chabon's epic tale of comic book makers Josef Kavalier and Sammy Clay. Riding the wave of the golden age of comic books, the duo create a series of superheroes, beginning, just before World War II, with the Escapist, who "comes to the rescue of those who toil in the chains of tyranny and injustice." While fighting the war against Hitler with pen and ink, Joe and Sammy do not, however, become superheroes themselves. If you are looking for a how-to literary mentor, we know someone who does.

Richard Novak, in A. M. Homes's *This Book Will Save Your Life*, is left emotionally numb after a divorce causes him to leave his young son, Ben, behind in New York. His new life, in Los Angeles, is filled with modern-day artificiality and alienation: he lives in a glass box house on a canyon wall, splendidly sealed from the world with a noise-canceling headset, and he interacts only with his housekeeper, his nutritionist, his masseur, and his personal trainer. One day, he starts to *feel* again—beginning with an overwhelming and undiagnosable physical pain—and gradually new people start coming into his life. The next thing he knows, he's breaking his rules—drinking coffee ("Real coffee?" asks his nutritionist, aghast. "With regular milk?"), snacking on doughnuts, bursting into tears, taking naps. And he wants to "be more, do more . . . to be heroic, larger than life—rescue people from burning buildings, leap over rooftops." Be a superhero, in other words.

Richard's various heroic acts—including our favorite highway car chase in literature—will have you aglow with superhero awe. It takes his quack doctor, Lusardi, to point out that maybe all this saving of other people is really about saving himself. When Ben, now seventeen, finally pitches up on his doorstep, Richard is ready to try to rescue the most important relationship of all.

You can't become a superhero if you haven't suffered first. If, like Richard, you are motivated by correcting past wrongs and improving the lives of others, you can be a superhero too.

SWEATING

The Snow Child
EOWYN IVEY

Sweating can be an indication of many pleasurable activities. But there are limits. When dark circles appear beneath your armpits and you begin to exude an odor that even you can detect, you've crossed that fatal threshold from healthy glow to full glandular meltdown. Pick up this snowflake of a novel and let it caress you with cold like a winter sprite.

Mabel is so lonely and full of despair at her childless state that she deliberately walks out onto the unreliable surface of the freshly frozen Wolverine River (see: Children, not having). The ice makes a "deep, resonant crack like a massive champagne bottle being uncorked," but—unexpectedly—it holds and she crosses safely, returning to her cabin with a renewed sense of hope. Soon afterward, in the first flurry of new snow, she and Jack make a snow child together, its face whittled by Jack's penknife. But by the next morning it has disappeared—along with the hat and gloves they gave it. Footprints run from, but not to, the site of the sculpted snow child. As this magical child weaves in and out of their lives—leaving them when it's warm, and returning in a flurry of ice crystals when it's cold—Mabel worries about her "Faina" disappearing.

When your body heat rockets, return to a mental image of this wild and icy spirit, in whose hand snowflakes do not melt. Let her pervasive cold inhabit your body. Lose yourself in the enchantment of the Alaskan forest. Chase moose, catch snowflakes with Jack and Faina, and sketch with Mabel. By the end, you'll be so chilly that sweating will be a distant memory.

T

TASTE, BAD

Literature suggests it's never too late to learn good taste. Many a philistine within white borders has learned to dress in the fashions of the day, and to affect good taste even if they don't possess it. Yet it's interesting to note that an aesthetic sensibility doesn't align with worldly success very often in literature.

The Line of Beauty
ALAN HOLLINGHURST

Alan Hollinghurst's *The Line of Beauty* is no exception. Nick Guest is a bachelor aesthete who has a taste for high living, but lacks the means to achieve it. He becomes a lodger in the home of the MP, Gerald Fedden, the father of his best friend from university. Their Victorian mansion is full of beautiful and desirable objets d'art, but, as Hollinghurst delights in making clear, they consume art as a symbol of their wealth and power rather than possessing innate good taste. While looking for ways to survive in this world of people richer than he can ever hope to be, Nick gravitates toward the status—and physical beauty—of Wani Ouradi, a young millionaire he meets at one of the Feddens' parties.

Soon he and Wani, the son of a Lebanese supermarket mogul, have a plan to start an arty magazine. It will be named *Ogee*, after the S-shaped curve found to be present in many artistic standards of beauty, such as Islamic and Gothic architecture and Germanic clocks. (William Hogarth called it "the line of beauty"—hence the novel's title.) For Nick, this line is most sensually expressed in the curve of a young man's back, at the point where it cleaves to his buttocks.

Things start going wrong when various of the characters' sexual proclivities are exposed, with cataclysmic repercussions for Gerald Fedden. And though Nick plays a part in Fedden's fall, his genuine aesthetic sensibility ultimately redeems him.

As you read this novel, listening attentively to Nick as he waxes lyrical on music and art, your own sensibilities will open like a daisy in the sun. You might find yourself noticing that sinuous curve of beauty—in art, music, and perhaps the small of your lover's back.

TAX RETURN, FEAR OF DOING

Christie Malry's Own Double-Entry

B. S. JOHNSON

The April deadline is looming. Once again, you've left it to the last minute. You stare at your filing cabinet in horror, then back away from it as if from a rabid dog.

Sufferers from fear of doing taxes must forge an entirely new relationship with their finances— one that is nonthreatening and even friendly. This can be achieved by reading the shocking, toxic accounts kept by the simple, disaffected young man in *Christie Malry's Own Double-Entry*, by avant-garde author B. S. Johnson. Besieged by a sense that life is unfair, Christie Malry hits on the "Great Idea" of keeping track of the ways in which he has been slighted by others. According to the rules of double-entry bookkeeping as codified by the Tuscan monk Luca Pacioli in the fifteenth century—thus laying the foundations for modern capitalism—every debit must be balanced with a corresponding credit. And so Christie balances his accounts by taking revenge on the world—acts that start small (scratching an unsightly line down the side of an office block, for example) but quickly spiral out of control.

Christie takes pleasure in keeping his accounts in tidy order, and you should extract all you can out of this brief, bitter novel. By the time he enacts his most far-reaching act of vengeance, you'll see that the keeping of emotional accounts is the only real beast in the filing cabinet. Your own finances pale in comparison—they're just a harmless set of figures that won't bite when you open the drawer.

See also: **Procrastination**

TEA, UNABLE TO FIND A CUP OF

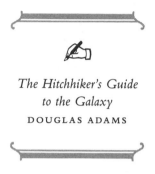

The Hitchhiker's Guide to the Galaxy
DOUGLAS ADAMS

We all know—or, to be more precise, those of us who are British know—the need for a good cup of tea. It traditionally hits at four o'clock, when our energy slumps. Luckily, it's usually fairly easy to make a cup. But what do we do when there's no kettle, boiling water, tea bags, or milk at hand?

Pick up a copy of *The Hitchhiker's Guide to the Galaxy.* Because your need cannot be greater than Arthur Dent's after one particularly trying Thursday. The day begins with Arthur prostrating himself before a bulldozer that's intent on demolishing his house. His protest is interrupted by his friend Ford Prefect—an alien from a planet somewhere near Betelgeuse—who insists he come to the pub to down three pints to anesthetize him against the imminent destruction of planet Earth. Duly anesthetized, they "hitchhike" onto a passing Vogon spaceship, in which they're tortured with poetry, before escaping to another ship. As Arthur, still in his robe, is blearily watching a binary sunrise over the legendary planet Magrathea and wondering what on earth—except there isn't one—is going on, that need for a good cup of tea hits.

The only source of hot drinks on the ship is a Nutri-Matic drinks synthesizer, a machine so sophisticated it claims to be able to produce a drink tailored precisely to your tastes and metabolic needs. But when Arthur requests a cup of tea, it produces a plastic cup filled with liquid that is "almost, but not quite, entirely unlike tea." Arthur throws away six cups of the stuff before finally, desperately, telling the machine everything he knows about tea—from the history of the East India Company to silver teapots and the importance of putting the milk in first. Only after the ship is all but destroyed do they find a small tray on the delivery plate of the Nutri-Matic, with three bone china cups and saucers, a silver teapot, and a jug of milk. It's the best cup of tea that Arthur has ever tasted.

All of which will help you bide the time between when the urge for tea hits and the moment you're reunited with kettle and teapot. Even if you've had to wait, at least you can sip your tea in the luxurious knowledge that the Earth, along with the contents of your kitchen and (come to think of it) you, haven't been demolished. Yet.

See also: Adolescence

TEARFUL, BEING

See: Cry, in need of a good • PMS • Tired and emotional, being

TEENS, BEING IN YOUR

THE TEN BEST NOVELS FOR TEENAGERS

Farewell, My Lovely
RAYMOND CHANDLER

TEETOTALER, BEING A

We know that being on the water wagon is no bad thing. Life on the straight edge gives you a clearer, purer view, and many health practitioners, unless they're French, advocate abstinence. But being a teetotaler in a world of drinkers is terribly dull. There are only so many mocktails you can get through before one of your companions will surprise you with a Death in the Afternoon. And what of that tricky moment when your future father-in-law suggests a manly moment with a malt whiskey? And how do you raise a toast to your great-grandmother on her one hundredth birthday? With a limp-wristed "Lemonade for me"?*

Literature's drinkers are generally more fun. And none more so than the great Philip Marlowe in Raymond Chandler's detective novels. Our favorite is *Farewell, My Lovely*, though any of them will do. It'll reacquaint you with the undeniable link between liquor and a certain louche, effortless cool as demonstrated by Marlowe at his most impressive: "I needed a drink, I needed a lot of life insurance, I needed a vacation, I needed a home in the country. What I had was a coat, a hat and a gun." People who find themselves pursued by Marlowe give him smiles that are at once "cozy and acid," because they know he'll extract compromising evidence from them somehow. But he does it with such panache that the baddies are almost honored to be found out. And living as he does by his own sense of justice—handing the culprits over to the police only if he knows them to be irredeemable—he manages to be a force for good but never a goody-goody. And it's partly down to drink.

Of course, you mustn't overdo it. But if you tend to be an abstainer, hang out with Marlowe for a novel or two. You'll find the wily sensibility of this quietly heroic detective will slip into your bloodstream like a rye whiskey highball. And as you turn the pages, go ahead and pour yourself one. Why not?

See also: **Goody-goody, being a · Killjoy, being a**

TENSION

See: **Anxiety · Stress**

---

* Yes, if you're a recovering alcoholic. In which case this cure is not for you. Please skip and go instead to: Alcoholism; and Dinner parties, fear of.

THIRTYSOMETHING, BEING

THE TEN BEST NOVELS FOR THIRTYSOMETHINGS

London Fields .... MARTIN AMIS

The Tenant of Wildfell Hall .... ANNE BRONTĒ

Middlesex .... JEFFREY EUGENIDES

The Sun Also Rises............................. ERNEST HEMINGWAY

The Best of Everything...................................RONA JAFFE

Of Human Bondage .... W. SOMERSET MAUGHAM

The Rector's Daughter.................................... F. M. MAYOR

The Jungle .... UPTON SINCLAIR

Miss Mackenzie................................ANTHONY TROLLOPE

All the King's Men........................ ROBERT PENN WARREN

The Friday Night Knitting Club

KATE JACOBS

TIRED AND EMOTIONAL, BEING

When you're tired and emotional, what you need is a comforting, warm, and well-told yarn—the literary equivalent of curling up in a hand-knit afghan wrap. *The Friday Night Knitting Club* is your cure.

Georgia is the owner of a knitting shop, Walker and Daughter, in downtown Manhattan. The single mother of beautiful, engaging Dakota, who is just beginning to spread her adolescent wings, Georgia was abandoned by the charismatic but unpredictable James when she got pregnant. So when he makes a reappearance in her life, wanting to make up for all the lost years, she is not exactly thrilled. She's far more interested in ensuring her business stays afloat and that her Friday night group is happily looked after and fed (with Dakota's wondrous cookies and muffins). Because clustered together in Georgia's shop every Friday evening is a rich and diverse mix of strong women she knows she can depend on. With James now back in the picture, her life enters a new phase of uncertainty, and she'll need the weft of family ties more than ever.

Yes, the yarn metaphors come thick and fast, but to read this novel is to be cable-stitched into a great warm skein of wool. The gentle nudges toward grannyish wisdom will set you back on course to recovery. As Jacobs writes, "Just grasp that yarn between your fingers and twist. Just start. It's the same with life."

See also: **Cry, in need of a good**

READING AILMENT *Tome, put off by a*

CURE *Cut it up*

If you are daunted by books the size of bricks, you'll be missing out on some of the most absorbing reading experiences known to humankind (see our list of Ten Best Big Fat Tomes, below). To overcome your block, break the book up into more manageable chunks. If it's a hardcover, stand the book upright and peer down: you'll see that the pages are divided into a number of "signatures," which are then stitched together. Make your divisions between one signature and the next. The pages of paperbacks are glued to the spine and can be attacked in a more random fashion; you'll need to carry a supply of paper clips with you to keep the loose leaves together. Suddenly the big fat tome has metamorphosed into a dozen slim tracts, each about the size of a long short story and no longer intimidating at all.

And don't be too precious about the loose pages, by the way. Once you've read them, throw them away. We're fond of the notion of blithely letting the pages fly one by one out the window of a fast-moving train (although to recommend such littering would be irresponsible). Either way, shrink the book as you read and thus gain the upper hand. Far better a copy of *A Suitable Boy* existing in noncorporeal form inside your head than left intact but destined to spend its life propping open a door.

(continued)

THE TEN BEST BIG FAT TOMES

TONSILLITIS

The Empress of Ice Cream
ANTHONY CAPELLA

Gone are the days when they whipped them unceremoniously out. Now it's all about endurance, antibiotics, and sweat.

When the dreaded tonsillitis strikes, here's a smooth, ice-creamy novel to slip down your throat. *The Empress of Ice Cream* begins in Florence in the seventeenth century when Carlo Demirco, a young boy of lowly origins, comes to assist Ahmad, the Persian ice maker, with his craft. Ahmad's secrets have been passed down through his family, and he sticks to the traditional recipes: only four basic flavors—orange, rose water, mastic, cardamom—can be used to create four different kinds of ice: *cordiale, granite, sorbetti,* and sherbets.

Carlo, on the other hand, experiments by making frozen delights from wine, *pesto genovese,* almond milk, crushed fennel, fruits, syrups, and all manner of different creams. He attempts to unlock the deepest secrets frozen into the ice. Then he takes these secrets into the innermost chambers of the court of Charles II, where sex, sorbet, and politics make a potent mix.

So celebrate the continued existence of your tonsils. When infection strikes, relieve your pain with this syllabub of a story, downing spoonfuls of soothing coolness as you read.

See also: **Pain, being in**

TOOThACHE

If you're suffering the exquisite pain of a tooth-ache, you will sympathize with Vronsky in Tolstoy's *Anna Karenina*: "He could hardly speak for the throbbing ache in his strong teeth, that were like rows of ivory in his mouth. He was silent, and his eyes rested on the wheels of the tender, slowly and smoothly rolling along the rails."

Anna Karenina
LEO TOLSTOY

What cures Vronsky, in the very next moment, is the displacement of the physical pain by a searing emotional pain—a memory that sets his "whole being in anguish" and makes him forget his toothache completely. Looking at the rails, he suddenly recalls *her*, or at least "what was left of her," when he found her sprawled on the table in the railway station cloakroom, among strangers, her body bloody and limp, the head lolling back with its weight of hair, the eyes awful in their stillness and openness, the mouth still seeming to emit the "fearful phrase" that she had uttered when they had quarreled: that he would be sorry.

If this image of Anna's broken body hasn't done the job, think of another shocking tableau from the pages of literature (for our own favorites, see: Hiccups). Then meditate on it while you schedule an appointment with your dentist.

See also: **Pain, being in**

TRAFFIC COP, BEING A
See: **Nobody likes you**

The Millstone
MARGARET DRABBLE
. . .
Notes from an Exhibition
PATRICK GALE

Sometimes, when we find ourselves seeking refuge in the closet beneath the stairs, our children rampaging around the house, we read Margaret Drabble's *The Millstone*, kept there for just such emergencies. Because even the happiest of parents can feel trapped by their children at times.

Rosamund Stacey is catapulted into motherhood by her very first sexual encounter. She nevertheless has a brisk approach first to her pregnancy, and then to life with her unplanned child. While not initially thrilled to be pregnant—she makes vague, botched attempts at an abortion (gin, a hot bath)—in the end she "fails to decide not to have it." And though she has plenty of other calls on her attention, she becomes utterly devoted to the beautiful creature she produces. So much so that she never feels the millstone around her neck that her friends predict. Suddenly, in our closet beneath the stairs, we realize we are not trapped by children, but surrounded by love.

You'll find more of this sudden, unexpected joy in Patrick Gale's *Notes from an Exhibition*, in which we meet bipolar mother Rachel. Rachel's mothering style is unique. She spends months locked away in her studio, painting and more or less ignoring her children. But on special days such as birthdays, she plunges in with total body and soul, keeping them home from school and letting them choose the pleasures of the day. On top of this, she is most inspired artistically when she's not on her medication, and loves being pregnant—when she's forced off the drugs—for this reason. And so through her children, and children to be, she heads to her biggest highs.

Of course, it's not as easy as that. After the highs come the lows, and the consequences of those live on in the bones of your children. But there's an encouragement here to live more intensely with our children than we, perhaps, always remember to do—to delight in them and celebrate them for whole days at a time.

See also: **Children requiring attention, too many** • **Claustrophobia** • **Fatherhood** • **Identity crisis** • **Jump ship, desire to** • **Motherhood** • **Single parent, being a**

TRUST, LOSS OF

In the Cut
SUSANNA MOORE

First of all, we have to decide whether someone is worthy of our trust or not. Most of us have a fairly good idea of this from the start. Trust this first impression. After that, continuing to trust someone when things get bumpy is an act of generosity. When in doubt, remember this: the degree to which you are prepared to trust is a measure of the degree to which others can trust you. Give up on people too easily, and they'll know that you, too, will let them down.

When you're a single girl in New York with a gift for the combative one-liner, you're making decisions about whom to trust all the time. When you also have an interest in risqué sex, making the right decision can mean the difference between life and death. Susanna Moore's *In the Cut* follows such a character in Frannie, who teaches English at a school for gifted low achievers. When the fast-talking, anecdote-rich Detective Jimmy Malloy calls on her to investigate the murder of a young actress in her neighborhood, she is immediately attracted to him, despite his many quirks (and cheap drugstore cologne). As Frannie becomes involved with Malloy and meets his colleagues at the homicide bureau—including his partner, Detective Rodriguez, who carries a yellow plastic water pistol in his holster—the first murder is followed by a second, and the tension ratchets up fast.

Test yourself with this novel: whom would you trust, and when and why would you stop trusting? It's worth getting good at it. As Frannie's fate testifies, one day your life might depend on it.

See also: Lying

TURMOIL

Home
MARILYNNE
ROBINSON

To be in turmoil is to be in a state of great and terrible disturbance. Perhaps you're at a fork in the road and you don't know which way to turn. Overwhelmed and confused, you need to find calm and clarity—the still center at the eye of the cyclone. Lucid, clear, and cool, the prose in Marilynne Robinson's *Home* will provide that calm in the storm.

At the age of thirty-eight, Glory has returned home to look after her dying father, a Presbyterian minister, after a disappointment in love. Once there, she begins to think the lifestyle suits her, and she discovers some much needed peace. But then her brother Jack turns up after a twenty-year absence. Jack's prodigal return fills his father with delight—he is a strong, silent type, and has a calm about him. But his silence is a complicated one: dark secrets lurk within, and there are things that cannot be discussed in front of their dogmatic father. Glory becomes increasingly troubled by what may or may not come out.

Yet she finds some comfort in Jack's presence, her thoughts drifting back to pleasant childhood memories. Once, she recalls, Jack taught her the gentle word "waft" while breathing on a feather. When Jack entered the room, the "stir of air" had floated the feather out of her hand. He'd stood in the doorway and watched the feather circle against the ceiling in the air, then caught it lightly in his hand and gave it back to her.

As you let the prose of this novel do its work on your troubled psyche, notice how turmoil coexists with calm. *Home*, an elegy to forgiveness, is that still room in which a single feather can waft unharmed, floating on a gentle current of air, then return to your hand.

See also: Anxiety • Cope, inability to • Stress

TWENTYSOMETHING, BEING

THE TEN BEST NOVELS FOR TWENTYSOMETHINGS

Old Man Goriot	HONORÉ DE BALZAC
The Stranger	ALBERT CAMUS
The Mysteries of Pittsburgh	MICHAEL CHABON
I Cannot Get You Close Enough	ELLEN GILCHRIST
The Buddha of Suburbia	HANIF KUREISHI
One Hundred Years of Solitude	GABRIEL GARCÍA MÁRQUEZ
The Group	MARY MCCARTHY
Goodbye, Columbus	PHILIP ROTH
The Secret History	DONNA TARTT
Sexing the Cherry	JEANETTE WINTERSON

U

UNEMPLOYMENT

Those out of work need a dose of quintessential Murakami. Because Murakami, the most popular Japanese novelist to be translated into English, specializes in passive protagonists with a lot of time on their hands and a tendency to get mixed up in entrancing, dreamlike adventures.

The Wind-Up Bird Chronicle

HARUKI MURAKAMI

The Wind-Up Bird Chronicle begins in suburban Tokyo with Toru Okada, who has left his legal job for no particular reason, doing the sort of things unemployed people do—cooking spaghetti at ten o'clock in the morning, listening to a radio broadcast of Rossini's *The Thieving Magpie*, fending off his wife, Kumiko, who calls to tell him about jobs for which he's unsuited and wouldn't enjoy. He goes out to look for their lost cat, Noboru Wataya, so named because it has the same "blank stare" as Kumiko's brother of the same name, whom Toru hates because he believes he's a sellout.

The search for the cat leads Toru to two strange women, down a dried-up well, and into the arms of yet another strange woman. What matters in all this is Toru's response: however bizarre and unconnected the events seem, he accepts them with neither surprise nor judgment—as we, too, become trained by the novel to do. And though the meaning of all the incredible events eludes him—and us—it is his openness to this transforming, liberating journey that will inspire.

See also: Ambition, too little · Bed, inability to get out of · Boredom · Broke, being · Job, losing your · Procrastination · Seize the day, failure to

UNHAPPINESS

See: The Novel Cure (Ella Berthoud and Susan Elderkin)

UNPOPULAR, BEING

See: Traffic cop, being a

V

READING AILMENT   *Vacation, not knowing what novels to take on*

CURE   *Plan ahead to avoid panic purchases*

Don't make the mistake so many of us do of thinking you'll find the perfect novel to take on vacation with you at the airport bookshop. You'll be in a rush, you'll have a limited selection to choose from, and you'll probably end up grabbing the nearest heavily promoted best seller. Don't waste your precious vacation on pulp. It's the perfect opportunity to tuck into something that transports you to another era. Hang out with something eminently readable and gorgeously, hedonistically historical.

THE TEN BEST NOVELS TO READ IN A HAMMOCK

Island Beneath the Sea ....ISABEL ALLENDE
Jack Maggs .... PETER CAREY

(continued)

VANITY

Gone with the Wind
MARGARET MITCHELL

• • •

The Picture of Dorian Gray
OSCAR WILDE

One problem with being vain, although it's not the only one, is that it makes you selfish and stupid.

Scarlett O'Hara, the southern belle at the heart of Margaret Mitchell's *Gone with the Wind*, is so aware of her green-eyed beauty that all she can think of is pretty gowns and winning the heart of not just the man she wants to marry, Ashley Wilkes, but of every young man in the vicinity. When she hears that Ashley has become engaged to his cousin Melanie—an undeniably plain girl—she can't believe it. Obsessed as she is with outward beauty, she can't begin to see Melanie's other qualities—or the need to nurture them in herself. And so she remains stuck as a spoiled, petulant teenager, continuing to use her looks to get what she wants. As oblivious to the importance of kindness as to plight of the slaves all around her (as, indeed, the author herself at times appears to be), Scarlett runs roughshod over everyone, including her husband, Rhett. Finally, the truth dawns on her. The flawless Melanie has belatedly won her admiration, respect, and love for the same reasons she won Ashley's all those years ago. And it has nothing to do with looks.

Vanity also makes you ugly in the end. In Oscar Wilde's classic tale, when the incandescently beautiful Dorian Gray starts to realize that everybody loves him for his looks, he becomes so worried about losing them that he pledges his soul for eternal youth, arranging that the handsome portrait of him painted by Basil Hallward deteriorates instead. He then embarks on a life of heedless hedonism under the tutelage of Lord Henry Wotton, and when a young actress whose heart he breaks commits suicide, an ugly sneer appears on the portrait. For our face bears testimony not just to the passing of the years, but to the evolving character of the person behind it. And as Dorian's disregard for others leaves more and more wreckage in its wake, his portrait becomes correspondingly hideous.

Do we really even have to say it? Beauty is what's on the inside.

See also: Arrogance • Well-read, desire to seem

VEGETARIANISM

Cold Mountain
CHARLES FRAZIER

Every now and again you bean lovers need to get down off your high horses and admit that death is an inevitable part of life. Eating only living things that grow from the soil is all very worthy, but the body cries out for blood every now and then. And although we admit that these days much meat is farmed in reprehensible ways, there are times—not least when you find yourself out in the wild without a picnic—when it might just be imperative to snack on a beast.

This is something that Inman, the protagonist of Charles Frazier's *Cold Mountain*, knows better than most. Injured in Petersburg during the Civil War, Inman decides to journey back to his North Carolina home in the hopes of being reunited with the woman who holds his heart. He walks all the way, avoiding roads for fear of re-conscription into the Confederate army. He needs to eat, and his adventures largely spring from his attempts to procure himself a meal: stealing a basket of bread and cheese from women washing at a river, saving a widow's hog from the feds and eating its brains, shooting a bear cub whose mother has died (which does leave him with some remorse).

Halfway through his travels, he meets a goat-herding woman who has lived in a rust-colored caravan surrounded by her herd for twenty-five years. Her relationship with her animals is one of total symbiosis. When she strokes the goat she cradles in her arms, then gently slices its throat, its death is portrayed as a completely natural part of the cycle of life—loving and respectful, rather than cruel or wasteful. As Inman leaves her caravan with a bellyful of goat and forges on toward his beloved Ada, he clutches a drawing of a carrion flower plant that the goat woman has given him. The carrion flower emits a stink of rotten flesh in order to attract its carnivorous pollinators, which serves as a reminder of the tricks nature plays on itself to survive. With this, Frazier puts the carnivores among us firmly into the natural order of things.

VENGEANCE, SEEKING

Wuthering Heights
EMILY BRONTË

Taking revenge is always a bad idea. It sets in motion a chain reaction of revenge and counterrevenge that inevitably escalates and becomes hard to stop.

Such a domino effect is played out in full, terrible glory on the tormented, windswept moors of Emily Brontë's *Wuthering Heights*. When Mr. Earnshaw, lord of Wuthering Heights, brings the orphan Heathcliff into his home, his own children, Hindley and Catherine, resent it (see: Sibling rivalry). And when Mr. Earnshaw starts favoring Heathcliff over Hindley—while Catherine and Heathcliff fall in childish love—Hindley is even more put out and takes revenge on Heathcliff. Seeing this, Mr. Earnshaw takes revenge on Hindley by sending his son away to college, and shortly afterward he takes revenge on all of them by dying. Hindley inherits Wuthering Heights, and immediately sets about taking revenge on Heathcliff by reinstalling himself and his new wife, Frances, there and sending Heathcliff out to work in the fields.

Frances dies giving birth to a boy named Hareton,* and Hindley becomes a gambler and hits the bottle, and in his drunkenness takes revenge on Heathcliff even more. At about this time, Cathy, despite loving Heathcliff, marries Edgar Linton, who lives with his sister Isabella on the other side of the moor at Thrushcross Grange, and Heathcliff takes revenge on Cathy by

---

* Frances's dying could be interpreted as her taking revenge on her newborn child for the pain he inflicted on her. It's just an idea.

VENGEANCE, SEEKING

running away. Then he comes back and takes revenge on Hindley by arranging for Hareton's education to be discontinued, so that the boy grows up illiterate. He also lends money to Hindley so that Hindley gambles and drinks even more and eventually dies. Heathcliff inherits Wuthering Heights and then gets his revenge on Cathy for marrying Edgar by marrying Edgar's sister Isabella, which means he's in line to inherit Thrushcross Grange should Edgar die. He is vile to Isabella as a way of getting revenge on Edgar for marrying Cathy.

Then Cathy, who lives at Thrushcross Grange, gives birth to a daughter named Catherine and dies* and Heathcliff runs over the moor wishing he had not taken revenge on Cathy, or she on him, and shortly afterward Isabella takes revenge on Heathcliff by running away to London and giving birth to a boy named Linton.† We then fast-forward thirteen years to when Cathy's daughter Catherine crosses the moor from Thrushcross Grange to Wuthering Heights and meets Hareton, Hindley and Frances's illiterate son. Then Isabella dies‡ and Linton goes to live with Heathcliff at Wuthering Heights. Heathcliff is horrible to him, presumably in revenge against everybody. Then Catherine meets Linton at Wuthering Heights and they fall in love, although it turns out that Heathcliff has talked Linton into seducing Catherine because if Linton and Catherine marry, Linton will inherit Thrushcross Grange as well as Wuthering Heights and Heathcliff's revenge on Edgar Linton will be complete.

One day Heathcliff holds Catherine prisoner at Wuthering Heights until she marries Linton. Soon after, Catherine's father, Edgar Linton, dies and then so does Linton, perhaps in revenge against Heathcliff for forcing him to marry Catherine. Heathcliff therefore inherits Thrushcross Grange and forces Catherine to live at Wuthering Heights with him and Hareton.§ While Catherine and Hareton fall in love, Cathy's ghost continues to take revenge on Heathcliff by driving him mad. One wild night Heathcliff dies, presumably in revenge against Cathy, but also in revenge against himself. Hareton and Catherine inherit Wuthering Heights and Thrushcross Grange and decide to get married and the reader takes revenge on Emily Brontë by gun-

* Cathy's death could be interpreted as an act of revenge on Heathcliff for taking revenge on her by marrying Isabella.

† Interestingly, Isabella does not die after giving birth. This could be interpreted as her taking revenge on Heathcliff. However, she does die later.

‡ See?

§ We are not sure whether this is an act of revenge, or, if it is, whom it is an act of revenge against.

ning for Heathcliff all the way through because of his overwhelming love for Cathy, despite the fact that he's been vile and taken revenge on absolutely everybody ever since Hindley first took revenge on him for something that wasn't, in fact, his fault.

Do you see? Don't do it. The revenge that comes back to you will be worse than the revenge you inflicted in the first place. And it may start a cycle of vengeance that goes on all your life.

See also: Anger · Bitterness · Murderous thoughts · Rage

VIOLENCE, FEAR OF

The Strange Case of Dr.
Jekyll and Mr. Hyde
ROBERT LOUIS
STEVENSON
· · ·
Musashi
EIJI YOSHIKAWA

There is violence from without and violence from within. Let's deal with the latter first. Most of us are aware that every now and then in a flash of rage we have a brief fantasy of committing a violent act. Most of us quash it immediately. But if you find it hard to resist the urge to lash out physically, and harder still to stop thinking about, *The Strange Case of Dr. Jekyll and Mr. Hyde* will allow you to explore and reflect upon your inner violent streak.

Robert Louis Stevenson's famous novel is a deep excavation of the latent possibility of violence within us. Dr. Jekyll, a respectable doctor and experimental scientist living in London, has long been fascinated by the opposing natures of man, and so he decides to divide his own two natures using a homemade drug. The temporary schism will allow his dark side to operate independently of his moral, respectable self. And because he looks completely different when he transforms into Mr. Hyde—shorter, hairier, younger—Jekyll need not answer to the consequences of Hyde's actions.

We don't actually witness most of what Hyde gets up to; his ominous disappearances, sometimes lasting several months, remain shrouded in mystery. But we soon gather that he is a monster capable of the utmost depravity. As Hyde begins to dominate Jekyll, making it harder and harder for Jekyll to maintain his respectable facade, soon he can no longer control whether he's

Jekyll or Hyde. It's a powerful message about what happens when our own darker natures begin to take over.

If it's the violence of others you fear, acquire the strength of a samurai by reading Eiji Yoshikawa's epic novel *Musashi*. This nine-hundred-page masterpiece about the noble pursuit of samurai swordsmanship takes you on a journey from punishing mountaintop training rituals with Zen Buddhist teachers to the battlefields of sixteenth-century Japan and thence to the discovery of love, humility, and wisdom. Our impressive hero eventually realizes that committing a violent act is the last thing he ever wants to do. But the knowledge of his inner strength means that he'll never need to. Absorb the legend of Musashi. Let his fearlessness—if not his martial art prowess—inspire you. Show the kind of inner confidence and unconquerable demeanor he does, and would-be aggressors will leave you well alone.

See also: **Confrontation, fear of** • **Murderous thoughts** • **Rage**

W

WAGON, FALLING OFF THE

See: Alcoholism

WAITING ROOM, BEING IN A

The Stars My Destination
ALFRED BESTER

Waiting rooms mean hospitals, doctors, dentists, train stations, bus depots, airports. Joyless, drab, stained with worry, echoing despair. It is crucial to be armed for this dead zone with the perfect novel cure.

Which is Alfred Bester's hugely influential 1956 novel *The Stars My Destination*. What makes it perfect fodder for a waiting room is Bester's unique "jaunting." Jaunting, developed unintentionally by a man named Jaunte, is the technique of transporting yourself to another location. As long as you have the coordinates of where you are now and where you are going, and you can visualize your destination, you can jaunte anywhere on this planet, either instantly or in stages. The only limit is that it must occur within space: it is impossible to jaunte through a vacuum. Jaunting is all about the mind: it works by focusing very clearly and *willing* the leap through space. Once Gully Foyle comes along, the entire jaunting system is challenged by his dauntless roaming through the galaxies.

The novel is set in the twenty-fifth century, when Gully, the sole survivor of an unexplained catastrophe, is clinging to life in the only airtight room left intact in the wreck of his spaceship, the *Nomad*. His locker is four feet wide, four feet deep, and nine feet high—a "lightless coffin" in which he's been incarcerated for five months, twenty days, and four hours. When a ship appears in space that could save him, Gully is galvanized into action. But *Vorga* passes him by. Gully swears vengeance, and this is what drives him to survive. When we next see Gully, he is at a jaunte training school back on Earth, playing AWOL with his coordinates and going countries farther than he is strictly allowed.

As you read this in your waiting room, be grateful, at least, that it is (we hope) a little bigger than "four by four by nine." Harness the power of your mind and feel possibilities surge through you as you imagine all the places you would jaunte to if you could. You may not get your full jaunte certification, but you may discover, like Gully, new skills waiting to be used in the chambers of your mind.

See also: **Anxiety · Boredom**

WANDERLUST

The Alexandria Quartet
LAWRENCE DURRELL

So you are gripped by the desire to go to Africa.* For the sake of argument, let's say that you want specifically to go to Egypt. And within Egypt, the city that enthralls you, calls to you, is Alexandria, the city founded by Alexander the Great.

Reader, consider the expense. First of all, there are all the things you will have to buy in advance: luggage, digital camera, safari trousers, etc. It all adds up. Then there's the cost—and let's not forget the environmental cost—of the flight. At either end there will be trains, taxis, trams, camels, feluccas. Then there are the hotel bills—and if you're anything like us, you'll convince yourself you should stay in the nicest room you can find, so you can make the most of it,

---

* Replace as required with relevant country/city/founder/transport method/tourist attraction/climate as required, and with the relevant novel cure from the Ten Best list. These novels have been chosen for their length (i.e., to incapacitate for two or three weeks at a time), as well as their ability to transport the reader without leaving home.

splurge a bit, now that you've come all this way. And we haven't even begun to add up the cost of the food—three meals a day, in restaurants and cafés—and the mosquito repellent and the medicines. And what about the shopping? You will almost certainly want to buy an expensive shawl or rug or bowl as a souvenir. And go on excursions—to the pyramids, the Red Sea, the desert. Again, now that you've come all this way.

Consider, also, the discomfort. Alexandria in the height of summer is stiflingly hot. And at night it can be freezing cold. And that's not even to start on the winds.

And finally consider the strain of all this on your relationship with your traveling companion(s). Hot, tired, perhaps suffering from digestive troubles, you will be at your most irritable—and so will they. Only the naive would expect to come home from such a trip with their marriage/friendship intact.

Now consider the alternative. Stay at home and read about Alexandria in the first three volumes of the Alexandria Quartet: *Justine*, *Balthazar*, and *Mountolive* (skipping, for now, the fourth, which is set in Corfu). Together with the narrator, Darley, your guides to the city will be Alexandrian natives: the vain, goddesslike Justine, magnificent with her dark skin and white dresses, every particle the Alexandrian society woman; her husband, the humorless but faithful Prince Nessim; the fragile, sickly Melissa; the serene, solitary artist Clea; and Balthazar, with his "deep croaking voice of great beauty," yellow goat eyes, and monstrous hands. Darley himself, an itinerant schoolteacher, falls in love with them all.

And as you visit every corner of this dusty city in their company, wandering aimlessly from the cafés to the sandy beaches in the fast fading afternoon light, so will you. The best way to know Alexandria is to know its people. Durrell believed we are formed by the place we're from, but also that we then inform that place further. These richly drawn characters make this city what it is. Luxuriate in the layers, then, of the characters and the city they cannot exist without. By the time you emerge, not only will you intimately know this ancient city, but you'll have saved yourself a bundle in time, hassles, and discomfort.

THE TEN BEST NOVELS TO CURE WANDERLUST

Save the planet and your pocket by traveling the world from your armchair.

See also: Itchy feet

Fabulous Nobodies
LEE TULLOCH

WARDROBE CRISIS

Many of us face this ailment at the start of every day. Gazing at a chaos of bobbly, hole-ridden, ill-fitting, and faded relics, alongside a few classy numbers completely unsuitable for everyday wear, we shiver in our undies trying and discarding random alternatives one by one. As we slip resignedly into whatever we had on the day before, we dream of that ideal outfit—comfortable yet well made, flattering yet relaxed—that can take us anywhere. Or, even better, a perfectly thought-out collection of stunning, coordinated pieces for every occasion, plus lots of clever accessories. If this fantasy strikes a chord, *Fabulous Nobodies* is the novel for you.

Reality Nirvana Tuttle has a huge responsibility. As fashion enforcement officer at the Manhattan club Less Is More, she must let in the fabulous and turn away the drab. Reality, known as Really to her friends, is infallible on the subject of fashion fabulousness. Anyone wearing angora, acrylic, or peach chiffon is *out*. Anyone wearing Thierry Mugler or an old Pucci print is *in*. And on top of that, Reality has to recognize the Somebodies who look like unfabulous Nobodies, and let them in too.

Reality may come across as an insufferable fashion victim, but her love affair with frocks is endearing, and she does show genuine concern for her style-challenged acolytes. Like them, you'll learn a lot from her. Not only will she steer you through common fashion mistakes, but she'll also open your eyes to the potential for the clothes already in your wardrobe. As with friends, you'll need to choose well—and then look after them, appreciating their special qualities, and finding ways to support and encourage what they do best. Ultimately, the novel acknowledges the folly and absurdity of fashion, but let's face it: clothes are a fact of life. So get to know your own wardrobe inside and out. Identify and source any omissions. Give the useless ones away. Your mornings will be forever easier.

WASTING TIME ON A DUD RELATIONSHIP

The Transit of Venus
SHIRLEY HAZZARD

It is deeply painful to watch someone you love throw his or her life away on someone unworthy. We grieve for the loss of potential, for the self-inflicted pain, for the inevitable suffering. And yet it's an error that's all too human, and many of us make it ourselves.

Victims of this sorry predicament—and you'll know who you are—need to fall in love with the grave, raven-haired beauty of Shirley Hazzard's *The Transit of Venus*. Caroline Bell suffers in the inferior embrace of Paul Ivory. Caro, as we come to know her, is one of two orphaned Australian sisters who have emigrated to London in the 1950s to take up new lives—Grace into a conservative marriage and kids, Caro into a government job and independence. Caro is loved—devotedly, hopelessly—by Ted Tice, an academic of modest means. But it is the tall, graceful, upper-class Paul to whom she succumbs. Paul is a dashing young playwright tipped for great things, whose easy manner and pleasure in his own good health and good looks makes him bound to outshine his red-haired rival.

When they meet, Paul is engaged, and soon marries Tertia, heiress to a castle. But he is drawn to Caro's "somber glow," and their mutual attraction is overpowering. We know from the start that he is not good enough for her—he's dazzled by his own success, and his shallowness evidenced by his marriage to the empty-eyed Tertia. Paul and Caro both know she can see through him, and that her love is mixed with contempt. Clearly, nothing can come of their affair. But Caro cannot seem to resist.

Hazzard's dense, extraordinary prose drives home the anguish we feel for

Caro's wasted years. You will find yourself forced to submit, as the author masterfully dissects emotions with surgical precision, elevating you to new levels of understanding about your own self-deception. Ache for Caro as you read, but as soon as you've turned the last page, ache for yourself. Then cut your losses and get out before it's too late.

See also: **Love, doomed** • **Mr./Mrs. Right, holding out for** • **Mr./Mrs. Wrong, ending up with**

WEDDING

See: **Broke, being** • **Children, under pressure to have** • **Jealousy** • **Shelf, fear of being left on the** • **Wardrobe crisis**

READING AILMENT   *Well-read, desire to seem*

CURE   *Ten novels for the literary fake*

While we sympathize with your desire—a well-read individual, particularly of novels, is likely to be more balanced, more mature, and of course more interesting to talk to*—we do not condone this pitiful failure of integrity. Like Nick, the narrator of *The Great Gatsby*, who after embarking on a career in the city buys "a dozen volumes" that promise to unfold the secrets of "Midas and Morgan and Maecenas," you probably have every intention of reading the books you claim to have read at some point in your life. And maybe, once you've finished bluffing your way through another earnest conversation about them, you really will. But the chances are you'll be bluffing next time too.

The good news is that you don't have to have read *that many* books in order to seem well-read—even strikingly well-read.

(continued)

* Not that we are biased or smug.

You just have to pick the right ones. The following ten will stand you in excellent stead for a lifetime of good first impressions. Be careful, though, not to mention any one title more than twice to the same person, and even then, let several years go by in between. With luck, by the time you read to the end of this list, you'll have acquired the taste for more. And then you won't have to bluff anymore.

THE TEN BEST NOVELS FOR SEEMING WELL-READ

The first five are simply essential; the second five will imply the existence of vast literary landscapes in your head.

Wuthering Heights .... EMILY BRONTË
The Great Gatsby .... F. SCOTT FITZGERALD
The Recognitions .... WILLIAM GADDIS
Independent People .... HALLDÓR LAXNESS
The Magic Mountain .... THOMAS MANN
Moby-Dick .... HERMAN MELVILLE
The Radetzky March .... JOSEPH ROTH
War and Peace .... LEO TOLSTOY
Voss .... PATRICK WHITE
Beware of Pity .... STEFAN ZWEIG

WIDOWED, BEING

Do not underestimate the enormity of what you are going through. Losing one's life partner will set in motion a series of seismic shifts in every sphere of your life. Before, you had a companion; now you live alone. Before, you were, perhaps, one half of a set of parents; now you are

The Same Sea
AMOS OZ
(continued)

The Widow's Tale
MICK JACKSON
. . .
Major Pettigrew's Last Stand
HELEN SIMONSON

parenting alone. Your relationship to your child or children will undergo changes. As will the relationships with your friends. And you will also have to build a new relationship to yourself. Because without that other person to prop you up, fill you out, add whatever it was they added to your sense of self, you will sometimes wonder who you are.

To help you navigate these sad and difficult times, we offer you Israeli author Amos Oz's transcendentally beautiful prose poem *The Same Sea*. Written in short, gentle vignettes, it tells the story of Albert Danon, a "mild" accountant whose wife, Nadia, has died of cancer. Their only son, Rico, has gone off to Tibet, thinking the world needs some sorting out, leaving his girlfriend, Dita, to look in on his dad. Albert does not have an entirely platonic reaction to pretty, bold Dita in her short orange skirt, and when she suddenly finds herself homeless he invites her to move into his spare room. Meanwhile, Albert's friend Bettine—herself widowed for twenty years—keeps a watchful eye on the pair, not without a vested interest for herself.

In times of grief and loneliness, we must take life moment by moment. And this is how Oz proceeds, capturing with wondrous clarity the time-suspended moment between Albert's turning off the computer and his going to bed; or the moment when Nadia, woken in the night by a blackbird, wonders who she will be when she dies; or the moment when Bettine lays her cards on the table. Oz gives equal attention to the banal and the beautiful, the touching and the lustful, side by side. For sensitive, understanding company that allows you access to the vast and complicated terrains of emotion inside your heart, *The Same Sea* can't be beat.

The Widow's Tale by Mick Jackson offers an opportunity to reflect on this remaking of the self by examining the past, this time from a widow's point of view. The widow herself remains unnamed, but through diaries and interior monologue we know her every thought. Wry, humorous, and mildly aggrieved, she is angry at the way her husband died and directs her anger, uselessly, at him. Her way of dealing with it is to flee to the Norfolk coast, where she rents a cottage and, under the pretense of being a bird-watcher, begins spying obsessively on the house of a former love, fantasizing about the life she could have had with this other man.

Her behavior may seem bizarre, but her stint as a stalker turns out to be cathartic. In her attempt to reawaken a largely fictitious affair, it makes her realize the good things she had in her marriage and purges her of the negative emotions that were threatening to swamp her memories. Let this novel encourage you to examine both the good and the bad in your years of marriage, accepting and forgiving the past and leaving you with an honest, open heart.

New beginnings are always possible, however jaded we might feel. In Helen Simonson's *Major Pettigrew's Last Stand*, Major Pettigrew—a retired military man in the stiff-upper-lip mold—is about as rigid in his habits as a man can get. But when, after losing his wife, he also loses his brother, the sixty-eight-year-old major is so tripped up by grief that he begins to see the familiar in a different light—including the kindly Mrs. Ali, the woman who runs the village shop. On the surface the two could not be more different, but they're drawn together by their mutual widowhood, clashes with their similarly small-minded families, and a shared love of books, particularly Kipling. Anyone reading the book that you're holding in your hands will appreciate this as a basis for a new relationship—and it may encourage you to leave the door open, just a crack.

See also: **Death of a loved one** • **Loneliness** • **Sadness** • **Yearning, general**

WORDS, LOST FOR

Lolita
VLADIMIR NABOKOV

If you're lost for words because you're in shock, wait for the shock to pass and the words will return. If the words won't come because you have a stutter or a stammer, see: Speech impediment. But if you're lost for words because eloquence is not your strength, and the right words seem to desert you whenever you need them most, then take as your companion the narrator of *Lolita*, Humbert Humbert, a man who is as far from being afflicted with this ailment as a person can get.

By rights Humbert Humbert should be the one shamed into silence. He has used a young girl for the selfish pursuit of his own illicit pleasures. But instead, as he waits in prison for the trial that will determine his fate, words are his greatest friend. In fact, Humbert Humbert can't wait to speak. Here, in prison, he no longer has to keep secret the despicable self he has been repressing all these years. At last he can indulge in the rapturous specifics of what, and who, he has loved.

And one of those things is language. For Humbert Humbert, words are a plaything—he loves allusions and double meanings, and finds in them both an outlet for his humor and a catharsis. But they are also a tool of seduction—and this time it's the reader who's being seduced. What Humbert Humbert is famously doing is seducing us with his tongue. From the very first paragraph, with its sensuous dismantling of her name into its three delectable syllables—"Lo-lee-ta"—we are as entranced by his descriptions of Lolita as he is by the girl himself. We want more of this "exasperating brat," because we want more of the language in which she's revealed to us. Thus ensnared into the rhapsody, tainted by the joint titillation, how can we condemn Humbert Humbert without condemning ourselves? Such is Nabokov's cunning game. By the end, we are captivated by this confession of rape, murder, pedophilia, and incest, with its "bits of marrow sticking to it, and blood, and beautiful bright-green flies," as if it were an aboveboard romance between two consenting adults. Nabokov has made a sordid thing into a divine work of art.

What separates you, tongue tied and anxious eyed, from Humbert Humbert—erudite, literary, a French speaker with a predilection for *le mot juste* as well as little girls—is that this loquacious criminal has an unwavering sense of his right to speak. Take a page from Humbert Humbert. Steep yourself in his elegant rhythms—though not his inelegant activities. Think of words—though not nymphets—as your playthings, as sources of private and shared amusement. Let his charm—though not his charming of young girls—become your charm, tripping off your tongue from the palate to the tip "to tap, at three, on the teeth," giving your anxious tongue license, at last, to speak.

WORK, NOT HAVING ANY

See: Job, losing your · Unemployment

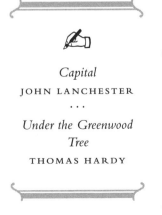

Capital
JOHN LANCHESTER
· · ·
Under the Greenwood Tree
THOMAS HARDY

WORKAHOLISM

One of the most vexing dilemmas about being a workaholic is that, were you to turn up to a Workaholics Anonymous session seeking support for your addiction (yes, such sessions exist), nobody else would be there . . . Well, being workaholics, they'd all decide they were too busy to go to the meeting. And face it, so would you. The hamster wheel of workaholism is hard to jump off, particularly when your workaholism yields status, nice possessions, a roof over your head, food for your table, and school fees for the children. As a result, the only surefire way to exit the wheel is to be pushed.

In John Lanchester's novel *Capital*, his dazzlingly perceptive overview of the contrasting lives of a handful of Londoners of wildly divergent backgrounds, a workaholic City banker named Roger Yount realizes first gradually, then suddenly, that his unending toil has been in vain. His spoiled, grasping, frivolous wife, Arabella, complains endlessly about the time he spends at the office, but spends every penny he earns (or she anticipates him earning) on the trappings of privilege she takes as her due. Roger has counted on his one-million-pound Christmas bonus to cover their mogul excesses. Waiting for his envelope, he entertains hopes that his bonus might be even higher than expected: two and a half million pounds "would, once he'd paid for all the things he had to pay for, salted some away in the pension . . . and all that, leave him with a fair few quid left over. It was said you could get somewhere pretty habitable on Ibiza for a million quid. Worth thinking about." But it's not worth thinking about once Roger, feeling sick, sees the real figure: thirty thousand pounds. With so "little" money, any thought of a second (or third) home flies out the window—they might not even be able to hold on to their first. Can they possibly make do with less work, less money, less *stuff*? You could almost pity Roger if you didn't feel he had it coming—and Arabella certainly needs to learn a lesson or two. But how can they learn to cope once Roger jumps off the wheel?

The answer is to wean themselves from relentless acquisition (see: Greed) and steep their overachieving, overcraving souls in something very simple, very rustic, very small. To effect this transformation, we suggest Thomas Hardy's gentlest, most innocent novel, *Under the Greenwood Tree*. The members of the Mellstock parish choir are a motley crew. Gathering in rain or shine with their fiddles to sing and play—a labor of love, not money—they have not forgotten the important things in life: a little music, a little cider, a little cheer for old and young alike.

Realistically, it's too late for the Younts to find much relief in such humble escapism; Arabella's interests don't include nineteenth-century novels, just the stately country homes in which they are set. But, assuming a vacation home in Ibiza is not in your sights, it's not too late for you to reform your workaholic ways. Take a lesson from Roger's comeuppance: downsize your workday, connect more fully with the life outside your desk, and take a page from Hardy's soothing prescription.

WORRY

See: Anxiety

WRITER'S BLOCK

I Capture the Castle
DODIE SMITH

The remedy for writer's block inflicted upon the novelist father in *I Capture the Castle* is nothing short of genius. But—darn it—to tell it would be to give away one of the plot twists in this unutterably charming novel. Mortmain, as he is known by his second wife, Topaz, achieved great critical success with an experimental novel called *Jacob Wrestling.* But he has not been able to put pen to paper since an unfortunate incident involving a next-door neighbor who foolishly intervened when Mortmain brandished a cake knife at his first wife while they were having tea in the garden. He ended up spending three months behind bars, writer's block set in, and the family has been penniless ever since.

While Topaz and the three children struggle to feed and clothe themselves and their ruined castle crumbles around them, Mortmain drifts around reading detective novels and the *Encyclopaedia Britannica* and staring into space. He's ditched all his friends and has more or less stopped talking to his family. Eventually Rose, the elder daughter, can stand it no more and decides to marry her way out of poverty. But the younger, wiser narrator daughter Cassandra soon realizes it's time to force their father's writing hand. Her plan—which involves a Freudian regression to the moment at which the block began—works to a T.

Sufferers of this unfortunate condition should not necessarily attempt to copy Cassandra's cure. It is somewhat extreme and in any case would not work with your own consent. But read between the lines of this book and a fuller, more complete picture of how Mortmain's block dislodges will emerge. As you read, gather the things you need around you: a person of like mind, someone to do the cooking, and, yes, the *Encyclopaedia Britannica.*

Feedback on the success rate of this remedy would be greatly appreciated.

XENOPHOBIA

If you find yourself fearing or even loathing those from countries other than your own, bathe in these books from foreign parts. Written by authors native to the setting, they reveal the essential sameness of us all beneath the skin and will remind you of the humanity common to us all.

THE TEN BEST NOVELS TO CURE
THE XENOPHOBIC

Once Upon a River .... BONNIE JO CAMPBELL
See Under: Love .... DAVID GROSSMAN
The Blind Owl .... SADEGH HEDAYAT
Waltenberg .... HÉDI KADDOUR
The Garlic Ballads .... MO YAN
Cities of Salt .... ABDELRAHMAN MUNIF
Q & A .... VIKAS SWARUP
Harp of Burma .... MICHIO TAKEYAMA
House of Day, House of Night .... OLGA TOKARCZUK
Cutting for Stone .... ABRAHAM VERGHESE

Y

YEARNING, GENERAL

To long—painfully, endlessly, fruitlessly—for something you believe will satisfy a deep, persistent need in you is a painful, endless, fruitless way to spend your life. It's also irritating to all who have to witness it. Life is too short. Luckily, we have a cure so short that we needn't spend much time prescribing it and you won't spend much time administering it.

Silk
ALESSANDRO
BARICCO

It is not that Hervé Joncour doesn't appreciate his loving wife, Hélène, who waits for him patiently when he makes his annual, hazardous trip by land and sea to the Japanese village of Shirakawa to smuggle back silkworm eggs, an illegal trade at the time. It is just that, were it not for the yearning he feels for the young concubine who captures his heart in Shirakawa—and with whom he exchanges only missives written in Japanese—he would have appreciated her even more.

Do not prize what you do not know above what you know. Love and cherish your true friends and family rather than cultivating some distant, impossible dream.

YEARNING FOR HOME

See: Homesickness

Z

ZESTLESSNESS

Ragtime

E. L. DOCTOROW

Z estlessness is a notoriously difficult ailment to diagnose. Easily confused with boredom (which is really a failure of the imagination; see: Boredom) and apathy (which manifests as physical sluggishness although it, too, has a mental cause; see: Apathy), zestlessness can appear, to the untrained eye, to be simply a case of having a dull personality. Left untreated, it can ruin entire lives—and we're not just talking your own. To live without zest is to live without an appetite for new experiences, to miss out on the spice, the juice, the edge that makes life thrilling. It is to live with deadened, flattened senses, with your passions unaroused and your curiosity untapped. It is to depress the hell out of those around you—and, frankly, us too. Do us all a favor. Read this novel and switch yourself on.

Ragtime takes as its subject the dawn of the twentieth century in the United States—a time when the entire nation was in the exhilarated grip of commotion, invention, and change. Sparkling new railroads sprung up across the country. Model T Fords spilled off the assembly lines. Twenty-five-story buildings shot skyward and aircraft zoomed people away. Telephones connected people as never before. Skyrockets and cherry bombs exploded in the skies. In ordinary homes, sneezing powder and squirting plastic roses tickled people's noses and made them laugh.

In among all this is the story of a well-to-do family in New Rochelle, New York. The son—known simply as "the little boy"—is fixing his gaze on a bluebottle fly crossing a screen one day when Harry Houdini crashes his car outside and is invited in for tea. Soon after, Mother discovers a black baby in the garden, and takes the child in—thus breaking the first of several cultural and gender taboos. When Father returns from an expedition to the Arctic to find her running his fireworks business, he becomes increasingly alienated from the domestic scene, and the family begins to fall apart.

By turning his lens from vivid close-up to great, sweeping vista and allowing real and fictional characters to meet at the junctions of a vast, complex cobweb, E. L. Doctorow injects the novel—and the reader—with enormous zest. As immigrants from Italy and Eastern Europe, such as Tateh and his beautiful daughter, pour into squalid tenements on the Lower East Side, the financier J. P. Morgan sets new standards of wealth and power, and Houdini defies death with more and more terrifying feats. Freud puts America on the couch, and the boy's uncle, known as Mother's Younger Brother, stalks the country's first sex goddess, Evelyn Nesbit.

As you read, notice how Mother and the little boy say yes to progress and change. Watch how Father, conversely, says no, refusing to move with the times. Like Tateh, let the tumult and tumble of Doctorow's startling sentences remove you from what is familiar and failing. Board the train to a new life. Take with you the boy's curiosity for recent inventions. Appropriate Grandfather's joy at the sight of spring (though take care, if you're getting on in years, that you don't slip and break your pelvis doing a spontaneous jig). Put yourself in a place where change is a given, and feel the zest flood back in.

See also: **Disenchantment**

ACKNOWLEDGMENTS

Thank you to our team of readers, who valiantly tested our literary cures and reported on their efficacy: Becky Adams, Miranda Alcock, Tim Bates, Josh Beattie, Nichole Beauchamp, Chris Berthoud, Colin Berthoud, Lucy Berthoud, Martin Berthoud, Veronique Biddell, Amanda Blugrass, Gael Cassidy, Sarah Cassidy, Sarah Constantinides, Belinda Coote, Stephanie Cross, the Danny House Book Group, William Davidson, Sandra Deeble, Mel Giedroyc, Gael Gorvy-Robertson, Teresa Griffiths, Gill Hancock, Jane Heather, Belinda Holden, Charlie Hopkinson, Grahame Hunter, Clare Isherwood, Lou James, Tim Jones, Sarah Leipciger, Annabel Leventon, Rachel Lindop, Hilary Macey-Dare, Sam Nixon, Emma Noel, Anna Ollier, Patricia Potts, Joanna Quinn, Sarah Quinn, Janaki Ranpura, Lucy Rutter, Carl Thomas, Jennie Thomas, Morgan Thomas, Clare Usiskin, Pippa Wainwright, Heather Westgate, and Rachel Wykes.

For G&Ts, nurturing, and hands-on help, we would like to thank Damian Barr, Polly and Shaun at Tilton House, Pippa Considine, Tim Jones, Natalie Savona, Laurie Tomlinson, and Olivia Waller.

Thanks to our Bibliotherapy Advisory Board for ideas and suggestions over the years, including Terence Blacker, Rose Chapman, Tracy Chevalier, Abi Curtis, Nick Curwin, Ashley Dartnell, Geoff Dyer, Piers Feltham, Patrick Gale, Sophie Howarth, Alison Huntingdon, Nicolas Ib, Lawrence Kershen, Caroline Kraus, Sam Leith, Toby Litt, Anna McNamee, Chiara Menage, Stephen Miller, Tiffany Murray, Jason Oddy, Jacqueline Passmore, Bonnie Powell and her Facebook friends, Charlotte Raby, Judy Rich, Robin

Rubenstein, Alison Sayers, Anna Stein, Chris Thornhill, Ardu Vakil, S. J. Watson, Rebecca Wilson, and Charmaine Yabsley.

Special thanks go to our colleague and friend Simona Lyons at the School of Life; and Morgwn Rimmell, Caroline Brimmer, Harriet Warden, Clemmie Balfour, and all those at the School of Life who supported us throughout the period of writing the book.

Thanks also to our bibliotherapy clients past and present, who gave us ideas for books we had not yet read, and allowed us to practice our medications on them.

Thank you to our agent Clare Alexander, our editor Jenny Lord and all at Canongate, plus Colin Dickerman, Liesl Schillinger, and all at Penguin USA.

A posthumous thank-you to our tutor at Cambridge, David Holbrook, who set us on our way.

And most of all to our families: Martin, Doreen, Saroja, Jennie, Bill, Carl, and Ash, for their love and support throughout this process; and to our children, Morgan, Calypso, Harper, and Kirin for putting up with our mental absence.

READING AILMENTS INDEX

TEN-BEST LISTS INDEX

AUTHOR INDEX

NOVEL TITLE INDEX

NOVEL TITLE INDEX

NOVEL TITLE INDEX